THE CHILD

Development and adjustment

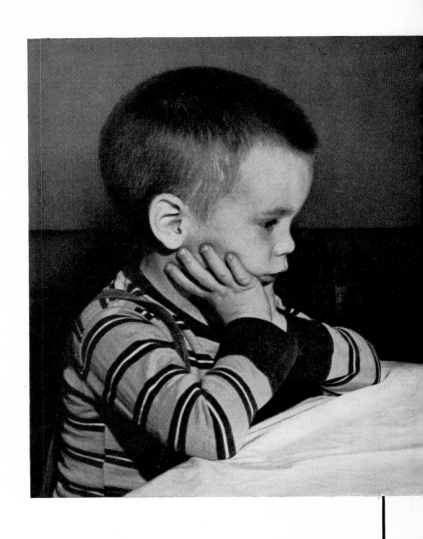

Allyn and Bacon, Inc.

BOSTON

1959

THE CHILD

Development and adjustment

MAX L. HUTT *Associate Professor, Department of Psychology, University of Michigan, Ann Arbor, Michigan*

ROBERT GWYN GIBBY *Chief Clinical Psychologist, McGuire Veterans Administration Hospital, Richmond, Va., and Lecturer, Graduate School, University of Richmond*

First Printing . . . . . . April, 1959
Second Printing . . . . . . January, 1961
© Copyright, 1959, by ALLYN AND BACON, INC.,
150 Tremont Street, Boston. All rights reserved. No part of this
book may be reproduced in any form, by mimeograph or any
other means, without permission in writing from the publisher.

Printed in the United States of America.

Library of Congress Catalog Card Number: 59-8670

Preface

THIS IS A BOOK ABOUT THE DEVELOPING CHILD. In discussing development we have tried to put the focus where we think it properly belongs—on the child himself, and not on his physical development, or his language development, or his emotional development. It is not that these latter topics (and many others) are not critical in significance, for indeed they are; but it is vital, we feel, to keep constantly in the forefront the fact that it is a real child with whom we are concerned, and not some abstractions about hypothetical children. Moreover, since, as we demonstrate in many ways, the child develops as an integrated individual whose needs, goals in living, and diurnal variations in motivation may have a profound influence upon his growth, his structure, and his functioning, we cannot fully comprehend these aspects of his growth without first understanding him as a total person. Hence our primary consideration is the way in which the child's personality matures and develops. Once we have this conceptual anchorage we are better able to consider in detail the child's physical, emotional, social, and intellectual growth.

In selecting material from the extensive resources that are now available, we constantly posed the question: "How important are these data for gaining a deeper understanding of the child and for forming more accurate generalizations about principles of human development?" These two purposes guided us in the selection and emphasis we have given to various topics as we assembled the findings from child psychology, social anthropology, medical and psychiatric literature, and education. An additional guiding principle we followed was to give emphasis to each topic at the developmental level at which it had the greatest pertinence. With these criteria in mind, we have discussed the child from the prenatal stage of development through the early stages of adolescence.

v

At each stage we have then considered those findings and those topics that are most relevant.

The authors are clinical psychologists and have drawn heavily upon their experience in clinical work with a wide variety of children and parents. Our views have been tested in the crucible of the classroom, where we have taught courses in child development and child adjustment to teachers, supervisory school personnel, psychologists, social workers, psychiatrists, medical students, parents, and others. In the give-and-take of both clinical and classroom settings, these views have been modified and have matured. Contrary to popular conception, our experience with children has been primarily concerned with the so-called "normal" and "fairly normal" child. Our clinical population certainly contained a major proportion of such children who came (or were brought) not because they were severely maladjusted, but more commonly because they or their parents or teachers had questions about the most effective programs of guidance in home or school, or because of transient problems which are characteristic of almost all children. The emphasis in this book is clearly upon the "normal" child, but it must be noted that he, too, has many problems in the course of his growth and adjustment. Hence, some of our illustrative material is based upon somewhat more severely disturbed children, for they help us to see, because of the exaggerated phenomena they manifest, the very same problems in less extreme form in the average child.

The authors are inclined, in their view of personality theory, toward the psychoanalytic orientation; nevertheless we recognize that no present-day theory can do full justice to the problem of child development and are eager to make use of the contributions of all other personality theories that have some general or special merit in connection with some aspect of child behavior. We have asked ourselves again and again: "What contribution to understanding does this particular theoretical explanation offer?" We have asked, further: "What evidence is there in favor of this explanation?" Therefore, although we have been extremely eclectic in sampling views and findings from all available sources, we have tried to integrate this material, as meaningfully as we could, in terms of a dynamic conception of the growing child. The psychoanalytic view, which is itself constantly in a state of change, is most congenial to us in organizing present-day knowledge; at the same time, we are keenly aware of its limitations and do not hesitate to indicate these or to utilize other findings and explanations to improve our over-all conception of child behavior. Without some personality theory as an organizing force in interpreting the data of child behavior, we would be like the person with considerable financial resources from many different countries who did not know their values and did not know how to utilize them. Our theory gives an orientation and a consistent way of organizing our findings and thereby enables us to put them to better use.

We are under great obligation to the scholars, researchers, and practitioners who have studied, pondered about, and dealt with children of all ages. We hope that our specific citations will acknowledge, to some extent, the nature of this obligation. We are deeply indebted to the organizations that kindly supplied photographs for use in the book: The American Mutual Liability Insurance Company, the Cleveland Health Museum, the Gesell Institute of Child Development, the H. J. Heinz Company, the Merrill Palmer School (Donna Harris, photographer), and the University of Michigan News Service. We are also extremely grateful to Mrs. Catherine E. Gibby who worked tirelessly and enthusiastically in transcribing our rough draft into a finished manuscript. Our thanks are also due to Mrs. Barbara Windecker who assisted in the extended typing process.

M. L. H.
R. G. G.

To Brett, Casey,
Robert, and Carole

Contents

10   *Childhood disturbances—prevention, correction, and treatment*   352

1

Personality and the patterns of child development

THE PHENOMENA of growth and development are an unceasing source of wonder, although many aspects of growth, especially growth of the human being, have been thoroughly and scientifically studied for a long period of time. It is amazing how growth occurs: from the beginnings as a minute fertilized ovum in the mother's womb, through the process of birth when newborn children seem to look and act very much alike, to full development in young childhood when each individual has a unique personality.

What forces are responsible for the incessant movement onward and upward? Why do certain stages in the child's physical and emotional development occur in a particular sequence? Why, despite all of the fascinating and intricate differences among human beings, are there so many fundamental constancies, such as similar basic organs, fundamentally constant proportions among the component parts of the body, similar physiological processes, and similarities in this thing we call human nature?

Other aspects of development are also intriguing. Consider the highly complicated development of language functions. At first, the infant responds passively to the mother's cooing and coddling; later he responds differently to mother and non-mother and he makes his first gurgling and gasping noises; still later he learns to say words and sentences; and finally, after much additional development, he acquires the complex abilities of reading, writing, and mature oral communication. Under what conditions is this development facilitated? Why do some adolescents develop the "gift of language" while others have difficulty in making their thoughts and feelings known? Another process, that of emotional development, is equally fascinating. Why do babies differ in emotional responsiveness? What makes some children characteristically sad while others are characteristically happy? Why are some pleasant while others are hostile? Similar types of questions may occur to us about development in physical size, motor coordination, perception, thought and other patterns of social behavior.

A KEY TO UNDERSTANDING
CHILD DEVELOPMENT

In this volume we propose to consider the central and important aspects of the growth and development of the child, but before embarking on this journey we should decide upon some plan of procedure. What shall our main organizing theme be? How can we put the facts of human development into some sensible and integrated scheme? Above all, how shall we look at these phenomena so as to make them more understandable and functionally more useful? We might proceed by discussing each aspect of growth and development separately. According to this plan, we might start with the *neonate* (the newborn child) and move through the successive stages of development, discussing, in turn, the neonate, the infant, the preschool child, and so on. In this approach by *developmental stages*, we would consider within each stage each of the several *topics* of child psychology, such as physical development, growth in language, emotional development, and so on. We might, on the other hand, take a look at the longitudinal development of each aspect of the developmental process from birth through maturity, thus employing a completely *topical* approach to our problem. Here we could consider how physical growth proceeds from birth through maturity, then discuss next, for example, the total development of language, and the like. The former approach would keep the facts of each stage together and permit us to discover what various aspects of behavior looked like at a given time. However, we would lose some of the sense of continuity in growth and find it difficult to gain a proper understanding of the total child at a given stage of development. The latter approach would give us insight into the development of each aspect of the child's behavior and would prove particularly valuable to the person who wished to know something of the major topics of child psychology but it would make even more difficult an appreciation of the whole child; it would be a logical analysis of topics in development rather than an analysis of the psychological development of the child. As we can see, both types of organization of the material of this field would limit our understanding of the developing human organism as a growing, adjusting, integrated human being.

It is a real problem to decide how to meet this dilemma. The moment we begin to dissect total development into its component parts we are in danger of losing sight of the whole. Moreover, each of these approaches fails in a singularly important respect, in our opinion. It does not organize the data of child development in terms of the personality processes and dynamics that are constantly influencing them. We shall see that the child's biological and psychological drives, his conflicts and the ways he attempts to resolve them, his self-perceptions, his peculiar traits, and the like are sometimes crucial and always relevant in determining how development proceeds and in making understandable how he reacts to this development. Although we would have norms of development we would not be able fully to understand their meaning. It is therefore important that we try to resolve the dilemma and obtain the clearest possible perception of human development.

To concretize our discussion, let us consider a common phenomenon that occurs during prepubertal development. At this stage of development the growth curve in weight shows typical changes. There is a change in the steepness of the curve, that is, the rate of growth changes. (See Chapters 4 and 9.) If we were tracing the growth in weight we might be able to learn what the norms for weight were at each preceding stage and what shifts typically occurred at the prepubertal stage. We would also learn that there were exceptions and that certain children showed variations from these norms. We would then have two kinds of facts at our disposal in relation to the growth of weight: normative development and variations from normative development. However, we would not necessarily know what factors influenced a *particular*

child's spurt in weight, how a *particular* child reacts to this sudden spurt, or why he reacts as he does. For one child, excessive gain in weight might be a resultant of emotional frustration; for another, it might be a normal prepubertal spurt. For one boy, obesity might be a source of worry and discomfort. He might think of himself as "fat," he might be highly sensitive to the jibes of his playmates, or he might tend to withdraw from social participation and become depressed. Another boy, who was equally obese, might acknowledge the fact of his obesity; he might take some measures to overcome this condition, but he might continue to regard himself with equal favor and would not worry or modify the scope of his activities.

The phenomenon of obesity and its possible implications for the individual was selected to illustrate our problem because it is not too infrequent in our times and in our culture. We might just as well have selected for our illustration such phenomena as motor awkwardness, the eruptions of pimples, or reading difficulties, problems in spelling, and the like. The point of the illustration is to highlight an interesting fact: *evaluation of the meaning and significance of any growth phenomenon cannot be complete without reference to the organism that shows the phenomenon.* This thought might be more accurately expressed by saying that almost any isolated phenomenon occurs to and has significance to the individual in relation to the kind of personality that he has. We wish to emphasize that it is not the fact alone that produces a particular reaction, but the total way in which the individual *perceives* that fact and *responds* to it.

In view of such considerations as these, we believe it is best to organize the discussion of the development of the child around the central, unifying theme of the child's personality. With this theme constantly in the forefront, we shall proceed by discussing child development in terms of the successive stages through which it passes. Within each stage we shall then select the topics that are central in the development of that stage. Thus, for example, physical development proceeds so rapidly and its patterning is so critical during the stage of infancy that we shall devote major attention to this aspect of development during this stage in the child's growth. We shall give varying emphasis to physical development or to some aspects of it again at other stages in which its importance becomes central again. Thus, we shall not discuss each topic of child psychology in each chapter (or at each stage) merely because this would be a logical presentation of this material, but shall discuss it when it seems most relevant to do so. We hope, in this way, also to avoid some of the repetitiousness that might otherwise occur, and to give prominence to critical principles and findings as they emerge from the study of a living, adjusting human being. Thus we hope to combine the advantages of the topical approach with the approach through developmental stages. Our core question

will always be, however, "What meaning does a particular pattern of development have?" and an implied question will always be, "Why does the child behave this way at a particular time in his development?" Since we cannot properly understand the child by considering the separate aspects of his development alone, we shall attempt to understand him in terms of the dynamic meaning of the interdependence of his drives, his conflicts, his physical equipment, and the social environment in which he is developing. Personality thus becomes a key to our understanding of the child.

We shall subsequently discuss in detail the concept of personality, but at this point we may define it roughly as the integrated pattern of typical perceptions by the individual of himself and his environment and the accompanying typical response tendencies. Each individual learns to think of himself in characteristic terms (he has a *self-image*), whether or not this perception accords accurately with the facts. Similarly, each individual learns to *interpret* his environment (to perceive it) in characteristic ways, again not necessarily completely in accord with the facts. Finally, he learns to react in characteristic ways to a wide variety of phenomena (his habitual response tendencies). As we shall see, even the infant soon shows some signs of his unique personality, and the older child has an even more completely integrated pattern of perceptual and response tendencies. If we understand how these patterns of personality develop we may be better able to understand how the total organism functions. Hence, we shall consider the successive stages in the development of the child in terms of, and with constant reference to, concurrent development of his personality. This, we believe, will furnish a basis for a better understanding of child development.

PRELIMINARY OBSERVATIONS CONCERNING PERSONALITY

The characteristic ways in which a person behaves constitutes his personality. As we have seen, these methods of responding are based, in part, on how the individual perceives himself because these self-perceptions influence his behavior. If we illustrate this point its meaning may become more intelligible. To do this we shall select two examples of an extreme kind. In the first, a child who ordinarily behaves in a self-confident manner and is reasonably assertive while conscious of the rights of others has just received a severe tongue-lashing from his teacher, who was greatly upset by some severe trauma in her own life. He has been told that he is very mean, that he is inconsiderate of others, that he is aggressive, and that he is therefore a worthless, disagreeable specimen of childhood who is no longer liked by his teacher. As one can imagine, he feels humiliated, angry, and depressed. For the next few days he responds in a meek, passive, dejected and insecure manner; he does not feel sure about anything he does; he is no longer self-confident nor appropriately assertive. The impact of the verbal criticism from someone whom he valued has resulted in a "deflation of his ego" and he perceives himself differently from the way he did before. In

turn, his behavior is modified to accord with his temporarily changed self-image.

As another example, let us consider the behavior of a timid and fearful young man who has joined the marines. During training his leaders constantly impress upon him and the other members of his company what gallant men *all* marines are. He learns that he is a member of a highly respected group with a very proud tradition. He is told that marines "never say die" and that they are constantly able to surmount almost impossible obstacles. He finds that other members of his company, who had confessed some of their own self-misgivings, begin to believe these things and to behave in a confident manner. He soon perceives himself as a vital member of his company who shares their characteristics. During a training mission he finds, surprisingly, that he, too, is behaving aggressively, confidently, and without his former fears.

In both of these examples an individual's changing self-perceptions influenced the ways in which he behaved—at least for a time. In both, there was a change, perhaps a reversal, of the traits that he had previously manifested. Which of the patterns of behavior, the former or the latter, constitutes the "true" personality of the individual? Should we say that the personality is characterized by the changing patterns of an individual? Would all individuals respond in the same manner to the changed circumstances of their lives as these two did? If we think deeply about these questions, we can begin to see what psychologists have learned: that underneath the *overt* behaviors or *traits* that an individual displays there are *covert* or *latent* determiners of behavior. In the examples given, other individuals subjected to the same circumstances might have reacted differently. Thus, if we attempt to characterize persons in terms of the patterns of traits that they manifest, we have to define or describe these patterns with at least two additional variables. One of these deals with the *consistency* or *inconsistency* with which these patterns are displayed under varying circumstances, and the other is the kinds of *needs* that motivate these behaviors. The *needs* may be fully conscious to the individual, in which case he has a *conscious awareness* of them, or they may be only partially conscious to him or not conscious at all, in which case they are said to be *unconscious*.

This leads us to a consideration of the motivations of behavior. All behavior is motivated; that is, all behavior is based on the underlying needs of the individual. In Chapters 2 and 4 we shall discuss in detail how these needs or motivations develop. We can anticipate these discussions in a few respects, however. A person is born with a certain innate, biological equipment. At birth people differ in weight, length, complexity of nervous system, color of skin, type of blood, and so on. However, they are all born with the same types of *basic drives* (sometimes called *instincts*). These original drives constitute the raw material of human nature. We do not have to specify,

at this point in our discussion, what the precise nature of these drives is or some of the ways in which their intensity differs in different people—we shall get into that later. We do wish to make the point, however, that all people have the same types of drives—and that in the beginning human nature is pretty much alike in all infants. However, humans have different drives from subhumans, and hence we can talk about the different drives of humans and animals. In some respects humans and animals have similar drives, like the drive for food and the drive for temperature regulation. In other respects it is thought that they have quite different drives, like the drive for love and the drive for emotional security.

At birth the individual is not consciously aware of his drives. He is driven to behave in a certain way, and has to behave in that way even to survive. As he meets gratification or frustration of his drives, they begin to become modified and simultaneously the individual begins to become conscious of his drives—or as we call them at this point, his needs or wants. Thus conscious awareness of one's needs arises out of the context of living in a real world in which gratification and, especially, frustration occur. Some drives may never become conscious or fully conscious (such drives as those involved in heart action or those involved in digestion or peristalsis); others may become conscious but later be *repressed*. It is highly important to understand the nature of repression for, as we shall learn, much of our behavior is motivated by repressed and unconscious drives. Here, again, we shall anticipate a little of our discussions in later chapters.

When an individual engages in behavior that is opposed by or criticized by someone who is very important to him, he feels uncomfortable about it. We say that he feels *guilty*. Guilt is derived from two indispensable preconditions: awareness of the wishes of others and a need on the part of the individual not to displease these others because he is dependent upon them or values their good will. Thus, to avoid disapproval from others or because others (*important others*) have already disapproved, the individual automatically and unconsciously inhibits the behavior he would otherwise have shown. In this way the drive is said to be repressed in order to avoid conflict or guilt. Nevertheless, the drive is not entirely eliminated since it has important reasons for being and has to find some outlet or discharge. Only its *direct expression* is inhibited and only *conscious* awareness of its existence is eliminated. The drive finds an outlet, if not immediately then eventually, in some indirect or roundabout manner. In these ways the individual tries to avoid tension or guilt: by repressing the direct expression of a drive (or drives) and by finding substitute ways of gratifying the drive in a more or less acceptable fashion.

Thus we can begin to see that an individual's behavior is motivated by two sets of drives, *conscious* and *unconscious*. If we understand this fully we can understand why some individuals show highly variable behavior and why some individuals engage in highly inexplicable (to them) behavior which they apparently did not intend. Variability in behavior is partly dependent upon the kind and amount of repressed drives; the more repression the less consistent a person is likely to be in his overt behavior. The degree and type of repression govern the degree and irrationality of behavior. We shall later try to understand why a youngster who is very pleasant and overtly extremely compliant to the wishes of others suddenly and apparently inexplicably behaves like a "demon"; we would at least suspect that this is related to the emergence of repressed drives that were unable to find other, more suitable outlets. For similar reasons we might find that an adult who shows a "tough" and "hard" exterior manifests a surprising "heart of gold" when the "chips are down." The concept of repression will prove to be a highly useful tool in understanding many types of motivations and behaviors that might otherwise be bewildering (1).*

An individual's personality is usually described in terms of the *traits* that he characteristically displays. A trait is a more or less pervasive mode of behavior. We can think of many popular terms used to describe a person's traits, such as amiability, honesty, cooperativeness, emotional stability, independence, and the like. If we listed all of the terms for traits that are in the dictionary, we would compile a very long and confusing list. Some of these terms would refer to the same thing, and some would be included with others in some more general terms. In order to bring some order out of the

---

* Numbers in parentheses indicate bibliographical references cited at the ends of the chapters.

chaos that would result if we simply used all available terms for traits, psychologists have attempted to establish a list of the *primary traits* on the basis of which most behavior that is observed can be described. Different lists have been compiled by different investigators, but recent research, making use of modern methods of measurement and statistical analysis, has yielded a list of a few *primary traits* upon which there is fairly common agreement and which are largely independent of each other; that is, each one describes an aspect of behavior not described by the others. Table I gives a list of such traits (2).

We should like to make one additional point in this introductory discussion. This concerns the problem of what a healthy personality is. Usually, discussions of the *healthy personality* attempt to define it in terms of the absence of *symptoms* or the absence of *unhealthy traits*. Such a negative approach does not tell us much about the positive features of the healthy individual. For our purposes we shall consider the healthy personality (the one with a good adjustment) as that which is able to provide adequate satisfaction of an individual's basic needs while at the same time enabling the individual to meet the demands of his society in a pleasurable and cooperative manner (3). This concept should not be confused with the concept of conformity. Conformity of itself is no guarantee of good adjustment; moreover, it may lead to a high degree of rigidity and unproductive stereotypy in behavior. There are even situations in which it is healthy and mature to rebel

Table I. *Cattell's list of primary (source) traits*

   A. Cyclothymia *vs.* schizothymia (slow *vs.* abrupt shifts in mood) *
   B. General mental capacity *vs.* mental defect
   C. Emotionally stable *vs.* neurotic emotionality
** E. Dominance-ascendance *vs.* submissiveness
   F. Surgency *vs.* desurgency (energetic, cheerful *vs.* anxious, agitated melancholy)
   G. Positive *vs.* dependent character (persevering, responsible *vs.* fickle, immature)
   H. Adventurous cyclothymia *vs.* withdrawn schizothymia
   I. Sensitive, infantile, imaginative emotionality *vs.* mature, tough poise
** K. Socialized, cultured mind *vs.* boorishness
   L. Trustful cyclothymia *vs.* paranoia (composed, trustful *vs.* suspicious, bashful)
   M. Bohemian unconcernedness *vs.* conventional practicality
   N. Sophistication *vs.* simplicity

---

* Material in parentheses is explanatory of the trait names.
** Traits D and J have been omitted since these have not been confirmed by other research. Traits L, M, N have been established only tentatively, according to Cattell.

against an unwise proscription. Nevertheless, the individual must be able to live comfortably with his community, under ordinary circumstances, adapt to its mores, and *at the same time* attain satisfaction and be uniquely creative and productive in terms of his own needs and talents. This conception of the healthy personality is a dynamic one; it assumes that personality is healthy when there is a give-and-take and a constant interaction of the individual's needs and the needs of society. The healthy and mature personality strives constantly to balance inner needs with external realities in a manner that takes both into account and finds a stable but constantly varying pattern of responses. It is stable in that the basic modes of adaptation are consistent; it is variable in that the specific means that are utilized take properly into account the variable qualities of the reality situation.

SOME EXAMPLES OF CHILD BEHAVIOR

Discussion of the general principles and findings of child psychology needs concrete examples to be really meaningful. We have selected some cases that will help to illustrate what child behavior looks like, or how it came into being, or what the behavior means when we get a closer look at the underlying phenomena. Our sample of cases will not be representative of all children, but we hope the cases presented will contain some of the more important elements that are common to many. Some of the cases represent normal patterns of behavior, but a few are concerned with more abnormal behavior in order to illustrate the differences and similarities of such behavior with that of the well-adjusted child.

Harold: A four-year-old's reaction to tonsillectomy

Harold was a fairly healthy four-year-old who had lived a well-sheltered life. Both of his parents were intelligent, busy people with well-developed interests and activities. Both loved Harold, who was an only child. The father was a fairly successful businessman who had established a small but growing concern. Quite often he would remain at the office in the evening to clear up problems that could not be taken care of during the day. Usually, he would devote the entire week end to his family. He had a very good relationship with his wife, who also loved and respected him. Harold's mother was a secretary for a law firm. She had gone back to work about six months after Harold was born in order to help with finances until her husband's business was well established; she was looking forward to leaving her job in about four months since things were beginning to work out well for her husband's business. Both parents hoped to have another child within the near future but were waiting until the mother could spend all of her time at home.

Harold was a full-term baby of normal delivery. About two weeks after birth he began to gain in weight and soon was a lusty, thriving baby. The maternal grandmother lived with the family from the time that Harold was born and devoted much of her time to his care. Harold seemed to be quite fond of his grandmother and seemed to favor her over his own mother. His mother accepted this state of affairs and felt that this good relationship made it easier for her to resume employment when Harold was six months old.

During his infancy Harold seemed to develop quite normally, occasionally having mild sore throats, and once having a mild colic condition. Dentition proceeded normally, too, although he did show considerable irritability and restlessness when his first tooth erupted at about seven months of age. He seemed to adjust better to the eruption of his later teeth. By 30 weeks of age he began to crawl a little and by 13 months he was able to take his first independent steps. At a year and a half he developed an ear infection, and his mother stayed at home with him for ten days until this condition cleared up fully. He was a happy infant, and loved to play with his grandmother and mother.

During Harold's second year the family moved into a new home in the country. The parents felt that raising a child in the country provided important advantages and bought their home with this thought in mind. The house was located about 20 miles outside of the city (where both father and mother worked) in an area where the builder had said other homes for young families would soon be built. However, the builder's plans for the other houses collapsed and no other homes were built in the immediate area until Harold was almost four years old. Meanwhile, the family lived a fairly isolated social existence since the nearest neighbor lived almost half a mile down the road. This neighbor had a boy who was three years older than Harold. No other children lived nearby. Harold seemed quite happy in his home environment, but as might have been expected was a little timid and shy when taken for a visit to relatives and encouraged to play with cousins of about his own age. The first such visit away from home occurred when Harold was slightly more than two years of age. The mother recalled that he paid no attention to the other children and when they approached him he began to cry. On subsequent visits of these cousins to his home, or on Harold's visits to theirs, he gradually began to share in play activities with them, but he did not do so eagerly nor did he play well with them.

Because the parents realized that Harold's social activities were unduly restricted they made two plans to try to help him in this respect. The first of these was to enroll him in a nursery school in a little town about five miles from where they lived. Unfortunately, the teacher who organized this school and taught it became very ill and the school had to be discontinued some two months after it was opened. Harold was frightened about being left in this school when he was first brought there, but by the time the school closed he was reported as making a "pretty good adjustment" to the other children. He was a little shy and was somewhat passive but otherwise got along satisfactorily. He expressed some dissatisfaction when he could no longer attend the school. The other plan was to get Harold a dog which he could call his own and take care of. Harold was given "Inky," a cocker spaniel puppy, when he was three years and two months of age, and he soon learned to love it. When nursery school was no longer possible, he would spend more time playing with his dog than he would with his toys.

Just about two months before Harold's fourth birthday he developed a sore throat again and he began to have some difficulty in breathing due to enlarged and cryptic adenoids. When the pediatrician was consulted he advised tonsillectomy and adenoidectomy. The parents hesitated, but about three months later, after Harold was well again, he was taken to a hospital in the city for the operation. He was taken there by his parents, who noticed how frightened he was. Neither parent remained for the operation; in fact, they were told that it would be better for all concerned if they returned to see him in the evening after the operation had been completed. And so Harold was left in the hospital at about 8:30 A.M., after he had been taken from his home that morning almost an hour previously, and the operation was performed early in the afternoon. The parents saw him that night and every night thereafter while he was still in the hospital. He seemed to be sad and frightened; he cried muffled sobs a great deal of the time; he had two hemorrhages; and his convalescence was a very slow one. Some eleven days after the operation he returned home.

The real trouble seemed to begin then. He seemed to resent his mother and would call frequently for his grandmother. He became a very "finicky" eater, whereas he had been a very good eater previously. He would refuse to go to sleep at night unless his grandmother stayed with him, and then he would sleep restlessly. He began to wet his bed again at night (*nocturnal enuresis*) although he had learned to "keep dry" almost a year before this.

When this pattern continued without abatement the parents took him to a "child

The traumata of injury or illness can be lessened in many ways. (U. of Mich.)

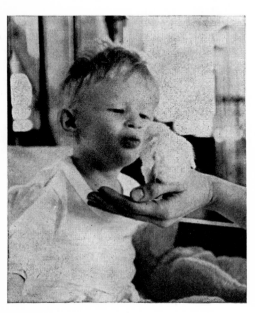

guidance clinic" for diagnosis and recommendations. Since the family lived so far from the clinic it was decided not to attempt *release therapy*, which seemed to be indicated (a form of psychotherapy in which the recent emotional traumata of the child are expressed in play and "discharged"); instead, after a careful study of Harold and the family situation, the parents were seen a number of times and the problem was discussed with them carefully and sympathetically. It took more than three more months before Harold resumed his previous modes of behavior and no unfavorable aftereffects of the experience could be detected.

It is not our purpose in this case to consider in full the *etiology* (causation) of this problem or the nature and effects of guidance for Harold and his parents. However, we should like to point up some important phenomena. (The reader may wish to do his own speculating about etiology and treatment.) Certainly, Harold lived a very sheltered life and had insufficient contact with children of his own age. Nevertheless, he displayed a pleasant, happy personality. He matured normally in the physical sphere and in most respects made a good emotional adjustment. He was stable emotionally and usually was outgoing. He did show some timidity in new (for him) social situations but this might have been expected in view of his limited social experience. Perhaps he would have made a good adaptation to social experiences in time. There was, however, no preparation for the traumata of the hospitalization and operation, he was frightened by the separation from his home and parents (see Chapter 6 for a discussion of these problems), and he *regressed* in behavior to previous modes of adaptation (his bed-wetting, for example) and developed *phobias* (fears of the dark and of being left alone). His mood and other behavior traits changed, for a time, after the operation. Fortunately, he subsequently appeared to make a good adjustment. The case illustrates the effect of rather severe traumata upon the personality and adjustment of a reasonably well adjusted child of four years, and will offer us some data to consider in the next section of this chapter when we discuss types of personality.

Henry: "The Little Monster"

None of the children liked Henry. He was always ready to "pick a fight." While walking down the aisle in school he would suddenly, for no apparent reason, hit a child on the arm or push him out of his seat. It was the same way in the play-yard. Other boys would get into arguments and fisticuffs on occasion, but Henry could *always* be expected to get into a fist fight or would start wrestling someone to the ground. He did not apparently need any provocation. He would seem to get the impulse to get rough with someone and then it would begin. At first he selected bigger boys to tangle with, but later he had trouble with just about anyone. There was only one boy with whom he seemed to get along, and even seemed to protect. This was Jimmy, who was much smaller and thinner than he. All the other children had learned to leave Henry alone; in turn Henry seemed to resent almost everyone.

When a fight would start, Henry would keep at it whether he was winning or losing. Usually an adult would have to separate him from his antagonist. Sometimes the other children intervened. Occasionally Henry would lose the fight or would give up even before this happened, but this was rare. The children had nicknamed him "The Little Monster."

Henry was almost two inches shorter than the average of his classmates in the kindergarten class. Only Jimmy was shorter than he. Henry was the youngest boy in a family of four boys; all his brothers were above average for their age. His fighting tendencies had emerged rather suddenly when he was just a little less than five years of age, and just before he had entered the kindergarten. Previous to this he had been quiet, and almost meek. His brothers would make fun of his small stature and Henry would silently resent this. About a month before Henry had become so aggressive he had been fitted with a pair of glasses. He had fought in vain against getting them. He pointed out that none of his brothers wore glasses, but his mother insisted that he was nearsighted and that the oculist had advised glasses.

Henry was regarded as mother's baby. When he was smaller the other children had babied him, too, but now they seemed to take pleasure in pointing out how he was "mom's boy," and that he was smaller and weaker than his classmates. Henry did not like this but seemed to take the ribbing he was given fairly well. It was only when he felt that his mother had betrayed him by insisting that he wear glasses that his belligerent tendencies began to crop out. He even resented his mother's attention or her special favors. He wanted to be a "big boy" like the others, and he learned to dislike the other children who were bigger and usually stronger than he.

Many relatively easy answers can be suggested to explain Henry's belligerency, but none of them might be sufficient to account in full for his changed behavior. He fought, possibly, to prove that he was as "big" or as "tough" as the next boy.

He fought to try to defend himself against the jibes about his physical status. He wanted to be accepted, but his behavior produced more rejection instead. He wanted punishment for his deep feelings of insecurity and his feelings of difference, since they resulted in the production of hostile impulses, which he had always been taught by his mother to regard as "bad." He may even have resented the feeling that his mother was trying to make him into a girl because she wanted so much to have a female child; he recalled that his mother had not permitted his long, curly blond hair to be cut until he had been almost four years of age.

All these reasons might be relevant and yet even together they might not explain adequately why Henry behaved as he did. All we can say for certain is that Henry was an aggressive boy because he was troubled and that his aggression was some kind of defense against conflicts that he himself was not able to understand.

How are we to become more certain of the meaning of his behavior? A careful and much more complete history of his life, of his relations with the other members of his family, of his physical history, of the values in the home, and of the social conditions under which he was reared would be of help. So too would interviews conducted by a sensitive and understanding person—a teacher, a school psychologist, or the like. Possibly an evaluation of his free-play behavior and of his play activities during psychotherapeutic play sessions would prove diagnostically useful. An evaluation of his fantasies, of his wishes, and

even of his dream life might prove rewarding. These and other technical methods of evaluating his personality problems and his conflicts would enable us to form a more adequate evaluation of the whole story.

Mary: She has lost interest in her school work

Mary had always been an above-average pupil in her school studies. In some of her classes she had been near the top in all of her academic work. She had always been regarded as bright and had earned superior ratings on intelligence tests given in school. But ever since she had entered the eighth grade, her school work had fallen off and

Hospitalization does not have to be a frightening experience. (U. of Mich.)

she had progressively lost interest. When asked about this she had no explanation. She did not dislike her teacher nor did she admit to any negative feelings toward her classmates. She claimed that she tried, but her mind would wander away from her studies, both in school and at home. She would forget to bring her homework to school even when she had completed it; more often, she left much of her work undone. She had begun to believe that she would fail the eighth grade and have to repeat it.

Mary's folks tried to do everything they could to encourage her. They tried to get her to organize her study program at home. They told her that she was the oldest child in the family and that she had to set an example for the others. They pointed out that they knew she was smart and compared her present marks with her former grades. They obtained the cooperation of Mary's homeroom teacher, who was also concerned about the problem. All of these and other approaches seemed to be of no avail. Mary's work continued to be poor and her behavior was listless.

At this point a careful medical examination was given. It was thought that Mary might have some metabolic disorder; possibly she was suffering from some infectious process; even a neurological condition was suspected. Mary had a complete check-up. The result: negative. The doctors could find no explanation for her condition.

One day at home, Mary's mother found her carefully examining a small mole on her face. To the mother this mole, which Mary had had for some years, seemed attractive. It gave Mary's face a certain degree of piquancy. Obviously it was disturbing Mary, but when she was asked about it she denied that it was troubling her. However, her mother took a very patient tack and gradually encouraged her to disclose her feelings. It turned out that Mary was quite worried about menstruation! She had not begun to menstruate, was worried that she never would, and was worried about it if she did. It was learned that her concern about the mole was a displacement of her feelings about these other problems. She had become more sensitive to her appearance and, with the usual problems in heterosexual adjustment at this stage, was concerned lest boys dislike her. No one of these problems by itself was overwhelming, but together they seemed, to Mary, to be more than she could bear.

Mary and her mother had quite a number of talks after this and a few additional things came to light. For a period of five months before Mary's school work had begun to fall off, Charlotte, Mary's younger sister, had been ill with an attack of virus pneumonia. At first Mary was worried about her ten-year-old sister, but gradually she began to resent the almost constant attention her mother gave her. At the same time she felt guilty for feeling this way, "knowing" that the sister was ill and needed special care. Her father, too, seemed to give unnecessary attention to the sister. Mary's guilt about her jealousy and resentment troubled her. Beyond this, she was worried about when she would begin to menstruate, what she would do about it, and how she would feel. Her mother, who would probably have been alert to these concerns of Mary's, was so preoccupied with the sister that she did not think of them. And Mary had begun to think that her mother did not care about such problems, or perhaps was even ashamed to talk about them.

Thus, her problems grew and seemed to be insoluble to Mary. Her mind became preoccupied with fantasies. School work seemed unimportant, and social activities only served to point up even more her difference from other girls. Many times she wanted to talk things over with mother, but each time she felt guilty about her hostile thoughts and feelings. It was only when mother in her patient, understanding way helped to prepare the way for discussions that Mary could talk about her feelings and begin to explore their meaning.

Mike: Teacher's favorite

Mike, a nine-year-old boy, was always well liked by his teachers; he was very agreeable and cooperative. He could be depended upon to discharge his responsibilities promptly and with enthusiasm. He always looked as if he had just been scrubbed! His clothes were immaculate; he was carefully dressed and seemed to take pride in his appearance. He kept his books and his papers in the same fashion—tidy, organized, and neat. He was almost always well behaved, as one might expect, and he tended to be rather quiet in demeanor.

Mike had attended the same school from the time of his registration in kindergarten. His second-grade teacher had told his mother, in one of the parent-teacher conferences, that she thought Mike was a little bit inhibited, but when pressed for an explanation by his mother had to confess that this was something she found hard to explain. He seemed to be eager to please and did not seem to respond spontaneously and to yield to his own impulses as she believed a healthy seven-year-old should. And yet he was interested in people, was fairly outgoing, and seemed to be content. She had to say that perhaps there was really nothing wrong but that sometimes a child could be too well behaved. Mike's mother said that she had tried to give him everything he needed, that she had learned the value of strict discipline (but not harsh discipline) after she had been too indulgent with his older brother (who was eleven years old), and that she was highly pleased with the way he responded at home and in school when he was seven years old.

The mother was accurate in her description of Mike's behavior at home. He was liked by both parents although he seemed to be the focus of occasional, and sometimes heated, arguments with an older brother and a six-year-old sister. It was true

that he did not have any close friends in the neighborhood but he did have playmates. There was only one boy who was at all close to Mike and who would sometimes visit his home. This was a rather quiet boy who was timid in group situations and who seemed to want to cling to Mike.

Mike had one problem that concerned his mother: he suffered from frequent constipation. This had grown more serious and the usual measures that the mother had employed were gradually of less avail in providing relief. Previously, laxatives or rectal douchings had been effective. Now, the constipation recurred more frequently and was somewhat more severe. Mike had therefore been placed under a physician's care for this problem but it was too soon to determine how effective his treatment was.

There was another peculiarity in Mike's behavior, which the mother had been concerned about previously but seemed to take for granted now. Mike had nightmares. Some nights he would thrash about violently in bed, and occasionally he would scream out in his sleep. No one in the family ever spoke of these things. The parents assumed that it was "just one of those things" and that Mike would outgrow them. Meanwhile, he had been given a separate bedroom so that he would not be as likely to disturb the other children. The mother remembered that she had suffered from nightmares during most of her childhood and had "outgrown" them.

Mike's parents, and especially his mother, could be described as highly compulsive people. Everything at home was done on a close schedule. Closets and chest drawers were carefully arranged. No part of the living quarters could be used for play purposes; there was a recreation room in the basement for that purpose. The mother was obsessively concerned about dirt and cleaned her house overzealously.

Mike's difficulties may be understood as stemming from overly severe and restrictive home training. As we shall see later, on the basis of clinical and research evidence, very strict home discipline may produce conformity to social standards, but it is likely also to produce disturbances in emotional security and in reduced mental creativity (see Chapters 4 and 5).

Suzan: A speech problem?

Suzan was almost three years old when her speech difficulties began. Her speech and language development had been superior in all respects up to this time. At the age of two years, for example, she was able to employ sentences of four or five words and had begun to ask almost interminable questions about everything that happened around her. Moreover, she had overcome those usual "infantilisms" in speech that are so characteristic of preschool children; her speech had become fairly precise and mature. Her vocabulary was quite extensive. But suddenly, or so it seemed, she had begun to stutter.

Her father, who was a dentist, at once thought that this might be related to her dental development, but on further consideration recognized that this could not be the case. He was seeing too many other children, just like Suzan, whose dental development was similar and most of whom showed no serious repetition in their speech. Her mother felt that the stutter was due to the fact that Suzan thought so rapidly that her speech could not keep pace with her thought production.

Suzan's stutter was not very serious, nor did she stutter all of the time. Only when she was excited or somewhat fatigued did her difficulty manifest itself. It was noted that she was more likely to stutter toward evening. She also stuttered more frequently when there was company in the home. Her stutter was characteristically *clonic* in type; that is, she would tend to repeat rapidly the first letter or syllable of a word. However, the condition was not extreme and sometimes there were days when her speech showed no trace of a stutter.

Suzan was taken to a speech clinic. There a careful medical examination showed no abnormalities. The social worker who compiled a *case history* found that the home situation was essentially normal. Suzan was an only child in a happy home. Parents and child got along very well with each other and Suzan was given sufficient attention and appropriate discipline for her age. Her social experiences were good, and her physical history was not unusual in any respect. The clinical psychologist had two play sessions with Suzan which she seemed to enjoy very much. She had no difficulty in going with the psychologist into his examining room and leaving mother outside. She seemed to have confidence in herself and in her relationship with her mother; and her play productions disclosed no severe conflicts of any kind. Her intelligence was estimated to be very superior (the psychologist obtained but did not report to the parents an I.Q. score of 122). She did speak of her difficulty with her speech, but none of the observers in the clinic noted any speech problems while Suzan was there. Her speech was fluent and nonrepetitive. She said that "Mommie and Daddy were worried about my speech."

It was concluded that Suzan's stutter was part of the developmental pattern that was reasonably common among preschool children. It was felt that parental overconcern about this "normal" problem might possibly reinforce the very phenomenon that it was designed to overcome. Some simple mental hygiene measures were recommended, such as giving Suzan more frequent periods of rest and less physically strenuous activities in the late afternoon and early evening in order to reduce the temporary tension states that tended to promote the occurrence of stuttering. Above all the clinic recommended that no further attention be focused on Suzan's speech since this hindered rather than helped her speech development. It was suggested that even the usual praise that had been given for her superior language accomplishments be diminished and that she receive praise, instead, for her other notably good behaviors, such as her superior activities with blocks and paints, and her good adjustments to other children. It was believed that her speech difficulty was a transient problem that would soon right itself as her total maturity increased.

The clinic was right! In less than a year all traces of a stutter had disappeared. Suzan continued to make a good adjustment to home and to playmates.

FURTHER OBSERVATIONS

Analysis of the five preceding cases will reveal a number of pertinent findings about the nature of development and adjustment. In the first place, we saw that patterns of behavior are *variable*: they show fluctuation from time to time. In some instances such change in the overt behavior is precipitated by some emotional event in the life of the child; in others some physical condition triggers the change; in still others, growth itself produces variability. The case of Harold illustrates the first of these conditions— since the emotional experience in hospitalization and separation from the family was very important. The case of Mary demonstrates how the anticipation of physiological changes accompanying puberty can play its role in modifying behavior. Suzan's case illustrates that apparently normal development has its own hazards; in her case speech difficulty was

a transient manifestation of normal speech development.

A second generalization that we can make is that *overt* (directly observable) behavior is only a part of the total picture of child (and indeed human) behavior. Overt behavior is determined by the interaction of many types of motivations, some *overt* and some *covert* (not directly observable). A good illustration of this point is the case of Mike. Although his overt behavior was cooperative and pleasant, he suffered from some kinds of tensions. We can infer that there was considerable unconscious hostility, for example. It is quite possible, and even likely, that his violent nightmares with their thrashings about and screaming reflected some of these covert hostile feelings, of which he might have been completely or partially unaware. He might have been harboring some resentment against the compulsive regime in the home situation and much of his pleasant cooperativeness might have been a *reaction formation* or defense (see Chapters 4 and 5) against his own feelings of hostility.

Perhaps we have begun to see, also, that human development is a highly complex *interactive process* in which physical development has its psychological counterpart, in which the *social conditions* in which a person lives influence his behavioral traits, and in which the *stages* of a person's life during which certain influences impinge upon him may be crucial in determining the effect of these influences. Behavior is thus the *com-*

posite resultant of the interaction of internal and external events as they interact at a given stage in the life of the organism. A tonsillectomy has a different physical and psychological meaning depending upon the stage of development of the child as well as upon the nature of the operation itself. A deviation in height from that of one's peers as well as from the patterns of one's siblings means different things at different times in the life of an individual and with different kinds of individuals. The significance of puberty (and of other rather abrupt physiological changes) depends on the context of psychological conditions in which it occurs and upon the social context in which it is experienced. Conscious and unconscious drives interact in various ways, too, as we shall learn, and produce a resultant that may be difficult to understand without careful assessment of all the interacting forces.

To characterize the difference between *overt* and *covert* behavior, as we have

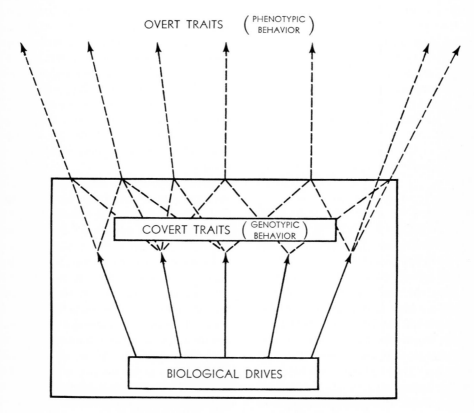

Figure 1. *The derivation of overt behavior traits.*

been doing, psychologists sometimes speak of *phenotypic* and *genotypic* behavior, respectively, to mean approximately the same things. *Phenotypic* behavior is that which we can observe directly in a person's actions. It does not have to be inferred; it can be seen, or felt, or palpated in some other direct manner. On the other hand *genotypic* behavior is that which has some underlying cause or causes, and must be inferred from observed behavior. Thus, Mary's worry about her mole was determined by some underlying conflicts relating to her self-image of which she was at first unaware. Genotypic traits are those that are more basic to the personality and have their source in the internal nature of this personality; we have to infer them, usually, from what a person does. We cannot see them in direct operation, but only infer them from the meaning the behavior has for the person. Genotypes are sometimes referred to, therefore, as the core of the personality, whereas phenotypes operate on the periphery.

The relationship of *covert* (genotypic) traits to *overt* (phenotypic) traits is illustrated in Figure 1. It will be seen that *biological drives* are the source of behavior and that *covert* traits are derived from this source. Since such *drives* and *covert* behavior are not directly observable, they are represented diagramatically as being *within* the box, concealed from our view. From the *covert* traits, singly and in combination, are derived the *overt* (phenotypic) traits which constitute our observable behavior.

If we evaluate the case illustrations in the earlier section of this chapter we can

find some other interesting things about the types of data that were presented. When we spoke, in Harold's case, of the relatively early development of his crawling and walking, we were comparing his development to *norms* for children in these areas. Child psychology has developed norms for many aspects of growth and behavior. Norms usually represent the average in some characteristic for a specified population of subjects. Thus we have norms for height, norms for vocabulary, norms for reading ability, and so on. It should be stressed that a norm is simply a statistical score derived from a sample of cases, and like all such scores has meaning only in terms of the sample from which it was derived. The use of norms can be quite helpful, but as we shall see their function in understanding child behavior can be easily exaggerated or even more easily misunderstood.

Child psychology also makes use of various methods of obtaining data about children. One of the simplest of these is to measure a sample of children on some characteristic, physical or psychological. If we take such measures on a sample of one-year-olds, and do the same for a *comparable* group of two-year-olds and another group of three-year-olds, for example, we can then have not only norms but data on the development of the measured characteristic. Such an approach then enables us to plot a curve of growth in the characteristic. Many curves in height and weight have been constructed in this way. This method is known as a *cross-sectional* approach to the study of development. It has certain important advantages. We do not have to wait for the children to grow up in order to construct our curves of growth, but assume that the norms at each age represent what growth would look like at later ages if we measured the same children at those times. It is often difficult to obtain the same children for *repeated* measurement, and the cross-sectional approach eliminates this difficulty. It has some hazards of its own, of course. For one thing, we may not be certain that our successive samplings at different ages are truly comparable. For another, we are not certain that the conditions of growth will not change over a period of time and thereby modify the results that would be obtained. Even more important than either of these two difficulties is that cross-sectional study of groups of children tends to obscure the irregularities in the individual growth curves of children, since the curves are based on averages derived from large samples.

To obtain a more accurate picture of how an individual child grows or develops in some characteristic, the *longitudinal* method may be employed. As the name implies, a child is measured repeatedly over a period of time and his growth curve is then constructed from these measurements. Psychologists have found, as we shall see later in Chapter 6, that such curves are highly irregular and that different children show different types of irregularities when they are studied over a period of time. Of course, if repeated measurements are made of a number of children over a period of time, the scores of children at each age may be averaged and thus norms may be arrived at, and group curves of growth may be obtained.

Observations of the behavior of children are likely to be influenced by a number of types of errors. One of these is the error due to poor control over the data to be observed. Another is due to the bias or incompetency of the observer. A third is that due to lack of precise definition of what is to be observed. We noted in the case of Suzan that the child was brought to a speech clinic for study. At such a clinic trained observers (speech diagnosticians, psychologists, social workers, and the like) are able to make trained observations under controlled conditions. Other types of agencies supply similar types of opportunities for trained observers' observations under specified conditions. Among these are the psychological clinic, the psychiatric clinic, and the hospital clinic. In recent years special types of laboratories have been established for careful observation and measurement of normal as well as disturbed or sick children. Sometimes these are called laboratories, sometimes they are called child development institutes, sometimes they are called child welfare or child research institutes, as well as many other names. We shall have occasion to comment on their specific methods of work and some of their findings in later chapters of this book.

In a laboratory, methods of observation and measurement may be greatly refined. Special equipment may be provided to note children's reactions. There may be a one-way mirror or one-way screen through which the child may be observed or photographed without awareness on his part that observations are being made. Children's speech may be recorded, and samples of play photographed for analysis later under better conditions of more leisurely evaluation. Special equipment may be available to measure such phenomena as amount of perspiration, level of blood pressure, cardiac reactions, and the like.

Psychologists are particularly interested in the mental, emotional, and social reactions of people. For purposes of measurement with some degree of precision a

great variety of tests and test equipment has been developed and *standardized*. Among the important kinds of tests that are available are *individual intelligence tests*, personality tests of the *objective type* (in which children are asked standardized questions about their feelings and wishes) and of the *projective type* (in which the child is asked to interpret some ambiguous picture or other type of stimulus to determine how his needs color his perceptions), and *interest questionnaires*.

Behavior can be observed through a one-way viewing mirror. (Merrill Palmer)

Less formalized methods of observing children include: *play therapy* (in which children can play out their problems with toys or other inanimate objects), such as *paint* and *clay* materials (through which children can express their inner feelings). There are tests of sensory and motor functions, and tests of imagination and of aptitudes. In fact almost any kind of skill or capacity can now be measured with some degree of close approximation to the function itself.

In this brief survey of types of data used in child psychology, we should not neglect to mention *interview methods* used with the parents of the children. Modern psychology uses various kinds of *controlled interviews* in which *structured* (specific and focused) types of questions as well as *unstructured* types (open-ended questions designed to explore the respondent's own organization of the material) are carefully tested out in advance and are then known to have certain degrees of *accuracy* or *reliability*. Even their

Personality and behavioral reactions can be observed in painting. (U. of Mich.)

validity may have been previously established (the degree to which they can predict certain criteria).

In the course of this book we shall have many occasions to comment on and to illustrate these and other methods of child study.

GENERAL READINGS

1. Hutt, M. L., and Gibby, R. G., *Patterns of Abnormal Behavior*. Boston: Allyn and Bacon, 1957.
2. Cattell, R. B., *Personality*. New York: McGraw-Hill, 1950.
3. Jourard, S. M., *Personal Adjustment: An Approach through the Study of Healthy Personality*. New York: Macmillan, 1958.
4. Dennis, W., "Historical beginnings of child psychology," *Psychol. Bul.*, 1949, 46, 224-235.
5. Pressey, S. L., and Kuhlen, R. G., *Psychological Development through the Life Span*. New York; Harper, 1957.

2 | *The birth of a child*

IN CASUAL THOUGHT, we think of the life of an individual as beginning with his birth. In actual fact life begins with the incident of conception, the moment when the *ovum* of the mother is fertilized by the equivalent germ of the father, the *spermatozoön*. Moreover, the influences that affect the life of an individual were present long before conception—influences transmitted directly through heredity from the parents and indirectly through the cultural traditions and practices which affected the parents and which will later affect the infant in his relations with his parents and other persons.

PREPARATION FOR LIFE

We shall begin our discussion of child development with the *gestation period*—the period before the child is visible in the world and during which many of his characteristics are formed. This period starts with the union of the two parental cells and ends, on the average, some 280 days later, when the lusty cry of the infant announces his arrival. Unless we understand the nature of this prenatal development we shall be less than adequately prepared to understand what follows. We shall try to avoid getting bogged down in the technical details of this process, which are indeed complex, but shall sketch only the facts that are of fairly central significance as a foundation for understanding child personality and behavior.

As we have said, the prenatal period usually lasts some 280 days, or ten lunar months, but it may vary from approximately 180 to 334 days and the infant may survive. Because of the nature of biological development, it is customary to divide the total prenatal period into three subsidiary periods: the *germinal period,* about two weeks in duration, before the rudimentary shaping of the potenial human being is discernible and before the ovum is physically attached to the mother (also known as the *period of the zygote);* the *embryonic period,* for about the next six weeks, during which rapid development of the major structures and organs occurs; the *fetal period,* the final period which terminates at birth and during which the nervous and glandular systems and the muscles and sense organs show very rapid development and attain considerable maturity.

The zygote

We shall now consider each of these three periods in turn. The germinal period begins with conception or fertilization. The mother usually produces a single ovum once each twenty-eight days, and about halfway between her menstrual periods. Since the ovum lives only for a short time, usually a day or so, it must be fertilized during this brief interval. On the other hand, the father continuously produces spermatozoa, millions of them, and these live for several days. The spermatozoa locomote up the vaginal canal and remain near the uterus, toward which the ovum also drifts. Hence, intercourse need not take place precisely at the time of formation of the ovum (the period of *ovulation)* for fertilization

to occur. Only a single spermatozoön can penetrate and fertilize the ovum, since, immediately after this penetration, a covering is formed around the ovum and no other male sperm cell can enter it. Occasionally, two or more ova form at the same time, and each of these is penetrated by different spermatozoa. In such instances two or more separate zygotes will develop and the mother will have *fraternal twins* or *triplets,* and so on. Such twins or triplets are known technically as *dizogotic* or *trizogotic,* respectively. In contrast, *identical* or *monozygotic twins* may develop when a single, fertilized female sex cell forms into two separate zygotes or organisms, for reasons not yet fully understood. Ordinarily when a single union of the male and female cells has taken place, the combination or single zygote begins a process of division and multiplication. The original, recombined cell divides into two identical cells, then these divide into four, the four divide into eight, and so on. The pace of development is amazingly rapid. Moreover, growth proceeds in "fits and starts," as it were, so that although it is continuous there are periods of activity and periods of rest. Before the two weeks are up the organism sends out tendrils by which it attaches itself to the wall of the uterus. When this has occurred, the developing baby has become a parasitic organism, since it now obtains its nourishment from the mother. It should be noted carefully that the zygote develops its own circulatory system which is independent of the mother's circulatory system. Thus, there is *never* any direct interchange of blood between mother and developing child, in normal circumstances. Nutritional material is brought by the mother's blood stream to the *placenta* (a vascular structure) where a semi-permeable membrane separates this circulatory system from the "baby's." Nutritional substances are absorbed by capillary action and are then carried into the developing organism by the organism's own blood circulation. Similarly, waste products are discharged through the placenta by the arteries of the *umbilicus* (a cord or tube from the zygote to the placenta).

We are now faced with one of the major riddles of growth. How does it happen that the original fertilized cell subsequently not only divides and multiplies but also *differentiates* into different kinds of cells and different kinds of organs and structures? When the first cell divides into two cells both have the same genes, for instance. The most probable answer is that while a single, unified organism is developing by the process of cell division, the cells in the different parts are being subjected to *different internal conditions of growth*. One of these differences is in nutrition received by the cells; those nearest the umbilicus are nearest the source of food supply. Another internal condition that differs among the cells is that of pressure; those on top have different pressure from those on bottom. Thus, the *internal environment of the various cells is variant*. Moreover, as differentiation of structure develops, these internal differences become increasingly more pronounced and some cells grow much more rapidly than others. The first major differentiation is into three layers of cells: the *ectoderm* (or outer layer) from which the skin and nervous system are formed; the *mesoderm*

(or middle layer) from which the heart, muscles, circulatory and lymphatic system develop; and the *endoderm* (inner layer) from which develop the stomach, some glands such as the thyroid and pancreatic, and the respiratory system. The nervous system grows proportionately more rapidly than other structures and becomes one of the major centers of dominance in controlling growth throughout the organism. There are, of course, other centers of dominance, each of which influences growth processes in the immediately adjacent areas more than in others.

From the very beginning, when there is only one cell, growth proceeds by *differentiation* and by *subordination* of the developing parts to the whole. No part, no matter how differentiated its structure, is entirely independent in its growth and in its function from the operation of the whole mechanism. The remarkable feature of the process of differentiation, which might have been foretold from the fact that the original cells were at first identical, is that any cell (at least in theory) which might have developed a given function could as easily have developed some other function if it had occupied some other region. Quite a number of studies have shown, particularly with animals, that when certain cells are transplanted *before* their specialized functions or structures have developed they acquire the characteristics of the new region (10, 11). Thus, there is a *critical period* before which interchange of functions may develop. Such findings again support the principles of subordination of the part to the influences of the whole. Later, we shall discuss this and related propositions in more detail.

We wish to cite one more fact which is paramount in importance. During the germinal period, the developing organism obtains a special kind of insurance. It does this by becoming encased in an *amniotic sac* (a double-membraned pouch) in which it literally floats in amniotic fluid (reminiscent of modern types of oil-cushion suspension!). In this way the organism is largely insulated within the uterus from obnoxious external pressures, changes in temperature, and the like. It has an ideal, stable environment in which to pursue its only function: to mature as effectively as possible without trauma or accident.

The embryo

If the first two weeks of life are characterized by rapid growth so are the next six during which, spectacularly, the organism develops from a "germ" to a clearly distinguishable human being. At the beginning of this period the embryo is about ¼ inch long whereas, at the end, it is about one inch long or slightly more. Nevertheless, within this little bit of living organism (about the size of the outer portion of the thumb!) the major human structures are discernible. Gesell characterizes this period as one of "structural organization" (3). The fully developed embryo has crude arms and legs and also has rudimentary fingers! Muscles have

begun to develop, and the internal organs, such as the heart, the lungs, and the kidneys, have begun to take definite shape. Although the embryo has a tail (a vestigial feature which will later be discarded), it also has a head (about one-half the length of the total organism) with definite facial structures such as mouth, eyes, and ears.

It has been reported that some embryos of six weeks have definitely shown movement (reflex responses). Such evidence is based upon direct observation of embryos that have been removed surgically from the uterus because of medical reasons. However, the mother is hardly likely to be able to perceive such movements. (Remember how tiny the embryo is and how well insulated it is in its hanging sac within the uterus.) The phenomenon of the "quickening of the fetus" occurs later, at about 17 weeks after conception, and then the mother may be acutely aware of fetal movements, and the changes of position of the whole fetus. Nevertheless, the mother may be clearly aware of the fact that she is pregnant. A common experience is that of *morning sickness* or nausea. Moreover, the breasts may feel full and changes in the size and appearance of the nipple may have become visible (enlargement and darkening). In addition, she is no longer menstruating.

The tiny, curled-up, living and moving bit of humanity is now ready for embarkation on the third stage of its journey to freedom, the fetal stage during which finer differentiation within structures occurs and the organism prepares itself for an independent, nonparasitic existence.

As we have said, the fetal period is marked by very rapid differentiation of structure and function. A major portion of this type of development occurs during the third through sixth lunar months. By the time the organism is 28 weeks of age it is so well equipped to exercise its various physiological functions that it is now said to be *viable*; it is capable of surviving in an extrauterine environment provided it obtains appropriate care. From this time on a large proportion of growth is concerned with increase in size and weight, and with increase in complexity of organization.

The activity of the fetus has been described as *mass activity*, a tendency for the whole organism to respond to any stimulus (12). Although this may be true, it should be noted that it also is capable of many reflex responses and that much of the mass activity is more apparent than real, being due to heightened response of segmental portions and muscle groups. Nevertheless, a great deal of generalized, mass activity does take place in the fetus.

Of special interest is the growth and development of the nervous system which, as we have pointed out, influences the way in which the fetus develops by setting up an appropriate communication system. The brain, in particular, develops more rapidly than other portions of the body, so that by the time of birth it is

Figure 2. *Relative body proportions at different stages (total size equated).*

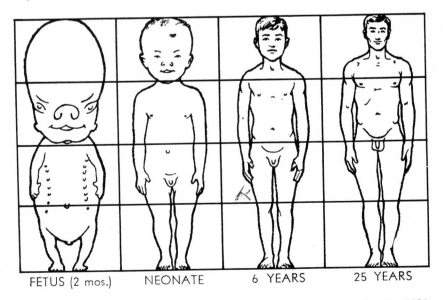

FETUS (2 mos.)   NEONATE   6 YEARS   25 YEARS

Adapted from Robbins, W. S., *et al., Growth.* New Haven, Yale University, 1928.

approximately 10 per cent of the total body and weighs some 10 to 12 ounces. Three main divisions of the brain become differentiated: the *cerebrum*, at the upper end of the neural tube, which is the largest portion of the brain and in which association (and later, thinking) takes place; the *cerebellum*, just below and partly behind the cerebrum, one of whose chief functions is the control of postural adjustment; and the *brain stem*, below the cerebrum, which acts as a kind of control switchboard, regulating incoming and outgoing neural impulses. All of the nerve cells, having first multiplied rapidly in number *(hyperplasia)*, differentiate in form, size, and function. By eight weeks of age the fetus can respond to tactile stimuli. Shortly after this it can move its lips, head, and legs. More and more differentiated responses become possible as the sensorimotor system develops, until by the seventh lunar month almost all of the activities present at birth are available and present.

Sex differentiation has proceeded to such an extent that an expert is able to tell, at the end of the twelfth week, with some degree of assurance, what the sex of the child will be. By the end of the twentieth week hair has made its appearance on the head and body. About one lunar month later "true expirations and inspirations" are possible (3). There is a rapid development of other bodily activities, a catalogue of which may be obtained from the excellent descriptions of Gesell (3) and of Watson and Lowrey (8). The growth in size and weight are central features of the last two to three lunar months of fetal development. It is during this latter stage that the mother becomes acutely aware of her growing child because its increase in size and weight produces pressure and discomfort, and the fetal movements become more active and acute, so that the mother is usually quite willing if not anxious to see the end of the gestation period.

Some factors influencing prenatal development

Before we consider the next general event in the life of the organism, the event of birth when the fetus becomes a *neonate*, let us stop for a moment to evaluate what is known of factors that may influence prenatal development. For a long time, that is throughout the history of man, almost nothing was actually known about the nature of prenatal factors, until recent years when scientific studies of this problem were made. As might be suspected, when ignorance abounded superstition flourished. Hence it was that each culture developed its own brand of "old wives' tales" and myths. Among the commonly recurring myths was one "explaining" that a specific emotional experience of the mother had a direct and sometimes devastating effect upon the embryo or fetus. The specific content of this type of belief varied: if the mother was frightened by a blind man the child would be likely to be born blind; if the mother was terrified by a rat the child would have some special markings resembling the form or color of a rat; and so on.

From what we already know of the remarkably stable and simple conditions of prenatal environment, as well as from our knowledge of the separateness of the circulatory systems of mother and embryo, it should be clear that such beliefs are unfounded and unlikely to have any basic veracity. Conditions affecting the mother can never *directly* influence the growing organism within, although some substances absorbed by the mother may be transmitted to the embryo under certain conditions. Nevertheless, the experiences that occur to the mother, especially extreme or prolonged conditions, may have a highly indirect and complexly wrought effect upon the fetus. Knowledge of these possible effects and how they may be transmitted is only slowly accumulating, but we already know enough to state that the prenatal environment of the child may have profound effects upon the fetus and later child in certain areas. For example, there is the general principle that the tissue or organ that is in rapid process of differentiation is likely to be most influenced by noxious conditions occuring at the time. That organ will not be affected if the time of the trauma occurs before or after this peak period of its development.

We have said previously that there is no direct connection between the mother's blood stream and the embryo's. However, just as certain chemicals and nutritive substances may be absorbed through the semipermeable membranes of placenta and umbilicus, usually with benign effects, so may other noxious chemicals and toxic agents be transmitted. Such noxious types of transmissions may injure the embryo. We shall consider some of these conditions first. When the mother suffers intense or prolonged anxiety or emotional distress, there is an effect upon her physiological responses. In turn, the increased cell activity and hormonal discharge indirectly affect the embryo. Thus, although there is no direct connection between mother's and embryo's nervous system, the embryo may show increased bodily movements, and at birth, under the conditions described, the baby may be underweight or be hyperactive. In more serious cases stillbirth, eating difficulties, gastrointestinal upset, and sleep disturbances may be some of the postnatal aftereffects. Some babies seem to show increased need for affectional gratification. (See references 13 and 14 for specific research findings.) Moreover, not only conscious experiences of the mother, but unconscious conflicts and attitudes, if severe enough or prolonged enough, may affect not only the mother's autonomic activity but the behavior and development of the fetus and neonate (15, 16).

Another condition that has recently been studied is the Rh blood factor. About 15 per cent of mothers have an Rh negative blood factor. If such a mother mates with a man having an Rh positive blood factor and has a fetus with Rh positive, she will develop antibodies. If these are produced in sufficient quantity and enter the baby's blood stream (as they may) great harm may result including mental deficiency, miscarriage, and maldevelopment or deformity. Fortunately, such conditions can be prevented entirely if the condition is known in advance and preventive measures are taken (19).

Another general condition that may affect the fetus is severe malnutrition of the mother. Such a situation may indirectly affect the diet of the fetus and produce the effects of retarded development or deformity. A few diseases, too, may adversely affect the fetus. Among the more important are German measles (especially if present before the end of the fourth month) and syphilis. Such effects are uncommon, but they should not be overlooked for they may result in cataracts, stillbirth, heart disease, and other conditions. The age of the mother at the time of conception may also have a bearing upon the health of the fetus and neonate, although here again it is probably not age as such, but the indirect effects of age upon the mother's health and upon her metabolism, in particular. The effects of drugs taken by or given to the mother have also been studied. Normally such drugs as barbiturates and narcotics taken in reasonable amounts, as they may be needed for medical reasons, have only a temporary effect upon the baby. However, excessive dosage (that is, excessive for the particular mother) may cause the infant's death by asphyxiation (since the oxygen intake may be seriously reduced) or brain damage or

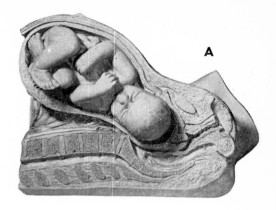

A

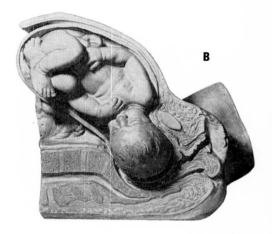

B

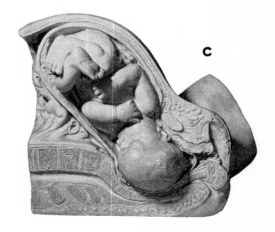

C

Six stages in the process of childbirth:

A. *The uterus at term—cervix not dilated.*
B. *Cervix dilating as the uterus contracts.*
C. *Progress of the head to pelvic floor.*

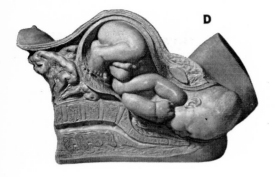

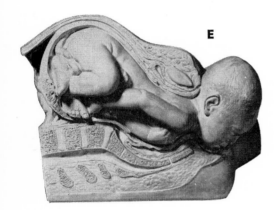

some less serious disturbance of the nervous system (17).

We wish to emphasize that we have been considering certain extreme or unusual conditions and their effects upon the embryo. Our original proposition that the prenatal environment of the infant is remarkably stable and simple (as compared with his postnatal environment) is true. We should not forget, however, that prenatal environment differs for different embryos and that these differences are sometimes very significant. We should also note that although the studies of such factors as emotional states of the mother yield significant results, their findings must be interpreted with caution since it is difficult to separate the effect of the baby's prenatal environment from his postnatal environment which may also produce or contribute to the deviant condition. Knowledge in the whole area of prenatal environment is in need of great extension and confirmation.

THE BIRTH PROCESS

" 'The birth is hard,' said the Tchambuli, 'because the mother has not gathered enough firewood' " (5). This quotation from Margaret Mead is used to illustrate the belief that the nature of the birth process may be influenced by the previous

D. *Emergence of the head as it rotates.*
E. *The further extension of the head.*
F. *The shoulder begins its emergence.*

(Courtesy Cleveland Health Museum)

experience of the mother. Not only such factors as the amount of her activity and the nature of her nutrition, but also such factors as the mother's "race," her conscious and unconscious attitudes and the culturally derived attitudes and practices attending childbirth may condition the nature of the birth process. It is interesting to observe how the pendulum has swung from the primitive position when childbirth was natural, to the position of being strapped on a delivery table in a hospital, back to the position in which "natural childbirth" is once more gaining in popularity.

Obstetricians speak of the beginning of the birth process as the onset of *labor pains*. Another indication of the imminence of birth may be the appearance of a clot of blood that has been loosened from the cervix just below the uterus. Sometimes there is a flow of amniotic fluid from the ruptured amniotic sac. Before these events have occurred, the position of the baby within the uterus has usually changed so that its head is now turned down in the direction of the cervix and vaginal canal. When birth begins the baby is no longer able to obtain sufficient nutrition and oxygen in the usual way and ejection of the baby from the uterus becomes essential. Labor begins as uterine and abdominal muscles contract to assist in the passage of the baby through the cervix and down the vaginal canal. Labor pains occur every 15 to 20 minutes at first, and during this stage the mother is able to ambulate. The duration of this stage of labor varies

greatly, being longer for first deliveries in general and depending on many physiological and anatomical factors in the mother. The frequency of labor pains increases gradually until, perhaps half a day later, the baby's passage down through the cervix begins.

The pains or contractions gradually become more frequent until they are only three minutes apart and are much more intense. Birth is impending! The baby is forced through the cervix and the pelvic region and through the vaginal canal. Contractions speed up still more until finally, some hours after they began, the head of the baby protrudes. The doctor now assists the baby in its passage through the vulva by pulling it gently as it rotates its position so that its lateral axis (the axis of the shoulders) parallels the longer axis of the vulva, and soon the baby has "escaped" into this world. This normal type of passage is known as a *vertex presentation*.

The final stage of the birth process is the expulsion of the placenta and amniotic sac, the *afterbirth*. Before this has occurred the doctor has clamped and cut the umbilical cord, and even before this the baby may have been held by its heels and given a sharp slap to encourage its extrauterine breathing. The doctor is now ready, once again, to give his attention to the mother, massaging her abdominal muscles, giving some medication to assist the uterus in its shrinkage back to normal size and to stop any small internal bleeding that may have occurred.

From the viewpoint of the neonate, it has had a "rough passage." It has been subjected to severe pressures, its position has altered radically, it has had to adjust to the sudden change in temperature, and it has had to begin independent breathing. It is now subject to a great variety of new stimuli. According to Bernfeld, the physiological phenomena that accompany birth are: a choking fit caused by initial oxygen deprivation, followed by deep inspiration; another spasm with vigorous expiration, then more regular breathing; concomitant paralyses and spurts of the circulatory system; then convulsive movements, twitching, and shivering (18). We shall have occasion to comment on the significance of these phenomena in a later section.

And what about the mother? In part, her reaction depends upon the attitudes of her immediate family and her culture. She has endured pain, although recent evidence suggests that much of this pain is needless in most cases if appropriate prenatal care is available, but she has also endured psychological anxiety—most mothers have some anxiety about whether the baby will be a normal, healthy infant, and some fear about the phenomena of childbirth. Some recent medical thinking encouraged the use of abundant sedation in some areas with diminution in the pain experienced by the mother, but this also reduced her capacity to cooperate in the process of delivery and may also have caused unfavorable effects upon the baby in its initial adjustment to the outer world. In some cases the mother may not only have been sterile, but she may have been excessively isolated from her husband and others upon whom she could lean and with whom she could share in terms of emotional experience. The rituals of birth vary tremendously, not only from primitive to modern societies, but also between successive decades and in different regions of our own society. Some doctors have decried the excessive use of sedation and have indicated that, on occasion, the psychological need of the obstetrician, rather than the medical need of the mother, may have produced some of the disadvantages of hospitalization. Certainly, more humane as well as more scientific practices are now generally emerging.

We have been discussing normal deliveries which not only occur in the vast majority of births but which are also increasingly common with improved medical care. Just a few words may be in order concerning the exceptional or abnormal delivery; it should be noted that abnormal delivery does *not* necessarily mean an abnormal child. Some babies do not pre-

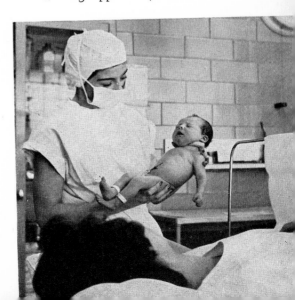

An infant shortly after birth. Note how he is being supported. (U. of Mich.)

sent the vertex position but, instead, the *transverse presentation* in which the baby's body is at right angles to the mother's longitudinal axis. The buttocks may appear first in a *breech presentation*. In such cases there is danger of asphyxiation, or of brain injury if excessive use is made of instruments for delivery. Surgical delivery through the abdominal wall, *Caesarian section* (so called because of the belief that Julius Caesar was thus delivered), may be used to avoid danger to mother and child in these and other cases. There may be *abortion* or early expulsion of the fetus due to accidental factors or induced medically for appropriate reasons. *Stillbirth* may occur, in which a mature fetus is born dead for some unfortunate reason. Let us emphasize, to avoid any possible misconception, that unfavorable effects of childbirth have been markedly reduced and that competent medical care is further reducing these effects through constant research and improved obstetrical methods.

PREMATURITY AND POSTMATURITY

We have learned that not all babies are born at the same biological distance from conception; some are born prematurely and others postmaturely.

Technically, any baby born less than 280 days after conception is premature, although it can be understood that it is difficult to determine the fact of prematurity when the deviation from the norm is only a few days. One of the criteria of prematurity is that of appearance since a baby born during the normal fetal period looks different from one born at the normal time of gestation; usually if the weight is less than about five pounds and the over-all length is less than about 19 inches, the baby is said to be premature.

The specific effects of prematurity, *per se*, are not too clearly established. It is difficult to disentangle the effects of prenatal conditions from conditions during birth, and especially from postnatal conditions when the mother may be oversolicitous and overprotective. All of these, singly or in combination, may contribute to the baby's subsequent development. Insofar as physical status is concerned, evidence indicates that premature children catch up to children born at the normal period within six months to a year, with the exception of postural control which may take another half year or so before normal controls are established. The picture is quite different with respect to emotional and intellectual maturation, where there is suggestive evidence to indicate that premature children are likely to be slightly retarded for a longer period of time; they tend to be more irritable, more aggressive or submissive, and have more feeding difficulties. Howard and Worrell's study on 22 premature children is indicative of such findings (19). However, in this study as in others, the control factors of a matched sample of "normals," the postnatal environment, and prenatal conditions were not adequate. Gesell has indicated in one of his studies that premature infants tended to rate *higher* on his personal-social scale (20). However, not only were these infants given unusually superior care but also the degree of precocity was taken into account in evaluating the findings.

There are both advantages and disadvantages to being born prematurely. For one thing, the premature child has less difficulty in passing through the birth canal because of his small size. On the other hand, the greater softness of the skull and the consequently greater possibility of cerebral trauma may produce brain injury during birth. And brain injury at birth, associated with prematurity, may produce mental retardation. Another condition that was unnecessarily associated with prematurity during recent times, but that is rarely encountered today, is a form of blindness known as *retrolental fibroplasia,* which appears to have been due to the excessive or prolonged use of oxygen.

We may conclude, in terms of our present knowledge, that prematurity is not of itself necessarily abnormal, although accidents associated with this phenomenon or effects due to unfortunate postnatal care because mothers may be unduly anxious may contribute to retardation or maladjustment.

Our knowledge concerning postmaturity is fairly adequate with respect to physical factors but is quite limited with respect to psychological consequences. Technically, most authorities refer to the condition of a baby at birth as "postmature" when it is delivered more than 280 days after conception. However, as in the case of prematurity, it is not an easy matter to establish the fact of postmaturity. The vast majority of postmature babies are less than 305 days old (from the point of conception), roughly three weeks or less postmature. Contrary to the popular supposition, most postmature infants are not oversized; only about 10 per cent are. The reason for this is that the placenta has usually degenerated before birth and the fetus does not continue to obtain normal amounts of nourishment. Many postmature babies are even undersized. However, if the infant weighs more than nine pounds and there is other evidence to substantiate it, postmaturity may be suspected.

In most cases, the birth process of postmature infants is similar to that of norm l-term babies. Labor may be somewhat more difficult or prolonged in the final stages. Otherwise, since size and even the stage of ossification are not essentially different from normal-term babies, what differences there are may be regarded as insignificant. If there is a marked increase in size, or if the fetus has lost its protective covering (the *vernix caseosa*), or if gestation has been unduly prolonged, the chances of mortality or of serious damage increase.

Postmature babies are somewhat advanced in their capacities for adjustment to the external world, although this difference from normal-term babies soon becomes unimportant. The unique reactions of the mother who has such a baby (especially her anxieties, unfounded beliefs, and the like) may influence the adjustment and behavior of the infant more than the simple biological fact of postmaturity. This may occur if the mother becomes oversolicitous or overprotective in her care of the newborn infant.

THE PSYCHOLOGICAL MEANING OF BIRTH TO MOTHER AND CHILD

We have already commented briefly on the physiological stresses to which the baby is subjected during the birth process and have noted some of the experiences of the mother during this event. Now we are ready to consider more fully the psychological significance of birth to these two individuals.

There can be little doubt that extremes of conditions during the birth process may have severe effects upon the subsequent psychological development of the

Weighing the baby is an important part of developmental care. (U. of Mich.)

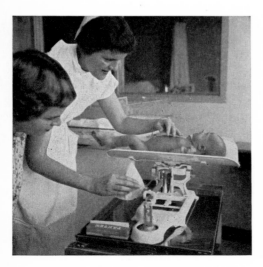

child, for as we have seen such sequelae as blindness, mental deficiency, irritability, and insomnia may follow. It is much more difficult to assess the psychological effects of more nearly normal or normal birth. At one extreme is the position of Rank who felt that the shock of birth was always so great that it created a reservoir of anxiety which served as the basis of all later anxiety throughout life (21). Freud, who disagreed with Rank on this matter, believed nevertheless that birth trauma produced "the first prototype of the anxiety reaction. . . ." His position was that the child could not yet consciously experience anxiety, as such, and hence could not have a truly valid anxiety reaction although the severity of the physiological reaction was significant in providing a neurological reaction pattern (a prototype) (22). Greenacre, who carefully reviewed the evidence up to the time of her 1943 paper, had the following to say about this problem: "The anxiety response which is genetically determined probably manifests itself first in an irritable responsiveness of the organism at a reflex level. . . . How much this total reaction is potentially present but not elicited before birth, and how much birth itself may, even in the individual life, play a reenforcing or organizing role, is not clearly determinable at present. . . . Variations in the birth process may . . . increase the (organic) anxiety response and heighten the anxiety potential, causing a more severe reaction to later (psychological) dangers in life" (23). This cautious statement is still a good summary of our present knowledge on the subject.

Recent research has confirmed the conclusion that the severity of the birth trauma is correlated with irritability and general hyperactivity in the infant's behavior. (See, for example, the study by Wile and Davis, 24.) The results are equivocal, however, with respect to any "permanent" aftereffects of birth trauma except in extreme cases. Research is difficult in this area not only because of problems in controlling for such factors as the severity of labor, the influence of prenatal conditions, and the biological readiness of the fetus for the trauma of birth, but also because it is difficult to evaluate the relative severity of birth trauma in spontaneous versus surgical delivery. Readiness for subsequent anxiety reactions may in some way be related to the normal trauma of birth, and heightened nervous irritability may be increased by it, but beyond such general statements we can say little else with assurance, at present.

We know more about the nature of the mother's reactions to her child's birth. In a recent study, it was reported that from 18 to 34 per cent of mothers were displeased or had mixed feelings about their pregnancy (6), the frequency of reported displeasure being positively related to the ordinal position of the child (less displeasure was reported for "first children"). We can be sure that the frequency of unconscious conflict about the birth of a child is much higher than these figures reporting conscious conflict. The mother's attitudes are conditioned by her conscious and unconscious concepts of her role as a "woman." For some women, there is great difficulty at an unconscious level in accepting the idea of becoming a mother even though they may con-

sciously wish to become a mother. Such a change in status or role may mean, for them, losing their glamour, becoming submissive to man, finding a competitor for the affection of their husbands, giving up their real or fantasied goal of following a career. The period of pregnancy may cause not only its normal physical discomfitures but may produce exaggerated reactions to the changes in physical size and shape. The act of childbirth may be unduly frightening and unfounded fears about the consequences of childbirth to health and attractiveness may be present. These are only a few of the many and varied reactions of mothers to childbirth (2, 36).

Even when a mother appears to consider her participation in the act of bearing a child with equanimity, her reactions may be far from placid or favorable. The way in which her husband relates to her and shares in all of her experiences may be crucial in determining how well she is able to accept and work through the normal problems of having a child. Further, the mother's attitudes and reactions to childbirth may have a very significant bearing upon her relationship with her infant and upon his personality development, as we shall see in the next chapter.

"HE WAS BORN THAT WAY"— HEREDITY AND CONSTITUTION

We are all familiar with some of the variations in the story of the mother, distraught by the behavior of her son, who exclaimed to her husband, "That son of yours gets all of his bad traits from you!" When the father, in rebuttal, pointed out what a well behaved and sensible little girl he had, the mother said, "Well, of course, she inherits those things from me." The story illustrates how often we tend to think of hereditary factors in ways that are consonant with our own feelings, but it also points up the fact that siblings usually are different from each other in many ways. How are we to explain this? Through hereditary factors, or environmental conditions, or through an interaction of the two? To understand the problem we should know something of the *mechanisms of heredity* and something of the results of research studies on heredity and eugenics. Our discussion will necessarily be a presentation of only the main principles and findings in this difficult and complex area.

In the previous section dealing with the embryonic development of the child we have already indicated that although the prenatal environment is basically stable and similar for most children, there are variations—some moderate and some extreme. We pointed out that the child reacts to these prenatal factors and that, in fact, he learns some kinds of responses even before he is born. Moreover, the intra- and intercellular influences, as well as the extracellular factors, condition the growth process. Hence, what a child is at birth is not entirely a matter of heredity.

Nevertheless what a child is born with —his biological constitution—is primarily a result of hereditary factors, the remaining influences before and during the birth process being *congenital*. We will recall that the human organism results from the union of two germ cells, the spermatozoön and the ovum. The carriers of heredity are in these cells. More specifically, the carriers are contained in the *chromosomes* of these cells—rod-like structures which are visible under the microscope. Each germ cell has, in fact, 24 pairs of chromosomes, or 48 chromosomes. Germ cells, like other bodily cells, grow and divide in the usual way up to the point when they are about to become recognizable spermatozoa and ova. At this time, unlike all other cells, they undergo a process known as *reduction division* wherein the pairs of chromosomes, one of each pair having come from each of the parents, split up into two groups. The split is not into one cell with the chromosomes from the male parent and the other with chromosomes from the female parent, but appears to be random so that the 24 which remain in one cell may have come in a unique pattern from each parent. Then when the spermatozoön and ovum unite, each with its 24 chromosomes, the zygote once again contains 48 chromosomes. Hence it is that different zygotes formed during different conceptions of the same parents are likely to be different to some degree—in fact are almost sure to be different.

Moreover, the mechanism of heredity is still more complex. The specific traits transmitted through heredity are thought to be embodied in the *genes*, great numbers of which are present in each chromosome. Before the stage of the spermatozoön and the ovum has been reached, there has been a process of cell division

during which a great amount of reshuf-
fling of the genes has taken place. Hence,
each germ cell is different from every
other germ cell. When a particular germ
cell of the male unites with that of the
female the chances are exceptionally high
that the particular combination will
never be repeated. This explains why all
siblings (*identical* twins excepted) are
unique. It also explains why siblings tend
to have much in common—since the pool
of genes from which they ultimately
emerge is different from the pools of

genes from which children of other parents emerge. We noted previously that
fraternal twins, developing from the fertilization of two different ova during the
same ovulation period, inherited *different*
characteristics, since they were not produced from the same ovum or the same
zygote. In this respect fraternal twins are
like other pairs of siblings. The case of
identical twins is different. Such twins

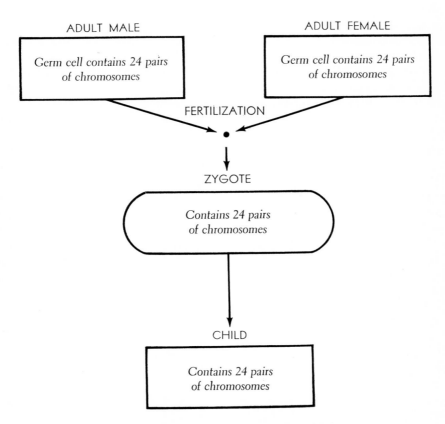

Figure 3. *The basic genetic process in inheritance.*

are produced from the union of a single male germ cell and a single female germ cell. In this case, there is a split in the zygote *after* it has formed and two different organisms, with presumably the same combinations of genes, develop. It must be remembered, however, that even identical twins may and probably do have somewhat different prenatal environments (position, pressure, nutrition) so that they are not entirely alike at the time of birth.

Now we must introduce two additional complications in this abbreviated discussion of the mechanisms of heredity. The first of these has to do with the notion of inherited traits. Geneticists speak of *unitary traits* by which they mean, most often, a specific biological structure; sometimes they mean other things with the same term. Presumably, genes determine the presence or absence of many structural properties, and may determine the predisposition for others. Many of these biological characteristics still depend upon environmental conditions for their subsequent development or the degree of their development. However, the problem is not as simple as this for psychological traits (as we shall see shortly). It has been extremely difficult to pin down specific psychological traits which are determined by heredity; almost all, if not all, psychological traits are specifically the resultants of postnatal experience and only based in a general way on the biological constitution with which an individual is born. Moreover, even physical traits may be the result of combinations or patterns of genes rather than of single genes.

The second of the complications is that resulting from the fact that some traits are *dominant* (tend to dominate in manifestation when the contrasting or recessive characteristic is present), whereas others are *recessive* (tend to be subordinate in manifestation to the dominant trait). For example, the characteristic of black hair is dominant and that of red hair is recessive. This means that when an organism inherits two genes for hair color they may both be dominant, or they may both be recessive or there may be a combination of a dominant and a recessive gene. In general, when mixed dominance is present, the dominant gene predominates but the recessive gene is, of course, carried in the "germ stream." Some examples of dominant traits are: brown eyes, blood types A, B, and AB, susceptibility to tuberculosis; some examples of recessive traits are: straight hair, absence of allergic sensitivity, color blindness in women.

The determination of the sex of the child is a problem in dominance-recessive characteristics. One of the pairs of chromosomes in the male and one in the female carries sex determinants. In the male, this pair of chromosomes consists of one X and one Y chromosome. In the female, the parts of the pair are always alike, there being two X chromosomes. When the germ cell in the male splits before maturation, one has the X factor and the other the Y. Thus, the zygote may contain two X's or an X (from the female ovum) and a Y (from the male sperm). In the former case, the child will be a girl, and in the latter case a boy.

Thus far we have spoken of genes as if they developed inviolate in the bodies of the parents. There was a time when the doctrine of *the inheritance of acquired traits,* promulgated by Lamarck in the eighteenth century, was widely accepted. According to this view, the genes could be modified by training or specific experiences of the parent. At the extreme such a doctrine would suggest that a virtuoso of the piano, through long and intensive experience in playing the piano, would so modify his genes that his offspring would inherit not only more supple and facile hands and fingers but a sensitivity for piano music.* That such a conception is false we now know largely as the result of experimental evidence accumulated by Weismann near the end of the nineteenth century (25). However, we also know now that the genes are not entirely immune to external influences. There may be spontaneous changes in the genes over long periods of time, that is over many generations (a process known as *spontaneous mutation*), but there may also be changes resulting from certain kinds of severe trauma. For example, recent evidence has indicated that the genes may be adversely affected by exposure to nuclear radiation in certain amounts, with resulting deformities or deficiencies in later generations. Direct X-ray exposure in excessive amounts may have a similar effect. Some types of chemicals may also produce changes in the genes. Thus, the genes are not quite inviolate nor are they immune to certain extreme conditions.

From the above we can get some idea of how complex the problem of inheritance is. Nature never determines completely the development of any trait; nurture always plays its role in the way in which a trait or a predisposition toward a trait develops. *The interaction of the two factors is always to be reckoned with in the development of human features.* Now, to see to what an extent hereditary or environmental factors contribute to specific traits, we may look at the results of the most recent research. Some of this evidence is highly inferential since it is based upon experiments with plants and animals, the results of which can only be applied by analogy to humans. Much of the most pertinent evidence is based upon comparative studies of identical twins, fraternal twins, siblings, and unrelated children.*

We can begin with a generalization: *the more we move in the direction of psychological characteristics and away from physical characteristics, the more specific environmental factors are influential in determining the nature and the extent of the developmental pattern.* The classic studies by Newmann, Freeman, and Holzinger on twins were the first to elucidate this principle (26). Recent research on severe mental illness has demonstrated that the old belief in the inheritance of such illness (or psychosis)

---

* A recent revival of this theory was favored in the Soviet Union by Lysenko and his followers but was not accepted by authorities in the Western world.

* A very readable exposition of the problems of heredity may be found in the revised book by Scheinfeld (7).

is unfounded and most researchers in this field now believe that there *may* be an inherited predisposition for some types of mental illness or for mental illness in general, but that most cases of psychosis are environmental in origin.

It should be noted that studies comparing identical with fraternal twins on the assumption that identical twins have a much higher degree of similarity in inheritance also tend to make another assumption: that there are no differences in the postnatal environments of these

The baby will "sop up" both nutrition and affection readily. (U. of Mich.)

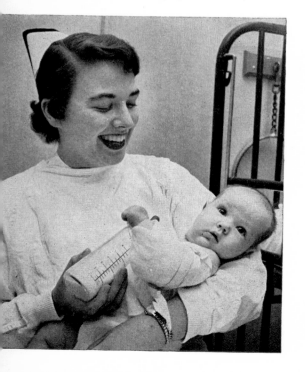

two groups. When it is recalled that fraternal twins may be different in sex whereas identical twins are always of the same sex and when it is noted that there are other differences in the appearance of the two groups, it can be appreciated that the parents may react more differentially to fraternal than identical twins and thus provide different "environments." This is not the only methodological difficulty in such comparisons, but it may serve to emphasize the difficulty in designing appropriate studies and in interpreting the results.

Most studies have shown that there is greater similarity in the physical and physiological characteristics of identical twins than in that of fraternal twins and that there is a *tendency* for the similarities of fraternal twins to be greater than that of siblings. One of the interesting reports deals with eye movements of the two types of twins. Studies of such phenomena (and there are still very few of them) are important because it is far less likely that this type of factor is as directly susceptible to ordinary postnatal experiences as are other learned or complex skills. In a report by Stern, identical twins were found to be more alike than fraternal twins (27). In general, studies in this area support the proposition offered above, except that results are generally inconclusive for most complex motor skills—in which learning may play a significant role.

A number of other studies have dealt with specific physiological indices, such as blood pressure. These have indicated that there is an interactive relationship between heredity and environment. One series of studies by Jost and Sontag used a combined index based on a number of separate measures of physiological behaviors, such as blood pressure and pulse rate (28). They called this an index of *autonomic stability.* They compared identical twins with pairs of siblings and pairs of unrelated children and were able to show that the twins were most alike on this index and that the unrelated children were most dissimilar. Thus there is the possibility that hereditary factors play a significant, *contributory* role to what we may call excitability or nervous reactivity. We have said "contributory" because the size of the correlations that they found (the measure of the degree of similarity or relationship) for identical twins was only of the order of 0.4 (and a correlation of 1.0 would represent perfect similarity).

The research studies dealing with the contribution of hereditary factors to personality traits that have been conducted up to the present have yielded findings that are far from conclusive. Heredity seems to play a part, as it does in mental illness, perhaps contributing to a predisposition to develop in one direction rather than another, but specific environmental experiences seem largely responsible for the degree and specific form of such traits or of mental illness. This viewpoint is strongly supported by cross-cultural studies of personality and of mental illness.

APPEARANCE AND BEHAVIOR OF THE "LITTLE BUNDLE"

The beguiling, full-colored advertisements of the newborn baby appealing to all the world to buy a very special type of talcum powder are, unfortunately, not true to life. The often scrawny, wet, awkward-looking, sticky-covered newborn just doesn't look so attractive, although he may look like that in a few weeks or a few months!

The period from birth to the time when the child has made a stable adjustment to the extrauterine world and has perfected the functioning of his vegetative system is known as the *neonatal period.* As might be guessed, authorities differ in the limits they set for this period, perhaps the most common being two weeks, with variations from one week to one month. At birth the neonate usually weighs about seven pounds and is about twenty inches in total length. Boys average about 4 per cent more in weight and about 2 per cent more in length than girls. The neonate has a coating, or protective layer, over his skin which dries and rubs off in a few days. He is a complete human being insofar as structure is concerned and he has all the organs necessary for human functioning, but he is still helpless, fragile, and in need of protection against sudden changes in temperature, pressure, and stimulation. His skull still has several openings covered by tough membranes (fontanels). Of course, his appearance will differ if he is premature or postmature.

Although all neonates may look very much alike at first glance, they are actually very different in appearance and even "feel" different. They differ in weight and size; they differ in the characteristic position they assume, although most lie with the head on one side; they differ in how they "feel" when they are held up, some being quite stiff and others loose and relaxed. The eye color of the neonate may differ from the later eye color of the child. Both the male and female neonates have enlarged breasts which produce a "milk" or secretion.

The spontaneous or provoked birthcry ushers in the baby's independent breathing and is symptomatic of its beginning of a nonparasitic existence. It is probably capable of taking in food very shortly after birth, for the stomach enzymes that help in digesting food are already available. In fact, some anthropological studies have reported that, unlike our culture, in some cultures babies are fed almost immediately after birth. In any case, it won't be very long before the neonate's blood pressure and blood oxygen level are established at normal postnatal limits and blood circulation is fully adequate to maintain an independent life.

Babies not only look different and feel different, but act differently from each other; they have unique personalities, albeit of a most rudimentary sort. These differences may be hereditary or constitutional (resulting from prenatal or birth experiences). We previously noted the results of the work of Jost and Sontag on autonomic stability of children. Fries has shown that babies differ in the characteristic amount and pattern of gross activity from birth on (29, 30). She classified them in this respect as: "active," "moderately active," and "quiet." These differences predispose them differently to

their earliest experiences, so that the active child is less able to tolerate restraint, whereas the quiet child tends to withdraw unless given extra stimulation. What is even more significant, possibly, is that these trends tend to become exaggerated when the mother is unstable or excitable whereas trends "toward the mean" (more moderate, balanced behavior) develop when the mother is warm, accepting, and affectionate. It has also been noted by other workers that the neonate's pattern of behavior tends to influence the way in which the mother responds to him, consciously or unconsciously. From such data one can infer, again, how complex and intricate is the process of personality development.

The neonate is rather easily susceptible to respiratory and gastrointestinal infection. Hence, careful pediatric and medical care is necessary to prevent such occurrences. On the other hand, if, during and following the neonatal period, the baby lives a too-sheltered existence, so that it is not *gradually* exposed to some irregularities and stimuli, the process of maturation and the development of resistance may be significantly retarded so that later infection cannot be coped with by the organism. A healthy environment is not necessarily the most aseptic and protected one.

Immediately after birth the baby sleeps most of the time, awakening only when disturbed by tensions: hunger pangs, intense noise or light stimulation. Even during sleep it may manifest "fits" or convulsions as it responds more or less diffusely to internal stimulation. It has fully or nearly fully developed internal sense organs which respond to stimulation from within the body. These sense organs are of two kinds: the *proprioceptors* (nerve endings in the muscles, tendons and joints), and *interoceptors* (nerve endings in the internal membranes of the stomach and the like). Thus, the neonate is able to respond to (and perhaps experience in some way) movements of the body, hunger pangs, and so on.

We have stressed the fact that the baby's behavior is *mass* and *diffuse*, except for certain reflexive behaviors. Two of these reflexes are particularly interesting. One is the *Moro reflex* in which the baby responds to sudden and intense sounds by throwing out its arms and then embracing itself tightly—which can be interpreted as a protective response. The other is the *Babinski reflex*, which gradually disappears, and in which the baby responds to stroking of the soles of its feet by an upward and fanning movement of its toes. (Later, the response to this stimulation is a downward and curling movement of the toes.)

Now that we have obtained an over-all picture of the appearance and behavior of the neonate, let us look at some selected aspects of other behaviors. We shall not attempt a detailed or technical description of all aspects of gross behavior and physiology, such as is available in a number of excellent manuals and books. (See, for example, 31.) Of special importance is the intake of food. The sucking response is highly developed at birth. Tactile stimulation of the side of the cheek, for example, will evoke sucking movements, especially when the baby is hungry. When the baby is hungry its stomach muscles will contract and it will become restless and perhaps cry. As

Gesell and Ilg have shown, babies vary greatly in their hunger needs and hunger responses (32). When the baby is hungry it will tend to grasp anything that comes within reach and it will begin to suck. If a sugar ball is put in its mouth, it will not only become more quiescent but it will even become impervious to pain. (This method is used during circumcision with great success.) Different cultures respond in different ways to the baby's hunger and sucking needs, and in our own country we have changed our attitudes drastically, from practices of *schedule feeding* to *demand feeding*. Psychoanalysts have suggested that adequate sucking experience is necessary, aside from its relation to food intake, for appropriate stimulation of the infant through his *oral zone* (see Chapter 4). They have postulated that adequate experience of this kind helps to produce

An examining crib. Note the test materials suspended out of view. (Gesell)

such character traits as confidence, optimism, and stability whereas insufficient experience helps to produce such traits as pessimism, suspiciousness, and impatience. Some of the critics of such propositions have tried to assess the effect of differences in oral gratification by itself, without consideration of the *total constellation* in which such experience appears. It appears to make considerable difference under what circumstances the feeding is done—what the total pattern of the oral gratification involves. Recent experimental evidence by Goldman-Eisler, in an investigation of feeding and weaning experiences of middle-class individuals, strongly supports the general postulate given above (33). Experimental evidence with puppies, in a study by Levy, points in the same direction (34).

The neonate is able to see, although the movements of its eyes are nonsynchronous and poorly controlled, so that its eyes often cross over. It is apparently unable to focus in the beginning or to discriminate the outer world from itself. That it can see and respond to light shortly after birth was demonstrated in an experiment by Pratt (31). The neonate is also able to hear—the Moro reflex is indicative of this behavior capacity, for example. These capacities make the possibility of early learning more significant. Several studies have shown that neonates learn, although some of the results of this learning do not last very long. One of the earliest studies was that of D. P. Marquis who demonstrated that babies could be conditioned to the sound of a buzzer if this sound was made a number of times immediately after the presentation of the bottle and nipple. Subsequently, some of the babies responded to the sound of the buzzer with sucking behavior (35).

We have stated that the neonate sleeps most of the time except when it is hungry or tense. When it does become restless, it will clutch diffusely, it will squirm while making waving movements of the arms and perhaps of the legs, and it will suck. The baby will often cry a great deal when awake, and it will hiccough and cough, sometimes responding to being picked up, even when it is not fed. Its respiration is poorly developed at birth, and mucus may further interfere with easy breathing. It will eat but it will also regurgitate much of its food. It will defecate, usually shortly after birth, with waste products and glandular secretions that have accumulated (and been swallowed) during its prenatal existence.

By and large, however, during the neonatal period when the transition from a vegetative to an "independent" status is being made, the neonate is passive. We shall have more to say about the possible significance of this passivity in Chapter 4. We shall also leave to Chapter 4, after a further discussion of variations in cu'-tural practices, the analysis of some general principles of development.

GENERAL READINGS

1. Berne, E., *The Mind in Action*. New York: Simon and Schuster, 1947.
2. Deutsch, H., *Psychology of Women*. New York: Grune & Stratton, Vol. I, 1944, Vol. II, 1945.
3. Gesell, A., in collaboration with Amatruda, C. S., *The Embryology of Behavior, The Beginnings of the Human Mind*. New York: Harper, 1945.
4. Gesell, A., and Ilg, F. L., *Child Development*. New York: Harper, 1949.
5. Mead, M., *Male and Female*. New York: Morrow, 1949.
6. Sears, R. R., Macoby, E. F., and Levin, H., *Patterns of Child Rearing*. Evanston, Illinois: Row, Peterson, 1957.
7. Scheinfeld, A., *The New You and Heredity*. Philadelphia: Lippincott, 1950.
8. Watson, E. H., and Lowrey, G. H., *Growth and Development of Children*. Chicago: Year Book Publishers, 1954.
9. Whiting, J. W. M., and Child, I. L., *Child Training and Personality*. New Haven: Yale University, 1953.

SELECTED BIBLIOGRAPHY

10. Stockard, C. R., *The Physical Basis of Personality*. New York: Norton, 1931.
11. Spemann, H., "Organizers in animal development," *Proc. Roy. Soc. London*, 1927, 102 B, 177-187.
12. Irwin, O. C., and Weiss, A. P., "A note on mass activity in newborn infants," *J. Genet. Psychol.*, 1930, 38, 20-30.
13. Sontag, L. W., "The significance of fetal environmental differences," *Amer. J. Obstet. and Gynec.*, 1941, 42, 996-1003.
14. Squier, R., and Dunbar, F., "Emotional factors in the course of pregnancy," *Psychosom. Med.*, 1946, 8, 161-175.
15. Despres, M. A., "Favorable and unfavorable attitudes toward pregnancy in primaparae," *J. Genet. Psychol.*, 1937, 51, 241-254.
16. Sontag, L. W., "War and fetal maternal relationship," *Marriage and Family Living*, 1944, 6, 1-5.
17. Montagu, M. F. A., "Constitutional and prenatal factors in infant and child health," in Senn, M. J. E. (ed.), *Symposium on the Healthy Personality*. New York: Josiah Macy Jr. Foundation, 1950.
18. Bernfeld, S., *The Psychology of the Infant*. New York: Brentano, 1929.
19. Howard, P. J., and Worrell, C. H., "Premature infants in later life: a

study of intelligence and personality of 22 premature infants at ages 8 and 19 years," *Pediatr.*, 1952, 9, 577-584.

20. Gesell, A., "Behavior aspects of care of premature infants," *J. Pediatr.*, 1946, 29, 210.
21. Rank, O., *The Trauma of Birth*. New York: Harcourt, Brace, 1929.
22. Freud, S., *The Problem of Anxiety*. New York: Norton, 1936.
23. Greenacre, P., "The predisposition to anxiety," Chapter 3 in Tompkins, S. S. (ed.), *Contemporary Psychopathology*. Cambridge: Harvard University, 1943.
24. Wile, I. S., and Davis, R., "The relation of birth to behavior," *Amer. J. Orthopsychiat.*, 1941, 11, 320-334.
25. Weismann, A., *Essays upon Heredity and Kindred Biological Problems*. New York: Oxford, 1899.
26. Newmann, H. H., Freeman, R. N., and Holzinger, K. J., *Twins: A Study of Heredity and Environment*. Chicago: University of Chicago, 1937.
27. Stern, C., *Principles of Human Genetics*. San Francisco: Freeman, 1949.
28. Jost, H., and Sontag, L. W., "The genetic factor in autonomic nervous system function," *Psychosom. Med.*, 1944, 6, 308-310.
29. Fries, M. E., "Factors in character development, neuroses, psychoses, and delinquency," *Amer. J. Orthopsychiat.*, 1937, 7, 142-181.
30. Fries, M. E., "Psychosomatic relationships between mother and child," *Psychosom. Med.*, 1944, 6, 157-162.
31. Pratt, K. C., "The Neonate," in Carmichael, L. (ed.), *Manual of Child Psychology*, 2nd edition. New York: Wiley, 1954.
32. Gesell, A., and Ilg, F. L., *The Feeding Behavior of Infants*. Philadelphia: Lippincott, 1937.
33. Goldman-Eisler, F., "Breast feeding and character formation," in Kluckhohn, C., and Murray, H. A. (eds.), *Personality in Nature, Society, and Culture*. New York: Knopf, 1953.
34. Levy, D. M., "Experiments on the sucking reflex and social behavior of dogs," *Amer. J. Orthopsychiat.*, 1934, 4, 203-224.
35. Marquis, D. P., "Can conditioned responses be established in the newborn infant?" *J. Genet. Psychol.*, 1931, 39, 479-492.
36. Hall, D. E., and Mohr, G. J., "Prenatal attitudes of primaparae: a contribution to the mental hygiene of pregnancy," *Ment. Hygiene*, 1933, 17, 226-234.

3

The child
"inherits" a culture

In this chapter we shall consider the problem of the interaction of the biological organism with the cultural milieu in which it develops. We have already seen that the child inherits the tendency to develop certain specific physical structures, and also inherits *potentials* for developing a wide variety of human traits. These tendencies do not simply unfold. They are nourished, conditioned, modified, and molded by postnatal experiences. As we have seen, they have already been modified before birth by prenatal experiences. Their limits and their direction may be fixed by biological inheritance, but their actualization, their specific patterns, and their specific values will depend on the total interaction of the organism and its environment. When we say that a certain characteristic is "human nature" we often think we are referring to some innate, biologically determined characteristic, whereas this characteristic may be as much, or even more, a function of the cultural heritage with which an individual is born and the particular way he responds to it and to other cultural experiences that he seeks out and *internalizes*. In short, we are born not only with a biological but with a cultural heritage.

THE MEANING OF CULTURE

The term *culture* has been defined in many ways by anthropologists. Boas once defined it as that "which embraces all manifestations of social habits of a community, the reactions of the individual as affected by the habits of the group in which he lives, and the products of human activity as determined by these habits" (9). This is a very comprehensive concept of culture and is a quite technical definition. We may think of culture, more simply, as the pattern of living shared by a group of people. This pattern includes such things as language, habits of dress, ethics, implements, art, social controls, and daily routines. The Yale Cross-Cultural Survey has defined a wide variety of categories which go into the total pattern of cultural modes. These culture patterns are transmitted by society through its customs, its laws, and the ways of life that are impressed upon its members. Each society may have many *cultures* and the cultures of a society tend to change as the society evolves and effectuates new modes of living. (Compare the Deep South with New England, for example, or compare the Deep South of the nineteenth with that of the twentieth century.)

Culture is not a thing apart from and above the life of the members of a society, although some anthropologists have conceptualized it in just that way for purposes of more rigorous methodological study. (See, for example, White, 10.) All members of a cultural group share and are influenced by the cultural heritage of that group, so much so that it seems "quite natural" to the members of that group to behave that way—in fact, it almost seems inborn. Analysis of this quality of apparent "inbornness" will indicate that the cultural pattern has been *interiorized,* or *enculturated* as the an-

thropologists say. In other words, the habitual cultural ways of reacting have been absorbed (or, more accurately, learned) so that they function automatically in the lives of many or most members of the group. At the same time, although all members of the group may be exposed to the group's culture, all do not react to these influences in the same way. In fact, it can be said that no two members of a group respond to its culture in exactly the same way. The manner in which an individual responds to his culture is dependent upon the nature of his biological characteristics, his unique pattern of needs, and the subjective way in which he experiences the culture. From a biological viewpoint, the individual's intelligence, the kind of autonomic activity he has, his sensory equipment, and even his rate of metabolism influence his reaction to cultural factors. Similarly, a person's needs influence his perception of cultural experiences and determine the ways in which he reacts to such experiences in many other ways. Finally, the total subjective state of the individual, that is the way he feels, the significance for him on both conscious and unconscious levels of his experiences, and his particular goals in life may modify his reactions to his cultural experience (10).

We can see, therefore, how complex is the interaction between culture and organism. There is still another dimension to this problem that we must not fail to consider. An individual may not be a passive respondent to the cultural experiences of his group. It has been demonstrated that individuals vary in the ways in which they reach out and make use of other cultural phenomena than those that are inherent in their own cultural group. They may be influenced by what they see and hear about other cultural groups. They may travel and intermingle in such ways as to maximize their contacts with a variety of cultural experiences. Their already formed or developing personality characteristics may influence such additive acculturations in a variety of ways (11).

To begin with, however, the individual at birth is "born into" a particular culture, and is largely captive with respect to these influences that he experiences. (In Chapter 2 we indicated how culture may affect prenatal development.) Group differences in such early postnatal cultural effects, the cultural heritage, may profoundly affect early child development. It is to this problem that we next turn our attention.

CULTURE AND PERSONALITY

In our detailed examination of the interaction of culture and personality in early infancy, we shall begin with the proposition that there is no ubiquitous, fixed cultural pattern in which the baby is reared or even in the ways in which biological needs are met. For example, it is not always the biological mother who takes care of the baby or who feeds him. Among the Alorese, an Indonesian people, the baby is frequently taken care of by the father while the mother is occupied in the fields with her chores. At other times a sibling or a grandparent may be responsible for the baby. During these times that the mother is away, sometimes as early as the second week after its birth, the baby is given pre-masticated food or it may remain hungry until the mother returns (12). At the other extreme are the Hopi Indians of our own country. These Indians are extremely indulgent in their care of the baby, who is breast-fed by its mother whenever it shows any inclination to want nourishment (13). In this respect, the use of the breast as a pacifier or as a comforter is also practiced by Okinawans (14) and the Comanche (12). Our only point at this time is that there are great variabilities in the kinds of interactions between mother and infant which are related to culture variabilities.

Some constancies in the culture of infants

Despite the marked differences that exist among cultures in respect to early patterns of child-mother interactions, there are also marked constancies. After all, the newborn child is a helpless, dependent individual who will die unless its nutritional needs are met and unless it is protected from injury and disease. Hence, with few exceptions, there has been a *minimal constancy* in the relationship between infant and mother (or the adult who takes care of him). This type of constancy makes it very difficult to know what is inborn in the infant, what is "instinctive" in the mother, and what is the learned effect of the persistent modes of interaction. An illustration of this difficulty in the case of subhuman species will make this point more explicit. Psychologists had long assumed that animals as well as humans were born with certain

The culture influences the child's appearance and behavior. (U. of Mich.)

instincts: certain inborn ways of behaving to reach specified goals without opportunity of learning these behaviors. Most of the texts in psychology of a few decades ago contained the particular author's list of such animal or human instincts, and psychologists vied with each other in compiling more complete and exhaustive lists. These instincts were assumed to be present because of the apparent, unvarying behavior of the particular species. However, when in experimental studies the conditions of "minimal constancy" were varied, surprising results were obtained. For example, Schneirla found, in a review of the experimental literature of maternal behavior of lower animals, that much of the so-called instinctive maternal behavior was not instinctive at all but was the result of interactions of learning, socialization, and specific types of chemical excitation (15). It was learned that when a cat is prevented from licking parts of its body that are *customarily* licked during parturition or when the cat is prevented from licking at the afterbirth, its interest in licking its neonate and even its very interest in the neonate may be entirely lacking; i.e., such interests are not automatic and instinctive. Many studies have now demonstrated that, in fact, there are no true maternal instincts in animals, although some authorities do not accept this proposition entirely. In a similar way, studies have shown that what was formerly assumed to be instinctive in the infant animal was attributable to the combined effects of development, learning, and socialization. Again, merely by way of illustration, a study by Scott may be cited (16). In this study, it was reported that a female lamb, separated from its mother and from usual mothering experiences for the first nine days of its life, failed to respond in the "instinctive" manner of young lambs. It did not suckle and did not graze with the other lambs. (In fact, it seemed to prefer people and was rejected by other lambs!)

From the foregoing we can begin to see that the behavior of a newborn organism is considerably influenced by the early experiences to which it is subjected —by its cultural heritage. We have tried to indicate, too, that the interactions between infant and culture are highly complex, embracing such *patterns* of behavior as methods of giving nourishment, methods of giving affection and sensual stimulation, methods of control and discipline, and experiences in interactions with single individuals or with groups of individuals in constant or inconstant ways. Each of these units of interaction and many others contain many complexities within themselves. For example, methods of giving nourishment may vary in terms of what is fed, the amount of food offered, the frequency of feeding, the salient factors determining the times of feeding, the concomitant behaviors of the mother during the feeding, and the like. This complexity within the units of the pattern and within the total pattern makes it difficult indeed to isolate the precise relationship and the causal influence, if any, between an individual factor in the infant's early experience and the immediate or long-term resultants in personality. This does not mean, however, that early experience is unimportant—indeed all the evidence is to the contrary. It does mean that we shall be doomed to disappointment if we try to predict resultants in personality development from individual, isolated, specific factors in the child's cultural experience. Orlansky attempted to review the evidence on the relationship between specific aspects of infant-mother interactions, such as duration of breast-feeding, and was unable to find any direct, simple correlations with subsequent personality (17). This might have been expected because of the reasons we have suggested above.

Patterns of feeding

To illustrate and clarify the significance of the culture-organism interaction, we shall now discuss two of the many patterns that are significant. Later in our treatment of the development of the infant we shall have occasion to examine some other patterns affecting the general personality and socialization of the child (see Chapter 4). Two of the most important sets of experiences for the newborn center around the intake of food and the early controls of body functions. Let us consider the nutritional intake of the baby first. As Scupin points out: "When (the infant) is hungry it sucks loudly on its fingers, but this pacifies it only for a short time. Before it is placed at the breast, its head rolls back and forth restlessly, the mouth seeks eagerly, and the eyes are open wide. When it finds the nipple, it utters satisfied grunting sounds, sucks hastily until it chokes, and sighs as if it were doing the most strenuous work" (18). Presumably this pattern of responses by the infant is ready to function at birth. How it develops, becomes modified, and finally gets integrated into later forms of food-seeking and food-intake is a matter that is very much affected by the nature of the *total pattern* of the infant's relationships with its mother. Equally important, this total pattern of relationships involves much more than the development of food-intake habits; it affects the way in which the early personality characteristics of the infant develop. For, along with the intake of food, the baby "takes in" the earliest (for him) culture patterns of the mother. The nature of the attention he gets, the nature of the deprivation he suffers, the kinds of affection he is given and the amount and kind of fondling and "handling" which may be part of the food-intake relationship with the mother affect his reaction patterns. As Fries, for example, has shown, when babies are taken care of by compulsive, rigid nurses they tend to develop startle (or anxious) reactions and show other signs of tension and anxiety, whereas when babies are taken care of by gentle, secure nurses they show far less of such reactions (19). Observations by Escalona of infants who were high-strung, showing that their mothers were also high-strung, support the same conclusion: that babies take in more than nourishment; they "take in" also many of the attributes of the mother (20). Exactly how this interiorization of attitudes and other behaviors occurs is not thoroughly understood as yet, but much of it is explainable by the process of *empathy*, a nonverbal means of communication through which the infant shares some of the mother's psychological experiences.

In our own American society, by and large, the feeding of the baby is now on a demand basis. Much permissiveness is practiced on the assumption that under such conditions the baby will develop more adequate emotional security and *basic trust* in its relations with the world. Such a practice, which is in opposition to the previously held practices of scheduled feedings, allows for individual differences in the nutritional and physiological needs of the youngsters and also allows for individual differences among mothers. We have apparently learned, in this country, that such a permissive relationship does not necessarily mean complete indulgence of the baby. The baby has to learn very slowly, and later the infant also has to learn, to tolerate frustrations and to compromise its needs with the needs of mother and family. If this beginning of reality-testing is not practiced, very slowly to be sure and with the individual tolerance limits of the baby or infant, the baby can learn to become the tyrannical master of the household and fail to learn methods of secure and reciprocal relationships with others.

Although the trend in this country is toward permissive or demand feeding, such a practice will not automatically solve all of the problems of good infant-mother interactions. As we have already indicated, much depends on the emotional security of the mother who can do what she feels is right for the infant because her observations of the infant, and not because some arbitrary norms from some authoritative sourcebook, tell her what to expect and what to do. In addition, the mother is, herself, part of a culture, which greatly influences the ways that she has "available" for dealing with and relating to her child. These general culture patterns have been dichotomized as *fetusphile* and *fetusphobic* by Bernfeld (21). By the former term is meant a culture that attempts to reproduce the "natural" conditions of infants so that it is most comfortable, warm, and protected. By the latter term is meant a culture that traumatizes infants or shocks them so that through physical frustrations they will become hardened. These two extremes of culture patterns may be termed overindulgent and overtraumatic, respectively. Another way in which cultures may be classified with respect to the general pattern of infant-mother rela-

tionships is the following threefold division described by Honigmann (5): *symmetrical*, in which the infant is treated like an incomplete adult; *complementary*, in which the infant is regarded as essentially different from adults; *reciprocal*, in which the infant receives certain things from adults as due to him and owes other things to adults (such as achievement) in return. It is probable that an infant living in a particular culture will tend to form personality characteristics that are different from another infant living in another category of culture. More specifically, each of Bernfeld's or Honigmann's categories of culture patterns is likely to lead to different types of per-

Cultures vary in the kinds of experiences they may provide. (Merrill Palmer)

sonality resultants. The mother living in a fetusphile culture will tend to feed her child differently from one living in a fetusphobic culture. It is not our intention, at this time, to trace the types of specific personality outcomes from each category of culture pattern but only to emphasize the general principle that these differences are highly significant.

To make the foregoing discussion more concrete, we shall now describe one pattern of cultural practice of feeding children and discuss the particular outcomes in that instance. We have selected a culture that the anthropologists have called a very indulgent one: the Arapesh of New Guinea. In this group, suckling of the baby is provided, especially during the first two weeks, whenever the baby seems to wish for it. The mother encourages suckling by manipulating her breast for the baby so that it vibrates while the baby is feeding. There is continuous playing with the baby while it is suckling for long periods. Nursing continues until the child is some four years old unless the mother becomes pregnant. The infant is always attended by a familiar adult, usually the mother or, if she has to work in the fields, by a nurse who accompanies the mother and child to the fields. As Margaret Mead, who reported on this group, says (7): "The infant is never left alone . . . comforting human skin and comforting human voices are always beside him." Any hurt or injury the baby or infant suffers is responded to with cuddling and with breast-feeding. The whole pattern of food in-

take is part of a larger pattern of great indulgence for the infant by the mother and the immediate adult community. Weaning is slow, delayed, and gradual. Meads reports that the older Arapesh child ". . . grows up with a sense of emotional security in the care of others . . ." We cannot conclude from this account that the total food-intake process produces this type of emotional security, but the relationship, when considered in the light of all the other evidence about the Arapesh, does seem to *imply* such a *possible* and *complex* type of causality.

Patterns of training of body functions

The ways in which a child learns to control its body functions is also culturally determined to a large extent, and in turn the cultural pattern influences the emerging personality. One of the important types of body controls is that of sphincter behavior. In a biological sense *sphincter control* refers to the ability to regulate the muscles that open and close a natural opening of the body. We shall use this phrase, however, to denote the learning of the total act of retaining or expelling feces, including all of the ancillary functions which go along with this in a particular individual, such as where and when he defecates, what the conditions of defecation are, and the like. In American middle-class society, sphincter control is usually established early in the child's second year of life, although there are considerable variations. The time when a particular culture begins to try to establish such control varies greatly, too, but in general it does not begin before the middle of the youngster's first year.

The importance of how sphincter control is established with respect to early tendencies in personality development can hardly be overestimated, and we shall have much to say about it in our next chapter. However, we can easily understand, at this point, *why* it is important if we remember that during this general period the youngster experiences his first lessons in *socialization*. He has begun to learn to communicate with the people who take care of him (and by the end of the second year he has a considerable although immature vocabulary) and can begin to understand verbal communications with some accuracy. Moreover, unlike suckling in which the actual presence of the mother was necessary for his effective gratification, defecation is an activity the child can complete by himself. At the same time, since he has to learn an appropriate pattern for bowel movements (appropriate to the particular culture in which he lives), he learns to *inhibit* as well as to *gratify* (to withhold as well as to expel) in terms of cultural requirements as represented by his mother. In this process, he also learns, sometimes implicitly, the meaning of prohibition and the kinds of punishment to which he may be subjected. He has to learn to satisfy his mother as well as himself, since he can no longer express his impulses as freely as he might wish. Thus, through these and many other lessons he learns to give up his self-centered state and begins to become a *social being*. In this process he also learns how to express or suppress other impulses through the process of *generalization* (the utilization of

the same or similar responses in related situations). It is believed, further, that he lays the foundation for important personality traits such as orderliness and self-inhibition. Finally, he also learns to adapt to a particular, explicit culture pattern. (Consider, for example, the wide difference in sphincter control in a primitive culture where there is no fancy plumbing and the modern, civilized type of culture where fancy tile bathrooms and exquisitely lovely bedspreads are the housewife's dream.)

The type of pattern of sphincter control that is used sets certain trends in the personality, although again we caution the reader not to expect that these trends imply that the personality will continue to develop along the same lines. At one extreme is the Tanalan pattern in which toilet-training is begun very early, perhaps at two months. Before the infant is even able to sit up or maintain adequate postural control and before he has established any preparatory pattern of bowel movement which the mother can understand or learn to anticipate, he is forced to learn control. The Tanalan culture has an unusually high standard of cleanliness which reinforces the need to develop rigid controls. It is not surprising to learn, then, that the Tanalan adult is highly compulsive, overly rigid, and ritualistic (31). These latter outcomes are congruent with the early training and the requirements of the adult culture. On the other hand, a culture that has a highly permissive attitude toward toilet-training, one which follows the baby's needs and physical maturation rather than anticipates them, may be expected to inculcate different early personality trends. An illustration of this type of pattern may be found in the Alorese or in the Kaska Indians. The lack of concern among the adults of these cultures with tidiness and cleanliness again seems congruent with the early pattern of socialization in toilet-training.

We have said that we should not expect to find a one-to-one relationship between a specific factor in the culture and later personality since the whole pattern has to be considered and factors other than culture have to be reckoned with. To illustrate the first part of this problem (that of other factors), we may examine the situation among Great Whale Eskimos (3) and the Hopi Indians (13). These people are quite indulgent with respect to toilet-training, the Hopi people paying very little attention to it, in fact. However, although the adult Eskimo is tidy but compulsive, the adult Hopi is highly argumentative and quite distrustful of others. To understand these generalizations (and we must remember that they do not apply to *all* members of these cultures), we have to consider many other factors in the respective cultures and not their toilet-training practices alone. Hopi children used to live in the constant fear that they would be taken from their parents and sent away to live with whites and attend white schools. They were also subjected to severe fright and punishment through rituals in which they were "scared into being good" by Kachinas (horrible-looking, masked figures) and "spider women" who threatened them with dire consequences if they misbehaved. These and other experiences were in conflict with the indulgent experiences of infancy and may have produced the unfavorable effects that could not have been predicted from the nature of the earlier experiences alone.

Nevertheless, we can say that undue harshness, strictness, and "forcing" in connection with toilet-training tend to produce unfavorable personality traits. Many clinical and survey studies bear out this conclusion. In one clinical study made by Huschka it was found that when toilet-training started very early (before eight months) or was completed very early (before eighteen months) the children showed such signs of emotional disturbance as problem behavior, elimination difficulties (such as constipation), and excessive fear and rage. By contrast, a control group of children who were not given such strict training showed significantly less of all these phenomena (22).

We began our analysis of culture and personality wth the proposition that there is no ubiquitous pattern by which babies are reared and we followed this by the assertion that the nature of the culture-organism interaction in early life exerts considerable influence upon the developing personality. We may now close this introductory treatment of culture and personality with another general and important proposition. The nature of the effect of the culture upon the personality is, in part, a function of the continuity or discontinuity of the sequence of cultural experiences. When the sequence of culture experiences is continuous, that is

Learning to use one of the many "implements" of our culture. (Merrill Palmer)

an early childhood of great severity in the demands made by the culture. (We shall have occasion to comment further on this principle in later chapters.)

CULTURE AND SOCIAL CLASS

A child is not only born into a culture but he is also born into a *social class*. By social class the sociologist means the status position within a community which an individual or his family has. A family may be in the topmost position, which is referred to as *upper-upper* class, or it may be in the lowest position, which is referred to as *lower-lower*, or it may be somewhere in between, in the *middle* classes. (The three general social classes are: *upper*, *middle*, and *lower*.) The concept of social class is important because the amount and kind of direct contact between different classes within a general culture is usually limited in some way—sometimes severely limited. When this occurs, the different classes are likely to develop different patterns of living. Since communication across class boundaries is limited, each class is likely to develop a distorted perception of the behaviors and values of the other groups. This discussion should not be taken to mean that all societies or all communities are highly stratified in terms of social class, but rather that most are. In rare instances, communities may have little or no stratification. This is most likely to be the case in small villages. In most communities, however, a "class curtain" (somewhat like the "iron curtain") screens one class from another.

when successive experiences are consistent, they encourage the development of strong, permanent and generally well-adaptive (to the culture) personality traits and adjustment. On the other hand, when an individual is exposed to experiences that are inconsistent or in sharp contrast, some disturbance in personality development is likely to ensue. Such *discontinuities* may be of different kinds and the differences may be small or large and hence the kinds of disturbance they produce may vary considerably. We are not yet in a position to evaluate precisely the effects of varying patterns of discontinuity, but present evidence, mainly from anthropological sources, suggests that the most disturbing type is that in which an infancy of great indulgence is followed by

Sometimes it is easily possible for an individual or a group to move upward from one class to another, and individuals in such a society may easily develop the motivation to try to move up. Such a tendency toward upward movement from one class to another is termed *upward mobility*. When an individual shows a tendency to move downward from one class status to the next lower one, the tendency is known as *downward mobility*. To the extent that opportunities for mobility exist, distortion of the values and behaviors of one group is less likely by the members of another group.

Class-linked personality characteristics

It has been fairly well established that personality characteristics are *class-linked*, that is, that different classes have characteristically different ways of behaving and perceiving things. Sometimes such differences lead to well established *class prejudices* and *class attitudes*. The reader will easily think of many examples of such class differences in attitudes. One of the writers had occasion to witness an unusual example of such a prejudice which affected the logic of an otherwise realistic and intelligent community. This example will be illustrated by a conversation with a member of this group, in a small village in the southern part of Maine. The discussion had turned to an evaluation of the significance of W.P.A. projects in and near this community during the latter days of the Great Depression. The writer (who will be identified as speaker A) had

asked what the respondent (identified as B) thought of these projects.

A. And how do you feel about the W.P.A. projects?
B. I think they're scandalous, a waste of the taxpayer's money, and it's a movement that encourages laziness.
A. But do you have any W.P.A. projects in this community?
B. Oh yes, we surely do. One of them is the construction of a much needed road around the far side of this lake.
A. How is that one going?
B. Oh, fine, fine. Lots of our boys and men who've been out of work for a long time have now got a job. And they're doing a mighty fine job at that. They're good workers all right. The road will help us out a lot. And the money will certainly come in handy around here.
A. Could you have gotten this road without the W.P.A.?
B. Naw, I guess not. We've needed it for a long time but we couldn't get it going.
A. But I thought you didn't think such projects were any good.
B. Nope, they're no damned good. They waste the taxpayer's money and put a drain on future generations. They make people lazy. And they just do things that don't need doing.
A. Have any of your men on W.P.A. become lazy?
B. By golly, I guess not.

The respondent was a man from a community that had always prized independent effort, shunned "charity" and believed in hard work as the salvation of most of men's ills. He could not see the lack of logic in his convictions although he did not lack for good logic when discussing problems in which his class prejudice did not operate.

These introductory remarks have been intended to convey some idea of the extent to which culture practice is bound to class membership . . . and as we started to say, the baby is born into a particular class. By that fact, the probability that he will receive a particular type of training rather than another is very great. The type of training received in infancy, as we have seen, can influence the way in which the personality develops. To illustrate this last statement insofar as it pertains to class, we shall cite a few facts obtained as the result of recent research.

One of the clearest sets of findings relating to class differences is reported in a study by Davis and Havighurst (23). Using observational methods and comparing middle-class and lower-class families with respect to many aspects of child training, they found that middle-class mothers are more exacting than lower-class mothers in such things as methods of feeding and cleanliness training, and that they begin most of the training routines for infants at an earlier age and expect their children to assume many kinds of responsibilities around the home at an earlier age. Table II gives a condensed summary of some of the major findings of this study. Davis and Havighurst concluded that ". . . middle-class children are subjected earlier and more consistently to the influences which make a child an orderly, conscientious, responsible and *tame* [italics ours] person." In general, their data indicate that middle-class children, as compared with lower-class children, learn to inhibit or even *repress* their impulses more frequently.

In an earlier study, Ericson, using interview methods with middle- and lower-class mothers found the same kinds of differences between these two groups (24). It is interesting to note that he found three times as many cases of

Table II. *Comparison of training practices of middle-class and lower-class children in the United States* *

Type of training	Lower class	Middle class
Feeding and weaning	More often breast-fed; use pacifier more frequently	More often given supplementary feedings; children more often held for feeding
Toilet-training	Training starts late	Bowel and bladder training starts earlier; whites begin training before Negroes
Strictness of home regime	Children go to movies earlier; stay out later	More frequent daytime naps; come home earlier
Responsibility	Children work less around home; freer to play on street	Children required to work in home earlier; girls expected to care for younger children

* Adapted from Davis and Havighurst (23).

thumb-suckers among the sample of middle-class children as among the lower-class children. This study also indicated that middle-class mothers stressed the assumption of responsibility by their children at an earlier age and that these children showed higher achievement drives in general. The problem of class differences in *achievement motivation* is a particularly interesting one, especially since our culture emphasizes the doctrine of "equal opportunity" for all of its citizens. It seems to be a clearly established fact, however, that middle-class children have better psychological opportunities for achieving because of the nature of their early infancy and childhood training. (See, for example, the work of Hollingshead, 25.) Not only do such children learn to assume responsibility earlier and become more accustomed toward upward striving, but when they get to school they find these values are stressed there and school is, therefore, more congenial to them than to lower-class children. In addition, of course, such children are more likely to have had better and more enriched cultural opportunities in the home with respect to language, music, and exposure to scientific and literary phenomena. Hollingshead says: ". . . the class system is maintained in part by the control of institutional offices by the upper classes . . . (and) by allowing only upward mobile persons who have the 'right attitudes' to have access to them." The point that we are stressing is that being born into one class rather than another determines the probabilities that certain kinds

Children in the early years do not manifest race prejudice. (Merrill Palmer)

of personality characteristics will be developed.

Social class and mental illness

Perhaps the most striking data with respect to the influence of social class upon personality are those dealing with mental illness. In studies that attempt to show the relationship between class membership and the frequency or type of mental disturbance, great care has to be taken to control for all other relevant factors such as physical condition, racial origin, and economic stability. Enough studies have now been completed with adequate attention to such controls so that we are in a position to make some definitive statements. These include the following: (a) membership in a particular social class influences the probabilities with respect to the frequency of occurrence of mental disturbance; (b) membership in a particular social class influences the probabilities with respect to the type of mental disturbance that develops; (c) membership in a particular social class influences the *content* of the mental preoccupations of delusional patients (that is, for example, their delusions differ from those of other social classes).

A series of studies by Faris and Dunham in Chicago showed that *schizophrenia* (a type of mental illness or "insanity") occurs more frequently among the poor than among the rich and that *manic depressive* (another type of mental illness) does not show this distribution (26). Moreover, these studies indicated clearly that the probability of occurrence of schizophrenia was independent, to a large extent, of the national or "racial" origins of the people involved but was dependent, in part, on the specific nature of the living conditions of particular socioeconomic classes. This kind of conclusion, that type of mental illness is partly dependent on the living patterns of class (and of culture, therefore), is clearly shown in a recent study of Eaton and Weil (27). They examined very carefully samples of ten populations of Hutterites. This sect is interesting to study because

it operates almost like a closed religious order, living in economic interdependence, with very well developed in-group behaviors (the patterns of life are well delineated for all) and with little group contact with other American and Canadian groups. These people who had real social security had a relatively low incidence of personality disturbance, ". . . as low as or lower than that of any contemporary Euro-American group within the Judaeo-Christian complex of cultures...." It was also found that the Hutterite emphasis on community concern for all members of the group and strong cohesion of the group yielded personality traits congruent with such living conditions: little free-floating anxiety (that is, diffuse anxiety), little aggression and little violence, little tendency toward impulsive or antisocial behavior. On the other hand, when mental disturbance did occur, depression (perhaps as anger turned against the self rather than against the group) was common.

In concluding this section let us remember that we are not trying to establish what is "good" or "bad" about an individual social class; rather we are trying to demonstrate that social-class membership has important consequences for the type of personality that is developed. Many other factors contribute to the development of personality, but the child who is "born into" one class rather than another automatically "inherits" different probabilities with respect to the kind of person he will become.

CHILD-REARING PRACTICES IN AMERICA

We are now ready to examine more systematically the specific patterns of child-rearing in this country. When we return once again to take up the story of how the child develops, in the next chapter, we shall, therefore, appreciate more fully the forces and practices with which he interacts. Fortunately for us, two recent books have summarized the results of two separate research projects dealing with this topic and we do not have to rely as much as we formerly did on hearsay evidence or fragmentary reports based upon questionnaires or interviews—second, third, or even fourth sources, far removed from the actual behavior of mothers and infants. It is surprising how little systematic data have been gathered about child-rearing practices in this country. Although anthropologists were busy observing such practices among Indian tribes in this country and among primitive and distant peoples in other countries, almost no data were being systematically assembled on the usual patterns in the United States (with the exception of Indian tribes and special groups). On the other hand, starting with Gesell (28), many investigators reported on their observations of the behavior and growth of children. The whole pattern of child-mother interactions or even of mothers' behavior was left unobserved. We shall discuss, first, the report of Brody (2) and then turn our attention to the work of Sears, Macoby, and Levin (8).

An observational study of mothers and infants

Brody's book is a summary of her research findings on a group of 32 mothers and their infants ranging in age from 4 weeks to 28 weeks. The study is part of a larger project, *The Infancy Research Project*, carried out under the auspices of the Menninger Foundation of Topeka and the United States Health Service. The mothers in the Brody research volunteered to have their rearing behavior observed during their visits to Well Baby Clinics as well as at home. In the 32 cases of infants studied there were four male and four female subjects at each of the age levels: 4, 12, 20, and 28 weeks. Although the total sample was small, it was hoped that intensive and direct observation of the infants and their mothers would yield insight into the kinds of reciprocal patterns of relationships that went into the total behavior of "mothering." At the same time, the division of the sample into four age groups would permit some generalizations about consistency of patterns over the age span of 4 to 28 weeks. The mothers were native-born and white. Eighteen of them came from the middle classes and fourteen came from the lower classes. They were predominantly Christian, thirteen being Protestant and seven Catholic.

Extensive data were obtained about the mothers through interview and observation of their behavior during various mothering activities. The interactions of mother and infant were observed directly in six categories of activities: feeding, cleaning, moving (i.e., postural shifts and other motor activities), touching (i.e., minor contacts with any part of the infant's body), offering objects, and speaking. In addition, the infants were given the Gesell-Amatruda Developmental Schedules (29). The observed behaviors were coded in various ways to allow for statistical treatment.

Before presenting some of the most important findings, we shall quote from one of the observer's reports of the feeding behavior of one of the mothers. The specific report is selected at random, but feeding behavior is singled out because it was demonstrated that it reflects, more than any other activity, some of the essential interactions between mother and child.

Male infant, 12 weeks old.

The mother and infant are very comfortably relaxed. The mother provides a good deal of physical contact without confinement and with freedom to touch the infant idly occasionally. She regards him, comments on his rapid sucking and on the values of breast-feeding. She rocks gently. The infant loses and by himself regains the nipple several times. Now and then the mother touches his cheek lightly or lays hers against his. The infant terminates the feeding.

In feeding the cereal (a fairly new experience for the infant) the mother's support is less adequate, but steady. She shows impressive ability to feed with good timing and rhythm as she waits for him to be ready for a next spoonful and as she wipes food around his mouth. Once she smiles at him shyly; throughout she looks pleasantly interested.

The mother breast-fed her other children successfully, finds breast-feeding easier, believes it more satisfying than bottle-feedings might be, and likes the fact that it gives her a chance to rest. She keeps a flexible schedule but tries not to feed the baby every time he cries. Her weaning plans are vague; she speaks of not knowing when her breasts dry up unless the baby cries during or after his feeding. She is in no hurry to introduce semisolids (fruits, vegetables, and meats) and will wait at least a month more.

This record is taken from observations of one of the mothers who is classified as belonging in the "A" group of mothers of this sample, by which was meant that the whole pattern of relationships of mother with child was evaluated as good; i.e., secure, comfortable, responsive, and the like. The report is discursive but it gives a vivid picture of the behaviors upon which it reports. The basic data of the research, subjected to statistical analysis, was based upon countings of specific behavior, ratings by one or more observers, and categorization according to well defined criteria.

One of the findings on feeding was that these mothers, who were under advice from pediatricians, for the most part did not follow their pediatrician's advice. It was also found that the mere practice of breast-feeding did not, by itself, insure "gentle procedures, intimacy, or restfulness." When mothers breast-fed willingly and when they *did not have conflict* about this practice, then the relationship between mother and infant was very likely to be good in most respects and the infant seemed to have a maximal opportunity of a secure and relaxed environment in which to develop.

We have said that the study indicated that the total feeding pattern was more indicative than any other pattern of the relationship between mother and infant. To illustrate how much feeding patterns may vary we have selected relevant data from two of Brody's groups of parents and presented them in Table III. We have already characterized the Group "A" mothers. The Group "D" mothers were generally at the other extreme in their maternal behavior as rated by observers on a scale consisting of a number of items. The "D" mothers were much poorer in the quality of their relationships with their infants than the "A" group; i.e., they were less secure, less comfortable, and less responsive to the infant.

We may note a number of important findings from Table III. It seems clear that the two groups of mothers varied in the essential consistency of their relationships with their children. If this is the case, the implication may be of the greatest significance for the effect this has upon the infants. When the relationship between mother and infant is inconsistent, there is far less likelihood that the infant will be able to learn appropriate methods of adjustment. (See Chapter 4.) In simple terms, since he does not know what to anticipate he is at a loss in learning how to adapt to his environment; he may even, under extreme conditions, fail

Table III. *Comparison of the feeding practices and interactions of mothers and infants in two groups* *

Behavior factor	Group A (N-7)	Group D (N-11)
Bodily contact	M ** holds I ** securely and close but does not confine; both M and I relaxed; feeding tempo consistently moderate; M does not interrupt I; waits for I to show cessation of interest in feeding	M does not use position that is comfortable for both M and I; tension state of M interferes with I's feeding; feeding interrupted abruptly; many disruptions of behavior by M
Communication	M responds to I but is able to respond to others; talks to I gently; frequent smiling of M and I to each other; M shows tenderness, pride, joy in her I	Frequently urges I to eat; frequently withdraws and restores nipple; occasionally teases or threatens not to offer food
Expressed attitude	M prefers breast-feeding and reasons: brought up that way, most natural, more satisfying; flexible schedule because moods of I vary; most M's consider latter part of first year best for weaning from breast to bottle or cup; none in hurry to wean	Most M's breast-feed for few days only and reason: insufficient milk, nervousness, nipple irritated; only one M had great desire to nurse; most said they preferred self-demand schedule but showed markedly contrasting behavior

* Adapted from Brody's findings (2).
** I is used for infant, M for mother.

to develop *basic trust* in himself or others. We can also learn from this table that the *verbal* expression of preference for breast-feeding by the mother is not *necessarily* accompanied by actual breast-feeding in *behavior*. From other data in this report it appears that this group of mothers had learned to report that they preferred breast-feeding, but this did not necessarily carry over into their behavior. Not only does this finding suggest that the verbal reports of mothers cannot be considered valid (or substantiated) without additional corroborating evidence but it also points up the inconsistency that often exists between a preferred practice and the actual practice. This table also demonstrates how complex the patterns of interactions in feeding can be. At the observable, conscious level, there may be very wide variabilities in the behavior of mothers who breast-feed their children. Such variabilities may include amount and kind of bodily contact with the infant, amount and kind of communication with the infant, and amount and kind of attitude that is expressed. There may be other variabilities in not readily observable behaviors, some of which may stem from differences in unconscious attitudes.

We should like to point up another general implication from these findings. We may note that Group "A" mothers are more *flexible* in their behavior than are Group "D" mothers. It may very well be that true consistency in the relationship between mother and infant implies *appropriate flexibility* (and hence spontaneity) on the part of the mother. It is not the mother who rigidly follows certain principles or rules who is likely to be secure in her relationship with her child,

but the one who can adapt and modify her behavior in terms of its actual meaning and significance to the youngster. Indeed, we have ample evidence from other sources to substantiate this conclusion.

Some other types of findings from the Brody study are of interest. Twenty-one of the 32 mothers expressed the intention of beginning toilet-training during the first year of the baby's life. However, seven of the "A" mothers also stated that they would wait for signs of the child's readiness for such training whereas only

An example of cooperative behavior in early childhood. (U. of Mich.)

two of the 11 Group "D" mothers expressed this attitude. The study did not follow through to observe the degree of agreement in actual behavior with the expressed attitudes. It will be noted, however, that there is overlap in the attitudes of Groups "A" and "D"; there was even more overlap between groups that were closer on the scale of maternal attitude.

With respect to methods of discipline that the mothers said they used or did use the findings are also interesting. All mothers said that *physical punishment* of some kind was acceptable, but only a minority of Group "A" mothers consistently accepted it although a majority of Group "D" mothers did so. Only 12 of the mothers favored the *use of reasoning* for these infants as a method of discipline, but it must be remembered that the oldest of these infants was only 28 weeks of age. Fourteen mothers favored *isolation and deprivation*. In general, Group "A" mothers favored more reasonable and more sensitive methods of discipline than the other groups.

In addition to the professional advice that these mothers received from their pediatricians, they used many other sources of guidance. They relied upon the opinions of relatives, friends, and neighbors. They used a variety of books and magazines as sources of information, notably Spock's baby book (30) and *Parents' Magazine*. The two main sources were self experience and husband's opinion, and literary sources of one kind and another.

Unfortunately, the small number of cases included in this study did not permit many kinds of generalizations that we should like to have had. As we have said, this was offset by the gain in intensity of the direct observations that were made. However, we cannot be sure how generalizable the findings are to other kinds of populations and we do not know what differences, if any, exist among different subcultures and different classes of parents. Nor do we know how consistent the findings are with practices of mothers with older children. Moreover, the author did not analyze her data for many other kinds of interrelationships among the factors studied, and a few of her statistical analyses may be questioned with respect to their appropriateness for the data. On the whole, however, the study has great significance for the light it sheds on specific patterns of mothering—about which much more has yet to be learned. Above all, even within this small and selected sampling, the study reveals how complex and how variable the individual patterns of each mother are.

A study based on interviews with mothers

Now let us turn our attention to the Sears study. In the book from which the following findings are cited (8), there are ample data worth repeated examination and detailed analysis, and we cannot pretend to do justice to the wealth of material that is presented. We should like, however, to discuss enough of this material so that the reader will get a fairly good picture of the major findings. Our major interest, of course, is to learn how mothers rear their children.

The nature of this study must be clearly understood if the conclusions are to be meaningful. The reported research is based upon carefully prepared, scheduled interviews (that is, containing certain kinds of questions to elicit certain kinds of data) that were conducted by trained interviewers. These interviews were recorded on an Audograph machine by the ten women who did the interviewing. In all 379 mothers of a like number of kindergarten children from two suburban areas near a large metropolitan city of New England were studied by this method. The interviews were subsequently transcribed and the material coded and rated in terms of 44 (reported) scales. These results were subjected to

factor analysis * in order to extrude the most common general factors. The project attempted to obtain a representative and equal sample of boys and girls and of mothers of children who were *only, first, middle,* and *youngest* in the family. All of the mothers were American-born and they and their husbands were the natural parents of the children who were studied. Protestant, Catholic, and Jewish faiths were represented among the respondents. The families were fairly evenly distributed socioeconomically from the upper-

* A statistical procedure used to determine common psychological elements.

Group play in the kindergarten encourages socialization growth. (U. of Mich.)

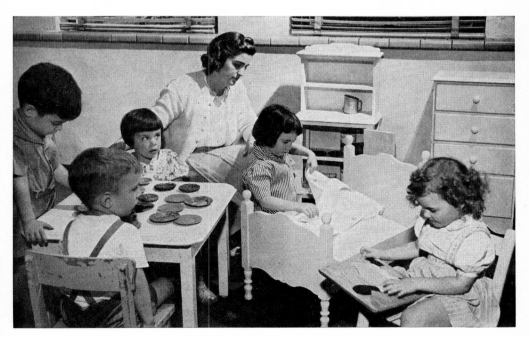

middle class through the upper-lower class. Some high-level professionals and some unskilled laborers were included.

We wish to emphasize that the data consist of *verbal reports* by mothers concerning their child-rearing practices with children about five years of age. What the mothers *said* they did and what they *actually* did are not necessarily the same. Some of the findings must be regarded with due caution because of this distinct possibility and some of the relationships or lack of relationships between various factors in rearing may be an artifact of this procedure. We must keep this possibility in mind in all studies seeking to establish relationships between reports of what respondents *said* they did and what they *actually* did. Otherwise, once the relationships among factors have been presented they are likely to be taken as literal; i.e., existing in the nature of the phenomena.

The Sears study attempted to answer three questions: (a) What are the rearing practices used by mothers? (b) What effects do these practices have on the children's personalities? (c) Why does a mother use one kind of practice rather than another? As to the first question, as the authors of the book say: "Asking questions about a natural phenomenon . . . implies the separating out of specific aspects of the phenomenon . . ." Although the book is titled *Patterns of Child Rearing* and attempts to explore the interrelationships among *specific* aspects of child-rearing, the study does not analyze *patterns* but rather attempts to

assemble these by statistical means. These are two entirely different procedures and may yield different sets of results. We are emphasizing this point because we believe, as we have repeatedly stressed, that the meaning of a specific behavior can be understood only in terms of the pattern of which it was actually a part. We also wish to emphasize the difficulty in discovering cause-and-effect relationships from the presence of the correlations between individual variables. Two things that are related may be related through cause-and-effect, or they may both be caused by some other factor, or they may be related for other reasons.

The first general finding of the Sears study is that there is considerable variability in the reported practice of these 379 mothers. With two notable exceptions, permissiveness for sexual behavior and permissiveness for aggression toward the parents, these mothers ranged through all the steps of the various scales. Variability among mothers is, therefore, the rule. Even with respect to sex and aggression, all steps on the scale were used, except that in these instances there was a bunching of the reported practices on permissiveness.

Five clusters of factors, called *traits* in this study, that were highly significant in predicting the personality characteristics of the children were isolated. Two other traits were considerably less valuable in this respect. All of these are traits of the mothers who were rated in terms of their reports of how they reared their children or in terms of their expressed attitudes. It was found that the most important trait, from the viewpoint of prediction, was that of *permissiveness-*

strictness. This trait was composed of such scales as severity of toilet-training, restrictions on making noise, use of physical punishment, and permissiveness for aggression among siblings. Another pervasive trait was *warmth of mother-child relationship.* It is reported that these two traits seemed to be closely related to important aspects of the child's personality. For example, *warmth* contributed to security in the child and *coldness* (at the other end of the scales) contributed to high aggression, feeding problems, persist-

ent bed-wetting, and the like. Similarly, *permissiveness* contributed to aggression, and to infrequent (rather than frequent) bed-wetting. It was shown that *punishment* (part of the trait of the mother defined as *aggression-punitiveness*) was ineffectual in the long-term effect it had in eliminating behavior that the mother wished to alleviate. In addition, physical punishment was associated with **in-**

Some forms of physical skill are developed unconsciously. (Merrill Palmer)

creased aggression toward the parent, feeding problems, aggression in the home, and a "slow development of conscience."

Other "major" traits that were established statistically were *general family adjustment* and *responsible child-training orientation*. The less powerful traits were *orientation toward child's physical well-being* and *perception of husband*. We shall not summarize the correlations of these traits with specific personality characteristics in the child. However, we should like to point out that, as the researchers are well aware, the strength of a trait may easily be influenced by the nature of the data that were gathered. For example, since the interviews in this study did not focus particularly on the behavior of the father, the trait *perception of husband* may have been seriously underestimated by that fact.

Some of the details of the reported child-rearing practices may now be summarized. About half of the mothers reported being "delighted" at becoming pregnant. The others expressed varying positions in their attitudes, ranging from strong negative feelings up to the strong positive position. Since about half of the mothers were less than "delighted" one can infer that these attitudes may have exerted some influence upon the ways in which they reacted to the newborn child. One wonders what the distribution of unconsciously held and consciously withheld attitudes may have been. Most mothers were extremely concerned with the rearing of their children. It was the

most important thing in their lives at the time. Another finding was that *love-oriented techniques* in child-rearing were more often associated with the use of *reasoning* than were other techniques used by mothers. Mothers were more tolerant of aggressive behavior of male children than they were of female children. This may, of course, be a reflection of current culture values about masculinity and femininity, but the fact is that the sex of the child influenced the way in which he was disciplined. Marked differences in child-rearing practices were reported by middle-class and working-class (lower-class) mothers. The latter were more restrictive, more punitive, and generally colder than middle-class mothers. This last finding is especially important because of the apparently high degree of relationship between the factors noted and child personality. We must be cautious, again, in accepting the finding as fact for a number of reasons. In the first place, the finding may apply to this sample, and not to others. More important, perhaps, is the possibility that middle-class mothers, because of greater sophistication, may have reported that they were less punitive and less restrictive whereas in fact they were not. Only direct observation of the behaviors of a wide sample of mothers would enable us to accept these specific conclusions, although we may tend to do so because of our own prior convictions on the subject.

From our review of these two research reports (Sear's and Brody's), as well as from a general review of available literature on the subject, we may come to the very clear conclusion that child-rearing practice exerts a profound effect upon the child's personality. (See, for example, the review of this evidence in Chapter 4.) We can also see that child-rearing practice is an interactive phenomenon, the condition of the child and the condition of the mother operating in reciprocal and reinforcing manner. We have learned that the nature of the rearing procedure is related to culture and to class and that the influence of these factors may be great indeed. Above all we have begun to realize what is meant by the statement: "The child inherits a culture."

GENERAL READINGS

1. Benedict, R., *Patterns of Culture*. New York: Penguin Books, 1946.
2. Brody, S., *Patterns of Mothering*. New York: International Universities Press, 1956.
3. Erikson, E. H., *Childhood and Society*. New York: Norton, 1950.
4. Fromm, E., *The Sane Society*. New York: Rinehart, 1955.
5. Honigmann, J. J., *Culture and Personality*. New York: Harper, 1954.
6. Martin, W. E., and Stendler, C. B., *Child Development: The Process of Growing Up in Society*. New York: Harcourt, Brace, 1953.
7. Mead, M., *Sex and Temperament*. New York: Mentor Books, 1950.
8. Sears, R. R., Macoby, E. F., and Levin, H., *Patterns of Child Rearing*. Evanston, Illinois: Row, Peterson, 1957.

SELECTED BIBLIOGRAPHY

9. Boas, F., "Anthropology," in *Encyclopedia of the Social Sciences*. New York: Macmillan, 1930.
10. White, L., "Ethnological theory," in Sellars, R. W., McGill, V. J., and Farber, M. (eds.), *Philosophy for the Future, the Quest for Modern Materialism*. New York: Macmillan, 1949.
11. Spiro, M. E., "Culture and personality: the natural history of a false dichotomy," *Psychiat.*, 1951, 14, 19-46.
12. Kardiner, A., *The Psychological Frontiers of Society*. New York: Columbia University, 1945.
13. Goldfrank, E. D., "Socialization, personality, and the structure of Pueblo society," *Amer. Anthrop.*, 1945, 47, 516-539.
14. Moloney, J. C., and Biddle, C. R., "Psychiatric observations in Okinawa Shima," *Psychiat.*, 1945, 8, 391-402.
15. Schnierla, T. C., "A consideration of some problems in the ontogeny of family life and social adjustment in various infra-human animals," in Senn, M. J. E. (ed.), *Problems of Infancy and Childhood*. Trans-

actions of the Fourth (1950) Conference. New York: Josiah Macy Jr. Foundation, 1951.

16. Scott, J. P., "Social behavior, organization and leadership in a small flock of domestic sheep," *Comp. Psychol. Monogr.*, 1945, 18, 1-29.

17. Orlansky, H. "Infant care and personality," *Psychol. Bul.*, 1949, 46, 1-48.

18. Scupin, E., and Scupin, G. E., "Babis erste Kindhert," 1907.

19. Fries, M. E., "The child's ego development and the training of adults in his development," in *The Psychoanalytic Study of the Child*, Vol. II. New York: International Universities Press, 1946.

20. Escalona, S. K., "Feeding disturbances in very young children," *Amer. J. Orthopsychiat.*, 1945, 15, 76-80.

21. Bernfeld, S., *The Psychology of the Infant*. New York: Brentano, 1929.

22. Huschka, M., "The child's response to coercive bowel training," *Psychosom. Med.*, 1942, 4, 301-328.

23. Davis, A., and Havighurst, R. J., "Social class and color differences in child-rearing," in Kluckhohn, C., and Murray, H. A. (eds.), *Personality in Nature, Society and Culture*. New York: Knopf, 1953.

24. Ericson, M. E., "Social status and child-rearing practices," in Newcomb, T. H., and Hartley, E. L. (eds.), *Readings in Social Psychology*. New York: Holt, 1947.

25. Hollingshead, A. B., *Elmtown's Youth*. New York: Wiley, 1949.

26. Faris, R. E. L., and Dunham, H. W., *Mental Disorders in Urban Areas*. Chicago: University of Chicago, 1939.

27. Eaton, J. W., and Weil, R. J., *Culture and Mental Disorders*. Glencoe, Illinois: Free Press, 1955.

28. Gesell, A., *Infancy and Human Growth*. New York: Macmillan, 1928.

29. Gesell, A., and Amatruda, C. S., *Developmental Diagnosis*. New York: Hoeber, 1941.

30. Spock, B., *Common Sense Book of Baby and Child Care*. New York: Duell, Sloan & Pearce, 1946.

31. Kardiner, A., *The Individual and His Society*. New York: Columbia University, 1947.

4

Development in infancy—
"As the twig is bent"

THE PERIOD FROM BIRTH to the beginning of locomotion and speech is known as *infancy*. The first few weeks after birth (about four weeks) are, as we have stated previously, the *neonatal* period, and technically infancy does not begin until this period has been completed. The end of infancy is even more difficult to define and authorities do not completely agree upon its terminal time or terminal characteristics. We may consider that infancy ends at about one and one-half to two years, when the child is ready, so to speak, to venture forth into the world.

Infancy is a period of prodigious growth and learning. Not only do physical structures and functions develop very rapidly, but personality characteristics also become well defined and patterned. What was first an *organism* has become a unique person, with his own appearance, his own needs and ways of meeting them, and even his own value system. By the time infancy has ended it is possible to make many kinds of approximate predictions about the particular individual—his future general level of intelligence (within broad limits), some of his special assets and deficiencies, his characteristic personality features, and even his types of likes and dislikes—so well crystallized is the unique individual by this time. Because so much occurs during this period and because it has so much importance for all later development, we can understand why it is very helpful to know as much as we can about it.

We must be ever on guard to avoid two kinds of error in analyzing infant development. One type of error is that which causes us to think about and evaluate the infant as a "little adult." This is far from the truth. If we make this type of error we are likely to attribute motives to the infant in terms of what we know about adult motives and we are likely to evaluate his behavior (as "good," "bad," "clever," or "dumb") in terms of adult standards. The other type of error is to fail to appreciate the enormity of the range or variability in the behavior and development of infants. We are likely to think in terms of "averages" or norms and evaluate favorably those infants who reach or exceed the norms and to think that those who do not are retarded. Although norms have their values in many aspects of child development, they tend to obscure the essential truth that each infant has a relatively unique pattern of development and, to some extent, even a unique sequence in the way the patterns develops. Not only is there general variability when we consider, say, the general population of infants of this country, but also different sections of the country, and different epochs in the same sections, show marked differences from each other. Hence, we must not think of the norm as defining anything other than the particular average for a particular (specified) population at a particular time under particular conditions. To make this type of error is to lose sight of the meaning of the specific development of a specified child under the particular conditions that characterize his maturation and learning.

We shall begin our discussion of infancy with an analysis of some general principles and patterns of development. Following this presentation, we shall proceed to discuss the *needs* of the infant and then his developing physical and behavior characteristics. It may be helpful to consider the need system first because much of the learning that takes place is influenced by these needs and the manner of their satisfaction. We shall consider how the infant learns to adapt, how he develops primitive techniques of coping with stimuli, how he learns to perceive his world, and how he begins to relate to people. After we have looked at the nature of his physical development we shall deal with such aspects of his interpersonal behavior as the development of language, emotions, and social-adaptive phenomena. Finally, we shall try to understand how the infant's identity develops as he acquires a self-system.

GENERAL PATTERNS OF DEVELOPMENT

It will help us to understand and to integrate many of the facts of child development if we first consider some of the general patterns and principles of development. Some of these patterns may have become evident in our discussions of the two previous chapters. When we described the growth of the embryo, for example, we learned that growth is discontinuous, that there are spurts and lags in the development of certain organs or organ systems. We also learned that there is a critical period in the growth of neural tissue after which its characteristics become fixed and before which it may be interchangeable with other tissue.

Similarly, in discussing culture and personality we learned that many aspects of behavior are dependent upon the specific cultural milieu that fosters them and that human traits do not develop in a vacuum. Now, we shall summarize some of the main principles of development in a more systematic manner.

Let us consider in more detail what is meant by the term *maturation*. This term refers to the unfolding of potentials that are inherent in the organism and, strictly speaking, refers to growth that occurs without opportunity for specific learning experiences. Some structures and functions will mature, at least up to a point, even though there is no opportunity for exercise, and will not become manifest or operative until the appropriate time in their development. Thus Dennis found, in his study of Hopi children, that infants were able to exhibit the same kinds of motor skills as children of other cultures although Hopi infants were so tightly bound that they were hardly able to move any part of their bodies except their heads (15). Although maturation is based upon inherent properties of the person, it is nevertheless greatly influenced in some instances by internal or external environmental conditions. Nutritional deficiencies, for example, can greatly impair or retard physical maturation. Nevertheless, maturation determines to a large extent when certain functions or certain structures will appear. (See some of the experimental evidence, for example, in 16 and 17.) We should like to emphasize that what we have said applies to *function* as well as *structure* and that *psychological* attributes as well as *physical* attributes are

Infants mature rapidly. (H. J. Heinz Co.)

subject to this principle. An example of psychological maturation is that of emotional behavior. It has been found that such behavior as crying, smiling, and laughing appear at approximately the same age in all children, even when opportunities for the children to observe such reactions in other persons is severely restricted.

Discontinuity in growth

As we have said, growth, in general, is *discontinuous*. Despite the common-sense notion to the contrary, growth does not generally take a steady, continuous course. Rather it is manifest in *spurts*, *lags*, and *regressions*. Gesell and Ilg have characterized this type of growth as the *spiral effect* (7). Instead of following a straight line of gradually increasing development, growth commonly proceeds in an irregular, almost spasmodic fashion. A phenomenon of this kind which we are well aware of is the rapid spurt in growth, especially height, that occurs in the pre-adolescent period. This kind of phenomenon is also characteristic of most other types of development. Thus a baby may show a gradually increasing amount of time spent in nocturnal sleep; then, just when the anxious parents expect that it will be able to sleep the whole night through, it suddenly reverts to its former pattern of waking up several times during the night. Sometimes, growth proceeds fairly regularly for a time, then a *lag* or *plateau* occurs during which no observable progress is made. Such a period may mark the time that integration of previous growth is taking place. Thus, plateau periods may be preparatory for subsequently more rapid learning. The saying, "We learn to swim in the winter and ice skate in the summer," illustrates this idea. During quiescent periods of learning the integration of previous learning expedites later learning. There is another observation concerning the principle of discontinuity in learning to which we might well call attention at this time; this is that some individuals' learning may be fast while others may be slow even though the latter group may eventually catch up with the former. This does not mean that *all* slow learners or slow developers catch up eventually with the fast group. It does mean, however, that the rate of growth does not *necessarily* indicate the ultimate level that will be reached. Some children may grow slowly in height yet attain an adult height that is equal to or better than the adult height of others who grew more rapidly when younger.

Integrative adaptation

Another general principle of development is that of *integrative adaptation*. The title we have given to this principle is intended to cover what are generally referred to in the literature of child development as two principles. However, as we shall see, the two principles may better be subsumed under one rubric: *integrative adaptation*. We learned when considering prenatal development that the organism tended to react as a whole and in a diffuse or mass way. As maturation of structure and function proceeds, the organism learns to make more *differentiated* responses, responses that are more specific and functionally more efficient. We can restate this phenomenon by characterizing early growth as that of *individuation* (another term for differentiation) in which part-functions develop out of the mass function. Much of early learning is characterized by this principle. Illustrative of this principle is the growth of ever more differentiated behavior in the grasping response: first rather clumsy movements of the whole body in the direction of the object that is to be prehended, later movements of one arm alone, and finally, after considerable development, the well coordinated grasping movement of the fingers in prehending the object. Similarly, in learning to ride a bicycle, the rider will first make clumsy movements of the whole body while attempting to maintain equilibrium and gradually learn to make finer and finer adjustments, sometimes involving only a single muscle group, in order to maintain balance. Psychological learning also shows this characteristic in the early stages of development. Thus, the infant first slowly learns to tell the "not-me" from the "me," then learns to distinguish his mother from all nonmothers, and finally, after much further development, is able to distinguish friendly from unfriendly faces, adults from children, male from female, and so on. The other part of *integrative adaptation* is equally important and is often referred to as the principle of *integration*. The process in *integration* involves putting elements of learning that have already been mastered into new pat-

terns of a more integrated character. Most adult learning is characterized by this principle but it also operates from the earliest stages of development although it is less important at this stage. All of us are familiar with many manifestations of this principle. For example, in learning to dive we may already have all the individual skills (the elements) in our repertoire of behavior *before* we learn this complex

An observation dome such as this facilitates not only visual observation but also motion-picture recording of the reactions of infants. (Gesell)

skill. We have only to learn to put them together in the proper sequence and with the proper timing to become efficient divers. Before we learn to dive we are able to stand erect, stretch our hands up, jump up, arch our bodies, move our head down, and so on. Yet we cannot deny that a great deal of integrative learning has to occur before we can finally execute a good dive.

The reason for putting these two apparently separate principles together under the general title of *integrative adaptation* may now be seen more clearly. We believe that all development is characterized by *both individuation* and *integration*. Although it is true that much of the development that takes place during infancy appears to involve individuation alone, closer observation of the developmental pattern will reveal that integration is also taking place but is overshadowed by the more impressive strides in differentiation that are taking place simultaneously. When a baby learns to crawl or creep before it learns to walk, for instance, considerable differentiation of behavior is occurring but integration of the differentiated skills is also taking place at the same time. In fact, every act of differentiation necessarily involves some reintegration of old elements or old patterns. Frequently we do not observe the integrative aspects in early life not only because the differentiating functions are then more prominent but also because the integrative functions may be less directly observable or may be latent. If we consider the development of the grasping re-

sponse we may be able to see that learning to use only the fingers to grasp an object also involves the *inhibition* of extraneous movements of the limbs and of the body and thus reintegrating the precise grasping movements into a new, more functional pattern.

The general principle of *integrative adaptation*, we shall learn, is highly important in understanding how an individual learns to adjust. In adjustment, there is a similar problem: how to make a more precise (differentiated) response that is more efficient, how to select the appropriate response and inhibit the irrelevant response, and how to integrate the total adaptive response to yield the maximal satisfaction. The same principle will be applied to our discussion (later in this chapter) of the phenomenon of *fixation*, in which failure to progress in psychological growth (and to learn to make more discriminating and appropriate responses) is due to failure to receive the necessary motivation to give up old patterns of behavior in favor of more differentiated and integrated patterns that would now be more efficient. The infant who has failed to learn to give up the breast in favor of the bottle and solid foods (and who is, therefore, *fixated* at the oral stage) has failed to learn to make an integrative adaptation to his changing biological organism. The principle is also significant in understanding that development and learning commonly are most efficient when the child proceeds from the *general* to the *specific* in his learning and from the *simple* to the *complex*. Again such development subsumes the two apparently separate principles of differentiation and integration, as may be seen in the following example. A mother, trying to teach her young child to avoid hot flames, carefully explains that he must not put his hand over the gas flames of the stove. But the same day, the child puts his hand in the fire in the fireplace! He was perhaps trying to obey his mother's instructions regarding fire but had not understood how the general concept of fire applied to the fireplace, since he had thought it referred to the gas stove only. He had to learn the specifics out of the general principle and then reapply the specifics to a new generalization: all fires burn and are to be avoided. At the same time that he was learning this new principle he was also learning by proceeding from the simple (one type of fire) to the complex (the concept of "fire"—all types of fires).

Directional sequence of growth

Development of human structure and function also follows the *cephalo-caudal* principle and the *proximo-distal* principle. Both of these may be subsumed under the principle of the *directional sequence of growth*. In studying prenatal development we learned that the cephalic end of the nervous system, which later becomes the brain, developed more rapidly and before the rest of the nervous system. In general, growth shows this kind of gradient, proceeding more rapidly in the portion near the head than it does near the opposite end. This, then, is the principle of cephalo-caudal development. After birth, the muscles that support the head develop before those that support the back or the legs. The other directional principle, the *proximo-distal* principle, indicates that development proceeds from the inside to

the outside, or in other words from the center to the periphery of the body. The growth of the limbs furnishes an example of this principle; first the limb buds develop, then the sections nearest to the body develop further, until finally the fingers and the arms become fully developed. Motor functions often develop in a similar fashion so that first the muscles near the center of the body function effectively, and later the muscles of the arms and still later of the fingers show efficient operation.

Total-organ involvement

At this point it is necessary to emphasize that although the individual's functions generally develop from mass to specific activity and that although finer skills become differentiated out of grosser skills and then become reintegrated into newer patterns, the individual always tends to react as a whole person, even though a special part may be carrying out the major activity of the moment. It is *not* an arm that responds to a pin prick, for example, but a whole person who moves his arm to avoid pain. Similarly, it is well to remember the principle that we may call *total-organ-involvement* as it applies not only to the organism as a whole but as it applies to a single organ or organ system. A very important example of this generalization is the way the brain operates. For a long time it was believed that individual parts of the brain acted independently and separately from other parts of the brain. This idea gained acceptance from the discovery of *localization of brain func-*

The development of surprise behavior in a very young infant. (Gesell)

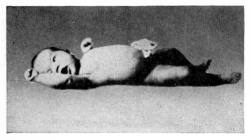

4 weeks

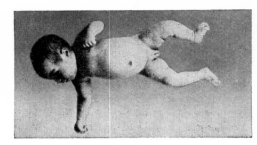

6 weeks

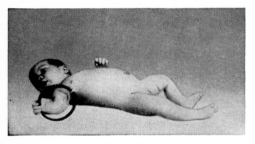

8 weeks

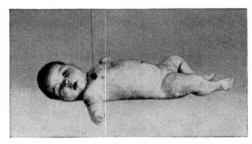

12 weeks

tion in which it was learned that different parts of the brain developed different and specialized functions. For example, motor activities are governed by an area in the forepart of the brain, the *frontal* area, and visual functions are governed by an area in the rear section of the brain, the *occipital* area. There is ample evidence for such kinds of localized brain functions. However, more recent evidence has also indicated that the brain tends to act as a whole. Such evidence, from brain injuries at birth and from experimental studies of animals, parts of whose brains were removed surgically, as well as from other sources, indicates very clearly that with adequate practice other parts of the brain can learn to take over some or all of the functions that were formerly governed by the destroyed area. There have been cases on record in which almost half of the brain tissue was destroyed and yet the individual was able to function so effectively that common observation could not detect anything wrong (18). Damage to the brain does not necessarily destroy memories nor does it necessarily destroy or reduce intellectual capacities, although such damage may otherwise interfere with maximal functioning. The most recent research on brain structure and brain physiology again lends some support to the concept that some tissues may be so highly specialized that their destruction may produce irreversible losses, but even this research does not suggest that such is always the case. We may conclude that, although specialized functions of various brain areas do develop, the brain still tends to act as a whole, even when one part *customarily* carries a specialized function. In this respect the brain is *not* like a telephone exchange (an analogy that has often been employed in describing the brain's functioning) for unlike the telephone exchange its functions are total, tend toward interchangeability, and functions lost through destruction of one section can often be recovered through utilization of another section. We believe, moreover, that this principle of *total-organ involvement* is likely to be true for other organ systems as well as the brain, as we shall see in later chapters.

Principle of continuous activity

A final principle of developing human behavior is that the human being does not simply *react* to external stimulation but rather *brings* to such a situation a *readiness* or a *set* or an *attitude* which significantly conditions the nature of his perception of and reaction to the stimulus. Stated more simply, the organism, and especially its brain, is *continuously active* and affects the nature of incoming excitation. Therefore, to understand the meaning of behavior, one must understand not only the nature of the external conditions that affect it but also the nature of the internal processes that are constantly going on *within* the individual. Hebb has pointed out with respect to the behavior of the brain that "an afferent (incoming) excitation must be superim-

posed on an already existent excitation" (11). This position is in sharp contrast to the extreme environmentalists and the theories of Locke (19) of yesteryear that conceptualized the individual as a *blank slate* upon which external experience marked its effects. It is in opposition to the position of John B. Watson (20) who believed that an individual was entirely the product of his environmental experiences. And it is different from the position that a given stimulus or stimulus situation, by its nature, has the same meaning to all of those who are exposed to it.

The principle of *continuous action* presupposes that there is a constant autonomous process going on within the individual. Some of the major evidence for this supposition is from studies of brain electrophysiology. There are other types of evidence, both direct and inferential, that support this position and from this principle we can derive far better interpretations of many kinds of human behavior and make more discriminating use of many types of observations of human behavior, as the following pages will show. Above all, recognition that individuals differ in the types of set or readiness they bring into the situations of their lives will enable us to avoid the error of thinking of the human being as a *passive agent* who simply *reacts* to events; we can begin to gain some meaning of the notion of human behavior as being *dynamic* in that humans *actively interact* with their milieus.

PSYCHOLOGICAL NEEDS
AND PERSONALITY DEVELOPMENT

We are now in a good position to begin our discussion of the development of the infant. It may seem strange to open this discussion with an analysis of the needs and personality development of the infant; it is more usual to begin by describing the infant's physical appearance, his motor development, his language development, and so on. As we have learned, however, these more conspicuous evidences of growth are sharply influenced by the ways in which the baby learns to adapt to his environment and the ways in which the environment is arranged for him. In fact, adequate attention to nutritional and other somatic requirements of the baby is no guarantee that he will develop normally or even that he will be able to live (as the studies of *marasmus* indicate). It seems to be at least as important to nourish the baby's psychological needs.

We can learn about a baby's needs only by observing his behavior. He has very few understandable ways of communicating his wants to us since he has not yet developed language skills. Even his body movements, through which he may attempt to convey his feelings, are rather diffuse and uncoordinated. Yet the mother who loves her baby and has spent much time with him soon learns when he is crying because he is hungry and when he is crying because he is in pain. She soon learns to tell by the "feel" of his body, by his looseness or stiffness, for ex-

ample, whether he is angry or pleased. And she learns how to adapt to her baby's needs just as he learns, very slowly, to adapt to her ways of gratifying his needs.

The infant has three major sets of needs: *physical* needs (especially needs for nutrition to sustain life and promote physical maturation); needs for *protection* against physical trauma, among which protection against extreme temperatures and against sudden changes in temperature are very important; and needs for *affection*. It is far simpler to provide for the first two sets of needs than for the last set, for scientific knowledge and scientifically arranged care are almost universally available in our country to insure adequate gratification of the former. To "feed" affection, however, requires a person who is capable of offering love. The biological fact of motherhood does not automatically qualify a mother as a good agent, nor do scientific rules about how to take care of the baby guarantee such a relationship. As illustrative of this principle we may refer to the findings of Brody, which we summarized in the previous chapter. We can cite the evidence of Bakwin, a pediatrician, who concluded, on the basis of his own observations as well as of the scientific literature on the subject, that infants who are brought up in hospitals and do not have adequate "mothering" fail to gain weight despite an adequate ingestion of foods. He also found that such infants slept less, smiled less frequently, had more frequent and more persistent respiratory infections, and tended to lose weight or gain less in weight (21). We can cite the impressive summary by Ribble in which she emphasized that without adequate "mothering" infants lagged far behind in their physical as well as their psychological development (22).*

To the authors, the most impressive evidence for the proposition that satisfaction of affectional needs is a *necessity* for effective growth is the history of the occurrence and treatment of *marasmus*. This is a "disease" of infancy in which the principal symptoms are: gradually increasing debility, physical atrophy, and aged-looking appearance including wrinkled skin, and *death*. Death used to be the expected outcome in advanced cases of marasmus not too long ago, and no cure was known for this condition. However, the frequency of the occurrence of this illness has been very sharply reduced (almost eliminated) and the inevitability of the consequence of death has been demonstrated to be entirely unnecessary. The most important single ingredient in the prevention and cure of this condition has been found to be "adequate mothering." The cause of marasmus was thought to be malnutrition. However, it was soon learned that it occurred frequently in large hospitals where there was good medical care and good nutrition but where there was insufficient fondling of the infant or inconsistent relationships between infants and nurses. A striking experience was reported in a Scottish hospital where marasmus cases had usually ended in death. It was learned by accident that children suffering from marasmus who were mothered by one of

the scrubwomen (whose lack of cleanliness was a matter of some concern to the hospital) recovered and became quite well. She was thereafter given all marasmus cases so that she might "handle" them into health! It is now widely believed that marasmus is usually the result of nothing more serious than severely inadequate mothering (in which lack of emotional warmth, fondling and other consistent forms of stimulation are lacking).

We have used the term *affection* to describe the set of needs that we have been discussing. This is not a very precise term and it certainly includes a whole range of activities. The baby is unable to *perceive* affection, as such, but it can and does respond to fondling, rocking, stroking, body warmth, and the like. It is likely that when a mother loves her child she will not only be able to communicate her feelings through these and other means but she will also be sensitive to the child's needs. Affectionate behavior on the mother's part probably means frequent and appropriate stimulation of the infant by various means, such as rocking and fondling. Moreover, rhythmic stimulations of this kind tend to promote the infant's growing and well-being. For example, the baby responds to rocking and fondling with improved breathing and blood circulation. There is ample evidence that lack of fondling retards growth (see the next section of this chapter). Moreover, an affectionate mother helps the infant to develop a sense of *basic trust* in himself and the

---

* Many studies in this area have lacked good or adequate experimental controls, but the weight of evidence of trained observers, fortified by recent studies that were better designed, strongly support the principle.

world because she is able to perceive and respond to his needs, without undue frustration on her own part, and because the infant, therefore, learns to expect that his needs will be gratified without undue frustration on his part. He learns to anticipate his mother's behavior just as she learns to respond to his. Thus, an affectionate relationship is not simply a condition that is important for sentimental reasons. It is also a scientifically desirable condition supported by "cold" research evidence.* ◄

Babies start off with different somatic needs and with different personality predispositions. For example, although all babies, directly after birth, sleep most of the time, there is considerable variation among babies. Even identical twins differ in the amounts of sleep they require and differ in restlessness and amounts of motor activity. Some babies seem to need less sleep than others. Most babies under four weeks of age have at least five periods of sleep each 24-hour day, interrupted by drowsy-wakeful states when they cry lustily until given food. Even at four weeks of age babies are rarely fully awake for any considerable length of time. By two years of age they are frequently able to sleep through the night for a period of 11 to 13 hours and stay awake during the day except for one or two nap periods of an hour or so each. The variations

among children in the patterns of sleep and wakefulness are very marked and even the same child shows a variable pattern from day to day, and week to week. In the beginning, the infant usually awakes because he is hungry and needs to be fed; later he awakes to play, to be coddled and comforted, and to watch the activity around him. Aside from needs for nutrition, the pattern of sleep and wakefulness depends on the *constitutional* needs of the infant with respect to autonomic activity. Although all babies are restless because their physiological stability is far from adequate, some are much more restless and generally more active than others. These constitutional differences in autonomic activity may be based upon prenatal experiences as well as upon hereditary factors. They may be further conditioned by the ways in which the baby, and later the infant, is gratified or frustrated.

So far as we know babies do not have the capacity to experience many differentiated emotional states. For one thing, the cerebrum is not sufficiently well developed for such fine perceptions to occur. They do, however, differentiate pleasure from displeasure or *satiation* from *distress*.* And they do differ, temperamentally, in both the amount and ease of irritability. Gesell and Ilg classify infants into three general categories: *solid*, *facile*, and *uneven* (8). The first, or solid, type tends to be less demanding, more self-dependent, and matures slowly. The second, or facile, type is somewhat more demanding, is less self-dependent, and matures rapidly. The third, or un-

---

* Our position is not accepted by some workers in the fields of child development and personality theory who remain critical of the general conclusion we are suggesting. See, for summaries of opposing viewpoints, references 23 and 24.

* Some prefer to call the initial conditions *excitement* and *nonexcitement*.

even, type is very demanding, is highly dependent, and matures irregularly. These appear to be constitutional differences that tend to persist unless the environment alters them through drastic means. These types are clearly related to *body build* and correlated differences in the proportions of *ectoderm, mesoderm,* and *endoderm* (roughly inner tissues, middle-layer tissues like the muscles, and outside layers like the skin and cerebrum, respectively). We shall have more to say about body types in later chapters, but at this time we wish to emphasize that: (a) infants differ in constitutional temperament, and (b) the differences in temperament which set the direction for differences in such development are tied in with the nature of the body build.

According to the psychoanalytic view, the further ways in which the personality of the child develops are conditioned by the nature of the *oral* and *anal* gratification. Freud suggested there were two periods of development that are crucial for the individual: the *oral period,* lasting from birth until about one and one half years of age, and the *anal period,* lasting from about the eighth month until well into the third year. The oral period is usually divided into an *oral receptive* and an *oral expulsive* stage, and the anal period is usually divided into an *anal expulsive* and an *anal retentive* stage. The oral and anal periods overlap, it will be noted, and merge into each other. Because Freud's theory has had so much influence in personality theory as well as in investigations by anthropologists and sociologists, and because the theory is so helpful in understanding normal and abnormal personality development, we shall

use it in viewing the conditions of personality development in infancy (5, 10).

Freud suggested that the sexual drives are the most important of all biological drives in personality adjustment.* By sex he meant those experiences that are pleasurable and that form the basis of emotional affiliation between people. According to Freud, sexual drives are biological in origin and operate in infants as well as in adults. They differ from other biological drives in that they produce more gratification when *sexual tension* is reduced. When satisfied they lead to *approach* behavior between people rather than *avoidance* or *flight* behavior. Sexual drives are not to be construed as simply those drives having to do with intercourse and procreation. They include fondling, sucking, soothing and being soothed, thumb-sucking, and the like. In short, they form the major basis of human relationships. In all instances, infantile or adult, the sudden discharge of these drives results in a heightened state of pleasure.

The oral stages

During the oral stages, the *zone* through which sexual drives are discharged is the *oral orifice*: the mouth and immediately surrounding regions including the teeth, gums, and upper extremity of the gastro-intestinal tract. Freud believed that this zone, because of its erotogeneity, is of

---

* We shall not discuss Freud's conception of death drives which we believe involves unnecessary assumptions and are not needed to explain any of the data of behavior.

primary importance in early infancy as an organizing region for discharge of sexual tensions. We have learned from our discussion in Chapter 2 that there are critical periods during which certain tissues develop special characteristics and satisfy certain needs. The oral orifice or the oral zone is in a critical period of primacy during the first eight months. The mouth is the region through which contact with the external world is developed and maintained. It not only takes in nourishment but it simultaneously takes in the attributes of the mother and through her the culture that she represents. This occurs because the total behavior of the infant is conditioned by the methods of handling when the hunger drives are most active. Thus, the mother's cultural modes of feeding her child greatly influence his behavior.

The first of the oral periods is known as the *oral receptive period*. The main *mode* (pattern of behavior) is *passive*, that is the baby is passive and dependent; he has to be helped to take in nourishment; he even has to be helped to find the nipple and he has to be "burped" to eliminate air pockets. Sucking, therefore, proves to be a very important activity not only for the intake of food but also as part of the initial pattern of a relationship with the external world. During this critical period the infant needs ample and prompt gratification of its sucking needs. There is evidence to suggest that breast-feeding gratifies these needs more adequately than bottle-feeding (although breast-feeding is *not* imperative). Breast-

feeding swells the spongy tissue of the mouth more completely, and is more satisfying, than bottle-feeding. Gesell and Ilg state: "Breast-feeding is the most favorable condition for the initiation of a self-demand schedule" (8). Breast-feeding more easily permits a close, relaxed, and warm (bodily-warm) contact between mother and infant under normal circumstances. While sucking, the baby explores the mother with his eyes and gets to know the "feel" of her body. Insufficient or delayed or inconstant sucking activity seems to encourage irritability; moreover, it may lead to a loss of basic trust in the world. Severe trauma during this period and in connection with sucking activity may lead to personality traits of depression and marked suspiciousness (or *paranoid attitudes*).

The second of the periods, the *oral expulsive period,* begins at about six months of age, and has a more *active* mode. Sexual primacy is now focused on the muscles of the mouth and on the teeth. The gums and teeth have matured and the baby gets pleasure out of biting and out of actively taking things into the mouth. If the mother cannot tolerate the baby's biting (and the reason may be soreness or sensitivity of her breasts rather than her unfavorable attitude toward the baby!), substitute objects may be required more often to gratify the baby's biting needs. The baby now has more active means of upsetting his mother because of his proclivity for biting. During this second stage of orality the baby's *identification* with the mother is making rapid strides, that is, the baby is learning both consciously and unconsciously to behave like the mother. He can now also react with more actively perceived irritation when the mother does not gratify his needs, and hence the baby is said to begin to be *ambivalent* toward the mother (even the "good" mother) at this time, both liking and needing her while disliking her and wanting to be rid of her at the same time.

We have said that the infant needs to gratify these early, oral sexual drives. Failure to do so may result in severe personality disturbance. These statements are supported by a considerable body of clinical evidence and are reinforced by experimental evidence on animals and humans. Trauma experienced in connection with oral development results in *fixation* of oral modes of behavior. Fixation may be defined as follows: over- or under-gratification (especially the latter) of oral needs *during the period of oral primacy* tending to result in abnormal persistence of the modes of behavior normally associated with development during this period. We have already given some indication of such types of abnormal development as a result of fixation during the oral receptive stage. Fixation during the oral expulsive stage tends to produce a heightened need for biting activities, stubbornness, and even "oral sadism" of which excessive use of sarcastic or "biting" language is an example.

Let us look, now, at some of the evidence supporting some of the assertions made in the preceding paragraphs. One of the important studies is that by Levy (25). Six puppies were subjected to varying conditions of adequacy of suckling during the period of their "oral primacy." Two puppies suckled at their mother's teats in the "normal" manner; two were

fed by bottles with nipples having moderately large holes; two were fed by bottles with nipples having very large holes. Thus, the conditions of suckling were varied systematically for the three groups. What difference in behavior, if any, followed these different types of feeding experiences? The first group, which engaged in normal suckling, developed well and were lively; they were able to rest contentedly after suckling. The second group, which had a mild degree of suckling frustration, engaged in many extraneous suckling activities, often chewing on solid objects, and they showed restless behavior. The third group, which had a fairly extreme degree of frustration of suckling needs since they obtained their nourishment too easily and had little suckling experience, showed poor general development. They were very restless and suckled almost all the time, even suckling each other's skin so severely that the skin bled. It should be noted that these differences could not, presumably, be attributed to insufficient nourishment for some of the puppies because ample nourishment was available for all. Rather, the differences may be attributed to differences in gratification of the oral needs of the puppies and resulting differences in oral frustration and in tension states.

Another source of information on this problem is the series of studies done by Spitz (26, 27). Although these studies were lacking in some methodological refinements (and we must remember how difficult it is to subject human beings to experimentally controlled conditions of frustration), and although the studies dealt with the total nature of methods of caring for infants rather than with oral gratification alone, the findings are of considerable pertinence. Essentially, Spitz compared three groups of infants: those hospitalized for a long period of time because, for one reason or another, their mothers were unavailable, those living in a nursery with other children, and those living in their own homes. In general, the last group had more consistent mothering and more opportunities for breast-feeding than the other two groups; they did not, however, have better nutrition or hygienically more adequate living conditions. The most important finding to which we wish to call attention, among the many findings of these studies, was that the hospitalized group with, we repeat, good to superior health conditions in their environment were retarded in development, showed many illnesses and even deaths, tended to become depressed and even developed psychosis (severe "mental" disturbance commonly known as insanity). This group suffered severe emotional frustration of many oral needs despite good medical care, and consequently built up tensions and resorted to abnormally defensive behavior. Similar in direction are the studies cited by Bowlby in his evaluation of the effects of frustration of the psychological needs of infants (2). More recently, Rheingold supplied data confirming the general implications of Spitz' and Bowlby's conclusions in studies in which the effects of only relatively moderate degrees of frustration of oral and mothering needs were evaluated (28). We should also like to call attention, again, to Goldman-Eisler's study, referred to in Chapter 2 (reference number 33), in which she found that oral pessimism was associated with too early weaning from breast-feeding. All of these studies, as well as manifold informal observations reported by trained clinical workers, lend strong support to the Freudian position on the importance of the "oral hypothesis" and the concept of *fixation*.

The anal stages

As biological development proceeds, the zone of primacy shifts to the *anal zone*. Now it is the anus, the buttocks, and the surrounding areas, as well as the lower end of the intestinal canal, that assume prominence in arousing pleasurable excitation and in organizing the discharge of erotic impulses. We have already given some attention to the problem of development during the anal period in our discussion of sphincter control in Chapter 3. Now we shall discuss the more general personality implications of development during this period.

In the first anal stage, the *anal expulsive* stage, pleasure is derived by the infant from the passage of the stools. The reduction of tensions accompanying this act as well as the tactile excitation that accompanies it are gratifying. Bowel control is also very important from the viewpoint of social learning since, as we have emphasized, it involves the highly complex interaction of infant and mother as the former learns to interiorize the cultural modes of behavior in regard to this act. It is also significant as a means of gratifying or displeasing the mother, so that the infant now has a powerful means of influencing his mother's behavior—far more so than his former resorts to crying. Furthermore, it is a social act that the infant can engage in by himself, being unlike eating in this respect (in which the baby was completely dependent upon supplies from his mother).

Expulsion of the feces may be painful as well as pleasurable. Thus the trait of ambivalence that began to develop in the previous stage of development may now become more pronounced. If gradual learning of sphincter control is not permitted, if instead the mother is tense or demanding or attempts to institute bladder and bowel control before the infant is biologically and psychologically ready for it, the total act of defecation may become a highly tense situation for the infant (as well as for the mother). A struggle for mastery between mother and child may ensue that is quite heroic in its proportions, as common observations may sometimes attest. The child may see the mother as hostile or even as an "ogre." The whole pattern of interrelationships between infant and mother may be profoundly disturbed, and, as a consequence, the infant may develop unfavorable personality traits. Since these traits occur so early in the life of the child and since they are so emotionally conditioned, they have a very good chance not only of persisting but of becoming gradually more and more pathological.

The second anal stage is known as the *anal retentive* stage. At about one and a half years of age the infant begins to be able to retain his feces if he so desires. The mode of behavior is now character-

ized by more active withholding and more active control in general. As we shall see in the next section of this chapter, the child has by this time in his life begun to be more accurately perceptive of the world around him, and by the end of the anal period he has a reasonably developed ego (that is, a nucleus of personality tendencies for perceiving himself, the world about him, and for knowing how to cope with conflicts between self-needs and the demands of others). He learns to derive pleasure out of his newfound ability to control bowel movements and learns to make even more effective social use of his new skills. He concurrently learns to value the excreta, per se, since it has been associated with important interpersonal events in his life. Hence, if undue emphasis has been placed upon it by his mother, he may attach excessive importance and emotional value to it. Just as the previous stage of anal development was a battleground in the *normal* relationships between infant and mother, so the second stage may be an even more intense battle situation and may become pathologically so if the issue is joined too early or toilet-training is too rigid. We must remember that although the infant's ego is beginning to develop he is, after all, only an infant and can easily misinterpret undue demands that are made on him.

Fixation during this period leads to a triad of personality traits: *parsimony* (or excessive thriftiness), *petulance* (or excessive stubbornness), and *pedantry* (or excessive meticulousness). Normal growth through the anal period will help to establish confidence in interpersonal relationships and sufficient degrees of skills in thrift, self-assertion, and orderliness, but frustration during this period is likely to be accompanied by an excessive development of these same traits and perhaps to *psychopathology* (disturbed emotional development).

During oral and anal phases of development the zones of primacy shift and the personality begins to emerge in more and more crystallized ways. These periods are important if for no other reason than that they come before later periods and thus are more likely to set the trends that tend to persist unless altered by other factors—always a more difficult task than the normal development of a favorable personality. All children and all mothers experience a certain amount of frustration during these periods; in fact, some frustration is necessary for growth to occur. Mild degrees of frustration serve as motivations since the individual tries to get rid of discomfort and, if successful, changes his behavior to more suitable modes according to his biological and psychological readiness. It is only severe, harsh, and inconsistent frustration that leads to fixations and unfavorable outcomes. These points may help to emphasize two things: (a) the need to *pace* the child according to his own rate of development rather than according to any normative schedule, and (b) the need to be aware of the principles of gradualness and discontinuities in development so as not to expect success in behavioral adaptations on the first attempts. In addition, the reader may have inferred from our discussion how ubiquitous is the need to express some of the hostile impulses in response to inevitable frustrations and how tolerant the parent must be to permit some overt expression of these needs. Otherwise, the infant is less likely to learn how to handle them appropriately.

Homeostasis, stress, and ego development

We have seen that the infant experiences many conflicts during the first years of his life. Conflicts of opposing impulses that arise simultaneously are ever present. The individual is never in a complete state of tensionless rest, not even during sleep when he most closely approaches this condition. Even during sleep conflicts and tensions arise as we have been able to learn from observations of the restless behavior of infants and from the fact that they often have dreams, sometimes of a nightmarish quality. Nevertheless, the organism continually strives for a state that is as *even* and as tension-free as possible.

This instability of the organism as it is developing and adjusting and the tendency to maintain a balance with a minimal degree of tension is known as the *homeostatic principle.* Physiologists have long been concerned with the various regulatory mechanisms of the body—ever since the time of Claude Bernard who published the results of his important research on this subject in 1859. He pointed out that the body made incessant efforts to remain constant despite the constantly changing internal and external forces impinging upon it. The principle of *homeostasis* was formulated by W. B. Cannon who described the self-regulating physiologic processes of individual tissues, organs, and organ systems (29). In this formulation, homeostasis referred to compensatory mechanisms undertaken by the body after disturbance by stimulus situations. The homeostatic tendency is thought to be innate in the organism and is a function of the autonomic nervous system. Behavior, according to Cannon,

total food content, increase its excretion of salt by drinking large amounts of water, or show a decrease of activity in the adrenal cortex with a resulting increase of loss of salt in the urine.

As the concept of homeostasis is now used in psychology it refers to the total behavioral adaptations of the individual

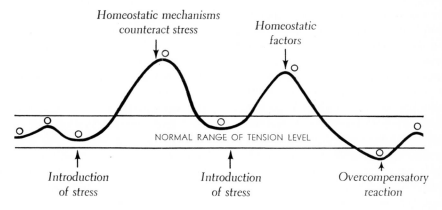

Figure 4. *Normal tension, stress, and homeostatic adaptation. (The small circles indicate that it is the whole person that reacts and adapts to stress.)*

is directed toward getting rid of disturbing stimuli or toward prolonging or reviving agreeable stimulation. The more recent work of Richter has substantiated the earlier hypotheses of Cannon (30). Richter showed further that even when the simple physiologic regulators of the body are experimentally removed the whole organism maintains homeostasis by changes in its total behavior. For example, an animal whose fodder contains too high a salt content will decrease its

—both physiological and psychological— as he attempts to maintain a balance in his tension state. After tension arises the individual adapts in some way, achieving an almost tension-free state when there is a further imbalance with corresponding regulatory mechanisms. The resulting new imbalance leads to still further adaptations, in a continuing manner, while the individual is attempting to maintain the minimal degree of unpleasant tension or conflict. Thus, homeostasis is a complex, ongoing process and results from adaptive efforts of the whole individual through his various regulatory mechanisms, physiological and psychological.

The concept of homeostasis is related to recent work on the concept of stress. Since 1936, Hans Selye, an histologist in Canada, has been experimenting with the effects of various kinds of stress upon the human organism. (Many other psychologists and physiologists have been doing work in the same general area.) Dr. Selye has developed what amounts to a revolutionary concept of stress in medicine and psychology: that stress is a common denominator in all biological activity (31). He has pointed out, for instance, that an agent invading the organism is not, by itself, responsible for the possible infection that follows, but rather that any resulting illness, disease, or maladaptation is caused by the nature of the adaptive mechanisms *of the whole organism.* It is not the germ that produces the disease; rather it is the way the organism adapts to this particular kind of stress that explains the specific and general reactions. Thus, Selye came to the idea of a *General Adaptation Syndrome* (G.A.S.) that is a *nonspecific,* habitual reaction of the whole person to the constant series of stresses to which he is being subjected. People differ in the nature and the intensity of their G.A.S., which has biological roots but which is influenced by *all* kinds of stresses in ordinary living, both psychological and somatic. Therefore, in evaluating how the person responds, whether normally or abnormally, healthily or unhealthily, one has to take into account three sets of elements: the *stressor* (or external agent which initiates the stress), the *defensive* measures (or hormones, emotional states, and defense mechanisms), and the *mechanisms for surrender* (or hormonal and nervous stimuli that tend to influence the body to give up). Selye has supplied a simplified formula to predict the total reaction:

$$\frac{\text{Local stress in any one part}}{\text{Total stress in the body}}$$

When there is local stress in one part of the body, the general reaction of the person tends to be minimal, if the organism is healthy and the stressing agent is not severe. When there is intense stress or general stress, the body as a whole is much more involved and we speak of the whole person as being "sick." We shall have more to say about Selye's ideas later in this book, but we can see that his theory of stress is a natural evolution of the concept of homeostasis: that the total person is constantly in a state of imbalance of some degree and that the total person tries to maintain the minimal degree of instability that is possible under the circumstances.

We have said that in early infancy there are only a few crudely differentiated emotional states—chiefly pleasure and displeasure, at first. The infant tends to act promptly to discharge his impulses. He is said to be, at this time, essentially a creature of instincts—biologically rooted drives that have little or no experiential component. The infant has not consciously learned, in the beginning, to make appropriate adjustment on the basis of cognition or thinking or reasoning. Rather he acts automatically, although, as we have seen, many of these automatic ways of behaving have already been conditioned by prenatal experience. The psychoanalysts use the term *id* to refer to these unconsciously, biologically rooted drives and consequent behaviors. Sexual drives are an important part of the unconscious id because of the role they play in adjustment. As the individual's biological and psychological maturation proceeds there gradually develops a set of skills that enable him to adapt to the changing circumstances of his life. The external world forces certain adaptations in the way in which the unlearned id drives express themselves, for the id does not know of reality or what is good and what is bad. The frustrations that the individual experiences compel him to inhibit, delay, or modify the ways in which he formerly "naturally" responded, and thus the ego is formed and developed. As the infant learns to become more and more socially adapted, as he learns to interiorize the demands of his mother and the culture she represents, he learns certain ways of mediating his id drives; he learns to perceive, to think, to choose, and to adapt. Thus, the ego apparatus (the set of skills that make this possible) consists of three kinds of abilities: the ability to perceive what the person feels and wants, the ability to perceive what the external reality involves, and the ability to perform integrated behavior to obtain the maximal adjustment to the set of circumstances.

The development of ego functions depends not only upon experience and concomitant frustration but also upon the

maturation of the biological mechanisms. Until vision has developed adequately, the perception of external reality is limited. Similarly, until hearing, sense of touch, and in fact all of the sense functions have developed, external reality can only be perceived grossly and inaccurately. Moreover, the development of the musculature also influences the rate at which ego functions can develop, since coordinated behavior involves various muscle groups. The growth of the cerebrum, and of the whole brain and the whole nervous system, also has important determining effects on how the ego emerges.

We can see how ego development is the result of an interactive process of biological and reality factors. We can also understand that many of the ego's functions are quite conscious; we are easily aware of much that we wish to do and, in fact, commonly do. Some of the learned ego functions operate at an unconscious level, that is some ego behavior is automatic and occurs habitually without awareness, whereas some of the motivations and feelings concerned with the behavior originally have been *repressed* (pushed back into a state of unawareness or unconsciousness because they are associated with painful experience of some kind).

Ego development is a gradual process, as we have said. The infant starts out at birth with no ego of any consequence, and the ego gradually becomes stronger and more appropriate to external circumstances under normal conditions, as the

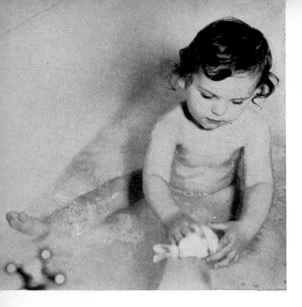

Infants like to do things for themselves.
(Am. Mutual Liability Ins. Co.)

child matures. In early infancy sensations of touch (both tactile and kinesthetic sensations) are thought to dominate ego functions. Later, as perception improves and as experience accumulates, the ego uses many sense modalities more accurately and uses cognition more fully. The individual learns to understand reality and to distinguish it from his internal world of fantasy, he learns how to overcome tensions, and he learns how to cope actively with his world. As illustrative of the differentiated ways in which the ego perceives, we can cite the work of Spitz who found that the infant is unable to smile appropriately (or in response to a suitable external object) until about eight months of age (26). Before this he could not differentiate known from unknown faces or masks of human faces from real faces.

One of the painful tasks of infancy and of early childhood is to learn to give up

belief in the idea of one's own omnipotence. (In fact, some adults never fully learn to give up this idea!) The infant acts as if he believes that the entire universe rests within himself and that he is the source of all power. After all, do not people come running at his bidding when he lets out a shrill cry? Isn't his mother always willing to do his bidding, especially if she is sensitive to his needs? How hard it is for the infant to give up this conviction that he is the center of all things. He invents fantasy to succor this notion and he has temper tantrums or convulsions when his wishes are not gratified immediately. Only as he gradually learns to delay gratification of some of his needs so as to gain greater rewards, only as he learns to tolerate frustration without subsequent deprivation, only then does he also learn to become more realistic and to replace his sense of omnipotence with an accurate perception of himself and of the world. Failure to learn in this way may result in retardation of many aspects of his development, and in severe cases may even result in serious types of maladjustment. We shall get to know more of these things as we now begin to examine other aspects of the infant's growth and development.

COPING BEHAVIOR—
RUDIMENTARY DEFENSE MECHANISMS

As the individual matures and learns to adapt to the circumstances of his life he develops certain habitual ways of coping with obstacles, frustrations, and deprivations. By *coping* we mean, in a simple sense, dealing with, adjusting to, or overcoming the physical and psychological problems that arise in the course of living. Certain of these coping methods have been given the name *mechanisms of defense*. These refer to specific coping methods having to do with ways of dealing with psychological conflict, and while present in both normal and abnormal developmental conditions are more prominent and more characteristic of the latter. That is why they are usually thought of as *psychopathological* (i.e. psychologically "sick"), although they are, as we say, utilized by all individuals to some extent. Although we still have to learn a great deal about the ways in which individuals develop coping methods, there is a considerable body of information available that is of interest.

The reader may have noticed that we have already referred to coping methods in various parts of this chapter without actually using that term. In discussing ego development, for example, we spoke of the infant's ways of dealing with external reality. Similarly, we shall find it necessary to refer to coping methods when we discuss the development of interpersonal behavior and other topics. In fact, coping behavior occurs in the context of all other behaviors; it does not have an existence that is independent of the rest of behavior. The very process of living constantly involves adaptation to changing circumstances, so that some kind of coping behavior is always present. Nevertheless, in order to conceptualize these processes more completely, it will be helpful to discuss briefly some of the most important modes of coping during the period of infancy.

As we have noted, the neonate, and later the young infant, is highly dependent and essentially passive in his orientation to his surroundings. This passivity does not mean that he is not doing anything actively in coping with his milieu. Even in the prenatal state the process of reaction was dependent upon the ongoing state—the ongoing processes—actively present in the organism. In postnatal life, reaction began to take on a more active characteristic as more differentiated ways of behaving became available. The young baby is so helpless and essentially passive because of his gross physical immaturity —he cannot do very much about changing the external conditions of his milieu. At this time, homeostasis is maintained most easily by immediate gratification of needs. When the needs of the infant are not gratified very quickly distress becomes apparent to the observer in crying, restlessness, and the like. The rationale for the self-demand feeding schedule which we have discussed is based upon the observation that an infant cannot tolerate any long delay in satisfaction of its needs. About the only general method the young infant has of coping with frustration is that of *withdrawal* which is best typified by sleep. When stress is not too great the comfort of sleep thus serves the double function of providing physiological rest and of coping for a time with minimal stress or discomfiture.

Incorporation—
a primitive defense

As the body matures and as the response potential becomes more diversified, the infant learns new, but still rather primitive, ways of coping with stress. He can cry out more vigorously when in distress, he can squirm more effectively, he can look (sometimes, we think, meaningfully) at mother, he can try to sit up, and so on. The first somewhat deliberate coping behaviors, then, develop out of increased control of behavioral responses—many of which were present in rudimentary form shortly after birth. Perhaps, above all, the first new way of coping involves the pattern of attempts at *incorporation* of objects so as to suck on them and ingest them if possible. Breast-feeding is, of course, the prototype of this pattern of incorporation in which the nipple can now be somewhat more actively incorporated as the infant tries to gratify its hunger needs. The incorporative coping mode soon involves grasping, holding, and various rhythmic movements as part of the total pattern. Development of the various sense modalities permits inclusion of responses involving these modalities in the total incorporative pattern. For example, as vision improves, visual skills become part of the pattern of coping—looking for the object to be sucked, fixating one's gaze upon it, and the like.

The development of motor abilities—even simple ones such as sitting up, pushing away, easy turning of the head volitionally—increases the range of possible coping behaviors. Long before locomotion becomes available, these simple motor skills increase greatly the varieties of behavior through which the external world can be "controlled" to some extent. If the rapport between mother and child is favorable, the infant learns to use new coping methods in a confident, happy manner and the reciprocal relationship between them is enriched and improved. Note that we said "confident" and "happy." Effective coping methods do more than permit some measure of control; they contribute to the dimly growing self-awareness of the infant as a confident or competent individual, and this type of developing self-image assists the infant in his further growth. During this stage, the infant also learns a more active way of dealing with some types of stress: he can push the disagreeable or unwanted object away, and can *avoid more actively* what is displeasing. Thus, the possibilities of *approach-avoidance* behavior become extended during this phase of development and are tied in, as more or less habitual ways of reacting, to the developing personality characteristics of the child.

We have discussed previously the concept of *psychological incorporation* as it applies to infancy. As the baby learns to adapt to the world through his mother (or mother substitute), he incorporates many of the personality characteristics of this person, and especially does he incorporate the prohibiting requirements of this person. The infant learns that his needs are not always gratified and he also learns that he has to begin to conform to external demands in some ways. During the periods of toilet-training, these prohibitive aspects of the mother become quite prominent, for the infant now has to learn to be a social person—one who can delay gratification or one who can find socially acceptable ways of obtaining gratification. During this stage of development, the infant also becomes aware of *consciously experienced anxiety* in a more personally meaningful way. Hence we shall now turn our attention to the role of anxiety in the development of coping behavior.

Anxiety and conflict

We shall use the term *anxiety* to refer to a stirred-up state of the organism involving apprehension and general discomfort, and in which the source of the condition is *not known* to the individual. We thus distinguish it from fear in which there is a *consciously* apprehended object or situation. We *fear* somebody or something, but we are *anxious* in general. Sometimes we may affix the source of our anxiety to something, *as if* this were the true cause (as when we are afraid of small rooms, but in reality do not know the source of this fear). We may do this to attempt to manage, in some way, the condition of anxiety, since it seems easier to deal with a known source of danger than an unknown source. Sometimes, anxiety may be transformed from a psychological state into a physical condition (for example, when we have rapid heart beat very often we may finally develop a chronically sick heart) so that we no longer experience the anxiety as vividly as before.

Anxiety is primarily caused by anticipation of being "hurt" psychologically. Failure in gratification of the basic needs of the infant may produce anxiety. The threat of being left alone may engender anxiety. The possibility of being hurt physically may also cause anxiety. Anxiety (as we are using the term) appears, however, only when the ego experiences threats of *separation* or of *mutilation* and

when the individual *anticipates catastrophe*. Such catastrophic reactions occur when basic needs cannot be satisfied—when the conflict is so great that it appears to the individual that his very ego is threatened.

As we have seen, the ego of the infant is quite weak and the ability of the infant to satisfy its biological needs is quite limited. The infant is dependent upon consistent and relatively immediate gratification of these needs. Once the infant has had such gratification, separation from the mother for an extended period (without suitable replacement) may have severe consequences—it is likely to engender severe anxiety and depression (26). In turn, the infant is afraid of displeasing the mother because he is so dependent upon her for gratification of his needs and because he has learned to love her. To avoid the anxiety that might be induced by displeasing the mother (through separation from her and even physical punishment by her), the infant attempts to conform. He has learned to do some conforming in the oral stages of his development, but it is during the anal stages that traumata are likely to be greater as he has to learn to conform still more. This is true because as he now, *more actively*, has to try to conform, he has to learn to tolerate the conflict induced by not satisfying his own needs. To please someone else, either because of love of or fear of becoming separated from the loved object, the infant has to displease himself—he has to give up some of his own satisfactions and find other ways of obtaining adequate satisfactions. This process always involves compromise-adjustment, and through this, if successful, maturation is achieved. If unsuccessful, the process results in regression.

Regression

Regression is one of the primary mechanisms of defense used by the infant in an attempt to maintain some sort of equilibrium and avoid anxiety. As we shall see, one of the functions of all defense mechanisms is to assist the individual in avoiding or reducing anxiety. In regression, the individual reinstates a former *mode* of behavior that was previously satisfying to him. This does not mean that the individual performs the behavior in precisely the same way as before—in fact he is now older and has other and perhaps better skills than formerly—but that he performs the behavior in the same mode. As an example, the infant who finds toilet-training too severe may regress temporarily, as many normal youngsters do, to excessive oral gratification, through thumb-sucking or some other form of oral satisfaction. Regression is an appropriate mechanism during infancy, because it can be resorted to *passively*; the ego does not have to choose to regress (in fact it doesn't) nor does it have much to do about the process. It "happens" as an expedient way of gaining more gratification when anxiety stimulates a return to formerly habitual modes. Regression is likely to be more severe and more persistent if *fixation* occurred at a previous mode.

In the other defense mechanisms that the infant may employ the ego is more active, that is the individual has "more to say" about the defense. As we shall learn in later chapters, cultural factors influence the choice of defenses. Moreover, certain kinds of defenses are more acceptable to one individual than they would be to another. That is not to say that an individual deliberately and consciously selects the particular defense to be employed, but rather that the selection turns out to be consistent with the individual's whole way of life.

Other early defenses

Among the other mechanisms that the infant may employ are *denial, repression, reversal, projection,* and *introjection* (4, 10). Usually repression is used in combination with one of the other defenses. *Introjection* has already been discussed as *incorporation,* a term that is often used synonymously. We shall discuss *repression* first since the use of the other mechanisms is often dependent upon it.

The term *repression* was first used by Freud to include "all of the techniques which the ego makes use of in conflicts which may lead to neurosis." The term is now commonly restricted to acts of unconscious forgetting or of being unaware of internal drives. An individual may *unconsciously* forget what he once knew in order to reduce the anxiety that would be stimulated by the memory. (A common example of repression is the forgetting of a person's name that one knew quite well, while, at the same time, the face is easily recalled.) Such an act of repression may be partial in that some parts of an experience connected with certain impulses (that is, some feelings or some content of the experience) may be repressed while other parts remain in conscious or preconscious awareness. This mechanism requires the constant expenditure of psychological energy (which in the end is biological energy) in order to keep the repression effective. A rough analogy would be that of a pot of constantly boiling water in which the lid could be held on only by constantly applying pressure. In this example, one can see that the energy of the boiling water has to find some outlet if the lid is sealed effectively and if the pot is not to explode. Similarly with repressed material; it constantly seeks to escape into consciousness and is, therefore, likely to find some substitute outlet. When this happens, and if the original conflict has not been successfully resolved, the individual begins to use other defenses to support the defense of repression and in this way a temporary stability or homeostasis may be achieved.

The mechanism of *projection* is one that is commonly if not universally employed during some phases of infancy. As we are using this term, it refers to the unconscious attribution of impulses, and associated characteristics, to other persons or objects. Usually, the impulses that are projected on to others are those that one regards as unfavorable or with which guilt is associated. The infant who feels frustrated by his mother when she tries to teach him toilet-training perceives her, for a time, not only as a frustrator, but perhaps even as an ogre. He attributes to her more than her objective frustration

would warrant. He attributes his own hostile impulses, to which has been added the increment of his mother's frustrations. Thus, he overreacts to his mother and perceives her, through projection, as wicked, mean, and unloving. Moreover, he then reintrojects this subjective image that he has of his mother and thereby feels even more guilty and anxious. Under normal, healthy circumstances, as the infant, or later the child, learns to gain control over his impulses and finds suitable channels for delay and substitute satisfaction, and as he tests reality and finds that his mother is, in fact, understanding, tolerant, and flexible, the use of this mechanism decreases gradually until it is no longer necessary. Projection may form the basis of some types of normal and healthy thinking processes, or it may lead to severe psychopathology if not gradually replaced by adequate reality-testing in a secure, adequate environmental milieu.*

Another very primitive defense is that of *denial*. Anna Freud, whose discussion of defense mechanisms is regarded as a basic authoritative source in this field, did not list *denial* as a mechanism of defense since it occurs before the full differentiation of id and ego (4). However, it is an important method of coping with conflict of the most elementary sort, in that the individual who uses this mechanism denies the very existence of the disturbing element in the reality. Reality

* See Chapter 6 for a discussion of the development of normal and abnormal thinking processes.

is falsified through the substitution of wishful thinking. Thus the infant fails to acknowledge one impulse whose gratification might be in conflict with the demands of reality and simultaneously experiences another impulse, perhaps in exaggerated degree; or a person or object that is objectively present to the senses may be *denied* so that the infant acts as if he were unaware of its presence. However, as the individual matures and his capacity for reality-testing becomes better developed, it becomes increasingly difficult to employ this mechanism—at least in its original form. It may be employed in adult life in other forms and may be used in certain kinds of psychopathology (32).

Reversal involves an alteration of the drive itself. It appears to be independent of reality and is presumed to be rooted in biological processes. It occupies a more speculative place in the account of early defense mechanisms and can only be inferred through changes in the infant's behavior when no outward conditions for the change are apparent. From our point of view, it is doubtful whether it ought to be included in the category of defenses; certainly it is not a defense of the ego.

When, in later sections of this chapter, we examine the behavior of children as they seek to establish satisfactory methods of developing adequate interpersonal relations, we shall see more concretely how all of these coping behaviors are employed.

THE INFANT'S PERCEPTIONS OF THE WORLD

The infant's first real relations with the outer world are made through stimulation of his sense organs by external stimuli—through his eyes, mouth, nose, ears, and skin. In these contacts he is first on the receiving end, being dependent on the stimulation he receives from without. During the first few days of his postnatal life, he becomes dimly aware of stimuli that are intruding upon him—he is having *sensations*, that is, direct, essentially uninterpreted responses to stimulation of sense organs. Even at this time, it is doubtful whether he responds without some primitive kind of interpretation or whether he responds only to a single sense stimulus. Certainly, very early in his life he begins to respond to the *interrelated impressions* derived from more than one sense modality, although one organ may be most prominent in the process; and he begins to respond by *interpreting*, even if in a very simple way, the stimulus (or stimuli) that he is receiving. The process of interpreting incoming stimuli is known as *perception* and is a conscious response to a total situation. We can speak, thereafter, of sensations as an abstraction, but in fact the behavior of the individual after birth involves, not sensations, but perceptions.

Thus, perception is a learned response and depends greatly upon the specific pattern of conditions in which the learner is involved. It is greatly affected by memory, since memory of past events conditions the meaning or interpretation of subsequent stimuli that are perceived. It is also greatly affected by the immediate *set, expectancy,* or *need* of the perceiver. These three italicized terms have very special meanings with which we shall become more fully conversant later, but we now wish to emphasize that the ongoing feelings, wishes, and goals influence the "reality" of that which is experienced. To illustrate this point, we may note that the size of a coin actually appears relatively larger to lower-class children than it does to middle-class children, presumably because the need for and values of money are greater for the former group (33).

During infancy we can learn about perceptual behavior only through the *responses* infants make to various stimuli. Hence, our observations of perception are, to a large extent, bound up with the motor responses that are made. Moreover, perception often involves some explicit motor response, such as withdrawal from a painful stimulus or approach to a pleasurable stimulus. For these reasons, many texts on child development speak of *sensorimotor* development as the topic that is to be discussed. It is also true that perception is related to more than motor response—it is related, as we have seen, to emotions, to memory; and it is part of a total response made by a whole human being. Nevertheless, we can study perception as a special topic and isolate it for scrutiny because of its own characteristics and significance.

In the beginning, the baby perceives primarily with his mouth and his stomach. He learns to distinguish pleasant from unpleasant taste stimuli and, consequently, these early experiences help him at the same time to learn to distinguish a "pleasant from an unpleasant" mother.

The mouth continues to be an important source of contact with the world for some years, but gradually the eyes assume an ever increasing importance in this role as the baby explores his world around him, first passively and later, in infancy, actively. The sense of touch and the thermal sense (sensitivity to changes in temperature), as well as the sense of smell also assume increasingly greater roles as the infant matures. Advance in perceptual development is limited by the rate of development of the skeleto-muscular system since active exploration of the world involves movement in general and locomotion in particular, and, in accordance with the cephalo principle, development proceeds from the head to the feet.

We have suggested how difficult it is to study the perceptual development of the infant because we are so dependent for our knowledge of this area upon the individual's motor responses to stimuli. Many ingenious experimental methods have been evolved for studying such responses, chief among them being the method of *experimental conditioning.* In this, the experimenter tries to learn whether the infant can learn to discriminate between two different stimuli by learning to make differential responses to them under controlled experimental conditions. Despite all of the experimental and observational work that has been done, our knowledge of perceptual development is still fragmentary, and unconfirmed in many instances. We shall attempt to summarize some of the most salient and well substantiated findings in this area.

It is difficult for adults to understand how primitive and undifferentiated the infant's perceptions are. He is unable to distinguish *figure* from *ground* (manifest content from background); his world is a jumbled, vague mass in which some objects only dimly emerge as they become significant to the infant and as his sense organs mature. He is vaguely aware of hunger pangs and of something that relieves his distress, but he cannot tell the outside from the inside world. The neonate can distinguish sour from sweet (by the end of the second week) and he responds differently to cold and warm milk. Sucking is interfered with when the temperature of the milk is excessive in either direction. In an important study done by Pratt (34), it was shown that babies in the age range from birth to 21 days showed avoidance reactions to such irritating substances as the smell of ammonia and acetic acid. We have also learned in previous chapters that the baby responds differentially to (and therefore perceives) compulsive nurses from noncompulsive nurses. We can therefore make a number of summary statements about the perceptions of the individual in early infancy. Perception is generally diffuse and rudimentary although the sense organs have been fairly well developed. Simple discriminations of sight, taste, smell and touch are available and are generally reacted to as pleasant or unpleasant (at first only unpleasant and neutral are distinguished). Shortly after birth the baby responds to sound, his activity becoming inhibited after exposure for some minutes to intense, loud sound. The mouth and later the eyes are perhaps the most important avenues for commerce with the outside world, but the outside world is not distinguishable from the inside world.

After the first few weeks, increasingly finer perceptual responses rapidly emerge. Color discrimination appears by about fifteen days of age and becomes well defined by about three months of age. By the end of the first year, the infant can discriminate saturated colors of red, blue, green, and yellow and shows a strong preference in response tendencies to red (35). Color thereafter is perceptually more important than form in visual preference and discrimination, being used as the basis of selective behavior (in preference to form) until about six years of age (36). Convergence of the eyes in binocular vision and fixation of an object in visual perception become possible at the end of the second month (37). Gradually, the infant begins to respond differently (for example, by smiling) to *mother* and *non-mother*, and to *tense-mother* and *not-tense-mother*. By one year of age, as the infant begins to locomote in space he also learns to locate objects in space and soon he shows overt signs of spatial memories (he seems to look for missing objects). Later in the second year he begins to be less distractible because he is less *stimulus-bound* (that is he does not have to respond almost automatically to any intruding stimulus and can use his memory better).

The other perceptions follow similar patterns of development, from gross to finer discriminations. For example, the sense of taste is well developed by one year of age and strong food preferences are present—usually the result of unconscious conditioning because of the mother's own food prejudices (38). Auditory perception develops rapidly after the first few months, so that pitch discrimination is often present at about five months, and the infant can discriminate pleasant from unpleasant sounds (angry from nonangry voices) during the second year. By the end of the first year, and certainly during the second year, the infant shows in his behavior how he regards the world —as a friendly, approachable place, or as a hostile and dangerous place. He has begun to develop a perception of himself as a secure, confident individual or as an insecure and perhaps depressed person. As we shall see in a later section, the perceptions that the infant develops mold the character of his *self-identity*. Above all, by the end of the period of infancy the healthy infant is well along the road of reality-testing—he is able to perceive reality as it is objectively (a good part of the time) and he is able to distinguish reality from fantasy to a significant degree.

In this discussion of perceptual development we have not meant to give the impression that the norms that have been presented are to be regarded as rigid guides. They are simply *average trends*, useful for scientific study, and reflecting the cultures from which they have been extracted. Infants vary tremendously in their rates of perceptual development and in the patterns that they exhibit, as in other aspects of behavior. If there is a useful rule that may be helpful in guiding the development of infants it is this:

follow the tempo and pattern of the child's development rather than some statistical norm.

GROWTH OF THE BODY AND DEVELOPMENT OF ITS FUNCTIONS

Physical development, both in terms of changes in structure and functions, influences the adjustment of the individual in many ways. If for no other reason, students of child development should become conversant with the major characteristics of the development of the physical organism. Moreover, there are other reasons for getting to know something of the nature of physical growth. Parental overconcern with the size and physical well-being of the child may also contribute to the nature of the child's adjustment. Further, not only the child's physical growth but also the ways in which he comes to regard his body (and in this he often reflects not only its relative adequacy but the unconscious as well as conscious attitudes of his parents toward his physical condition) may become a powerful factor influencing his total adjustment. Moreover, physical development during infancy is both directly observable (in many ways) and is startling in its rapidity and complexity. The baby seems to be, and in fact is, different every day, so rapid is his growth. An accurate understanding of the main findings concerning physical growth may, therefore, contribute to a better understanding of the child and help in guiding him more effectively.

General physical development

It may be surprising to learn that the characteristics of physical development (in which we include anatomical, physiological and motor aspects) are more complex than mental development. It has been found, for example, that the relative increments in growth of body parts are not highly intercorrelated, as Carter and Krause's factor analytic study of such measures has shown (39). Different parts of the body grow at different rates and in different patterns, as the accompanying figure demonstrates. The body does not grow as a single unit nor does it grow in all directions at the same rate. At one time Scammon suggested that there were four general types of growth curves for physical development that were characterized as: *lymphoid* (including the tonsils, lymph, and thymus glands), *genital* (including the testes or ovaries), *neural* (including the brain and its parts, spinal cord, head dimensions), and *general* (including the body as a whole, respiratory and digestive organs, and the skeleton) (40). Each of these four types of curves has its own distinctive shape. Some investigators have suggested that there are at least seven major, independent physical

Figure 5. *Four major types of postnatal growth curves.*

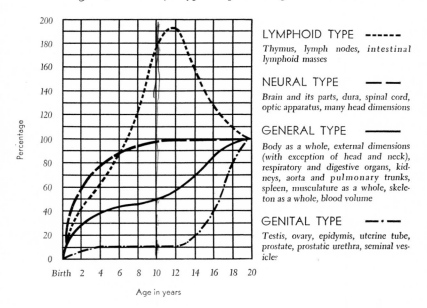

LYMPHOID TYPE ------

Thymus, lymph nodes, intestinal lymphoid masses

NEURAL TYPE — —

Brain and its parts, dura, spinal cord, optic apparatus, many head dimensions

GENERAL TYPE ——

Body as a whole, external dimensions (with exception of head and neck), respiratory and digestive organs, kidneys, aorta and pulmonary trunks, spleen, musculature as a whole, skeleton as a whole, blood volume

GENITAL TYPE —·—

Testis, ovary, epidymis, uterine tube, prostate, prostatic urethra, seminal vesicles

From Scammon, R. E., "The measurement of the body in childhood," in Harris, J. A., Jackson, C. M., Paterson, D. G., and Scammon, R. E., *The Measurement of Man.* Minneapolis: University of Minnesota, 1930.

factors (41). Not only do different parts of the body grow at different rates, but even the body type changes with age. We will recall that there are three major body types: *ectomorph, mesomorph,* and *endomorph.* Sheldon and his co-workers have submitted considerable evidence that body type (based on measures of the three major factors and on four second-order factors) remains fairly constant in adult life (42). Not as much work has been done on body type in children, but what evidence there is suggests that body type is not constant during this phase of development.

We should also note that there are important sex differences in amounts and rates of growth of children. For example, male infants are longer and heavier than female infants at birth and shortly thereafter. Subsequently, girls mature more rapidly than boys in physical development. However, the preadolescent growth spurt of girls is shorter than that of boys who then surpass girls, once again, in many physical measures. In the period directly after birth girls move ahead of boys particularly in skeletal development. After puberty, girls exceed boys in circumference of thighs and in length of legs but boys exceed girls in circumference of the thorax and in girth of the forearms.

Now let us consider gross or over-all physical growth. We must emphasize that we shall be reviewing average trends; there is marked variability among children, due especially to differences in constitutional factors (43). At birth, the average length of the body is approximately 20 inches and the average weight is approximately seven to eight pounds. At this time the head is more than one-fourth of the

length of the body. (At adulthood the head will be only one-tenth of the length of the body.) During the first postnatal year there is usually a gain of about eight inches in height and of thirteen pounds in weight, while during the second year the gains are about eight inches and fourteen pounds, respectively. (We will recall that during the neonatal period, while the physiological balance of the body is being established, there is usually some loss in weight.) During this same period, the brain increases in weight from an initial weight of about 350 grams to about 1,000 grams. The rate of gain in weight of the *cerebrum* gradually slows down during this same period. On the other hand, the *cerebellum,* which is important in postural control and balance, increases at a tremendous pace, there being a gain of about 300 per cent in its weight during the first year alone. The whole nervous system attains its adult status at about twelve years of age, having attained about 90 per cent of this status by about six years. General body tissues grow fairly rapidly during the first six years then slow down in rate of growth until about puberty when there is a new acceleration (the preadolescent spurt) for about six years or so, before slowing down occurs once again. In sharp contrast is the slow, almost inperceptible growth of the genital tissues until a very rapid acceleration occurs just before puberty.

The development of the skeletal system is also of interest to us. We have already discussed gains in length and weight. The legs begin to grow fairly rapidly during the first year and maintain a rapid pace during the second year. The bones of the body, which are very soft and pliable at birth (and therefore susceptible to change in shape because of restriction or cramping, as well as less likely to break due to trauma) gradually acquire more calcium (become *calcified* and *ossified*) and become stronger, so that by the end of the second year they are reasonably firm and strong. The bones have also begun to fuse with each other and as muscular growth proceeds they seem even more firm.

The growth of the teeth is a particularly interesting subject to parents and foreshadows weaning and the shift to the ingestion of solid foods. Some babies are born with one or two teeth (their deciduous or "baby" teeth); others acquire the first tooth as late as the end of the first year. Here again enormous variation among babies is the rule. On the average babies acquire their first teeth (the lower front teeth) at about the halfway point in the first year. Other teeth soon follow until all or most of the temporary teeth have erupted by the end of the second year.

Muscular development and motor behavior

During this period the muscular system develops at about the same pace as other *general body tissues*—fairly rapidly and steadily. (The muscles will increase in weight more than 40 times before their adult status is reached.) The *smooth muscles*, governing involuntary action, are fairly well developed at birth, but the *striped muscles*, governing voluntary movement (also known as the *skeletal muscles*), have a long developmental path to follow. Only as they grow in strength will various body movements and body positions become possible. (Postural de-

Figure 6. *Comparative proportions of adult height at different ages of girls and boys.*

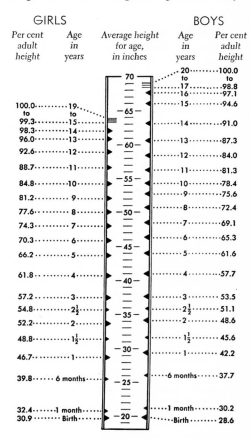

GIRLS			BOYS	
Per cent adult height	Age in years	Average height for age, in inches	Age in years	Per cent adult height
		70	20 to 17	100.0 to 98.8
			16	97.1
		65	15	94.6
100.0 to 99.3	19. to 15		14	91.0
98.3	14			
96.0	13	60	13	87.3
92.6	12		12	84.0
88.7	11		11	81.3
84.8	10	55	10	78.4
81.2	9		9	75.6
77.6	8	50	8	72.4
74.3	7		7	69.1
70.3	6		6	65.3
66.2	5	45	5	61.6
61.8	4	40	4	57.7
57.2	3		3	53.5
54.8	2½	35	2½	51.1
52.2	2		2	48.6
48.8	1½		1½	45.6
46.7	1	30	1	42.2
39.8	6 months	25	6 months	37.7
32.4	1 month		1 month	30.2
30.9	Birth	20	Birth	28.6

From Gruenberg, S., *Encyclopedia of Child Care and Guidance.* Garden City: Doubleday, 1954. © Copyright 1954 by Doubleday and Company, Inc. Reprinted by permission.

velopment also waits upon the development of the neural system and especially the covering or sheathing of the nerves, known as *myelinization*. That is why some writers prefer to discuss what they call *neuromusclar development* rather than *muscular* and *neural development* separately.) First there is a gain in strength of the grosser muscles and later of the smaller muscles and muscle groups governing fine coordination. The latter development continues through puberty. Because of the relatively slow development of the striped muscles, some motor and eliminative functions cannot be learned until the appropriate time has arrived. In particular, control of the sphincter responses, which has to shift from a purely reflex activity to a voluntary response, has to wait until the baby's muscular system is able to respond to both social and physical inhibition. Not only will prior training be unlikely to accomplish the desired result of early voluntary control but it may increase frustration, lower self-esteem and produce increased emotional irritability—these latter in turn delaying not only the training process but emotional and social maturation as well.

The development of motor behavior illustrates clearly the proximo-distal principle of development, as well as the principle of cephalo-caudal development. At the same time the growth of this behavior proceeds from the mass to the specific, from the gross to the fine. Local movements become differentiated out of general or mass movements, as many research studies have shown. Let us look at a few examples of motor development, which is at first highly gratifying to the parents

as the baby makes spectacular gains in voluntary control and then later becomes a little frustrating, to say the least, as the older infant seems to develop a compulsive need to explore everything about the house and "to get into everything."

The newborn baby's motor responses are not specifically directed to external stimuli; that is, they are diffuse or mass responses involving general activity. A little later some momentary eye fixation upon a stimulus and perhaps some increase in activity of the extremities occur. In a few weeks the baby's muscles acquire some definite *tonus*, that is they are not quite as limp-feeling as they were at birth. By four weeks of age his breathing has begun to be regular and he does not regurgitate as much as he formerly did. He has not yet developed coordination of the eyes; they seem to wander aimlessly, but the muscles that direct the movements of the eyeballs are slowly gaining some degree of control. Soon he is able to hold his eyes in a fixed position for a little while, although his perceptions are diffuse, since the cortex, or more precisely the nerve cells of that part of the brain, are not yet adequately developed. Whether asleep, which is most of the time—perhaps about 20 hours per day in all—or awake, his position is prone. He tends to keep his head to one side because the head muscles are not strong enough to hold it in any other position. He may show some reaching activity, but his arms do not coordinate for the task that his eyes may be trying to solve.

By about the third month he can sit up

Figure 7. Postural and locomotor development.

From Shirley, M. M., *The First Two Years, a Study of Twenty-Five Babies*: Vol. II. *Intellectual Development. Inst. Child Welf. Monogr. Series* No. 8. Minneapolis: University of Minnesota, 1933. Reprinted by permission.

with support; he will need another four or five months before he can do this by himself. By about the fourth month he has developed the ability to hold his head upright; he seems to enjoy doing this, but he tires readily. He can also rotate his head and explore his world more actively with his eyes. He also seems to like to sit up, supported perhaps by pillows. He engages in "finger play" by bringing his hands together and feeling the fingers of one hand with the fingers of the other. He has begun to explore himself. He does many other things in this process of self-discovery. A very prominent activity is that of putting things into his mouth—fingers or other objects. Through this process of exploration of his own body, he begins to get a crude concept of himself (a self-image) and he begins to learn where his own body is and where it ends in space. He gradually begins to differentiate between what is part of himself and what is not, between what is "inside" and what is "outside," in short between the "me" and the "not-me." Motor abilities are still awkward; he is unable to *clasp* an object but he is able to clutch it in a crude manner. However, the ability to manipulate objects develops quite rapidly.

Gesell and his co-workers at the Gesell Institute of Child Development, formerly at Yale University, made exhaustive studies of the motor development of infants, using repeated (*longitudinal*) testing and observation of many infants and recording the behavior during test sessions on silent and sound film for later, detailed analysis. Other workers have studied various specific aspects of motor development. We shall now summarize selec-

tively some of the representative findings dealing with locomotion in particular because of the importance of locomotion and because of the intensity with which it has been investigated.

In a study of 20 infants, Ames found that there are fourteen stages in crawling and creeping alone (44). Shirley, as well as Gesell, studied the sequence of activities from the first locomotor movements through independent walking (45). These workers agree on two important things: (a) training in locomotion is unsuccessful *before* the neural and muscular maturation make the particular locomotor skill available; prior training may produce some *temporary* improvement, but the long-term effects are insignificant; (b) for the most part, all infants move through a regular sequence in the development of locomotion regardless of practice or opportunity. It seems that maturation alone is responsible for the *appearance* of each stage in the sequence. However, the degree of skill and especially the psychological attitudes toward the activity may be greatly influenced, favorably or otherwise, by the kind and intensity of training.

In Ames' study, it was found that crawling, defined as progression with the abdomen in contact with the floor, appeared in about half of the infants who were observed at 34 weeks of age. The next stage of creeping, defined as prone progression in which the hands and knees are used to propel the body forward, occurred on the average about six weeks later. The next stage in the sequence, in which the feet and hands are used and in which the entire trunk is elevated, required an additional nine weeks.

Standing while holding on to some support begins to appear before the creeping sequence has been completed. By 15 months of age the average baby is able to stand alone and take a few independent steps. By this time he also seems to prefer this means of locomotion and will walk for a time if he can hold on to someone's hand. He can also climb, and will often attempt to climb anything he comes into contact with; ordinarily he does not as yet know the meaning of

fear in this activity. He also likes to perform many motor activities by himself, such as taking his shoes off, emptying dishes and baskets, throwing things out of his playpen, and he can, in an awkward fashion, pile one block on top of another. He may appear to be quite an independent person in many ways, and since he can usually communicate through language to make his wants known as well as "get about independently" in the world, many writers suggest 15 months of age as the end of infancy.

By two years of age, our infant is "quite a young man." He can now walk independently with considerable skill, although he will not have attained a fully erect position in this activity, and he can

Figure 8. *Steps in the development of prone progression.*

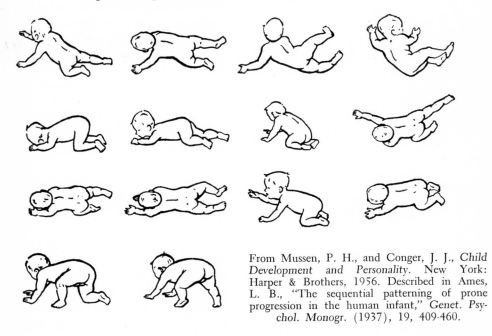

From Mussen, P. H., and Conger, J. J., *Child Development and Personality.* New York: Harper & Brothers, 1956. Described in Ames, L. B., "The sequential patterning of prone progression in the human infant," *Genet. Psychol. Monogr.* (1937), 19, 409-460.

climb and even walk up and down stairs. In the latter activity, he is likely to put the same foot forward each time to progress to the next step rather than alternating his feet. The tonus of his leg and other muscles has improved greatly, but there is still some flaccidity there, as trying to get him to keep his legs stiff or rigid while putting on his shoes or stockings will soon show. He can raise one leg while standing on the other so that he can kick things. At this stage of his development, parents are likely to become overambitious in motor training of their youngster and may produce fearful reactions, inhibition, and delay as a consequence. Again, we repeat, *practice makes for improvement only after the basic skill has matured and emerged.* Gesell's co-twin study in this respect may be interesting to consult if the reader wishes to have some detailed and convincing evidence (46).

We have mentioned briefly some aspects of growth in the ability to manipulate objects during the period of infancy. Manipulation involves more than the ability to grasp (*prehend*) objects; it also, especially in the beginning, involves the ability to integrate visual activities along with the necessary manipulatory ones. Even before eye fixation has become developed, the infant is able to strike out in the general direction of an object—at about 20 weeks of age. Gradually, specific prehensive skills and specifically directed, outward movements begin to emerge out of the previous mass and nonspecific activities. Sometimes, the new skill, or even a group of them, emerges suddenly because maturation has been silently doing its work of preparation. From the first

general movements in the direction of an object to mastery of the grasping response there appear to be ten stages (47). Between the eighth and ninth month the infant is usually able to make specific use of the forefinger in the grasping response. Later, the thumb and forefinger are opposed in grasping. By 15 months of age

Some test materials used in measuring developmental behavior in infants, from the Gesell scales. (Gesell)

the infant can hold and release small objects with considerable ease. He can make crude throws with a ball—it will take more maturation and many years of practice before he can become proficient in throwing. His grasping response is mature at about 60 weeks of age (47), but his manipulative skills are far from mature. At two years of age he can turn a doorknob, and he can make a very rough scribble and crudely imitate circular movement. Above all, at this time, his "engineering" talents have begun to emerge: he loves to take things apart! He can pull things apart and even use his hands alternately in putting things into each other or in fitting things together. As we shall see, true ambidextral coordination takes a much longer time to develop. (See Chapter 5.)

There are many other important aspects of physical and motor development —too numerous to summarize in detail here. The references at the close of this chapter will guide the reader to sources that offer additional information on specific topics. However, we hope we have made clear how the major principles of development apply to physical growth and have set the stage for further discussion of this topic in later chapters.

BEGINNINGS OF INTERPERSONAL BEHAVIOR

By *interpersonal behavior* we mean to refer to all aspects of behavior occurring between two or more persons. The most important types of interpersonal behavior are: language, emotional reactions, and social adaptations. We shall discuss each of these in turn.

Language and communication

The neonate makes its needs known in various ways but it does not have a language. The birth cry is a signal of some physiological distress. Later when the baby is hungry or thirsty it may cry reflexly. Nevertheless, these signals are not language. Language implies a two-way communication system—in which the sender is aware of the message he is relaying and the receiver is able to comprehend the message. Such two-way communication does not develop until the individual is aware of a "me" and a "not-me," is aware of "something out there" to which it directs its communication, and is able to formulate its message in some culturally understandable way. The parent may be able to understand the needs of the young baby, through its vocalizations, its postural adjustments, and its other behavioral gestures, but the baby has not matured sufficiently to satisfy the criteria we have specified.

Maturation and language. The vocalization of young babies appears to depend solely upon maturational factors. Research evidence shows that during the first year the pattern of vocalization follows a regular sequence irrespective of the culture into which a baby is born. The first sounds are reflexive and are associated with other responses of the baby, such as breathing and swallowing. The baby does not, at first, employ different sound combinations to express different needs, but as he matures he begins to employ different sounds. From the early neonatal sounds which include a few vowel sounds and a few consonant sounds, there is a regular progression through an ever greater diversification in the kinds of sounds that are produced (48). By about three months of age most of the vowel and about half of the consonant sounds that will be used as an adult are available (49). Toward the end of the first year the infant typically produces 18 of the 35 elemental speech sounds (*phonemes*) that are used by adults in our country. Both the variety and the frequency of use of sounds increase during the second year. American children, as well as those of other nationalities, use many sounds they will not employ when they have learned their native tongue. For example, our children use the French type of guttural *r* (as do children of all nationalities), but they do not use this sound in English when they have grown up. When walking begins, speech development is temporarily slowed up—a plateau has been reached. Later on there is another plateau in speech development, at about three years of age. It is not entirely certain why these plateaus occur, but like most plateaus that occur in learning these are probably periods in which integration of previous learning takes place. In addition, the first plateau is probably reinforced by the *interference* with speech because by the rapid development of locomotor skills that occurs at the end of the first year. In general, we find that the emergence of new skills interferes for a time with the regular development of other skills that have been progressing.

The maturational aspect of language development is affected by a number of factors. We shall cite a few of these to illustrate how general maturational factors influence the development of speech sounds. When the baby is able to sit up, the shape of the oral cavity changes as a consequence. When the baby begins to chew solid foods and exercise its jaw muscles, new speech sounds are again made possible by the concomitant physical changes. The beginning of dentition, the eruption of the frontal incisors, marks the advent of additional sounds. As chewing progresses, the sucking pads in the baby's cheeks are absorbed and the shape of the oral cavity changes again, making still other sounds possible. Later, a fully erect posture and better control of respiration and breath control make possible even more sounds that the younger baby was incapable of making. These and other aspects of physical maturation tend to govern the kinds of sounds the baby is able to produce and does produce in the course of *trial-and-error* learning.

Nevertheless, it should not be thought that maturation *alone* determines the early development of vocalization and speech. The hypothesis that only maturation is responsible for early speech development was, at one time, held almost universally by child psychologists, and is still held by some. Evidence indicates that, on the contrary, environmental factors condition both the rate of development and subsequent level of language growth. For example, the practice of cooing and singing to the baby by the mother contributes to the pleasure associated by babies with speech sounds. First through imitation and later by the additional *reward value* of sounds (since such sounds by the baby bring pleasurable responses from the mother), the baby learns to use certain kinds of vocalizations more regularly and frequently. Moreover, the total emotional climate in which the baby is reared can profoundly influence the nature and extent of language development. It has been established that children reared under conditions of deprivation show retarded language development. Spitz's studies, Goldfarb's studies (50), and observations by Freud and Burlingham (51) all point in this direction. The converse has also been shown. Mowrer's research with a talking bird (the Myna bird) is consistent with the hypothesis that a pleasant and gratifying relationship improves the nature of language development (52). In homes where more value is placed upon verbal skills children learn to speak earlier and more adequately. This is true of homes in the higher socioeconomic classes; the opposite is true of lower-class homes. (It should be noted that these findings are *contaminated* by uncontrolled factors since homes with higher socioeconomic status are somewhat more likely to have children with higher intelligence than are homes with lower socioeconomic status, and intelligence and language ability are positively correlated. The finding is nevertheless of value since it is consistent with other evidence.) Another type of evidence that tends to show that language development is influenced even in the earliest stages by environmental conditions is that female infants exceed male infants in this communication skill. Some psychologists believe that, in our culture, girls are rewarded more for speech than boys (boys are more likely to be rewarded for motor skills) and that this accounts for the sex difference. The interested reader will find a wealth of data reported by McCarthy which indicate the significance of environmental factors in early language development (49).

Thus, as with other aspects of development that we have already discussed, maturation sets the time and the limits while environmental conditions define the extent to which language development proceeds. The sequence of patterns of sounds is governed, in the beginning, by general maturation, but the subsequent rate and type of development and the level of skill depend upon the kind of learning that occurs.

Types of growth in language skills. We have already indicated how rapidly language proficiency develops during infancy. Now we shall point up some selected examples of the nature of this growth. A very impressive set of findings has been marshalled by Irwin and his co-workers, who systematically recorded the speech sounds made by infants in a series of longitudinal studies—studies in which the same children were regularly re-examined over a period of time (53, 54). During the neonatal period vowel sounds predominate over consonant sounds by the ratio of 5:1. The relative frequency of these two general types of sounds changes rapidly during the first year so that the ratio begins to approach that of adults by the beginning of the second year. Similarly, such sounds as *p, b,* and *wh* and such sounds as *t, d,* and *n,* which did not occur during the neonatal period, occur regularly by this period of time. (Note that these and other sounds depend upon the maturation of certain muscles, as, for instance, of the lips.)

Most workers in the field of language

development agree that the infant's first sounds occur spontaneously and that the sounds which persist and become part of the speaking vocabulary are the result of many complex learning factors. In the beginning the baby's sounds serve to stimulate him so that he tends to repeat the ones he vocalizes. This process has been called the *circular reflex*. Thereafter, those sounds that are reinforced by specific learning experiences are used more often than others. In this learning process the mother's careful and distinct repetition of the baby's uttered sounds appears to have a significant effect. However, it should be noted that until the baby is mature enough for such types of learning, practice not only has no positive effect but may even hamper further language development through interference (55). It should also be noted that the early babblings of children who are deaf soon decrease in frequency and disappear.

Sometime near the beginning of the second year or slightly later, the infant begins to use speech expressively as part of his total social adaptation. He uses nouns and interjective words to express his wants; commonly he uses a single word to express a whole thought. Thus, "Mama" may mean "Mama come here and give me food," or uttered in a different intonation it may mean, "I feel good when Mama plays with me." Previous to this (perhaps as much as two to five months previous), the infant has learned to respond to simple commands. Various studies have indicated, in fact, that language comprehension, or what has been termed by some as *passive language*, precedes *active language* usage in develop-

ment. After the child has learned to comprehend and to use single words to express his wishes, he begins to use phrases and, still later, simple sentences; that is, he begins to use *narrative language*. This generally develops some time about the end of the second year. Shirley has estimated that by the end of the second year the child's *expressive vocabulary* is about 37 words but the child's *effective vocabulary* (words that are either understood or used) is closer to 300 words (56).

The reader will have noted how many times we have used such expressions as "about," "approximately," "near the end of the year," and the like. This has been deliberate and we have tried to avoid the use of norms in a precise sense. There are several reasons for this. In the first place, there is enormous variability among infants in the way their language development proceeds. Perhaps even more important, patterns of total development vary greatly. Some children babble incessantly, then become silent, and then suddenly break out in a relatively mature form of language usage some months later; other children show a regular and steady progression through each of the stages of language development. Moreover, the various terms we have been employing, such as "words," "phrases," "interjections," and the like have not been employed consistently or even with adequate precision in the research literature (and are less rigorously employed by untrained people who wish to use the findings of language studies). For these reasons norms, without careful explanation of the precise meanings of the terms and the precise conditions under which they have been gathered, are likely to be misleading. The specialist or researcher in this field can make far better use of norms than can the parent.

We have spoken thus far of the development of various kinds of oral language. We should also note that other kinds of language are developing simultaneously. For example, *gestural language* is an important part of communication development for all infants, and is especially important for some. We could also have discussed development in accuracy of articulation, types of intonation, and other aspects of expressive communication. Instead, we have focused on the central core of language development, leaving these other topics for treatment in later sections of the book where they may be more pertinent.

Language development occurs in a real, growing, vital child and is an important characteristic of his total development. It is at the same time an expression of this development and a factor influencing the development. To understand the role that language plays in the life of a particular child one has to understand the whole child. In other words, *language development* is an abstraction; it is the child who develops and in whom language development is but one, although an important, expression of the many-sided and total interactive series of processes that are going on. To concretize this point, let us consider briefly how adjustmental factors may influence language expression.

A young boy of five years (let us call him Larry) was brought to one of the writers for clinical evaluation and guidance because he was mute. It turned out that he had shown apparently usual language development until about one and a half years of age. He had vocalized, said a number of words, and could comprehend language well up until this time. Suddenly, he lost all capacity for speech, and later he lost all capacity for vocalization of any kind. There was no discernible reason for this peculiar state of affairs. At first some kind of brain disease was suspected but after elaborate medical tests and observation a physical cause of this condition seemed to be ruled out. Nevertheless, the boy failed to resume speaking although he seemed to comprehend speech quite well. He was referred to a clinical psychologist for further study.

When the writer saw this boy, at the age of five and one half, he was not only unable to speak but was greatly retarded in all of his social skills; he played by himself and showed little interest in people. He was also given to violent emotional storms and temper tantrums. After extensive examination of the youngster and interviews with his mother, it was finally concluded that the boy's condition was truly *psychogenic* (resulted from psychological conflicts). Larry had been an only child and was the intense center of interest and almost constant attention not only by his parents but also by an aunt and an uncle who lived in the same house, in an upstairs apartment. Shortly before he became mute, the aunt and uncle had a child of their own. A month later, his parents had a second child. Attention was thus shifted rapidly and overwhelmingly from Larry to the new children in the household. The immense reaction of the unwitting rejection caused by the behavior of the four adults and Larry's increasingly understandable jealousy of the two newcomers produced more frustration than he could tolerate. He became mute in defense, as his play sessions in the clinic and other types of clinical data amply indicated.

The well-meaning parents were entirely cooperative in the clinic's plans for psychological treatment of their youngster. Through suggestions for guidance at home and intensive psychotherapy at the clinic, Larry's oral language skills re-emerged, in a reasonably mature form, in about nine months. Much additional treatment and guidance were necessary not only for Larry's speech development but also for his total adjustment.

This unfortunate and complicated case, which has been presented very briefly and simply here, is intended primarily to dramatize the assertion made above: that language development is but an expression of the total adjustment of the child and in turn influences all other aspects of development (49).

Emotional behavior

It may seem strange that a term like *emotions* is defined in so many ways by experts in child psychology that their pronouncements may seem like the voices of Babel, yet such is the case. Everyone else seems to *know* what emotions are, but psychologists cannot agree among themselves about the meaning!

The concept of emotion. We may think that emotions refer to a *state of feeling,* or as it is sometimes put to a *stirred-up state of feeling.* If this is our conception we may agree to call such behavior as rage, fear, depression, and love emotional behavior. Even such an apparently straightforward conception immediately gets us into difficulties, however. In the first place, people express, say, rage in quite different ways in different cultures. In one culture a person showing rage thrashes about with his arms, gets

livid in the face, breathes rapidly and deeply, and the like, while in another culture a person who may feel just as enraged may stand immobile, be expressionless, breathe normally, and show no overt signs of his inner feeling. This clearly indicates that emotional behavior or, more precisely, the expression of such behavior is culturally conditioned. Then we might say it is the *inner feeling* that characterizes the emotion—but this apparently neat solution to our problem leads us into a second difficulty. There is incontrovertible evidence that emotional behavior may occur *without* any concurrent conscious awareness of feeling (11). As a matter of fact, the feeling state may be induced without the overt, behavioral expression of that state, and the overt expression of emotion may occur without the feeling state. As illustrations, consider such examples as the rage expressed by an actor without the stimulus for or the feeling of rage, and the stirred-up physiological response of an athlete—which may physiologically resemble an emotional reaction without the occurrence of the emotional feeling.

There are other difficulties in defining the term *emotion.* Such problems as the following lead us into many difficulties: Do emotions *produce* disorganized behavior, or are they, in fact, an *expression* of disorganized behavior? (It is quite clear that the so-called pleasant emotions do not usually show such characteristics.) Is it only the extreme or violent emotions that lead to disorganized behavior? (There is evidence that some violent behaviors result in more efficient rather than disorganized responses, as in effective flight under conditions of fear.) Is the *seat* of the emotions the hypothalamus? (Work by Masserman and others has demonstrated that the hypothalamus may rein⸁force and coordinate the expression of emotional behavior but is not necessarily the agent producing such behavior.) Are emotions learned or acquired? (As we shall see the answer seems to be *both*.)

It is such difficulties as these that have led some psychologists to assume that emotions consist of a neural state the precise characteristics of which remain to be defined (11). In this type of conception emotion is *not* defined as a state of consciousness. This leads to other difficulties, chief among which is that many of the behaviors commonly termed *emotional* would not be included in such a conception. Another difficulty is that if we cannot define precisely or measure the neural state, how are we to know it is present?

For our purposes we shall, simply as a matter of definition, reserve the term *emotion* for those feelings, pleasant or unpleasant, in which there is heightened activity of the glands, circulatory system, and digestive organs, but which may or may not be accompanied by increased disorganization or organization. We are leaving aside the question of whether the feelings cause the physiological reactions (although we believe that this is not the case), but are merely specifying that the feeling state and the physiological char-

acteristics are part of the complex reaction we call emotion.

The differentiation of emotional behavior. It seems to us that, in the adult state at least, emotional behavior is indeed highly complex, involving such concurrent phenomena as perception, thought, and comunication, and that it is very difficult to isolate the emotional part of the response out of the total behavioral response. We are referring to the *affective* response, then, when we speak of the emotions—a response in which a subjective state of feeling is experienced.

It will be seen, at once, how difficult it is to study the emotional behavior of infants. We cannot possibly be aware of the subjective state of the infant, we can only *infer* it from manifest behavior. We can neither rely upon the judgments of observers as to the nature of this inner state (since they may impute their own meaning to the infant's experience) nor upon the older child's or adult's recollections of his emotions as an infant (since these are not accessible to memory so far as we know). However, we can rely upon the judgments of the observers under certain conditions: if they agree, if the total set of conditions in which the observations are made is carefully specified (such as the nature of the stimulus, the condition of the organisms, and the like), and if these observations are in accord with the known consequences or predictions of the inferred emotional behavior. It is on such types of evidence—still fragmentary and tentative—that the following discussion is based.

At the neonatal stage of development a variety of differential emotion-like responses are present. Babies cry, smile, and show distress, for example. These forms of behavior are not necessarily emotions, as we have defined the term, since the baby is probably unaware of the feeling state, and since these behaviors do not occur as responses to specific types of situations. Rather, these responses are at first haphazard reactions to conditions of distress and changes in tension states within the child. Sherman and others have clearly demonstrated that the so-called primary emotions of love, rage, and fear, postulated by John B. Watson, do *not* occur in infants as unlearned and specific responses to specific situations (57). Rather, it is best to characterize the first responses as those of *heightened* or *decreased excitement*. It is not until about three weeks of age that *distress* can be reliably observed to occur in response to an appropriately distressful situation. Stern has referred to the reactions of infants to distressful stimuli as "a dull undefined foreshadowing of consciousness . . ." and as "sense-emotional states" (58). He means by this that differentiation of sensory and emotional elements has not yet developed. Moreover, infants vary greatly, probably on a constitutional basis, and more specifically in terms of their original autonomic activity level, in the ways in which they respond to distressful stimuli. In one study, it was shown that only two out of 85 babies who were dropped a distance of two feet responded with distressful or *startle* reactions.

We have pointed out previously how passive and dependent the infant is and how much he needs immediate and consistent gratification of his basic needs for food, warmth, and affection. It is likely that these first distressful reactions are greatly increased when early conditions of rearing do not meet such criteria. In such cases the distress reactions soon develop into other unpleasant and emergency-type emotional responses, in which it should be emphasized the whole organism is involved—the visceral and skeletal system, in particular—and the pleasant emotions develop, if at all, in retarded fashion. As we have seen, general growth is retarded and, in extreme cases, death may result. This type of maldevelopment has emphasized the emergency nature of early emotional reactions.

Emotional development proceeds by the gradual differentiation of more specific emotional reactions out of earlier, less well defined emotional behavior. Thus *distress* is differentiated out of excitement, and subsequently *anger, disgust, fear,* and *jealousy* are progressively differentiated. On the positive side of the emotional ledger the following sequence of emotional differentiation appears to be the rule: *delight, elation* and *affection,* and *joy.* Figure 9 (page 122) presents a schematic summary of these types of emotional development.

At the same time that new emotions are gradually making their appearance, the response characteristics of the emotions already present become more sharply delineated. For example, patterns of anger, which are at first crude and sometimes difficult to distinguish from distress, become more distinct (i.e. more efficient), are more clearly directed out-

Figure 9. The differentiation of emotional reactions.

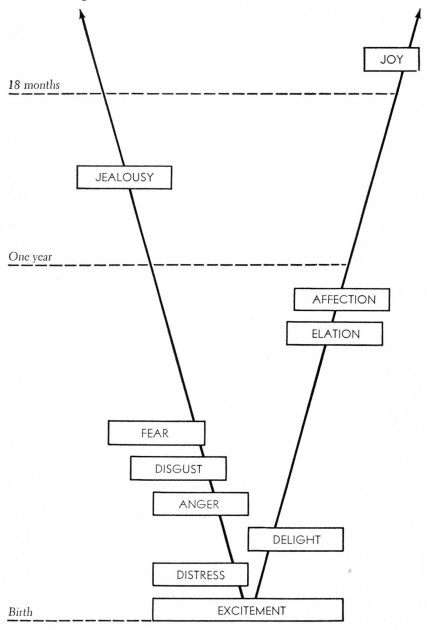

Based on data in Bridges, K. M. B., "Emotional development in early infancy,"
Child Develpm., 1932, 3, 324-341.

wardly, and come in response to more and more well-defined situations. Similarly, crying, which occurs quite frequently at first (estimated at about 15 per cent of the time by Bayley), and which appears to occur in response to internal stimuli, gradually decreases in frequency, and begins to occur more specifically in response to external agents (59). Thus, patterns of emotional behavior become more specific and better delineated.

According to Horney, the infant learns to adopt characteristic modes of emotional response involving approach, attack, or withdrawal (60). Gradually more specific methods of behavior within each of these three modes are developed. The development of the kinds and characteristics of emotional response patterns is greatly influenced by the conditions of the infant's life, that is, *they are learned.* They have an adjustive function in that they are attempts to meet conditions of frustration and gratification.

In the beginning, the visceral reaction is quite similar in all kinds of emotional responses. Later on these reactions differ in the various emotional conditions, and the emotion may be expressed predominantly at the visceral level or it may be channelled predominately through either or both motor or sensory responses instead. Still later, possibly somewhere around six years of age or possibly earlier, cognitive processes, and particularly thinking, play a prominent part in their influence upon the nature and content of the emotional behavior.

It appears likely that the general sequence in the differentiation of emotional reactions depends upon maturational factors. One of the convincing types of evidence for this assertion is that supplied by Dennis, who found that even children reared in social isolation during the period of infancy showed the same kinds of emotional responses as others reared under normal conditions (61). This is not to say, however, that the intensity or the content or the relative proportion of various emotional responses is similar under varied conditions of rearing. On the contrary, specific conditions of learning greatly influence these factors. It is possible to induce fear reactions to rats, which are not feared by infants without specific learning of such fears, by introducing a loud sound each time the rat is presented to the infant (62). Subsequently, under such conditions, infants *learn* to fear rats.

We have seen, in Figure 9, that emotions may be divided into two main categories—the pleasant and the unpleasant. The pleasant emotions, which emerge from a condition termed *nonstress* by some psychologists, and termed *love* or *affection* by others, facilitate growth and learning and assist in the over-all process of emotional maturation. When the infant generally finds his basic needs gratified and when he learns to anticipate, *consistently,* that such gratification will be the case, he also learns to feel secure, happy, and effective. He is also better able to tolerate temporary frustration and resulting tension. Further, even his physical development proceeds more effectively. Under such conditions the child learns to love himself appropriately and to love others as well. Gradually, his positive emotional feelings are extended to many other persons, animals, and objects. The quality of his affection also changes and with it the specific forms of affectional expression, leading to elation, joy, and a sense of well-being. They also become more and more differentiated and more and more enriched. In a very literal sense, the child has to learn how to enjoy most situations in life (63).

The unpleasant emotions, starting with distress, have been studied more extensively under experimental conditions than have the pleasant emotions, since they are easier to provoke and since their effects are more readily observable. Hebb maintains that fear, which emerges from excitement, results from three classes of events (11). One cause of fear is conflict produced by inability to discharge drives due to internal or external factors. A second cause is *sensory deprivation* which may be due to sensory defects or externally imposed sensory deprivation. A third cause is that of constitutional disturbances (arising out of original constitutional state or maturational disturbances). Although the latter two categories are important, the psychoanalytic view is that the first category is far more significant in most cases. Fear arises out of the general conditions of anxiety that we have discussed previously. Anxiety, due to loss of support of a loved one (especially when the infant is so totally dependent upon its mother), and due to castration situations (in which physical damage is perceived as tantamount to catastrophe or annihilation), underlies the later fear reactions in which anxiety is attached to or attributed to external objects or events. It should be emphasized that these external objects are not the essential cause of the fear reaction; the primary factor is inability to gratify internal needs or drives. That is why, as Jersild puts its, ". . . one cannot account for them [the fears] by analyzing the properties of the external stimulus" (63). An illustration of this principle is that children are far less likely to become afraid or even to be startled when they are held securely by someone whom they love and in whom they have confidence. Although it is true that some stimuli can arouse fear reactions more easily than others, it is not the nature of the stimuli, per se, that is responsible for the fear but the inner state of the individual and the subjective meaning of the stimuli to him. Most fears during the first year of life are "produced" by unfamiliar situations or events—those which the infant is unable to anticipate and which have the impact of *loss of support* (i.e., separation anxiety). That is why sudden loud noises, sudden movements, and sudden pain lead to fear reactions. During the second year of life the range of fear reactions normally increases (the infant attributes to more and different external objects the sources of his fears—so that he may more readily be able to cope with *them* rather than the unperceptible inner drives of which he is less aware and which he has not learned to control). The infant learns to fear more animals, more people, darkness, and the sensation of falling. An essential difference between such normal fear reactions and abnormal fear reactions

A developmental examination of a preschool child, showing a one-way vision screen arrangement. (Gesell)

is that the former are less intense. They are also more transitory and more malleable. Such fears are often unconditioned (unlearned) if they are subsequently experienced in the company of a loved person.

Experimental studies of emotions. One of the emotional responses that has received extensive experimental study is *anger.* Two main sources of data on this topic are Goodenough's systematic study of causes of anger in young children as reported by their parents (64) and Dollard and his colleagues' extensive experimental studies of a wide variety of subjects (65). Anger is differentiated out of distress, probably as the first outwardly directed response to internal or external conditions of frustration. It is, however, a matter of definition to decide just what to call anger. Shortly after birth, such responses as thrashing about and striking

might be considered expressions of anger, although at this time these responses are poorly coordinated and no external object is the focus of their expression. Even crying, screaming, and the like may be part of the pattern of behavior that means anger. It has not yet been determined what the essential manifestations of anger are. The anger response, in contrast to that of fear, is a movement toward an external object as a means of removing the external source of the frustration, whereas fear is an attempt at avoidance or a movement away from the object. However, it will be readily apparent that many responses that we call anger do not show much of this aggressive quality, but are rather a violent expression of distress or rage, even in adulthood. Hence, the term *aggression* is now more commonly employed to connote outwardly directed and focused expressions of anger, and the term *hostility* is more precisely restricted to connote the impulse that underlies any expression of anger.

Recognizable and reliably observable manifestations of anger usually emerge shortly after three months of age. As the individual matures the patterns of response in anger become more varied and more specific, so that we refer to such phenomena as *bullying, prejudice, sarcasm,* and the like to describe the specific pattern of behavior more accurately. The early manifestations of anger are unlearned responses to thwarting or frustration. As these responses relieve tension, and as they become reinforced or rewarded by social acceptance of the behavior, they are repeated; they have gained secondary values in the process even when they have not relieved entirely the original source of the frustration. This original source, we repeat, is frustration of basic drives so that the anger re-response may be conceptualized as a substitute expression of the discharge of such blocked drives. In early infancy, many frustrations arise as the child is given routine care. (Goodenough reports that about one-fourth of all anger responses are reactions to such problems during this period.) Another common "cause" of anger (again, according to Goodenough) is minor physical discomfort. On the other hand, physical restraint accounted for only six per cent of anger responses during the first year. During the second year anger responses occurred frequently in connection with training procedures (see our discussion of the anal stages, in this chapter), and as a result of various types of conflict with authority in areas other than training. During this period frustration in other social relationships also led to anger. In all of these situations the child is frustrated *not* by the external object or person but by *inability* to express his *internal drives*. When aggression develops, as an attempt to do "injury to an organism," a great deal of learning of anger responses has already occurred. It is then that we may say, according to Dollard and Miller, that aggression occurs because ". . . the child discovers that he can secure compliance with his wishes" (65). Aggression is thus a social response to social conditions in which "habits motivated by a drive" are blocked by an individual or by a physical obstacle. The expression of anger is modified in many ways and the external precipitants of anger are modified by specific cultural conditions in the individual's life. In some cultures, overt expressions of anger are frowned upon and the individual has to learn to inhibit such responses and substitute other more acceptable responses. If, nevertheless, anger is being evoked and cannot be channeled outwardly the individual may become excessively rigid or he may develop a *psychosomatic* reaction such as ulcers, depending upon many other physical or psychological factors within himself and in his culture.

Goodenough was able to show that frequent anger responses were associated with frequent illness, sleep difficulties, constipation, excessive fatigue, and the like. Such unfortunate outcomes of anger patterns may nevertheless provide secondary rewards for the child in that he becomes an object of more attention and concern. In other circumstances, the child's expressed anger patterns may be reinforced because they so distress his parents and others that they gain the ends he desires. Experimental and clinical evidence suggests that it is best to help the child avoid undue or too frequent anger responses and not to "reward" them unwittingly by succumbing to the child's demands. *Prevention is the best policy!* This can be achieved by helping to remove or reduce unnecessary sources of frustration. Correction is helpful, when prevention fails, through diversion of interest, assistance in dealing with frustration, offering substitute satisfactions when frustration seems imminent, and finally ignoring the anger as much as possible. In all of this, during infancy it is the personalities of the parents that are most important. The emotionally secure parent does not unnecessarily increase the child's frustration nor over-respond to the child's anger when it does occur. The parent does not need guide books to learn to respond calmly and to deal objectively with the child's anger or its source.

In closing this introductory treatment of the development of emotional behavior in infancy we should like to emphasize the interrelationship of the various emotional patterns which, as a matter of convenience, we have been discussing separately. Anger may occur in association with fear, and both of these may occur in association with love, for example. Patterns of emotional response are likely to be complexly interrelated not only with each other but with many other aspects of the child's total functioning. Emotions influence drives and become drives themselves. Emotions influence thinking and communication and are in turn influenced by them. It is always a whole child who is reacting, with his body and through his habitual personality modes, and never an emotion or a perception or a thought that is behaving as an abstraction.

Social-adaptive behavior

We have now seen how the passive, helpless, dependent newborn child has matured physically, how he has gradually learned to perceive himself and the world more accurately, how he has learned to communicate, and how he has learned to express his feelings. We have also conceptualized in terms of personality theory how this series of processes was motivated by basic needs and how it was either facilitated or hindered by disturbances in the interactive phenomena of the child, his parents, and their culture. Now we can examine the resultants of the integrated behavior of the infant as it is expressed in his social-adaptive relations—relations that involve awareness of his own growing and changing needs and adaptation to the social realities of his cultural milieu.

By the time the individual has arrived at the terminal phase of infancy he has become something of a true social creature. He has learned to delay, integrate and modify his own needs in terms of the physical realities of the world and the wishes and needs of a few others who live in it in very close proximity to himself. Social adaptation requires all of this and it implies some degree of reciprocity in interpersonal relations. It is a give-and-take affair in which the secure individual relinquishes something of his own need gratification in order to obtain the gratification of others and so eventually receive even more self-gratification in return. It is never without frustrations, but in a healthy child the process of social adaptation is a relatively smooth one which results in feelings of security and in adequacy in managing life's daily demands.

One can say that true social adaptation does not begin until the infant has begun to distinguish the "not me" from the "me." A few weeks after birth the infant begins to respond differently to animate objects than to inanimate objects. Probably the movement of people plays a role in this development, and certainly the fact that people, and especially his mother, can gratify his needs is highly significant. By the third week of age the infant usually begins to *attend* to human voices, but it is not until near the middle of the first year that he can *respond* to them with any degree of consistency. He responds differently to a familiar voice than to an unfamiliar one, to a pleasant voice than to an unpleasant one, and so on. When he has begun to cry he often stops immediately when he sees his mother or hears her voice. (In those homes where the father is familiar to the

Social-adaptive behavior as manifest at the end of infancy. (Merrill Palmer)

baby, plays with him, and helps to gratify his needs the same kind of positive responses may be made to the father at only a slightly later age than to the mother.) By the middle of the first year the baby has learned to differentiate strangers from nonstrangers and usually responds in a fearful manner to them. Before this time the baby has made known his demands for social stimulation. Observational data supplied by Gesell and others indicate that if he has had a pleasant relationship with his mother and others, he insists upon people paying attention to him, playing with him, coddling him, and the like—and does so more often in the afternoon and early evening (8).

By the middle of the first year, too, the infant has learned to use crying as a specific means of obtaining gratification of his needs. Formerly he was more likely to cry when distressed, and did so on occasions when restricted, when hungry, when cold, or when in pain. Now, he has learned that crying brings mother and play, attention or coddling and cooing. He has learned to demand these gratifications from her—and he does not cry as often only because of physical distress. If the mother-child relationship is a satisfactory one he gradually learns to use other, and usually more favorable, means of gaining attention and gives up crying as the sole means of gaining his ends. It is only when crying is unnecessarily rewarded—as when the mother is overly anxious or guilty about it, and so responds emotionally or perhaps too frequently to it—that it persists as the major technique of social communication.

Similarly, the infant is likely to learn not to fear most strangers if his basic needs have been met, if he is gradually exposed to a few strangers without undue excitement or unpleasant frustrations, and if he has found that strangers can contribute to his "fun." For by one year of age, most secure babies like to play, glory in getting attention, and have learned to enjoy the play pen, mother, father, and a few people who are not a regular part of the family picture.

During this first year the infant has learned to enjoy mealtime as a pleasant social event as well as a means of satisfying hunger needs. The conditions that give rise to this kind of reaction as the usual pattern (probably never as the only pattern) include a relaxed and secure relationship with mother, regular patterns of feeding experiences, and the association of happy moods of the mother with these feeding experiences. Self-demand feeding schedules appear most effective in such a program, but in any case regularity in patterns of feeding is essential if trauma is not to be associated with feeding experiences. Although it is possible to shift feeding schedules abruptly, clinical and experimental evidence indicates that such abrupt changes produce restless behavior, hyperactivity, and other manifestations of emotional upset (66).

There are now many experimental studies that support the Freudian thesis that appropriate gratification of the child's oral and affectional needs during these early periods results in better general adjustment; the few that do not support the thesis may indicate the great care that is necessary to study the whole pattern of need gratification rather than any specific aspect of it in isolation. One of the most convincing studies which shows the effectiveness of the total pattern of self-demand feeding on subsequent total patterns of good adjustment is that of Holway (67). In this study, Holway evaluated the adjustment of the subjects (three- to five-year-old boys and girls) by observing their patterns of play in a doll-play situation, one in which the children were allowed to play freely with miniature toys representative of people and objects of the home. Remarkably high correlations (of the order of .80) were found between ratings on the nature of early feeding experiences and on ratings of general adjustment.

Toward the end of the first year children have learned to play with their own mirror images and with adults who have taken care of them. They love all sorts of games such as peek-a-boo and pattycake. However, they have not yet learned

Development of a sense of self-identity begins in childhood. (Merrill Palmer)

to play with other children. Usually, babies who are placed in the same crib pay little attention to each other and do not make any attempts to play with each other. However, very shortly after this age period infants do begin to make advances toward other infants, so that by the end of the first year or during the early part of the second year infants try to attract each other's attention, touch each other, pull things away, and communicate in infantile speech (56). Buhler, who has made extensive studies of infants, notes that there are marked individual differences among children in their patterns of social interaction. She classifies children between the ages of six to eighteen months into three major social categories: the *socially independent* child, who is aware of the other child's presence, reacts to him, yet can carry on independent activity of his own; the *socially dependent* child, who reacts to the other child but is more or less completely dependent upon him, being inhibited or stimulated almost entirely on the basis of the other infant's behavior; and the *socially blind* child, who appears to be unaware of the presence of the other infant and is not reactive to him (68). Neither the cause nor the persistence of these patterns of behavior is known. We may suspect that each category of social behavior develops out of· the specific pattern of prior experience of the child and that the last category consists of children who are fearful and overly cautious in all interpersonal relations or who have had very limited personal contact with people, whereas the first category develops out of wholesome, satisfying, and effective interpersonal re-

lations with the mother and perhaps other members of the family.

Social imitation probably plays an increasingly greater role in the social adaptation of children after the first year. The infant now makes conscious efforts to imitate the mother. For example, when a child is afraid, the presence of a mother in a joyful mood is likely to dispel the child's fear and turn the reaction into a pleasurable one. Experiences such as these supplement the previous, more unconscious, interiorization of the mother's attitudes, moods, and prohibitions and serve to assist the child in better reality-testing, and in developing comfortable and secure models of behavior and later becoming able to adapt socially in his own unique way to the demands of various life situations. Such experiences tend to lead to greater adaptability and spontaneity in contrast to experiences in which frustrations and severe prohibitions administered in tense and angry moods lead to excessive conformity, rigidity, and undue anxiety. Thus, social imitation is likely to be most effective in leading to favorable personality traits when it has been preceded by secure and successful interiorization of the mother's personality traits during the period of earlier unconscious learning (69).

During the first part of the second year the child's interests in his social environment expand rapidly. He seems to lose the shyness he formerly showed and begins to explore everything he can. As Gesell puts it, "he gets into everything." He loves to watch and play with animals and tries to imitate their behavior and even their "speech." He tries to imitate the activities of adults, sometimes trying to "smoke," other times trying to use his breath to blow out match flames or to imitate coughing, and even mimicking facial expressions. He learns many skills in the process of observing and imitating animals and people. During the middle and later parts of the second year, as his motor and, more specifically, his locomotor abilities develop, he likes to move or "run" about, dumping things, taking things out of containers, grabbing things which he does not easily relinquish, and the like. This is likely to be a very trying time for mother since the infant is unaware of the dangers of his wild adventures into life space and since he resents restrictions. Social adaptation consists, in part, in firmly but gently applying restrictions, sometimes using diversion to accomplish this end, sometimes preventing the activity by providing for other activities ahead of time, and at other times using good humor, playful attitudes, and persuasion to restrict or terminate an undesirable bit of behavior of the infant. For along with the infant's "demandingness" there is also more responsiveness. He even enjoys the limits and safety of prohibitions if he has a secure anchorage in his relationships and he has not been subjected to strenuous "tugs of war" with his mother in contests over who is more powerful. By the end of the second year he has become a generally cooperative individual whose occasional flare-ups and transgressions can be largely overlooked. He delights in assisting with the chores around the house, he delights in company, and he also delights in demanding his nap when he gets fatigued. He has truly become a unique individual and, at the same time, a generally cooperative and adaptive one (8).

BEGINNINGS OF THE SELF-SYSTEM

Every individual has a psychological *identity* (and in some cases several identities) by means of which he experiences himself as "me." This identity consists of the integrated self-picture that one has of one's self or one's nature. It does not matter, from the viewpoint which we are discussing, whether this self-picture is accurate or distorted; in either case we act as if we believe in our own self-picture. We may think of ourselves as bright or stupid, quick or slow, even-tempered or irritable, vivacious or depressed, witty or humorless, assured or lacking in confidence, and the like. In addition to having this self-picture of one's psychological attributes, we also include in this identity our perception of our physical attributes—which, again, may have great or little correspondence with the facts of the case. The adult may believe that his perception of his self-picture is based quite accurately upon his actual behavior or performance in various life situations, whereas this perception is based, in the first instance, upon the ways in which *others* have appraised and reacted to him. That is, our sense of identity is formed, as Sullivan puts it, out of the "reflected appraisals" of the self by others (70). It is only after we have formed this preliminary sense of self out of such appraisals that we can later learn to evaluate ourselves accurately on the basis of what we actually do. Those of us who have not matured to this level are still too dependent upon the appraisals of others or are unable to form our own accurate judgments of our qualities based upon our actual behavior.

We noted above that an individual may act as if he had several identities. The well-known classic of *Dr. Jekyll and Mr. Hyde* illustrates what may happen in certain cases of psychopathology. There are so-called cases of *split personality* or *multiple personality* in which the individual may show the presence of two or more separate and *independently operating* identities within the personality. In all of these cases the individual failed to achieve a well integrated picture of the self—that is, a well integrated *identity*—or having once achieved it failed to maintain it in the face of severe stress or trauma. All of us are familiar with instances in which this has happened to others: during war conditions, during severe emotional crisis, during acute and intense physical illness. Under such circumstances, a "split" may occur and the individual may have *amnesia* of (or be unable to remember) what his *other self* did during the period of crisis. Such instances point up the importance of a well integrated identity.

We should also point out that even the well integrated adult, with a well developed sense of self, will show some variation in this sense of self or identity with variation in mood or activity. Thus,

during periods of moodiness or mild depression we tend to underevaluate ourselves (that is, our abilities or traits), while during periods of well-being we may do the opposite, thinking of ourselves more favorably. Other factors may also influence the self-picture momentarily. These normal variations cluster around our usual or average concept of ourselves and thus indicate how different such variation is from that of the person suffering from some form of psychopathology or reacting to some severe crisis.

Our present purpose, in this section, is to examine the process by which the sense of self develops in infancy. We wish to consider how a good or a bad self-picture is formed early in life. For once the characteristics of the self-system have become formed they tend to persist unless modified by later, usually drastic or very intense, experiences. Once having formed, they tend to influence how we feel and what we do to a considerable extent.

We can only speculate about what the neonate experiences of himself and can surmise that all he can experience, in the beginning, is a "great buzzing confusion." We have learned that until the nervous system has matured more completely and until the sensory processes have become established, little self-perception or perception of others is possible. Probably, the young infant soon learns, however, to know when he feels distressed and when he does not feel distressed. A little later he may also be able to experience pleasurable states. All of this certainly occurs before he is able to distinguish the source of his feelings—whether they come from outside or inside of himself. A well-cared-for, comfortable, secure baby soon begins to experience himself as in a pleasant state most of the time. Thus, the diffuse, amorphous base of the sense of self, in such instances, has pleasurable connotations. As his basic needs (and especially his oral needs) are gratified consistently, and he begins to distinguish the "not-me" from the "me," he also matures in his self-picture to the point at which he has learned to "trust" his world, i.e., his mother. In fact we can say with some justification that the infant feels "good" (even though he does not have any notion of the meaning of this concept), for he does feel good at a physiological level —homeostasis is relatively easy to maintain. Shortly, he begins to react still more specifically to the sensitivity and considerateness of his mother, by internalizing *her* good behavior in meeting his needs, as *his own capacity* for meeting his own needs. It is in this sense that we can say that the infant introjects the image of his good mother and thus identifies with her.

If the conditions of mothering are favorable, then, the foundations for a sense of trust in oneself as well as in the world are well established, and, as we have seen in previous sections, the infant tends to develop physically and psychologically in a sound manner. We can rephrase this statement in what the social scientist calls *operational terms* by saying that through the consistency in a pattern of good mothering the infant learns to anticipate that his needs will be gratified. The infant knows what to expect of himself because he has learned what to expect of his environment.

Even the best of mothers will sometimes frustrate her infant, wittingly or unwittingly. When this happens the foundations of self-trust in the infant are not shattered; they are only shattered when such foundations have never developed adequately or when conditions of frustration are extreme. On the contrary, such frustrations help the infant to learn to discriminate between gratification and nongratification ever more clearly and, since they are followed by gratification within a reasonable time— under favorable conditions—he learns to entertain an optimistic attitude toward himself and his environment.

It is during the second year of the infant's life, particularly, that frustrations come to have a different effect upon the emerging identity of the child. During the period of toilet-training, anal pleasures are necessarily interfered with by the mother, who prompts the youngster to learn to control his urination and defecation. Since the infant is now able to clearly differentiate his mother's frustrations from his own impulses, since in other words his mother is perceived as the source of the frustration, she is ever more clearly perceived as "bad." In situations involving a good relationship between mother and child, the bad mother is *introjected* (her prohibitions are internalized) so that the child may feel he has some control over the source of the frustration. *He* then acts as *she* would like to have him act. At this time, the infant has thus internalized two images of himself (or of his mother): the "good" image which "lets me do as I wish" and the "bad" image which "prohibits me from doing as I wish." As we have pointed out earlier, this conflict is resolved readily when the relationship between mother and child is good, when toilet-training is not instituted too early or too rapidly, and as the infant learns to satisfy both his mother and himself by gaining mastery over his sphincter reflexes. In the process he has gained a certain degree of what Erikson has called *autonomy* (71). He has begun to feel realistically that he has some degree of mastery and that he can function *independently*.

The consequences of the total process that we have been sketching, from birth through the end of infancy, include, under favorable conditions: a sense of confidence in the self, a sense of confidence in the world, a realistic sense of some degree of autonomy or independence, an ability to entertain two separate notions within the self (some part good and some part bad) *without any split* in the self-system, an ability to entertain generally positive attitudes toward mother while simultaneously entertaining some negative attitudes (without excessive ambivalence). These are tremendous assets as a base for further growth and development. They are the culmination of a happy infancy in which the reflected appraisals of a mother (and father) who is herself happy with her youngster lead to a beginning identity that is at once secure and confident, and that is relatively well integrated for that stage of development.

It has not been our purpose to sketch all of the possible unfavorable consequences in the sense of self and in consequent behavior when conditions of mothering and reflected appraisals are unfavorable. Some of these have been noted in previous sections of this chapter. However, a full analysis of such conditions must be left to books that have as their focus psychopathology in children. (See, for example, 2 and 30.)

GENERAL READINGS

1. Balint, A., *The Early Years of Life.* New York: Basic Books, 1955.
2. Bowlby, J., *Child Care and the Growth of Love.* London: Pelican, 1953.
3. Caplan, G. (ed.), *Emotional Problems of Early Childhood.* New York: Basic Books, 1955.
4. Freud, A., *The Ego and the Mechanisms of Defense.* New York: International Universities Press, 1946.
5. Freud, S., *A General Introduction to Psychoanalysis.* Garden City: Garden City Publishing Co., 1943.

6. Gesell, A., Halverson, H. M., Thompson, H., Ilg, F. L., Costner, B. M., Ames, L. B., and Amatruda, C. S., *The First Five Years of Life: A Guide to the Study of the Preschool Child.* New York: Harper, 1940.

7. Gesell, A., and Ilg, F. L., *Infant and Child in the Culture of Today.* New York: Harper, 1943.

8. Gesell, A., and Ilg, F. L., *Child Development.* New York: Harper, 1949.

9. Gruenberg, S. M. (ed.), *The Encyclopedia of Child Care and Guidance.* New York: Doubleday, 1954.

10. Hall, C. S., A *Primer of Freudian Psychology.* Cleveland: World, 1954.

11. Hebb, D. O., *The Organization of Behavior.* New York: Wiley, 1949.

12. Montagu, M. F. A., *The Direction of Human Development.* New York: Harper, 1955.

13. Mussen, P. H., and Conger, J. J., *Child Development and Personality.* New York: Harper, 1956.

14. Piaget, J., *The Construction of Reality in the Child.* New York: Basic Books, 1954.

SELECTED BIBLIOGRAPHY

15. Dennis, W., "The effect of cradling practices upon the onset of walking in Hopi children," *J. Genet. Psychol.,* 1940, 56, 77-86.

16. Sperry, R. W., "Mechanisms of neural maturation," in Stevens, S. S. (ed.), *Handbook of Experimental Psychology.* New York: Wiley, 1951.

17. McGraw, M. B., "Maturation of behavior," in Carmichael, L. (ed.), *Manual of Child Psychology.* New York: Wiley, 1946.

18. Rowe, S. N., "Mental changes following the removal of the right cerebral hemisphere for brain tumor," *Amer. J. Psychiat.,* 1937, 94, 605-614.

19. Locke, J., *Essay Concerning Human Understanding.* Philadephia: Kay and Troutman, 1849.

20. Watson, J. B., *Psychology from the Standpoint of a Behaviorist.* New York: Lippincott, 1919.

21. Bakwin, H., "Loneliness in infants," *Amer. J. Dis. Child.,* 1942, 63, 30-40.

22. Ribble, M. A., *The Rights of Infants.* New York: Columbia University, 1943.

23. Orlansky, H., "Infant care and personality," *Psychol. Bul.,* 1949, 46, 1-48.

24. Pinneau, S. R., "The infantile disorders of hospitalism and anaclitic depression," *Psychol. Bul.,* 1955, 52, 429-452.

25. Levy, D. M., "Experiments on the sucking reflex and social behavior of dogs," *Amer. J. Orthopsychiat.,* 1934, 4, 203-224.

26. Spitz, R. A., "The importance of the mother-child relationship during the first years of life: a synopsis in five sketches," *Ment. Hlth. Today,* 1948, 7.

27. Spitz, R. A., "Anaclitic depression: an inquiry into the genesis of psychiatric conditions in early childhood, II," in *The Psychoanalytic Study of the Child,* Vol. II. New York: International Universities Press, 1946.

28. Rheingold, H. L., "The modification of social responsiveness in institutional babies," *Monogr. Soc. Res. Child Develpm.,* 1956, 21, No. 2.

29. Cannon, W. B., *The Wisdom of the Body.* New York: Norton, 1932.

30. Richter, D. C., "Total self-regulatory functions in animals and human beings," *Harvey Lect.,* 1943, 38, 63.

31. Selye, H., *The Stress of Life.* New York: McGraw-Hill, 1956.

32. Hutt, M. L., and Gibby, R. G., *Patterns of Abnormal Behavior.* Boston: Allyn and Bacon, 1957.

33. Postman, L., "On the problem of perceptual defense," *Psychol. Rev.,* 1953, 6, 298-306.

34. Pratt, K. C., "The neonate," in Carmichael, L. (ed.), *Manual of Child Psychology,* 2nd ed. New York: Wiley, 1954.

35. Staples, R., "The responses of infants to color," *J. Exp. Psychol.,* 1932, 15, 119-141.

36. Brian, C. R., and Goodenough, F. L., "The relative potency of color and form perception at different ages," *J. Exp. Psychol.,* 1929, 12, 197-213.

37. Ling, B. C., "A genetic study of sustained visual fixation and associated behavior in the human infant from birth to six months," *J. Genet. Psychol.,* 1942, 61, 227-277.

38. Escalona, S. K., "Feeding disturbances in very young children," *Amer. J. Orthopsychiat.,* 1945, 15, 76-80.

39. Carter, H. D., and Krause, R. H., "Physical proportions of the human infant," *Child Develpm.,* 1936, 7, 60-68.

40. Scammon, R. E., "The measurement of the body in childhood," in Harris, J. A., Jackson, C. M., Paterson, D. G., and Scammon, R. E., *The Measurement of Man.* Minneapolis: University of Minnesota, 1930.

41. McCloy, C. H., "An analysis for multiple factors of physical growth at different age levels," *Child Develpm.,* 1940, 11, 249-277.

42. Sheldon, W. H., Stevens, S. S., and Tucker, W. B., *The Varieties of Human Physique.* New York: Harper, 1940.

43. Thompson, H., "Physical growth," in Carmichael, L. (ed.), *Manual of Child Psychology.* New York: Wiley, 1954.

44. Ames, L. B., "The sequential patterning of prone progression in the human infant," *Genet. Psychol. Monogr.,* 1937, 19, 409-460.

45. Shirley, M. M., *The First Two Years, A Study of Twenty-five Babies:* Vol. I. *Postural and Locomotor Development. Inst. Child Welf. Monogr.*, No. 6. Minneapolis: University of Minnesota, 1933.

46. Gesell, A., and Thompson, H., "Learning and growth in identical infant twins," *Genet. Psychol. Monogr.*, 1929, 5, 1-124.

47. Halverson, H. M., "An experimental study of prehension in infants by means of systematic cinema records," *Genet. Psychol. Monogr.*, 1931, 10, 107-286.

48. Chen, H. P., and Irwin, O. C., "Infant speech: vowel and consonant types," *J. Speech Disorders*, 1946, 11, 27-29.

49. McCarthy, D., "Language development in children," in Carmichael, L. (ed.), *Manual of Child Psychology*, 2nd ed. New York: Wiley, 1954.

50. Goldfarb, W., "Effects of psychological deprivation in infancy and subsequent stimulation," *Amer. J. Psychiat.*, 1945, 102, 18-33.

51. Freud, A., and Burlingham, D. T., *Infants without Families*. New York: International Universities Press, 1944.

52. Mowrer, O. H., *Learning Theory and Personality Dynamics*. New York: Ronald, 1950.

53. Irwin, O. C., and Chen, H. P., "Development of speech during infancy: curve of phonemic types," *J. Exp. Psychol.*, 1946, 36, 431-436.

54. Irwin, O. C., "Speech development in the young child: 2. Some factors related to the speech development of the infant and young child," *J. Speech and Hearing Disorders*, 1952, 17, 269-279.

55. Strayer, L. C., "Language and growth: the relative efficacy of early and deferred vocabulary training studied by the method of co-twin control," *Genet. Psychol. Monogr.*, 1930, 8, 209-319.

56. Shirley, M. M., *The First Two Years, a Study of Twenty-five Babies:* Vol. II. *Intellectual Development. Inst. Child Welf. Monogr.*, No. 8. Minneapolis: University of Minnesota, 1933.

57. Sherman, M., Sherman, I. C., and Flory, C. D., "Infant behavior," *Comp. Psychol. Monogr.*, 1936, 12, No. 4.

58. Stern, W., *Psychology of Early Childhood*. New York: Holt, 1930.

59. Bayley, N., "Mental growth during the first three years," in Barker, R. G., Kounin, J. S., and Wright, H. F. (eds.), *Child Behavior and Development*. New York: McGraw-Hill, 1943.

60. Horney, K., *Neurosis and Human Growth*. New York: Norton, 1950.

61. Dennis, W., "Infant development under conditions of restricted practice and of minimum social stimulation," *Genet. Psychol. Monogr.*, 1941, 23, 143-189.

62. Watson, J. B., and Raynor, R., "Conditioned emotional reactions," *J. Exp. Psychol.*, 1920, 3, 1-4.

63. Jersild, A. T., "Emotional development," in Carmichael, L. (ed.), *Manual of Child Psychology*, 2nd ed. New York: Wiley, 1946.

64. Goodenough, F. L., "Anger in young children," *Inst. Child Welf. Monogr.*, No. 6. Minneapolis: University of Minnesota, 1931.

65. Dollard, J., Doob, W., Miller, N. E., Mowrer, O. H., Sears, R. R., et al., *Frustration and Aggression*. New Haven: Yale University, 1939.

66. Marquis, D. P., "Learning in the neonate. The modification of behavior under three feeding schedules," *J. Exp. Psychol.*, 1941, 29, 263-282.

67. Holway, A. R., "Early self-regulation of infants and later behavior in play interviews," *Amer. J. Orthopsychiat.*, 1949, 19, 612-623.

68. Buhler, C., *The First Year of Life*. New York: John Day, 1930.

69. Sears, R. R., et al., "Some child-rearing antecedents of aggression and dependency in young children," *Genet. Psychol. Monogr.*, 1953, No. 47.

70. Sullivan, H. S., *The Interpersonal Theory of Psychiatry*. New York: Norton, 1953.

71. Erikson, E. H., *Childhood and Society*. New York: Norton, 1950.

5 | *The early formative period*

AT ABOUT THE AGE of two years the child emerges from the period of infancy and is ready to begin an active, and sometimes hectic (especially for the mother), exploration of his world. He has reached the stage of the *toddler*. For the next year or so he continues to learn how to live as a social human being and how to conform as well as how to resist conforming to the wishes of his elders and others. The problems and skills of the anal phase of development, which we discussed in the previous chapter, are still central features of this year or so of development. However, this period is different from the earlier one in two important respects: (a) *the child begins to interact with many new people* (more contact with his father is established, interest and play with siblings or with playmates of his own age group becomes important, relatives become more important in the life of the youngster); (b) *the child gains considerable mastery in bodily skills* (particularly in locomotion) which enables him to increase his sense of autonomy. Because these two sets of experiences are so important to the ways in which the child develops, we shall discuss them in a separate chapter, and leave for the next chapter development through the preschool years.

We shall begin by discussing the nature of the child's interpersonal relationships since these experiences tend to influence the rest of his development. We shall then discuss growth in motor skills, emphasizing the further development of locomotion which is of paramount importance. Finally we shall examine the nature of language development and see what consequences this has for the over-all development of the child.

We noted in the previous chapter that bladder and bowel training ought to wait upon the physical and physiological maturation of the infant. During the third year, that is from two to three years, the patterns of control usually become fairly well established. Full control and regularity develop first for bowel functions. Bladder control usually takes at least another year. During this year, the child's interests gradually widen to include adventures with father as well as mother, play and rivalry with siblings, and some degree of activity with other children outside the home (or in a nursery school, if the child attends one).

Relations with parents and other adults

Although the father may have been involved in the care of the infant, it is the mother who has had the role of maintaining an intense relationship with the infant and the responsibility for his care. She still continues these roles during the third year of the child's life but the nature of her relationships with the child changes and father becomes increasingly important to the child.

Let us look at the pattern of child-mother interactions first. During the day and early evening hours the mother cares for her youngster, watches over his physical well-being, feeds him, and plays with him. Teaching him to eat as well as teaching him to learn bowel control assume major proportions. Feeding becomes a matter of serious concern to most mothers because the child is given to extremes: he develops food fads and may insist that the food always be served in exactly the same manner; just as abruptly he refuses food that he formerly relished greatly; he seems to eat well on some days and then refuses all or most foods on other days. He appears to be obstinate, willful, and obdurate and coaxing seems to be of little avail. It is well to remember, first, that this is the typical pattern of feeding for normal children (and that it will run its course within about a year if no great issue is made of it). Lest the mother be unduly concerned about this apparently inexplicable behavior of her child, she might also like to know that children who are permitted to eat whatever they wish and whenever they wish (assuming no physical disease is present) will eat sufficiently over a period of time and will obtain a well balanced food intake, even without guidance (7). Moreover, this apparently inexplicable behavior does occur for good, if not easily understandable, reasons. This is a period in the child's life when he is exploring his limits and his controls. He varies in behavior because his internal control mechanisms (even his neurological mechanisms) are in imbalance. He is unable to choose in a consistent way because he is trying to please others and is simultaneously attempting to please himself. He therefore tends to go to extremes in his behavior—and his eating behavior displays these extremes to a pronounced degree. If the mother feels inadequate in dealing with the problems that arise, the trials of this period may add greatly not only to her own feelings of inadequacy but also to her child's feeding difficulties and consequent personality problems. If her own guilt or ambivalence about her child causes her to be too persistent in trying to get the child to eat just what he is given when he is given it, or too concerned about this "apparent" evidence in her child's behavior of her own neglect of his needs, she will be more likely to make feeding time a real battle of wills and so fixate or reinforce the very responses that she is trying to eliminate.

It should be clear, then, that the child is not necessarily obstinate when he refuses to eat or shows variable reactions at feeding time. He may *learn* that this normal, maturationally appropriate behavior on his part does upset his mother unduly and he may thus learn to use it for purposes of gaining control or attention. Taking the problem in stride, offering varied meals, gaining the child's good will by humor and play, helping the child to assist in selecting the foods he likes and helping him to feed himself—these and similar procedures may help to minimize the difficulties of this transitional period. Having a regular pattern of times for meals, and permitting snacks between meals when these are desired by the child, may also help (2). On the other hand, excessive rigidity and demandingness on the mother's part and emotionally distressing reactions by her are likely to aggravate the problems.

The discussion above should also help to point up the phenomena of introjection discussed in Chapter 4. All through the period of training in feeding, despite the outbreak of apparent (more than true or *voluntary*) negativism, the child is actually learning to do what his mother wishes. His active rebellion should be regarded as a phase of his reality-testing so that he does not simply become a rubber stamp or mirror image of his mother. As he varies his behavioral responses, he is also testing out his own uniqueness—his difference from his mother. Under normal circumstances he will introject enough of his mother's wishes and behavior, but he needs to learn also to be a unique person, one who is at least a little different from his mother. We shall return to a consideration of this aspect of development, which involves superego problems, when we next discuss the pattern of child-mother interactions in toilet-training.

Toilet-training, as we have learned, usually begins well before the start of the third year of the child's life. Bowel control is usually well established during this period, whereas bladder control takes some additional time. There are two principal reasons for this—both maturational in character. One of these is that the sphincter response in eliminating urine is reflexive and takes a longer period to inhibit than to learn to defecate, which requires the simpler, *voluntary* and *active* act of expelling. The other is that it is more difficult for the child to perceive his readiness to urinate; he first learns that he *has* wet and only later learns that he is *about ready to wet*. We shall center our attention mainly on bowel control, in which the mother's training of the youngster is an important supplement to the child's normal maturation in this respect.

The child needs only a little prompting to learn to defecate upon command. He will prefer a "pottie" to a regular toilet seat, at first, because he can climb into it more readily. He will learn to want to take his panties down, even though he may still need help in this or particularly in getting his panties up again. If the mother's attitude is relaxed and confident, the child will interiorize her wishes to learn to defecate regularly and he will also enjoy his increasing mastery over this function. In thus learning to internalize the mother's wishes he also learns to be self-confident and to be able to conform to authority. On the other hand, the mother's disgust with any of the aspects of defecation, her overly moralistic or overly rigid demands, may produce rapid training in bowel control but along with this an overly severe superego. The child is then likely to become fearful of his own impulses, to feel ashamed of the biological act of defecation, and to become afraid of authority and antagonistic to it. At the same time, his negative attitudes toward his mother will be strengthened and he will be less able to test reality—to determine his own capacities and his own unique ways of expressing them.

The problems discussed above encompass the phenomena of *identification* as well. As we have learned, identification is the resultant of the internalizations of the prohibitions expressed by the mother (although her approvals also play a minor part). When the mother has been excessively frustrating or demanding, and especially when she has been overly rigid, the child is unable to modify these internalized demands or reality-test them by

trial and error in his own behavior. The stage is thus set not only for the development of a severely strict superego but also for the repression of strong, hostile attitudes toward her which will later find their expression in excessive guilt, excessive and explosive rage reactions and a generally suspicious attitude toward people in authority.

Training in bladder control takes longer and is more gradual and irregular than bowel control. Control is established first over daytime wetting; near the end of the third year accidental daytime wetting becomes infrequent (8). Here again, the tolerant attitudes on the part of the mother will be helpful to both bladder control and to continuity of essentially pleasant relationships with the child.

It is during this year that the child, in our culture, takes an increasing interest in his father. He likes to play with him, likes to have him available as his ally when he is in difficulty with his mother, and tends to go to him more willingly than he formerly did. He also begins to imitate his father and notices ways in which he is similar to him in physical characteristics. The groundwork for later identification with the father, during the *oedipal period* (see Chapter 6), is thus prepared. Toward the end of the third year most children will have become aware of anatomical differences of fathers and mothers. They will be curious about these differences, and because of the usual modesty with which civilized people treat sex, will sometimes be shy about going to the bathroom in the presence of father or mother. In the area of sex interest and sex behavior, the same characteristic we noted in connection with food interests appears: marked variability in attitudes and behavior in the same child at different times.

Most boys will want to know how they are similar to their father and different from their mother, and may proceed to make inspection without any concern about propriety—for the child in his third year at first has no false modesty. All normal children are curious about their bodies and will examine the bodies of other children. If the parents look upon these exploratory interests for just what they are—finding out about oneself and one's world—and treat such behavior in the same way that they treat other evidences of the child's growing interests, no special problem will be likely to develop in this regard. Fathers can be especially helpful with their sons and mothers can be especially helpful with their daughters during this initial period of exploration in the area of anatomy and function. Some writers speak of the *exhibitionism* of children during this and later periods (in the preschool years), just as they speak of the children's *voyeurism* (9). Although it is entirely evident from various research studies that sex interests and behavior emerge, these technical terms (exhibitionism and voyeurism) should *not*, in the writers' opinion, be used to describe such behavior. They should be restricted to cases of individuals at much older ages, and especially to adults, in which there is a perverse need to exhibit oneself on a compulsive basis (exhibitionism) or a perverse need to look at the sexual parts of others (voyeurism). The behavior we are discussing, in the formative years, is *not* perverted, is *not* immoral, and is *not* immodest. It is exactly like the behavior of the child who wants to know how a dog is different from a cat or what is inside a refrigerator! It is the adult, who is ignorant of such matters or emotionally upset by such behavior because of his own problems in these areas, who is unduly concerned by children's explorations of their bodies, sometimes in full view of company, and who is the real problem. Such reactions by adults are likely to create unnecessary and unfavorable reactions on the part of the child.

The father is also important to the child, especially the boy, in another respect. We have indicated that all children tend to go through a period of "negativism" during the third year. The father is useful as an ancillary authority figure during this period and can act as a "court of last resort." Thus he can take some of the onus off the mother in her disciplinary role. This role of the father is particularly important in relation to the development of aggressive behavior of boys. Boys have to learn to identify with the sex-role of father and find socially appropriate ways of expressing aggression. When the father is unavailable physically or when he is not a good model of masculinity, we would expect that the son, particularly, would have greater difficulty in learning to master hostile impulses and express *appropriate*, aggressive behavior. There is evidence to support such a view. Sears reports on a series of studies based on the observations of doll play of children (starting at three years of age). In this study the amount and kinds of aggressive behavior among children from homes in which the father was physically absent was compared with that of children whose fathers were present. As expected, there was a significant difference between these two groups of children (although separation of the father at later ages was not productive of significant differences), the major difference occurring in the case of boys. Boys whose fathers were unavailable had much more difficulty in learning to handle their aggressive feelings (10). The evidence indicates that such children either did not develop appropriate aggression or handled it in inappropriate ways.

It is during this period that children become actively interested in other adults. Until age three or later they are likely to be fearful of such adults at one time and friendly at another time. They need time to learn to respond to the varied reactions of adults whose behavior may be quite different from that of their own parents. They may be shy in the presence of adults who are more assertive than their parents, for example, and they may burst out into tears when picked up or played with by adults who are brusque or whose physical appearance or techniques of manipulation or verbal play are very different from those of their parents. Although it seems wise to introduce children to a variety of adults, such increasing ranges and varieties of interpersonal experiences should be accomplished gradually. The introduction of too many new adults abruptly or the introduction of many new adults over a short period of time may result in withdrawal tendencies and even acute anxiety reactions. An ad-

mixture of the principles of common sense and of *pacing*, geared to the actual behavioral responses of the child, is helpful.

Sibling relationships

Thus far we have spoken of the family structure in terms of the parents and child. When the child has brothers or sisters, the family constellation becomes much more complex and the variety of interpersonal experiences becomes much richer and somewhat more hazardous.

Let us assume that we are dealing with the first child in the family and that the mother then becomes pregnant again. What may we expect of the first child's behavior and what should the parents do, if anything, to prepare the child for the newcomer? Perhaps we expect that the child will welcome his sibling with open arms, so to speak, and we may even insist that he have nothing in his heart for the newcomer except love. Such an expectation does not jibe with the facts and is a rationalized adult's viewpoint rather than that of the child. The normal response to a new child involves some degree of jealousy (11). On analysis, one could have predicted that such would be the case since the new arrival (even before he is on the scene) deprives the youngster of some attention, *seems* to the youngster to be the cause of some loss of love from his parents, and may even mean the loss of a crib or a room or some other personal possessions. As one youngster of three years put it, "My new brother came to our house. Mommy has only half her love left for me." The arithmetic may be wrong (since mother will give her love to three people in the family), but to the child's mind his logic is unassailable. Even adults sometimes act as if the new love of one of their friends for another person inevitably means some loss of love for themselves!

The emotionally secure child is able to express some of this jealousy quite openly and is able to express his positive sentiments as well. In time, the amount of jealousy will fade into insignificance or become entirely dissipated as good sibling relationships develop and good relationships with parents are continued. On the other hand, the child who is emotionally insecure, who is too dependent on his parents, or who is greeted with the accomplished fact of a new arrival in some traumatic fashion, is likely to regress in behavior and become quite disturbed. Or if expression of his jealous feelings is not permissible, he may repress his normal hostility, become sullen, and behave in a passively stubborn manner.

The intensity and duration of the jealous reaction depend on many factors in the family constellation. In general, the older the child is before the new arrival comes, the easier it will be for him to make a rapid and satisfactory adjustment. In one study it was shown that a four-year interval makes a significant difference in this type of response (12). Other studies have shown that the more dependent the child is, the more likely he is to become inordinately jealous (13, 14). It is also clear that the presence of older children in

the family tends to mitigate the response of jealousy of the youngest child.

There appears to be no *entirely* adequate preparation of the child for the new arrival. However, the adjustment can be facilitated and positive gains in emotional growth can be encouraged by a number of measures. When the child is able to recognize that mother is carrying a new baby, it is time to begin preparing him for the event. His questions about babies should be answered simply and in terms of the quite obvious meaning they have for him. (For example, when the child asks "Where do babies come from?" he does not expect a biological lecture on impregnation and gestation, but simply wants to know that a baby is growing inside Mommy, that Mommy and Daddy wanted to have a baby, and that when baby is old and big enough a doctor will help Mommy in seeing that the baby is born in a good condition and is healthy.) It seems to be helpful to let the child share in the family's preparation for the newcomer by participating in discussions of how he will be taken care of, what things he will need, where he will sleep, and what role each member of the family may be expected to take in relation to him. Such sharing not only helps to offer advantages to the first child, but also helps to differentiate the roles of this child from the newcomer in a positive manner.

Despite all of the preparations that one may make and even though the child is emotionally secure, some mild and temporary disturbance should be anticipated. In addition to overt expressions of hostility toward and jealousy of the baby, the older child may regress temporarily to bed-wetting, sleeping difficulties, fits of temper, infantile behaviors such as insisting upon going to the pottie, and the like. Relaxed but firm handling of the situation may be required if the hostility is acted out. Otherwise it is best to simply "weather the storm" for the normal child will soon make a good adjustment again.

The particular *ordinal position* that a child has in the family constellation contributes its share to the type of personality the child is likely to develop and to sibling relationships. The first-born is more likely than the others to have emotional problems in adjustment, especially in such behavior as shyness, withdrawal tendencies, and rapid swings in mood (10, 14, 15). This may be due to the fact that the parents are inexperienced in child-rearing, feel less secure in the process, may be overconcerned with the youngster and more variable in their treatment of him, perhaps going to extremes at times. The birth of the next child and the attendant problems that this creates, as we have noted, makes an additional contribution to the first child's problems. At the other end of the ordinal scale, the youngest child is likely to be more ambitious, more competitive, and more outgoing (15). Middle children tend to develop personality characteristics between these more extreme tendencies. We should emphasize that we have been discussing general tendencies of certain characteristics to be associated with ordinal position and that the overlap of the groups of children at various ordinal positions is quite marked. Moreover, ordinal position is only one of many factors, many of them far more important, that contribute to personality characteristics. Nevertheless, Alfred Adler's contention that ordinal position in the family does make a definite contribution is sustained by recent research evidence.

Play activities

We shall use the term *play* to mean what it is taken to mean by the layman: a pleasurable, spontaneous form of activity without the aim of reaching a particular objective other than of having fun, and a means of discharging tensions. One of the definitions given in *Webster's Collegiate Dictionary* (fourth edition) is: "To engage in sport or lively recreation; to amuse or divert oneself; frolic." In fact, as some authors have put it, play is a form of life.

Various theories have been spun to explain why children play. Perhaps the best known of these is the one offered by G. Stanley Hall, known as the "recapitulation" theory of play (16). This theory held that the child in his play recapitulates the history of the race, and therefore goes through successive stages in his development which can be identified in the history of man. The theory is probably of only academic interest today but its author served to stimulate interest in the whole field of child development by his careful analysis and explanation of this phase of child behavior. Another theory, widely held for a time and still accepted by some today, is that proposed by Gross in his book *The Play of Man* (17). In this theory, it was held

Having a picnic is fun and provides new learning opportunities. (U. of Mich.)

that play is an unconscious preparation for life. It was even assumed that the child played instinctively in certain ways in order to prepare for his specific role in adulthood; thus the girl *instinctively* played "house" to prepare for later roles as mother and housekeeper. One may cavil with these and other theories of play but one cannot deny that play is universal, although its forms and content vary in different cultures. In any case play provides for a considerable amount of learning and mastery experience and, during the formative period, is usually associated with fantasy.

Some authors suggest that the child begins to play at about the third month of life and that play is present at all stages of development thereafter. The infant is said to play with his feet, for example,

at about three months. About a month later he begins to play with objects of various kinds: the rattle, the teething ring, the sheet, and the like. These activities involve exploratory activities and often are accompanied by pleasure. It is questionable whether they are "sport" in the sense that we used this term above or whether they are deliberately, if spontaneously, engaged in for fun. However, there is little doubt that the kind of playful activities engaged in during the latter part of the first year come closer to our conception of the meaning of play. Certainly during the second year, when the child plays with blocks, enjoys imitating the facial expressions and vocalizations of mother, and uses various locomotive toys, like wagons, "chairs," and even pots (which can make wonderful wagons or trains in the child's imagination), the criteria of play are fully met.

It is during toddlerhood, however, that play really comes into its own. There appear to be two distinguishing features of the changed play interests and activities. One of these is the child's growing interest and participation in play with children of about his own age. Such play activities are especially likely to emerge during this period if the youngster attends nursery school. They will also appear in his interaction with other children in the neighborhood. The nature of the interactions is striking. The child quite obviously wants to have another child near him when he plays—not all of the time, but for short intervals, at various times—and seems to enjoy his presence. However, he usually goes about his own play activities without sharing them with the other child. The two children play together, but separately, being aware of, and sometimes even demanding in, the presence of the other, but being independent in what each is doing. This phenomenon has been called *parallel play*. It will be present with decreasing frequency for another two to four years. It is most characteristic of this period, however, when joint, interactive play is still infrequently present. Aside from parallel play, the only other regular use made of the other child in play is to explore his body as if it were any one of the numerous inanimate objects of the environment. Thus, one child will poke his fingers into any of the orifices of the other child's body that are exposed, he will touch and feel him, he will push and pull him, and he will even taste him! These are some of his ways of getting acquainted with other children. Such activity appears to be enjoyable and resembles much of the activity that the child previously engaged in with his mother as an object.

The other distinguishing characteristic of the play of this period is the almost exclusive use of the large muscles and muscle groups in the motoric manipulation of objects. The fine, delicate motor coordinations have not yet been differentiated, for the most part, and so play involves gross motor activity and hectic action. Shoving and pulling things and people are very important. Similarly, climbing any convenient object (without awareness of danger and usually without fear) seems to have a compulsive urgency to the child. Squeezing into small apertures has a peculiar fascination. Any open door of a closet or cabinet is also an open invitation to climb in or to squeeze in. He also enjoys being thrown

and bounced, juggled and jounced, "caught" and "freed." Mastery of control over large muscle groups is an important by-product of all of these experiences.

It is interesting to note that the play interests of boys and girls are similar during this period. As a matter of fact, significant differences in play activities will not appear until the later preschool or early school years. Differences in such interests may be encouraged at an earlier age by the practices of the culture and the particular motivations and playthings provided by the parents. Some parents insist upon having the boy do "boyish" things, and the girls do "girlish" things. Hence such parents will provide boys with tricycles and tools and provide girls with dolls and miniature articles for housekeeping. It should be emphasized that these are the preferences of the parents and culture and not those of the children. (And sometimes, in the case of a parent who is disturbed over his own sexual role, this is the psychopathological preoccupation of the parent!) Otherwise, toddlers of both sexes will enjoy and play with toys of all kinds irrespective of the sexual connotations these may have for adults.

When we discussed parallel play, above, we noted that it is characteristic of the period of toddlerhood. It should also be noted that a considerable amount of observational evidence, and some experimental evidence, is available to indicate that the duration and emphasis of this kind of play activity are related to the kinds of play materials that are provided. For example, in the nurseries of some countries in which very large, bulky (but light) play objects are provided, which require two or more participants for their manipulation, children develop more interactive and more cooperative play activities at an earlier age than is generally true in our own culture.

LOCOMOTION—
"WHAT A GREAT, BIG WORLD"

The child's body continues to grow at a rapid pace during the third year, and gains in height and weight are almost as great as they were in the second year (18). The small muscles are still not sufficiently well developed, with few exceptions, so that fine motor coordinations are still undeveloped and will not become part of the behavior pattern for another year, at least. Skill in the use of the large muscles develops rapidly during toddlerhood; this is demonstrated most strikingly, perhaps, in the marked difference in locomotor abilities between age two and age three.

Progression in walking, which at first involved putting the same foot forward before the next step could be taken, soon becomes a smoothly coordinated skill. The child learns to walk and run smoothly, he can walk (not climb) up stairs, he darts about, starting and stopping suddenly, he can jump, and he can even stand on one foot. This rapid progress is attained mainly by the development of more integrated, more smoothly functioning patterns of gross muscle control. Later when the finer muscles have developed, further differentiation in coordination, and especially in locomotor skills involving skillful body controls, will occur. Nevertheless, by the end of the third year the child is able to make symmetrical use of opposite sides of the body in locomotion, using the alternate swinging of his arms to increase his balance, and using the opposite sides of the body in alternate movements as he rapidly propels himself through space.

This is a period when it is very easy for the mother (or father) to fall into the error of overprotection—when the first stages of *Momism* are likely to be manifest (3). The child is full of energy and his movements in space appear to the observer to be unpredictable. He is likely to dart quickly into the street, unless watched continuously. Before one realizes it, he has climbed up on top of some precarious perch—perhaps to the top of a pile of boxes. He may grab at or pull down objects that are above his head, and in the process pull down some heavy or sharp object that would be dangerous if it struck him. The child certainly needs firm limits and he needs protection against his own impulses, but provision has to be made, at the same time, to permit him to explore his world, to get his share of mild bumps and small falls, and to learn from graded experiences what he can and what he cannot do. Overprotection, stemming from parental overconcern because of their own fears about physical pain or their own feelings of inadequacy in the area of physical coordination, as well as from a need to be dominant and in full control, may not only hamper the development of locomotor and other physical skills, but also may contribute significantly to the child's self-image as inadequate, fearful, and uncoordinated. Thus a skillful balance has to be maintained between permitting the child to explore his new world, getting into occasional difficulty as a result, and guarding him against severe or extreme danger situations. It is helpful if dangerous (or valuable) objects are kept out of reach, and if the child can be permited to explore and play freely in a protected physical environment (like a fenced-in back yard, or the properly arranged environment of a nursery school) so that he can obtain his experience without either serious physical damage or severe psychological frustration.

Another example of the development of skills in locomotion is the progression in the fine art of sitting. We adults, who take the act of sitting as a simple motor skill that "comes naturally," have only to observe the development of this skill in the toddler to see how complex it really is. The youngster approaches this problem as if it were, as indeed it is for him, a highly difficult obstacle. He may first survey the chair or couch he wishes to climb into, he may then push his "bottom" up into it and push the rest of himself up afterward, and then squeeze back into place. Or he may climb into the chair backward and then squirm around, uttering a great sign of satisfaction as he accomplishes this feat—sometimes even offering us a big grin in token of his success. Or he may develop other ingenious ways of getting into this space, showing both his imagination in coping with the complex physical world and his awkwardness in managing it. By the end

Play encourages fantasy and other intellectual abilities. (Merrill Palmer)

of the third year, and certainly in the fourth, he, like us, takes the act of locomoting into a chair for granted; he has *learned* to sit down!

SOME OTHER ASPECTS OF PHYSICAL DEVELOPMENT

We have selected for discussion two other important aspects of physical development during this period: dressing and handedness.

By the age of two years most children have developed some interest in dressing themselves. However, at this stage they are more successful in taking things off than in putting them on. Not only is

151

putting things on (and fastening clothes) more complex from a physical standpoint, but it is more complex from a perceptual standpoint. The child of two years is unable to distinguish front of clothes from back and is unable to judge whether to put both legs into one of the holes of the panties or both. However, he usually takes pleasure, at least, in taking some of his clothes off, or in helping to take them off. He can take off articles of clothing that slip off, such as shoes and pants, but he has more difficulty with unbuttoning and untying things. Frequently, he will make a game of undressing and try to repeat the procedure over and over, sometimes to the exasperation of mother. Nevertheless, as with other activities during this phase of development, tolerance, humor, and good will may make a productive endeavor with significant later "dividends" in personality as well as physical development instead of a battle out of the situation. Among other things to keep in mind with such activities is the need to allow ample and unhurried time for the undressing ceremony, so that mother does not become unnecessarily harried.

By the age of three years, the child has most likely gotten over much of his negativistic behavior in connection with dressing. At this time he is also much more helpful in getting his things off and he can usually be depended upon to put some of his things on. Gesell and Ilg state that the child may be expected to be able to unbutton most of his clothes (front and side, not back), and take al-most all of his things off by himself (2). He can now also put on his pants, sweater, and shoes. He may try to lace shoes but needs help in completing the act or doing a good job. Even more significant than the specific motor skills that have been learned is the degree of cooperativeness which is usually achieved and the pleasure which both mother and child take in the dressing and undressing behavior.

We now turn our attention to a fascinating and important problem in behavior development: the development of handedness. We can begin with two observations. The first is that the preference for the use of one side over the other side of the body is not unitary. By this we mean that an individual may prefer the right side for some activities and the left for other. No one is known to show universal preference for either side in all motor activities. Even within the more restricted use of one part of the body, say the hand, an individual is likely to prefer the right hand for some activities and yet prefer the left hand for others. For example, he may use the right hand for writing but use the left hand for throwing or catching a ball. The second observation is that infants do not exhibit any consistent hand preference until about three or four months of age, and then only for some limited activities, such as reaching (19). The latter conclusion has been amply confirmed so that we may regard it as factual. The implication of this finding is another matter. Workers are not agreed whether this means that some innate preference for one hand (or one side) over the other exists but does not manifest itself until a later stage of development, or whether the fact of gradual and late establishment of hand preference indicates that it is learned through cultural conditioning. Those who take the former view may argue that handedness is associated with cerebral dominance (since one side of the cerebrum is likely to be more dominant than the other) and that such dominance is inherited, or that anatomical features of the body (which have an innate basis) account for the tendency for the greater preferential use of the right hand. The evidence for this position is inferential and speculative and does not seem, to the writers, to be entirely convincing. Those who argue for the cultural conditioning viewpoint (among whom John B. Watson was a notable champion) point out that societies tend to favor the use of the right hand, and that even in primitive times warriors tried to protect the heart by carrying the shield over the heart area with the left hand and leaving the right hand free for combat. Whether this viewpoint is entirely correct is also a matter of opinion, but there is convincing evidence that: (a) learning greatly influences the choice of a particular hand in a particular act (and so does common observation of such activities as holding the fork in the left hand while cutting the meat with the right, or in catching with a glove on the left hand); (b) many individuals who originally preferred the use of one hand in some or many activities were converted to the preferential and more skillful use of the other hand, without any untoward results.

Consistency in the use of one hand for a number of activities develops gradually.

As one investigator has shown, when preference for handedness is examined for a number of activities (hand grip, tapping, steadiness, and dart-throwing), only about one fourth of the population shows *consistent* preference for *all* activities (20). (The research population ranged in age from four to twelve years of age. The proportion of persons showing consistency would be far less at four years than for the group as a whole.) At the age level of three years, with which we are concerned at the moment, there is apparently no significant preference in the use of the right over the left hand for complex motor skills. Gradually, as more skill develops *with practice* one hand begins to be more consistently preferred for that particular skill, so that a decided preference begins to be demonstrated for complex skills by about the fifth year (21). It has been estimated that about 90 per cent of adults are right-handed; i.e., prefer the use of the right hand for most activities in which one hand is used.

The problem of hand preference is important because of the implications many people draw about it. For some there is something sinister (hence the term *sinistral*) in the use of the left hand. For others, there is the belief that children who are left-handed are likely to stutter, or if they are left-handed and are converted to the use of the right hand, stuttering is likely to result. For still others, there is the implication that left-handed people are poorly coordinated and awkward. None of these beliefs is consistent with the research evidence (22). It is true that *some* cases of individuals who were converted to the use of the right hand in writing, after *left-*handed preference was clearly established, began to stutter. However, that conversion, even in such instances, does not necessarily cause stuttering is indicated by statistical studies which show that 90 to 95 per cent of those whose handedness is converted do not stutter (23, 24).

It has been demonstrated that the greatest incidence of stuttering occurs between the ages of two and four. We have already discussed the reasons for this—as part of the normal developmental pattern of immature speech, starting in later infancy. Since handedness begins to become dominant during the latter part of this period (two to four years), and since the child is frequently likely to show some stuttering as part of the phase of anal development, any attempts at conversion that are accompanied by emotional upheaval, abruptness, or other forms of trauma are likely to condition the speech difficulty and reinforce it. It is during this same period that the child begins to scribble or draw for fun. All of these factors lead us to the following generalizations and suggestions: (a) If the child spontaneously begins to show strong left-hand preference, do not interfere with it, except after careful clinical evaluation and competent professional guidance. (b) If the child shows some slight preference for the left hand, he may be encouraged to use the right hand by placing things at his right side or in his right hand, *without* criticizing him when he does use the left hand. (c) The choice of the hand is, after all, largely

A visit to the hospital calls for physical and social skills. (U. of Mich.)

a matter for the child to develop in accordance with his own convenience and competence. Help him to develop the trends that he clearly demonstrates (including his own hand preference) and avoid any emotional trauma in connection with the problem. (d) On the positive side, help the child to feel more confident in the preference that he seems to want to develop. Instead of regarding left-handedness as a liability, treat it as it should be treated, as part of the individual and unique, normal qualities of the child. A left-handed person can, after all, get along in this world as well as a right-handed person in most activities.

LANGUAGE AS A SOCIAL SKILL

It is during the third year of the child's life that language really emerges into its own as a social skill. We pointed out in the last chapter that by the end of the second year language has developed into the *expressive stage* and that the child has learned to use language actively for narrative purposes. In the next year there is a rapid flowering of expressive language, and language skills become significant in greatly extending the child's world. Through increased locomotion he is able to get about more actively and independently and to explore the physical world around him. Through language he can do much more. He learns to understand the world of immediate experience in many different ways, for once he has words to conceptualize these experiences he can begin to differentiate them more effectively, to compare them, and even to summarize and to integrate them. He can also extend his world be-

yond that of immediate experience. He uses words to remember past events and to anticipate future ones. He learns to differentiate experiences from within (*emotions*) from experiences from without (*external stimuli*) in ever more reliable fashion. He uses language to express his needs and to control the behavior of others. In these and other ways, language becomes a means of extending himself in time and space, and of enriching himself through direct participation with cultural experiences that can be shared with others. As a consequence he learns to use judgment more effectively; he can be reasoned with; he can explain himself. Although he may not always use these abilities constructively, he does learn to use them in more effective relationships with people, animals, and "things."

Some inkling may be gained of the rapid increase in language skills during the third year from the following selected facts. The size of the child's evaluative vocabulary probably increases, on the average, from about 300 words to about 900 words, a gain of 300 per cent (25). During the same period his ability to name objects on pictures increases from about one or two to about seven words (26). By the end of this period he has learned to understand and use at least three different prepositions; he can readily distinguish "in" from "under" and "above" from "below" (27). The typical length of his sentences increases from about one word, or occasionally two words, to about four words. By three years of age, although he is still confused about many words that sound the same but mean different things (such as "whole" and "hole"), he has at least learned that sometimes the same sound may be used for different words and the things that they represent. He is less "concrete-minded" in his use of words toward the end of this period, so that "brother" does not only mean his own brother but may represent the brothers of other children. His sentences contain more verbs and some adjectives and adverbs. He tends to use a greater variety of words within a given space of time. These are but a few of the many research findings that have been gathered over the past three decades (28).

It has become increasingly clear that language development is greatly influenced, once a sufficient degree of maturation has been attained, by a variety of environmental factors. One of these is the richness and variety of experiences the child has—experiences with things and with feelings. This principle has been recognized, and the importance of rich, personal experience as a foundation for good language development stressed, by the National Council of Teachers of English (29). Such factors as the kind of language used by the parents and siblings and the readiness of parents to answer questions and encourage the use of better verbal expressions by the youngster play important roles. There is convincing evidence that the age of associates influences the rate and quality of language development. An important argument for placement of children in a good nursery-school environment is based on the finding that when children regularly have children of their own age to play and learn with, their intelligence in general, and their linguistic skills in particular, develop more adequately.

Perhaps more important than the concrete types and varieties of physical, linguistic, and social experiences that the child has is the type of emotional climate in which he is developing. In the previous chapter we noted that children placed in orphanages tend to have retarded general development. Their language development is especially retarded. Goldfarb's studies showed that when children who have spent the first three years in an institution are compared with children who have spent their first three years in a foster home, the former group not only showed language development that was inferior to the latter group, but also, in terms of absolute standards, it was greatly retarded in *all aspects* of language skills that were measured. Even three to five years later, as measured on retests at that time, this retardation had not been overcome (30). The specific agent or agents producing this effect were presumed to be the nonstimulating, impersonal relationships of the institutional environment. Clinical studies by various psychiatrists have shown that when the child does not have a good emotional relationship with a mother, *autistic language* (noncommunicative, self-centered language) may develop as part of a total *schizoid* personality adjustment—a severely disturbed state of withdrawal (31, 32). Allen has demonstrated that specific types of emotional climates may be responsible for delayed speech and other types of speech and language defects (33). He characterizes these types of disturbed children as: (a) the "protest child" who has learned to reject food and has emotionally tense relationships with a parent, (b) the "overprotected child," (c) the child who has had insufficient emotional support, and (d) the "throttled child" who has not been permitted to express his feelings and impulses in appropriate manner.

The general point of these and other studies and reports is that language development is closely tied in with effective personality development. This conclusion is of particular concern to us in connection with the language development of the toddler for two very special reasons. The first is that during this period of rapid speech and language development the average child customarily experiences some difficulties. Many children first begin to stutter at this time—as part of their trial-and-error learning of speech and as part of the turbulence of emotional experiences during this time. Hence, it is doubly important to be patient when the child speaks and to maintain a relaxed and accepting emotional atmosphere. Most stutterers of this period overcome this difficulty spontaneously under normal circumstances. The second reason is related to the fact that the child is going through a period of socialization (the *anal* period) in which he has to learn gradually to accept certain prohibitions and frustrations. Language development may be unnecessarily disturbed by too severe regimes of toilet-training, by too much emphasis upon regularity and cleanliness, by too great

dominance in getting the child to conform rapidly, and the like. The child needs "room" for the expression of some of his "negativism" and he needs time and acceptance (understanding that this is a difficult time for him, too) in order to express both his impulses and his frustrations in language, as well as in other forms of behavior. Lewis, in discussing the increase in the child's use of questions during this period ("Why, Mommy?"), puts his finger on the crux of the matter: ". . . the growth [of the child in language] is determined by social cooperation working upon two powerful tendencies . . . to use language as play and as a means of satisfying vital needs" (34).

One of the most fascinating aspects in the development of language of children, closely related to the general issue we have been discussing, is the gradual transition from *egocentric* to *socialized* speech. The man most responsible for focusing attention on this problem, and who has contributed a great deal by way of both theory and research, is Jean Piaget. He classified children's speech into these two main categories on the basis of the function that language plays in the life of the child (35). By egocentric speech he meant speech that the child uses essentially for his own purposes without any concern about whom he is speaking to and without any intent to communicate to anyone. This type of speech was further subdivided into three subcategories: (a) *monologue* (in which the child speaks without interaction with anyone), (b) *collective monologue* (in which two or more children each engage in separate but more or less simultaneous monologues), (c) and *echolalia* (in which the child repeats the sounds made by others, without any necessary comprehension or any objective to communicate to others). Socialized speech was divided into five subcategories: (a) *adapted information* (in which some exchange in thoughts is taking place between the child and another person), (b) *criticism*, (c) *commands*, *requests*, and *threats*, (d) *questions*, and (e) *answers*. Piaget found that children's speech is predominantly egocentric between three and five years of age. During the next two years, socialized speech develops rapidly, and by seven years of age socialized speech becomes clearly and consistently more prominent. These findings are based on the child's spontaneous speech. It has been noted that the function of speech changes considerably depending upon the situation in which it is observed or measured.

On the whole these conclusions of Piaget's have been confirmed by other workers, although some have taken sharp issue with the kinds of interpretations of the data that Piaget made. One of those who has disagreed with Piaget's interpretations is Vigotsky, who stated that although a child's speech at three years of age is clearly egocentric in structure (and in this his data are in agreement with Piaget's), the function of such speech is nevertheless social in character. His essential point was that closer examination of the relations between speech functions and the social situations in which they were employed indicated that, even at three years of age, an important function of the child's speech was communication—or socialized speech. He did find that by seven years of age both the structure and function of speech were clearly socialized, but he believed that previous to this there was a maturation in the structure of children's language forms so that socialized speech was clearly shown to be present in greater degree than Piaget had indicated. The major characteristics in this type of maturation to which Vigotsky called attention was that of *inner speech*. As the child grows older, inner speech increases. By this is meant speech designed to test things out for oneself, to think things through, and the like. Hence, Vigotsky believed that, in fact, socialized speech really decreases as the child matures and as he is able to use the more mature form of inner speech. To demonstrate these interpretations, he designed a series of studies in which children's speech was examined under various conditions of *reduced* social stimulation and interaction, so that speech during free play was contrasted with speech in such situations as those involving a complete stranger, those with a deaf-mute child, and the like. In such situations egocentric speech, and not socialized speech, *decreased* (36). It seems to the writers that Vigotsky's results are really consistent with those of Piaget, but that attention has been called to two important distinctions: that function and structure of language are two different attributes, and hence have to be defined and interpreted more carefully than Piaget defined them;

and that although children's speech at the earlier level (say three years) is more egocentric in form than it is in later life, it clearly has important social functions in the behavior of the child.

This last point can be restated in another manner, as we have already done a few paragraphs back: the characteristics of the speech of children are greatly influenced by their social situations. Many studies have been conducted to test this conclusion and there is essential agreement that this is, indeed, the case. This fact, as we may now characterize it, also points up the importance in studies of language development of children of specifying rigorously the precise conditions under which the observations or measures of language are being made. In turn, this fact indicates the highly cautious interpretation one must make of language norms in terms of the conditions under which the norms were obtained. We shall have more to say about this important problem of defining norms in language in our further discussion of language development, in Chapter 6.

There is one additional observation about the development of language in the third year to which we should like to call attention. Linguistic skill and intelligence are highly correlated with each other, providing environmental and social conditions are kept constant, the correlation coefficient usually being in the range of .85 to .95. This helps to explain why most widely used intelligence tests for children, particularly those from two years of age and up, are so heavily based on language items. As a matter of fact many children's language or vocabulary tests are sufficiently valid to be used as

measures of intelligence, providing the conditions noted above are observed. For example, one of the fairly widely used vocabulary tests for children, which is also usable as an intelligence test, is that devised by Van Alstyne (37). The test consists of a series of cards on each of which there are four pictures of objects or situations. The child is asked orally to point out which of the four on each card is the appropriate answer to a question about that card, like "Show me the pen," or "Show me the boy who is running." The test takes only about fifteen minutes to administer and gives a reliable estimate of the child's evaluative vocabulary and therefore of his intelligence—providing the child's background is similar to that of the children upon whom the test was standardized and providing the conditions of testing are adequate. Another vocabulary test, and one that has had more extensive research done in devising it as well as in evaluating the significance of the findings, is the Williams and McFarland revision of a test originally published by M. E. Smith in 1926 (38). This test, known as the *Smith-Williams Vocabulary Test*, based upon samplings of words from Thorndike's word list for children (39), is available in two alternate forms, and involves both a test for *recall* of word meanings and the *recognition* of word meanings. This test has turned out to be one of the very useful research instruments for estimating the size of children's vocabulary at different ages and for inquiring into the types of conditions that facilitate vocabulary development.

GENERAL READINGS

1. Barker, R. G., Kounin, J. S., and Wright H. F. (eds.), *Child Behavior and Development*. New York: McGraw-Hill, 1943.
2. Gesell, A., and Ilg, F. L., *Child Development*. New York: Harper, 1949.
3. Levy, D. M., *Maternal Over-Protection*. New York: Columbia University, 1943.
4. Thompson, G. G., *Child Psychology: Growth Trends in Psychological Adjustment*. Boston: Houghton Mifflin, 1952.
5. White House Conference on Child Health and Protection, *Growth and Development of the Child*. New York: Appleton, 1932-1933.
6. Woodcock, L. P., *Life and Ways of the Two-Year-Old*. New York: Dutton, 1941.

SELECTED BIBLIOGRAPHY

7. Davis, C. M., "Results of the self-selection of diets by young children," *Canadian Med. Assoc. J.*, 1939, 41, 257-261.
8. Gesell, A., and Ilg, F. L., *Infant and Child in the Culture of Today*. New York: Harper, 1943.
9. Isaacs, S., *Social Development in Young Children*. New York: Harcourt, Brace, 1933.
10. Sears, P. S., "Doll play aggression in normal young children: Influence of age, sex, sibling status, father's absence," *Psychol. Monogr.*, 1951, No. 65.
11. Levy, D. M., "Studies in sibling rivalry," *Res. Monogr. Amer. Orthopsychiat. Assoc.*, 1937, No. 2.
12. Sewall, M., "Two studies in sibling rivalry. I. Some causes of jealousy in young children," *Smith College Studies in Social Work*, 1930, 1, 6-22.
13. Vollmer, H., "Jealousy in children," *Amer. J. Orthopsychiat.*, 1946, 16, 660-671.
14. Kawin, E., *Children of the Preschool Age*. Chicago: University of Chicago, 1934.
15. Cobb, E. A., "Family press variables," *Monogr. Soc. Res. Child Develpm.*, 1943, 8, 327-361.
16. Hall, G. S., *Adolescence: Its Psychology and Its Relations to Physiology, Anthropology, Sociology, Sex, Crime, Religion, and Education*. New York: Appleton, 1904.
17. Gross, K., *The Play of Man*. New York: Appleton, 1901.

18. Watson, E. H., and Lowrey, G. H., *Growth and Development of Children*. Chicago: Year Book Publishers, 1954.

19. Lippman, H. S., "Certain behavior responses in early infancy," *J. Genet. Psychol.*, 1927, 34, 424-440.

20. Heinlein, J. H., "A study of dextrality in children," *J. Genet. Psychol.*, 1929, 36, 91-119.

21. Wellman, B., "The development of motor coordination in young children: An experimental study of arm and hand movements," *Univer. Iowa Stud. Child Welf.*, 1926, 3, No. 4.

22. Wile, I. S., *Handedness, Right and Left*. Boston: Lothrop, Lee & Shepard, 1934.

23. Wallin, J. E. W., "A census of speech defects," *Sch. & Soc.*, 1916, 3, 213-216.

24. Parsons, B. S., *Lefthandedness*. New York: Macmillan, 1924.

25. Smith, M. E., "An investigation of the development of the sentence and the extent of vocabulary in young children," *Univer. Iowa Stud. Child Welf.*, 1926, 3, No. 5.

26. Cattell, P., *The Measurement of Intelligence of Infants and Young Children*. New York: Psychological Corp., 1940.

27. Gesell, A., *The Mental Growth of the Preschool Child*. New York: Macmillan, 1925.

28. McCarthy, D., "Language development in children," in *Manual of Child Psychology*, Carmichael, L. (ed.). New York: Wiley, 1954.

29. Smith, D. V. (ed.), *The English Language Arts*. National Council of Teachers of English, Curriculum Commission Series, Vol. I. New York: Appleton, 1952.

30. Goldfarb, W., "Effects of psychological deprivation in infancy and subsequent stimulation," *Amer. J. Psychiat.*, 1945, 102, 18-33.

31. Bradley, C., *Schizophrenia in Childhood*. New York: Macmillan, 1941.

32. Despert, J. L., "Schizophrenia in children," *Psychiat. Quart.*, 1938, 12, 366-371.

33. Allen, I. M., "Defect of the speech function in childhood," *New Zealand Med. J.*, 1947, 46, 297-307.

34. Lewis, M. M., *Infant Speech: A Study of the Beginnings of Language*, 2nd ed. New York: Humanities Press, 1951.

35. Piaget, J., *Judgment and Reasoning of the Child*. New York: Harcourt, Brace, 1928.

36. Vigotsky, L. S., "Thought and speech," *Psychiat.*, 1939, 2, 29-54.

37. Van Alstyne, D., "The environment of three-year-old children: Factors related to intelligence and vocabulary tests," *Teachers Coll. Contr. Educ.*, 1929, No. 366.

38. Williams, H. M., and McFarland, M. L., "A revision of the Smith vocabulary test for preschool children, Part III. Development of language and vocabulary in young children," *Univer. Iowa Stud. Child Welf.*, 1937, 13, No. 2.

39. Thorndike, E. L., *A Teacher's Word Book*. New York: Teachers College, Columbia University, 1931.

6

Early childhood—
the preschool years

JUST AS THE STAGE of toddlerhood was characterized by the emergence of interpersonal behavior, so the next general stage of development (early childhood) may be said to be characterized by a new, central theme. This new theme, the *socialization of the child*, may be understood as the crystallization of previous growth and learning. During the period between three and six years the child makes great strides in acquiring his basic personality. In Proverbs XX:1, of the King James Bible, we find the following: "Train up a child in the way he should go: and when he is old he will not depart from it." Modern psychology confirms this old truth, that the essential aspects of the personality have been well defined by six years of age and that they tend to persist as the enduring and basic ingredients of the later adolescent and adult personality—unless very marked changes in the conditions of living encourage a radical alteration. During the preschool period the child learns basic modes of social interaction. More than this, he acquires a well defined sense of self—a *self-identity*. Thereafter he tends to act in accordance with this identity—with the way in which he perceives himself. Later on he will add still additional identities as he increases the repertoire of his behaviors, but the essential core of his self-identity will tend to persist.

We shall, therefore, begin this chapter with a discussion of this socialization process and then turn our attention to physical development, language development, the development of thinking, school adjustment, and finally to the effects of various types of physical injury and disease upon the total development of the individual.

THE SOCIALIZATION PROCESS

During the preschool years the phenomena of ambivalence are at their highest intensity. We have noted how unstable the behavior of the toddler is; he may have rejected food one day that he seemed to enjoy the previous day; he was unpredictable in many other ways. The behavior of the preschool child at the beginning of this period is similarly unpredictable, but the nature of his instability changes gradually. As he matures he begins to show more general swings between such general traits as dependence and independence, passivity and hostility, babyishness and more maturity. By the end of this period, he has learned to integrate these opposing tendencies just as he has learned to reduce his ambivalent feelings toward each of his parents. He has acquired an integrated sense of self-identity made up of opposing trends and of different identifications that he has interiorized. He has learned to reconcile and to resolve his conflicting feelings toward each of the important people in his life. In the process, a stable and effective self-identity has emerged.

Personality conflict and personality development

Dr. Eric Berne, in his book *The Mind in Action* (1), tells the following tale about a mythical land of Brschiss:

In this land there are only giants, normal-sized women, and dwarfs. The dwarf lives with a woman whom he loves and who fully returns his affection. During the day the dwarf stays with the woman while she works around the house. The day is full of happiness as these two talk and play with each other and exchange evidences of affection. But toward evening, when the giant returns from his work, things begin to be different. As the giant approaches and his heavy footsteps are heard, the dwarf somehow feels a little frightened. When the giant enters the house, the woman embraces and kisses him and then gives him all of her attention while they talk about things that are of interest to them. The poor little dwarf is neglected, meanwhile. After supper, during which the dwarf gets only divided attention, the dwarf is sent to bed. The sound of the two adults in the other room can be heard by the dwarf who is trying to go to sleep. Later, the dwarf can hear these two in their bedroom. This sequence is repeated almost every day and the dwarf begins to get confused. He loves the woman but he resents her attention and affection for the giant. He feels jealous and hostile toward the giant, even though he knows he is a good man. Soon he loses his appetite when these two are together and he may even have difficulty sleeping, even having nightmares occasionally. The giant and the woman who love their dwarf cannot understand what is troubling him, and he is unable to explain how he feels, for he is very confused about it all.

This summarized and adapted version of Berne's myth depicts graphically the core situation that is usually involved in the *oedipal problem* of the preschool child. In turn, according to psychoanalytic theory, this problem is the crucial conflict situation which has to be resolved adequately if normal personality development and appropriate socialization are to occur. Even those psychologists and anthropologists who do not accept the universality of the oedipal problem recognize its importance in most cultures (especially where the familial structure is *monogamous* and *patriarchal*) and accept the validity of the significance of the interpersonal problems involved. Let us therefore take a closer and more systematic look at this conflict situation.

According to Freud, who first developed the theory of the oedipal conflict and the dynamics of its solution, the biological maturation of the child results in a shift of the erotogenic zone to the genital region at about three years of age. This shift has involved displacement of erotic primacy from the anal zone to the new zone. There is ample evidence that both the boy and the girl experience pleasurable sensations from stimulation of this region (7). In the case of the boy, the penis and, to a lesser extent, the immediately surrounding regions are thus excitable. Similarly, in the case of the girl, the clitoris, labia, and surrounding regions can now produce pleasurable sensations when stimulated. These respective zones of the body maintain erotic primacy until about seven years of age. The *oedipal period* (or the *phallic period* as it is sometimes called, to distinguish it from true genital primacy which develops during and after puberty) thus begins at three years and ends at seven years.

When Freud first introduced his psychosexual theory, it was met with disbelief and even with disgust by some individuals. To many, it was inconceivable that little children had sex drives. The fact that such sex drives occur during this phase of development is no longer disputed, although, as we have said, some

disagree with the central importance that Freud suggested for them in terms of over-all personality development. There is evidence that children frequently ask questions about sex functions and sexual anatomy, as the common experience of most parents will attest (8). There is evidence that sexual excitability, even the possibility of orgasm, occurs during the preschool period (9, 10). It is also probably true that all children engage in some form of masturbation by rubbing the genital area or by some other means, although investigations that seek to establish the extent of such practices, usually by asking mothers whether they have observed such behavior in their children, report the percentage of occurrence as below 100 per cent (8). Moreover, it must be remembered that Freud's psychosexual theory defined sexual behavior as that which has its roots in the specific, biological sex drives but which may be manifested in the general tendencies toward *cathexes* (establishment of emotional involvement in a person or object). Sexual drives are characterized by pleasure on being discharged, and may finally be *sublimated* through diversion into socially acceptable activities.

The crux of this theory is that *phallic* sexuality in both boys and girls exerts a powerful drive toward gratification and that intense emotional relationships and frustrations are produced as a consequence. The patterns of behavior through which these drives are satisfied are a central part of the nature of interpersonal relationships during this period. Hence, this is a theory not only of sexual development, as such, but of personality development, as well.

At the beginning of the phallic period, the boy has already developed a close and satisfying relationship with his mother (or mother surrogate). He has been played with, caressed, fondled, and cared for. He has been socially and emotionally dependent upon her. Under normal circumstances, he has interiorized her wishes, has learned to adapt and conform to her ways of behaving, and so has *identified* with her. We should recall that much of this learning (for learning it surely is) has been accomplished unconsciously and has produced a satisfying way of life for the boy. We may say that the mother has become the boy's first *love object*. During the phallic period this relationship has unconscious sexual meaning to the boy and is still a very dependent relationship, even under good familial conditions in which he has not been overprotected. If the boy is to acquire an appropriate masculine role he must, however, now learn a new identification. He must learn to identify with his father. Thus, a conflict situation develops and, as we shall see, it becomes quite involved before it can be entirely solved. The solution to this problem in both interpersonal and heterosexual relations sets the pattern for subsequent interpersonal and heterosexual relations. If the problem is not solved, a *complex* results (the oedipal * complex), and accord-

ing to psychoanalytic theory predisposes the child to psychoneurotic or disturbed emotional behavior at this or some later stage. We can, perhaps, see that this conflict contains the analogue of many types of human relationships: how to relate simultaneously to two or more people, both of whom are loved.

We will recall, from our discussion in Chapter 5, that the boy has already learned to relate to his father to some extent, even before the phallic period. He has also become aware of differences in the anatomy of father and mother or of boys and girls. Awareness of sex differences in anatomy and function is most likely greater in lower-class than in middle- and upper-class children because they have more opportunity to witness sexual behavior and because the roles and clothing of little boys and girls are more clearly differentiated (11). Cultural factors may increase or diminish the severity of oedipal problems in terms of the degree to which sexual behavior is *taboo* and sexual drives are expressed or prohibited. In any case, the boy is aware that he is like his father in some respects and unlike his mother in these same factors. The father is therefore perceived as an ally and as a similar kind of human being. However, at the beginning of this period, the boy has had only a moderately intense relationship with his father who has usually not had primary responsibility for rearing or taking care of him. The relationship has involved some positive elements but has also involved strong negative elements. For although the father may have liked the boy and been

---

* Psychonalaysts prefer the term *oedipal complex* to *oedipal conflict* to describe the oedipal problems. We prefer to reserve the designation of complex to *unresolved* oedipal problems only.

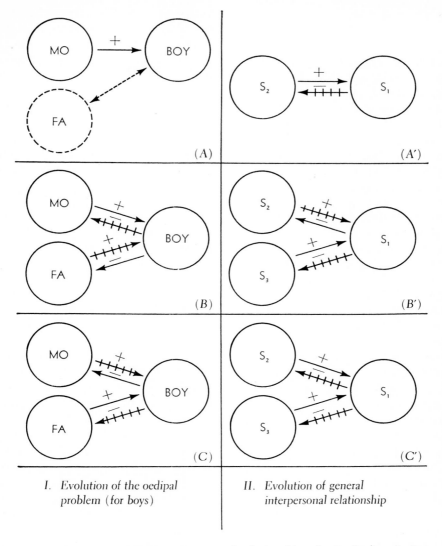

(A)

(A')

(B)

(B')

(C)

(C')

I. Evolution of the oedipal problem (for boys)

II. Evolution of general interpersonal relationship

Figure 10. Two models of interpersonal relationships. In I, the boy is first positively attracted to his mother (A), then when aware of his father still is more attracted to her than to him (B), and then positively identifies with his father (C). In II, S begins to learn to relate to two people (B') after a temporary decrease in the attraction to S_2, then learns (C') to develop realistic and positive relationships with both S_1 and S_2.

liked in return, he was not as intensely or emotionally involved in the rearing of the boy as mother was. Moreover, as the boy's erotic relationship with the mother became more intense, the father became a more likely rival, who was to be feared not only because he was bigger and stronger, but also because he might punish the son for his feelings and attitudes toward the mother.

We can see how ambivalence develops toward both mother and father: both are loved and hated, for both offer gratification and frustration. During the early part of the phallic period the boy's ambivalence toward his mother, under normal circumstances, is not very great, for he has already identified with her and perceives her primarily in positive tones. On the other hand, during this same early phase, the ambivalence toward the father is much more intense and contains strong negative elements. Eventually, the boy will learn to love both father and mother in different ways and will have reduced his ambivalence toward both, if the conditions for his personality development within the family (and outside) are favorable. In the process he will have resolved not only the oedipal conflict, but he will have learned that it is realistically possible to love someone and still have some negative feelings toward him. In short, he will have learned a most important reality principle, useful in many other life situations; namely, that love relationships involve a composite of *both* positive and negative components.

The boy tends to be fearful of the father. He is frequently literally afraid that his penis will be cut off and that he will become like a girl (who is seen by many boys as having lost her penis). Freud suggested that anxiety of this type may develop even if such threats have not been verbalized explicitly by the father. The child *acts* as though such threats are being made for he *feels* guilty about his feelings toward his mother, and he believes he ought to be punished. Such anxiety is probably increased if the father is assigned the role in the family of dispensing all punishment and if open expression of feelings is not tolerated. More often the boy's anxiety takes a less literal form. In such instances, the boy fears his body will be injured or mutilated in some way. (As we shall see later, his sense of the *intactness* of his body is not fully integrated at this stage of his development, and real or imagined threat of damage to his body may readily disturb this developing sense of body-intactness.) Sometimes his anxiety is transformed into more indirect and symbolic forms so that fears of large animals, fears of being bitten, or fears of breaking a limb become the derivative of the transposed anxiety. Because Freud believed that all of these fears had their roots in the boy's apprehension that his father would cut his penis off in punishment for having sexual drives, these behaviors were termed *castration anxiety*.

It is interesting to note that, even in modern society in which there is less moral prudery and suppression than in former days, the development of children's fears, as reported by child psychologists, offers interesting confirmatory evidence of Freud's theory. We would expect, according to this theory, that children's anxieties would first result predominantly in *separation* fears (during the oral and anal periods), and later result in *castration* types of fears (during the phallic period). Recent research indicates that prior to age four children's fears are predominantly those of being left alone, being abandoned, being kidnapped, and the like, whereas from about four years of age on, and especially after five years, the predominant fears are of being bitten, being attacked by large animals, suffering bodily harm, and of dying. It is very rare to find a child who is entirely free of these respective types of fears during these stages of development.

The solution to the oedipal problem depends upon repression of the boy's sexual longings for his mother, a partial renunciation of his identification with her, a new identification with his father, and finally an integration of the two iden-

Playing the role of the engineer of a freight train is fun. (U. of Mich.)

tities (with mother and father) into a suitable identity as a boy-man. This is a long and gradual process, with many "ups" and "downs," and with only a partial solution, in our culture, until early adulthood. The reason for the delay in its final resolution is that our society prevents the assumption of a fully adult role (including a marriage partner and the procreation of children) until the individual is economically (not necessarily psychologically) responsible and independent. During the oedipal period the boy will often rebel against his mother (or other females), he will once again show streaks of negativism toward her, or he may act inexplicably distant from her. He will sometimes try to oppose his father and will often try to compete with him. These periods of "acting out" should be understood for what they really are: attempts at mastery of the slowly emerging masculine role. The father can be especially helpful if, first, he is available to the youngster, and if he encourages him in trying out his new masculine role. Boys love to pretend to be "big" and "strong" and "brave." They love to go out with father and "act like a man." If these attempts are respected for what they are (partial trials at assuming a masculine role) and if the culture permits or assists the youngster in assuming a clearly defined male role, progress through the oedipal period is greatly encouraged. Often children will idealize cowboys, sheriffs, "space men," and other heroes and act out in play their need to be masculine and powerful. Boys, particularly those in the lower-middle and lower classes, will sometimes, either clandestinely or openly, compare and discuss the size and power of their penises. They will often engage in games of a phallic nature, playing "doctor," seeing who can urinate longer or for a greater distance, and the like.

This period is marked by intense curiosity, exploratory interests, and creativity. Intellectual activity shares in the total growth of the child toward maturity and assists him in reaching appropriate solutions. Children often seem "wise beyond their years," ask provoking and provocative questions, and master new experiences with astonishing rapidity. They love to wander about the neighborhood, exploring new places and things, and sometimes set out on explorations away from home—much to the anguish of the parents. All of these are signs, in part, of the healthy, surging vitality associated with phallic sexuality. Most good nursery schools capitalize on these interests and emerging capacities and put them fully to use. The hallmark of intellectual activity during this period, as we shall see later in our discussion of the development of thinking, is *integration*. Through previous experience and abetted by current curiosity and initiative, the "pieces" of knowledge which have been previously amassed are woven together into new and complex concepts and insights.

As we have said, the normal child gradually renounces his oedipal interest in his mother and identifies with his father. However, such progress assumes that familial conditions are satisfactory for growth. When favorable conditions do not obtain, the process of working through the oedipal problems becomes vastly more complicated and an *oedipal complex* may result. Such a complex means that the child has become fixated at the oedipal level and that he has retained most or all of his psychosexual attachment upon his mother (although he may be unconscious of this). We may note a number of specific conditions that contribute to the development of an oedipal complex. The first of these is the development of excessive anxiety in the child during previous stages of maturation. Such anxieties will have retarded emotional growth and have made the child less capable of dealing with current oedipal problems. Contrariwise, healthy and effective emotional growth during previous stages makes it much simpler for the child to weather the usual storms of the oedipal period. A second important condition is that of emotional disturbance on the part of either mother or father. Such disturbances may vary in type and intensity and thus contribute in varying degrees to the child's difficulties during this normally difficult period for him. A third general condition is that of inadequate acceptance of the mother (female) role by mother and of the father (male) role by father. When each of the parents does not exhibit in his daily personality manifestations clear-cut characteristics of his respective role, it becomes more difficult for the youngster to identify and to reconcile these two roles in himself. As we have said, the boy must learn to identify with his father, but he must also have previously identified with his mother; now, he must attain a clear self-conception as a male while still retaining some of the positive features of his previous female identification. (Parenthetically, it might be noted that no child has only androgen components—male hormones—or only estrogen components—female hormones—but has a combination of both. Typically, the male has more androgens and the female has more estrogens.) Finally, a fourth kind of difficulty is the absence or unavailability of the parent of the same sex during the critical period for identification with that parent. Substitutes, such as siblings, grandparents, and relatives, cannot as easily fulfill the identity needs during these important stages of personality development.

The resolution of oedipal problems in the case of the girl is more complicated and consequently takes a longer period of time. Whereas the boy had the relatively simpler problem of giving up his identification with his mother and learning to identify with his father, the girl has an additional step—and a most difficult one. After having identified with her father she still has to learn to reidentify with her mother. This means that she has to modify or renounce her boyish (phallic) traits and return to a feminine role which, in our culture, and also to some extent biologically, is a more passive or receptive type of role than that of the male. This is not only difficult because it involves another step in identification, but also because many of the consequences of the previous step involved considerable pleasure: erotic attachment to father, ability to express rebellion and aggression in tom-boyish activities, feel-

ings of mastery associated with gross muscular activity. Moreover, unlike the boy whose phallic excitement is focused in the penis during both the oedipal period and during later periods of development, the girl has to learn to obtain sexual gratification from the vagina (when she grows up) rather than from the clitoris (which is focal during the oedipal period). Perhaps the complexity of these problems helps to explain why girls' emotional attachments to their mothers, following the oedipal phase of development, is so much more intense than boys' attachments to their fathers; the girls' emotional experiences become more intense because, in part, of the longer and more intense learning experiences that they have.

One of the recurrent questions that is raised about the girls' psychosexual problems is whether girls experience castration anxiety. The most probable answer is that they do even though they do not have a penis to lose. The reason for such types of anxiety is that many girls worry about the fact that they do not have a penis * (and research as well as clinical evidence indicates that this is frequently the case), they worry that they might have been "damaged" because they were bad, and they do not yet have some obvious and distinguishing sexual characteristics (such as the later full development of breasts) which can compensate for

* This type of anxiety in girls is referred to as *penis envy*. Boys have a type of anxiety, somewhat comparable to this, that is known as *breast envy*.

their feelings of "loss." Research evidence on girls' fears indicates that their fears during the oedipal period involve castration types of anxiety although such fears may not be as intense or widespread as in the case of boys.

The development of a self-identity

If we stop to reflect about ourselves we are usually able to make some very specific statements about "what" and "who" we are. As adults, each of us believes in his own unique personality. We "know" that we are fearful or brave, that we are well or poorly coordinated, that we have much or little self-confidence in certain kinds of situations, that we are usually depressed or usually content, that we are slow- or fast-witted, and so on. This perception of what we are, of the usual roles we assign to ourselves, has not only a uniqueness but also a continuity. We are the same person we were an hour ago, two years ago, a decade ago, even though some things about us may have changed in the interim. Further, we expect others to recognize this continuity and basic integrity in our self-identity; we expect others to anticipate that we will behave in characteristic ways. In fact, without such a characteristic self-identity we would feel lost, fragmented, and helpless.

As we shall see, the nature of our self-identity greatly influences not only what we are but what we anticipate doing. We act in terms of our sense of identity and we attempt to retain a consistent self-image, strongly resisting change in this respect. Yet the fact is that this coherent,

Socialization and the differentiation of roles in group play. (U. of Mich.)

organized sense of self developed in us very gradually over many years before it became stabilized; and even though stability is finally achieved, the sense of self, even in adulthood, continues to change slightly in the course of normal development and further experience. A focal period in the development of the sense of self-identity, which had its roots in infancy and reaches a stable position only with adulthood, is that of the preschool years.

The development of the "self" began when the infant had his first awareness of himself as being different from the rest of the world. In the beginning, this sense of difference was extremely vague and diffuse. As his biological needs failed to be gratified promptly or adequately the infant began to become dimly conscious of a "me" that had tensions and some "not-me" that usually reduced these tensions but occasionally did not. Thus, we can see that the first glimmering of a self-identity was formed on the basis of frustrations which helped the infant to distinguish between his body (or bodily tensions) and "something out there" which was not part of the body. Some psychoanalysts believe that the first localization of the self is in the mouth, and partially in the hands, which serve as avenues of sensory communication during this early period (12). Gradually, very gradually in fact, the young child becomes aware of his body, in a very gross and undifferentiated sense, and later of things that are not part of his body. Still later, he becomes aware of *differentiated* feelings within the body. It is at this stage that *localization* of the self within the body begins to emerge. When young children

are asked where they "are," they tend to point to a circumscribed region on the body surface, such as the chin or the nose or the abdomen (13). Other parts of the body which have not been so identified with the "me" may be accepted as belonging to "me" but they are not "me." (In contrast, adults, in the same study, when asked "where are you?" characteristically pointed to the head.) Schilder has proposed that the gradually increasing and gradually more differentiated perception of the body forms the core of the development of the sense of self (14).

The next general step in the development of the sense of a self-identity probably involves an awareness of the inside of the body as differentiated from the outside. As sensory development proceeds, and increasingly more accurate perceptions of others become possible, the individual learns to distinguish between the outside and inside of the body. The interior of the body is then understood in terms of the child's experience with the interiors of things that he has seen (15). These may be interiors of toys or other objects or may be the interiors of animals or insects. Only as the child becomes increasingly sophisticated about his own exterior anatomy and experiences internal pain which can be localized can he gradually learn to differentiate various internal parts of the body. A somewhat more accurate perception of the interior will take a long time and considerably more knowledge than the child has at this stage.

During these early stages, the child has been learning to interiorize the demands of his mother (or of others who have had major responsibility for his care). Soon he begins to act the way she would like him to, even when she is not present. As we have already noted, this identification occurs at both a conscious and unconscious level. The model of his mother's behavior (as exemplified in her prohibitions, especially) is thus the first external model that is incorporated. When this has occurred, the child feels that "this is what I want to do." In turn, he feels that "this is the way I am." He now has the rudiments of a self-identity that exists in *time* as well as in *space*. For now, he knows how he will behave at different times, and he has acquired some sense of continuity. However, some indication of how rudimentary this sense of continuity is may be gleaned from the fact that he will be greatly disturbed by abrupt changes in clothes—in himself as well as in others—for he becomes confused over his sense of identity. He will sometimes express great concern over the fact that someone whom he has previously seen wearing an overcoat now appears before him without the coat, and he will wonder out loud whether it is the same person. Sometimes he will respond with terror at having his hair cut, not so much because of castration fears (which may sometimes be the cause) as because he no longer will be the same person without his usual hair. He tries desperately to hang on to his rudimentary sense of continuity in himself and in others!

It is during this same period that he begins to worry about the *intactness* of his body. Probably, the emergence of castration anxiety during the early stages of the oedipal period and the unstable sense of self jointly contribute to fears of mutilation. During ages four and five, especially, children worry a great deal about "hurts," broken legs, fingernails (in themselves and in their dolls), and broken objects. These fears are so intense during these stages that operative procedures that can be delayed because they are not urgent (and we are thinking especially about tonsillectomies which may have profound psychological impact upon the youngster at this time) should be postponed when possible, or should be counteracted by ample emotional preparation and support (16). Fears about dying and about death may also emerge at this time. Here again, emotional support for the fear (accepting the fear as valid but not becoming alarmed over it), together with simple, straightforward, and accurate explanation, may help the child not only to master the fear but also to become more assured with respect to the essential intactness of his own body.

During the later stages of the oedipal period, the child begins to adopt a truly socialized role, as he identifies with the appropriate role for which he is suited biologically and socially. A boy, for example, interiorizes the social roles which his father, his brother, his uncle, and others portray. The more clear-cut and acceptable these roles are the more stable is his sense of self-identity (17). He needs experience in portraying these roles so that he can learn to discriminate them more accurately and to use them more consistently. During this stage children will often fantasy themselves as a "superman" as part of their attempts at mastery. Indeed, sometimes they will refuse to admit they are not, in fact, the very "superman" they are playing, nor should this distinction be forced upon them too rapidly. Their own emerging experience and frustrations will teach them the truth, and they will have learned more in the process through self-discovery.

By the end of the oedipal period the process of development of a self-identity will have produced a substantial degree of superego development. In the normal youngster, this will mean that he has acquired sufficient internalized, inhibitory controls to be able to function, most of the time, in a fairly responsible social role. He will have learned a certain respect for the authority of others and he will have acquired techniques for co-operating with others. He will still need to be given definite limits with respect to what he can do, for his judgment about reality factors is far from fully adequate, but he will be able to manage himself in common, ordinary situations. He will experience some guilt when he has overstepped the limits, but if his superego development is not too extreme or too rigid, his guilt will be transient and produce only temporary anxiety. Through the internalization of a superego, he will have become a *social being* rather than just a *behaving organism.*

Of course, all youngsters during the preschool period will experience occasional doubts about the adequacy of their self-identity. They will meet situations for which they are still ill-prepared and with which they cannot cope adequately.

Under such circumstances, they will tend to resort to fantasy. When their real companions are frustrating or when their elders expect more than can be accomplished, they will imagine other youngsters or other elders who will meet their needs more easily. In these fantasy activities, youngsters will sometimes seem to believe in the reality of the fantasy, and they will sometimes "lie" when confronted with the more harsh reality. It should be clearly understood that a child's belief in his fantasy and his denial of reality is usually a perfectly normal phenomenon; it is part of the way of making the business of growing up some-

Preschool children like to assume the adult roles they observe. (U. of Mich.)

what more tolerable. Certainly up to the age of about five years, such fantasies and disregard of truth or reality probably occur occasionally in the majority of children, although accurate research data on this problem are lacking. It may be best to "play the game" with the youngster, giving him time to accept his own reality and the reality of his circumstances, rather than confronting him with his untruths or punishing him for his somewhat autistic behavior. By the age of six or seven, he will have given up his confusion between fantasy and reality and be more able to accept his own self-identity with its limitations. He will still engage in fantasy, and use it as a fertile source for ideas, but he will have become consistent in his discrimination of such behavior from that of reality behavior. Only when the child continues to employ fantasy excessively and is unable to distinguish it from reality, during the primary grades, should concern be felt about the possible psychopathological nature of this behavior. If such is the case, careful psychological study of the youngster and appropriate mental hygiene measures for him or his family, or both, may be advisable.*

Affective phenomena and growth

The discussion up to this point has clearly emphasized the role of emotions, conflict, and anxiety in growth. All of us

* A comprehensive review of the literature on *body-image* (which is roughly equivalent to the concept of self-identity) and a summary of their own research in this area will be found in Fisher and Cleveland's recent book (18).

are aware, in a general way, that our emotions, or the way we feel, have something to do with our growth patterns. In this section, we should like to document this general and valid belief with more specific evidence, and get to understand the interrelationship of affective behavior and growth more fully. We have already alluded to the highly significant effects of frustration and deprivation in infancy, in Chapters 2 and 4. We were able to see that when such conditions led to severe anxiety the child was likely to be greatly retarded in growth, learning, and adjustmental capacities.

A number of important studies bearing on the present question have been conducted at the Fels Research Institute. In one of these, Baldwin investigated the relationship of three general factors in the home upon the behavior of children in nursery school (19). The three factors, *democratic behavior, indulgence,* and *emotional warmth* are composites of ratings of parent behavior which had been shown to have fundamental importance for child-parent interactions. (See, in this connection, our discussion of these factors in Chapter 3.) The interrelationships of each of these three factors of parental behavior, and of these factors in various combinations, were studied in terms of the consequences for child behavior as rated in the nursery-school situation. The 56 children studied ranged in age from three to five years. It was found, as other studies have found, that a democratic home atmosphere usually went together with a home that was high in emotional warmth. Moreover, such a combination of factors was correlated with behavior in children that was socially outgoing, that was attractive to other children, and that was "high on activities demanding intellectual curiosity, originality, and constructiveness." On the other hand, indulgence (or, more accurately, overindulgence) was associated with physical apprehension and lack of skill in muscle activities. Although the study could not entirely separate each of the three main factors from the others and was not entirely successful in controlling for other relevant factors, its results were highly indicative of the significance on emotional behavior of conditions of the home climate (parent behavior), and of the consequences of the emotional state of the child for the type of growth pattern that emerged.

In another series of studies by Olson and his associates there was convincing evidence of the influence of emotional behavior on *all* aspects of the growth of the child (20). In these studies, Olson was first able to demonstrate that ". . . in all growth there is an underlying unity which is expressed in the various structures and functions that are measured." (We shall have further reference to this finding in a later section of this chapter.) From these findings he developed his concept of *organismic age*, a "central maturational tempo over time." This meant that although the various components making up the total growth varied in different individuals and at different times, growth tended to go up or to go down together, on an over-all basis. He then found that *anomalies* in growth, that is, deviations in the growth of behavior or of structures, occurred when there were disturbances in emotional

adjustment. In a specific test of this general conclusion, Mechem studied the relationship between the *affective* state and specific aspects of growth as well as of general or organismic growth (21). In this elaborative study, children were rated through interviews in terms of their positive or negative affective state. For example, one point was given for each response indicative of happiness or contentment. The central finding was that "substantial relationships . . . [were] found between changes in affective state and growth." Although the most significant relationships were found for reading age and mental age, *all* aspects of growth (including weight, dental age, and the like) tended to be affected by this state.

Over the past few years, a great number of studies have been made of the relationship between the amount and types of anxiety and the learning of various forms of behavior. The effects of anxiety are quite variable depending upon the intensity of the anxiety, the amount of ego involvement of the subject in the task, the *prior* anxiety state of the subject, and the like, but the overriding conclusion is inescapable: anxiety is intimately related to effectiveness of functioning and to the rate and amount of learning. The authors of the present volume have shown, elsewhere, that severe anxiety, especially during the very early and formative years, may have a crippling effect upon total personality development and may result in a predisposition to *psychosis* (insanity) or in actual personality breakdown (22). Hebb has pointed out that extreme emotional behavior (especially extreme negative emotional behavior) has a disruptive and disorganizing effect upon productivity and upon personal effectiveness (23).

It seems reasonable to conclude, in the light of our present knowledge, that although a child will profit from stimulation and mild degrees of frustration, which serve as motivators for effective growth and adjustment, extreme or continued frustration has a highly adverse effect upon these phenomena. This does not mean, it must be emphasized, that the child should be indulged or should be undisciplined, for such conditions also produce an unfavorable climate for healthy growth. Rather, the implication is that emotional security results from the conditions that favor rather consistent and pleasurable conflict solution, and that, in turn, such positive affective states facilitate effective growth and adjustment.

Social adjustment—relations to siblings and other children

We shall now consider how the total home climate affects adjustment and how the child inter-reacts with siblings and other children. It is assumed that how the child relates to other children is essentially a function of (is caused by) the child's personality (assuming a constancy in the characteristics of the other children, for the moment), but it must be recognized that the gratifications and frustrations the child experiences in his relations with other children also influence the further development of his personality.

There have been many studies of the effects of the home climate, most of them studies of the relationships of this factor to the child's adjustment in nursery school and in kindergarten. We have already referred to the studies of the Fels Research Institute which have traced the relationships of democratic, warm, and indulgent home atmospheres on some aspects of child behavior. We will also recall that, in Chapter 3, we discussed the relationships of early patterns of child-rearing to developments in the child's personality. From these and other studies we have gained the conviction that a secure home climate, one in which there is democratic discipline (acceptance of the needs of the child together with recognition of the needs of others), one in which there is warmth (emotional sensitivity and responsiveness to the child's needs), and one in which there is appropriate discipline, leads to a secure emotional development in the child. During the preschool period such security manifests itself in outgoing, cooperative but sometimes quarrelsome behavior, high intellectual curiosity, aggressive behavior (increasingly more appropriately so with progression in age), and physically secure behavior, together with increasing interest in making and maintaining social contacts with other children. These general conclusions have been borne out in extensive studies by MacFarlane who found, for example, that when a home was marked by the presence of a marked number of unfavorable features (from a psychological viewpoint), the child was

Fear may be conquered by the supporting presence of an adult. (Merrill Palmer)

likely to develop problem behavior (of many different kinds), whereas when there was a good home climate, or only one or two unfavorable features, the child was not likely to have such problems (24). Among the most significant unfavorable home features was that of marital discord, by which was meant emotional insecurity in one or both parents. In turn, marital discord led to other un-favorable characteristics of the home. Not only behavior is affected by home climate; there is considerable evidence that poor home climate influences general attitudes toward others and specific attitudes toward many social problems. For example, it was learned that when parents are *authoritarian*, children tend to develop strong ethnic bias (25). An authoritarian home is likely to be found

179

where there is insecurity or instability in the home climate; that is, authoritarianism is itself an effect of emotionally unsatisfactory conditions.

It should be noted that the characteristic democratic or authoritarian home atmosphere is largely independent of cultural practice. Even in those cultures in which strict discipline is practiced, homes vary in the degree to which they are either democratic or authoritarian, depending in large measure on the personality characteristics of the parents. Moreover, the emotionally insecure parent who merely consciously tries to be democratic does not succeed in developing or maintaining a democratic atmosphere (24). Home climate is more a matter of emotional security than anything else, even though it may vary in terms of socioeconomic and cultural conditions.

Among the home conditions, one of the features that may vary even when other conditions are constant is the number of children present. The number of children, their age spread, and the distribution by sex have an influence on the child's relationships with other children. The typical American family is small, the number of children varying inversely, in general, with the socioeconomic status of the family. Although the behavior of each child is largely determined, in the first place, by the nature of his relationship with the mother, later by his relationships with the father as well as the mother, and by the characteristics of the home climate that the parents develop, this behavior is also affected by the or-

dinal position and the total configuration of the siblings. As we have noted, older children tend to become jealous of "the new baby" and often regress in behavior when they feel more attention is being paid to the newcomer or when they feel that their previous status in the family is jeopardized. The youngest child tends to be more striving and outgoing. Other things being equal, the older child will be more likely to become jealous if he is a more dependent type of individual. Although there is no inevitability about it, an only child is more likely to become a problem child than a child who has siblings (26). Of course, there are many reasons why a family has only one child, some of these reasons being related to the personality characteristics of the parents, and it is not only the condition of being an only child that determines how the child will develop. The finding is nevertheless of significance and suggests that only children are more likely to be overindulged or overprotected (or through compensation because of parental fears in this connection, dealt with too austerely), and hence to develop certain personality problems.

Having older siblings in the family offers many possible advantages. Among these are: the availability of playmates and "protectors," the availability of models of behavior in siblings who have proved successful in meeting certain situations, a sense of family strength and family loyalty, the possibility of cooperative activities which may offset competitive drives, the possibility of learning adjustments to both sexes and of adjustment to small groups, at an earlier age. However, it should be repeated that if family conditions are unfavorable none of these advantages may obtain.* It is also clear that, aside from the conditions suggested, family size in itself has no *consistent* influence upon personality development. Rather, family size tends to increase the operation of factors *already present*. In other words, the way in which the size of the family is most likely to influence personality development of the child is already present in the personality characteristics and behavior of the parents. For instance, parents who have high status needs are more likely to have fewer children and focus more attention upon them, subjecting them to special kinds of pressures. As another example, large families are more likely to delegate matters of disciplinary control to older siblings, but such attribution of discipline was already part of the characteristics of the parents who were likely to have large families (27). Hence, in each family, the specific attributes of the parents and the specific ways in which they relate to or have needs involving their children must be evaluated if appropriate meaning is to be assigned to the influence of the family constellation.

During the preschool period children are likely to form their first friendships, sometimes as early as the third year and sometimes later. It has been learned that friendships are likely to be based on similarities in such factors as age, sex, type of social behavior, and type of physical skill. This means that children who are reasonably similar in such character-

* Indeed, in the case of Henry, described in Chapter 1, the presence of siblings provoked and increased Henry's feelings of insecurity and his aggressive behavior.

The four-year-old plays at gardening; the ten-year-old gardens. (U. of Mich.)

istics tend to play together and form emotional bonds more than those who are dissimilar in these things. In the beginning of the preschool period, friendships are few and transient. With increase in age, however, friendships become somewhat more enduring and certainly become much more intense (27). All children quarrel frequently with each other, at times. There may be sudden and apparently inexplicable shifts in the patterns of relationships, so that what was at one moment a very friendly play situation suddenly becomes a hectic argument the next. Two general conclusions of research in this area should be emphasized: one is that children who tend to get along better with each other, as compared with those who do not, are more stable emotionally and are more cooperative (even pliant) in their relationships with adults (29); the other is that while cooperation and competition alternate rapidly in the emotional relationships of preschool children, the preponderance of one over the other is clearly associated

181

with cultural patterns of behavior in which children live (30). The first of these conclusions points up, once again, the basic importance of home conditions for behavior outside the home, whereas the second points up how cultural factors affect the way in which drives are expressed. As a specific example of the last point, we can indicate that when the culture provides play materials in the nursery school or neighborhood, which because of their characteristics (such as large size, imitation of social mores requiring group participation, and the like) promote cooperative activities, then competitive behavior is diminished, and aggressive drives are channelized through group rather than individual goals (31).

PHYSICAL DEVELOPMENT

In physical development, too, the child comes into his own during the preschool years. By the time he reaches six years of age his body proportions are about what they will be when he is an adult, his motor controls are adequate for all but fine motor coordinations, he has a freedom and rhythm of movement which parallels his sense of self-identity and self-assurance, and he is basically able to take care of himself in very many, if not most, physical skill areas.

Although a great deal of physical development depends on maturation (just how much is still uncertain), increasingly more of it depends on training, both implicit and explicit. As we have already seen, the nature of the child's affective life influences his physical development. Additionally, the specific opportunities and encouragement he is given affect the course of this development. Moreover, the attitudes of the "important people in his life," notably his parents, his close relatives, and his teachers, will mold and condition the rate and character of many aspects of physical development. Therefore, it may be said with considerable justification that during the preschool years the child begins to *learn* to use his body in making an active adjustment to his environment.

Gross physical development during this period, in terms of such measures as height and weight, slows down considerably from the rate of gain shown in the previous years. For instance, the child will usually gain about nine inches or less in height during the three-year span from three to six years of age. It will be remembered that he gained more than this during the first two years and almost as much as this in the first year alone! In fact, the rate of growth has slowed down in such gross characteristics by about two thirds! At the same time, other aspects of growth development proceed at a relatively constant or even increasing rate. Muscle development and increase in muscle weight are very rapid during this period; capacities for physical endurance increase sufficiently to enable the child to maintain physical exertion for long periods of time and to decrease his needs for sleep time.

Not only is there variability among the several aspects of physical development, as we have emphasized in Chapter 4, but there is also variability or unevenness in the rate of development of any single

aspect. This truth has often been obscured by the normative charts or tables
of development. In such statistical tables
showing the average figures for each year
in a single physical characteristic, there
appears to be a smooth, continuous
growth in whatever physical characteristic is being portrayed. Reflection will
show why this is the case. Such tables are
based on the averages of measures obtained on *cross-sections* of the population, and such averages smooth out (or
cover) the individual variations shown
in the actual *longitudinal* growth in some
physical characteristic of an individual
child. The fact is that the actual growth
curve for any such characteristic for a
given child is uneven rather than smooth.
One of the best ways of demonstrating
as well as emphasizing this conclusion

is to plot the amount *above* or *below* the
average which a given characteristic
shows for a particular child over a period
of years. Such data are now available for
a number of physical features and we
shall discuss one set of findings, as typical, from the Fels Research Institute (32).

Figure 11 was constructed by Sontag,
of the Fels Research Institute Staff, by
determining how this particular child's
weight compared with the weight of
other children of the same sex at each
age from birth to ten years. Then, the
child's weight was given a variability
score for each age. This variability score
indicates the amount by which the child

Figure 11. *Weight of an individual in terms of variability units, from birth
to ten years.*

Adapted from data in Sontag, W. L., *The Fels Research Institute for the Study of
Human Development.* Yellow Springs, Ohio: Antioch College, 1946.

differs from the average in terms of a statistical unit of measurement known as the *standard deviation*. Reference to the figure will indicate that at birth this child's weight was almost two standard deviation units below the average of other children at that time. (The maximum possible variation in standard deviation units is approximately from +3 through zero to −3 units.) However, at age one year, this same child was exactly at the average for his age (since the deviation is zero). Thus, within the first year this child's weight shifted from far below average to just average. It will further be noted that after one year of age and until ten years of age the child was consistently above the average in weight for his age. Nevertheless, during this period of nine years, his weight varied from a maximum of almost +2 standard deviation units (actually +1.9), at ten years, to a minimum of only about +1.0 standard deviation units (actually +0.8), at seven years. Thus, in terms of *variability units*, the child's relative position or status with respect to weight was constantly changing. Of course, not all children show as much irregularity as does this illustrative case, but all children do show some irregularity. A *perfectly smooth growth curve is only a fiction of statistical abstraction!*

We commented earlier on the slowing-down in the rate of growth in height and weight. It may be pertinent to indicate that many studies have shown, contrary to popular belief, that neither of these measures, by itself, is indicative of the health status or of capacity for resisting disease of a child (33). Rather, the significance of either height or weight for such factors can only be evaluated in the light of the specific meaning these figures have for the particular child—and this requires competent medical judgment. Fortunately, the formerly popular fad of comparing the child's height and weight to tables of averages seems to be on the wane.

The rapid development of the musculature during the preschool years

Play on the jungle gym encourages physical development. (Merrill Palmer)

makes possible the development of good, adult-like physical controls during this period. By the age of four years, according to Gesell and Ilg, the child can throw a ball overhand, he can draw a circle and a square, he can use his arms in running, can cut on a straight line with a pair of scissors, can use a handsaw, and can engage in fairly rhythmical and graceful movements (34). He has lost his infant-like and his toddler-like motor characteristics and has begun to behave like an adult, to some extent. By the age of six years he has further developed gross and fine motor skills and has acquired a sense of physical security which realistically parallels his actual accomplishments. Now he can balance easily, can ride a tricycle (or sometimes a bicycle), and skip and jump smoothly, can draw a straight line easily, can jump rope, can engage in many carpentry and cooking activities, can build elaborate buildings with blocks, and can carry a glass of water without spilling any of the contents. Skill in fine motor coordination is now rapidly responsive to appropriate training (35). The youngster loves to help around the house, if mother or father is patient with him and teaches him to have fun while helping out. This is a good time to differentiate the sex roles by having the boy do some things with the father and the girl do others with the mother. Effective if limited use of children in helpful activities in the home is also important to their sense of belonging to the family. Moreover, helping with home activities enables the youngster to develop a self-identity appropriate to his age level and to develop a sense of responsibility. Too much skill

and care, of course, must not be expected from the youngster in the beginning when he first attempts such chores. Nor should the goal be to relieve the mother (or father) of some of the work—although this will be the ultimate outcome under favorable conditions. Rather, the goal should be to help the youngster mature through increasingly greater and more responsible participation in the appropriate roles of family living—and to have fun while doing so.

As the child develops his skills in physical coordination and seems to become ever more ebullient or even tumultuous in his behavior, with an apparently inexhaustible supply of energy, he also, paradoxically, requires less sleep. By six years of age he will only need about eleven hours of sleep (and this includes time spent in bed before he actually falls asleep), whereas some three years previous he needed at least one or perhaps two hours more sleep each night (34). As with all other norms, those just given for sleep should be regarded as statistical averages, and not as guides for an individual child. Children vary greatly in their requirements for sleep, and a particular child will show considerable variability in the number of hours he sleeps on succeeding nights. The parents should expect neither consistency in the amount of sleep from one day to the next, nor conformity to the norms. However, a gradual reduction in amount of sleep needed by the child may be expected as he moves through this preschool period.

A final word relating to physical development should be appended. During the preschool stage, children are more prone to a variety of physical illnesses, especially respiratory illnesses, than they will be during the rest of their childhood development (35). It is important that the child have periodic medical check-ups as preventive or precautionary measures. It is equally important that such check-ups and the attitudes toward the usual illnesses not be endowed with too great emotional meaning or concern. Such attitudes toward illness may leave more lasting imprints on the child, both physically and emotionally, than the actual illnesses themselves. We feel that this problem is of such great importance that we shall devote an entire section of this chapter to it, after we have discussed other aspects of development during this period.

LANGUAGE DEVELOPMENT

There is nothing especially remarkable about language development during the preschool years, but language does come more fully into its own during this period as a social skill. As we have seen, language served autistic ends in infancy when the child's first vocalizations and babblings served to satisfy his inner needs. As the infant developed he learned to use words, usually nouns, to obtain responses from his invironment; that is, he learned to make his needs known to others and to obtain some gratification of these needs in the process. In this process, although the first glimmerings of

the social use of language could be detected, language was still not being used to control the behavior of others, except in the limited sense of getting others to administer to one's immediate needs. Far less was language being used during this stage to respond to the needs, requests, or demands of others. Nevertheless, the child was learning the meaning of a wide variety of words, beginning to use them *as* sentences and then later *in* sentences of a rudimentary sort, and forming the groundwork for the use of *inflective, conceptual,* and *socially communicative* language. During toddlerhood, as we have seen, a large percentage of language was egocentric in many types of situations, but increasingly, language was being used in social settings and for purposes of social communication.

It is during the preschool period that the "miracle" of language becomes manifest. For, unlike all other species, so far as we know, in the human animal language becomes a truly social tool and serves many ends. The child learns to communicate his complex feelings and motivations to others, he uses language to solve problems he formerly solved by physical means, he substitutes thinking about problems for trial-and-error attempts at their solution, and he remembers, generalizes, and reproduces former experiences through words and applies them in the context of the present situation. Language becomes a means of understanding his environment (such as knowing the wishes of his parents and his playmates), of gaining further information about the world of people and events, and of acquiring other intellectual skills (such as reasoning, number concepts, time concepts, and the like). Above all, language becomes part of the pattern of complex social living, being influenced by social environment and, in turn, exerting its influence upon this social environment.

During the early part of the preschool period, most children enjoy language play. They seem to love to ask countless questions (even when they know the answers). They seem to enjoy hearing themselves talk and improve in their mastery over talking experiences. These uses of language continue to occupy a prominent position during the remainder of the preschool years, but they are gradually replaced by other uses (36).

It is during the latter part of the preschool period that the social function of language becomes most conspicuous. It is then, for example, that language is used in relating to others. Children ask the names of their playmates, inquire what they want to do or tell them what to do, and engage in the social task of accommodating themselves to others by means of language. Soon words and expressions become the means of expressing common social conventions and of managing social events. Words have *emotional loadings*, some connoting "good" things and others "bad" ones. Even ways of expressing oneself are "good" or "bad," not necessarily in terms of any intrinsic values, but in terms of social usage. Language thus becomes the carrier of a large part of the culture and is used to transmit this culture to others.

There is considerable evidence that language development, although it may be a good index of the intelligence of the individual under certain conditions, is significantly influenced by a variety of social factors (37). In general, social conditions that insure emotional security and social interaction facilitate language development, whereas conditions of deprivation, inconsistency, and rejection retard it (37, 38). According to the psychoanalytic point of view, a central factor in these social conditions is the nature of the child-parent relationships and particularly the freedom permitted the child to express and explore forms of behavior based on his developing phallic drives (39). When children are exposed to puritanical, rigid, and repressive environments during this period, they have difficulty not only in working through their oedipal problems but also in exploring their environments, expressing their emotions, and in maintaining an inquisitive and curious attitude toward the world around them. In the general repression that takes place as a consequence of such parental behavior, language development is also inhibited. Moreover, as we noted in the previous chapters, regression to anal modes of adaptation, with their hostile derivatives, encourages delay in giving up infantile speech and may result in blocking and stuttering of speech (40). We should point out that not only obviously repressive environments retard language development; even environments that fail to accept or tolerate children's inquisitiveness may produce some of the same effect. When mothers are too rushed to give adequate time to the "pestering questions" of their youngsters, or when nursery-school teachers have too large a group to supervise or have too much responsibility to allow for patient toleration of youngsters' repeated questions, both linguistic development and emotional responsiveness may be slowed down. This may be the reason for the findings in one study that although the kindergarten child is ". . . essentially a self-assertive individual . . . he reveals only slight evidence of intellectual curiosity and little interest" in more than the simplest forms of thinking (41). *Mass educational programs may retard spontaneity and growth through such subtle suppression.*

Other factors may influence language development. Among these socioeconomic status and the correlated emphasis upon language which such status involves is significant. The upper and middle classes show superior linguistic skills over the lower class, even when due allowance is made for differences in intelligence (37). A likely explanation for this finding is that better linguistic models and more reward value for good language are found in the higher socioeconomic groups; lower groups are superior in some other skills as we noted in earlier chapters. Another factor which leads to relatively slower language development is a bilingual background (37). However, this finding should be considered to have many reservations, since most studies of language of children from bilingual homes failed to control for many other salient factors. In some of these homes there was not only bilingualism but also inferior socioeconomic status and inferior language usage by both parents and siblings. Moreover,

failure to take into account the age at which the child was exposed to a second language and how well established the first language was as part of the child's skills leave the general conclusion about the effect of bilingual background open to question. It is possible that bilingual background may, under certain circumstances, not only *not* hinder but even improve language development. It is largely when the introduction of the second language produces confusion, because more than one verbal symbol has a given meaning, that retardation in language may result (42).

Some of the most extensive studies of language development have focused their attention on growth in vocabulary. Before discussing the general findings in this area, we should consider briefly what a *word* means. A *word* is only a symbol that stands for something by virtue of the fact that, for one or more reasons, culture has assigned a particular meaning to it. Moreover a word is likely to have not only more than one meaning (consider the word "trunk," for example), but within a particular class of meanings for a given word there is likely to be a variety of "shadings" in meaning. We can illustrate this by taking as our class of meanings for the word "trunk" that which refers to a chest or object in which to store or carry things. This subclass of the word "trunk" has many *representations*. It may refer to leather, wooden, or plastic containers; it may refer to a trunk of small or large size; it may represent a place in which to hide, or an object in which to carry something; and so on. When a child "knows" what the word "trunk" means, he knows at first only one class of such meanings and one shade of this class of meanings. He may respond to the word or use the word in such a way that "we know" that he knows its meaning, but he doesn't necessarily know the same things about it, nor does it have the same values, that we infer it does. In general, then, the child's representative meaning for a word is highly concrete and quite simple in the beginning. As he grows older, the child learns many differentiated meanings for words that he already knows. Thus, mere increase in size of vocabulary does not reflect the highly complex development in word meanings and word usage which also occurs (43).

One of the most extensive and most frequently referred to series of studies of vocabulary growth is that carried out by Smith (44). Her findings have been confirmed as representative with respect to the methodology she used. She tested children varying in age from 8 months to 72 months. Some of her samples were very small; for example her "norms" are based on only nine cases at the six-year level. Her test consisted of showing the child pictures of objects and asking the child to name them. If the child was unable to supply a name, he was questioned about the object and could thus demonstrate that he understood its meaning. Her norms represent, then, a special kind of recognition and, to some extent, *use* vocabulary. The results of the Smith studies indicate that vocabulary, as measured, increases slowly in the beginning (see Chapters 4 and 5), then increases more rapidly up to about three years, and then the rate of increase slows down slightly until six years of age. Smith also estimated that the average number of

words understood by her population of three-year-olds was 896; it was 1540 at four years, and 2072 at five years of age. She found that children could learn phrases as easily as words, but, in such instances, learned the phrases as if they were words. Usually the child has already learned some 100 to 200 words before he begins to use phrases in his speech.

As the child develops he learns not only words but sentences. Sentence length increases in much the same pattern as size of vocabulary. Smith's finding that at two years of age the average sentence length is 1.7 words (phrases or sentences) indicates that at this age children still tend to speak with single words rather than groups of words. By three years of age the average number of words used in response to questions is 3.4 words, and by four years it is 4.4 words (37). Sentence length increases gradually until at about four years of age complete sentences, of about 6 to 8 words, are common (45).

Verbs, adjectives, and pronouns are relatively late in their appearance. For example, according to the findings of one study, at 1½ years of age, in the spontaneous speech of one child, about 79 per cent of the words spoken were nouns, whereas 7 per cent were verbs, 7 per cent were adjectives and none were pronouns. By four years of age the respective percentages were: 58, 20, 13, and 1 (46). As the child matures during the preschool period he also learns to articulate more accurately (the correlation between age and accuracy of articulation being about .80), and he uses more complex sentence structure on an habitual basis (47). By six years of age the complexity of the child's language is sufficient to enable him to use it as a comfortable tool in social relations.

PLAY, FANTASY, AND INTELLECTUAL DEVELOPMENT

We have chosen to discuss the topics of play, fantasy, and intellectual development together because of the intimate and complex interrelationships they have with each other. We have already seen in the previous chapter how play is a part of intellectual development and how it stimulates it, and we have noted how inseparable are the play and fantasy activities of toddlerhood. Moreover, some of the best indices of mental development are derived from the play and fantasy activities of preschool children. We shall also see how discouragement of play and fantasy retard the development of thought.

Play

Freud stated that the dreams of adults are "royal roads" to the unconscious, since the ego in sleep is less capable of censoring or inhibiting the emergence of unconscious motives. For children, play may be conceptualized as the "royal road" to thought processes, for although children during the period we are discussing have not yet learned consciously to inhibit their thoughts, they are less able to communicate them to us directly through their verbalizations. During play, we may observe at first hand, if we observe carefully, both the conscious and unconscious thinking processes and thought products which would otherwise be more likely to escape our attention. Moreover, play reflects much more than some aspects of the child's personality; it also reflects some aspects of the child's culture. For example, we are accustomed to seeing children in this country play out domestic scenes or engage in play in which the children assume various roles, such as doctor, or street cleaner, or teacher. However, in other types of cultures the play activities of preschool children vary markedly both in content and in the level of reality they portray. Margaret Mead reports that the play of Mundugumor children habitually involves a great deal of violence and physical punishment, in contrast to the more cooperative and sociable play of American children (48). In our own culture such types of play would result in physical retaliation together with emotional resentment by the parents, whereas among the Mundugumor children resentment is neither expected nor expressed. It has been reported that the play of children of certain primitive cultures shows extraordinary (as compared with our own) mastery of complex skills. For example, three- to four-year-old children among the Kafirs are able to construct elaborate traps for game, whereas our children of a comparable age can only construct crude, unreality-like objects of blocks (49). In our discussion, therefore, we shall focus on the play, fantasy and intellectual accomplishments of American children as they have been studied and reported in the literature.

The nature of play activities undergoes

considerable change during the preschool period. Perhaps of greatest importance is the finding that play progressively involves less manipulation and more thinking during this period (50).

Whether the child uses blocks or whether he plays with paints or such objects as scissors, he tends to make fewer large muscle movements and to use his smaller muscles more (as in finer coordinations) and to use his cortex even more

than his muscles. Nevertheless he still likes to remake endlessly anything that he has once constructed. Moreover, he spends most of his time playing with objects rather than with children, although nursery-school children tend to play in groups more than children not in attendance at such schools. However, even nurs-

The preschool child often expresses something of his "private world" of feeling by his use of color and form in painting. (Merrill Palmer)

ery school children do not regularly engage in *cooperative play* (in which a common objective is aimed for in the play of the entire group) until five years of age. Still another general characteristic of the change in play activities is the marked reduction that takes place in *impulsive play* over the preschool period. Finally, as children progress in their differentiation of reality from fantasy they begin to require play materials that more closely or actually represent the things they are supposed to be. Thus a three-year-old will readily use blocks of wood or any other conveniently available objects to represent such real objects as chairs, or bedroom furniture, or people, whereas the five-year-old will want "real" chairs, or "real" articles of bedroom furniture, or toy people (in miniature or lifesized form). This last type of shift parallels the child's growing awareness of and accuracy in perception of reality. We can observe the same type of phenomenon (of greater acceptance of reality) in all other types of play activities. For instance, at the beginning of the preschool period the child will usually paint or draw things that are unrecognizable to himself or others, whereas at the end of this period he will insist on trying to draw something that he and others can recognize and that he can name and talk about.

The importance of play materials and play activities for preschool children can hardly be overemphasized. In the first place these are needed to enable the child to gain mastery over sensory responses. As the child (and to some extent even the adult) plays with things he learns something about their characteristics and their meanings to him. As his motor and perceptual abilities develop he attempts to duplicate the objects around him through construction in play. When he can use or make an object that he can *name* he feels that he has gained that degree of mastery over reality. Play leads to mastery of reality in many ways other than simply becoming able to name or define or duplicate it. The child learns through play to express his wishes, that is, his fantasy. In play he can make things come out just as he would like. Thus, he can avoid many of the frustrations of (for him) a very difficult reality. He can pretend that things are whatever he wishes them to be. (How frustrating it is to the three-year-old youngster to have an adult demand to know what it is that he has drawn or made. He hardly knows himself!) When he is disturbed emotionally or even when he has been restrained by some adult because of social requirements, he can act out his blocked wishes in play and accompanying fantasy. Sometimes, this acting out is the expression of some repressed wish; but more often it is likely to be the expression of some suppressed activity. Play therapy has been used with children to gain effective discharge of *both* types of needs (51, 52). He can try out under the "protected" conditions of play many situations he would not dare attempt in the more difficult reality situation. Play is also a means to greater socialization, even though in the beginning it may serve the ends of fantasy and solitary activity. It has been observed that when children are deprived of play materials they tend to become more solitary in their activities, whereas the opposite is true when they have adequate access to such materials (53). As children mature in play experience they soon demand co-operative play experiences with other children (54). Play also serves to assist the child in his identification with social roles. This is such an important aspect of play experience that we shall elaborate it more fully.

We have noted that children engage in play in which they portray the roles of important adults about whom they have had important, vivid, and concrete reactions and experiences. This may explain in part why the so-called *dramatic play* of preschool children centers largely around domestic scenes. Children love to play mother or father or both. (Until about six years of age children can assume either sex role with equal ease.) Often in playing out such roles they will faithfully recreate the values and other character-

istics they have observed in the people they portray. Thus, a strong mother (and most mothers seem strong to children at this age level because the mothers characteristically have so much responsibility for gratifying or denying children's wishes) is played out as just that, having even greater strength in the child's play than she has in reality. Then other people who are or seem important to children are dramatized. Such people are likely to include an older sibling, the doctor, the nurse, and others who have entered into the home picture in a vital way. Later, other people are dramatized, such as the policeman, the nursery-school teacher, and the minister. Sometimes, children will play such roles as the street cleaner or the garbage man just as readily and enjoyably as cowboy or space man, for

Group participation in games must sometimes be encouraged. (Merrill Palmer)

these former seem to be more real and vital and have been the source of many intriguing experiences. As an example of this, one youngster who loved to play garbage man and often actually did, or tried to, follow a garbage man around the neighborhood, "assisting" him in his chores (the youngster was 4½ years old), said of him, "He's a great man. He smells so good and he collects things that smell so good." To this youngster, the garbage man opened up a whole new world of experience! In all of such play activities the child learns to master and identify with various social roles, and so learns about both others and himself. The process is similar to that which the child experienced particularly during the toddlerhood period, when he was learning to master the *materials* of his environment through his manipulations in play. Now he is mastering the *roles* of society in much the same way.

Fantasy

One of the most important set of skills developed by the child during the preschool period is that of fantasy which is too often discouraged by parents and teachers in order to bring the child "back to reality." This is unfortunate since, as we have already seen in our discussions of language and of play, fantasy has definite values in the total development of the child. Severe or too early discouragement of fantasy may inhibit intellectual development and impoverish the personality.

Perhaps it would be well to attempt a more precise definition of *fantasy*. It has often been referred to as "pictorial imagination," and sometimes it has been confused with "imagination." Even though it has elements of both of these it is also really much more. Fantasy, in the first place, is the *product* of wish fulfillment. It first comes into being when the individual is unable to obtain adequate gratification from reality and therefore *substitutes* for this inadequacy an imaginary reality which is much more satisfying. Hence it is believed that fantasy is a sequel to the earliest forms of *hallucination* in infants and very young children. Such hallucinations occur in early life when the person or object through which gratification of basic needs was achieved by the infant is unavailable (55). Thus a child may normally hallucinate the mother's nipple or even the whole mother. At this infantile stage hallucination is essentially a passive process, supplying some substitute gratification for an unmet need. Later, the individual may deliberately conjure up an image of a person or situation as a substitute for or an alternative to a mildly or severely disturbing reality situation. In such situations, when fantasy has first come into its own, it is a much more conscious process although unconscious factors (unfulfilled wishes) still play a prominent role in its production. Thus we can see that fantasy has its beginning in mild or severe frustrations and that it is therefore always accompanied by affect or emotion.

Through repetition, emotional responses may induce fantasy behavior. We can observe this phenomenon in adults who sometimes "retreat" into a world of fantasy when they have been emotionally aroused (either unpleasantly—as when they are disturbed, or pleasantly—as when they are listening to a moving musical composition). Fantasy is not only a withdrawal from reality, however; it is also a technique for understanding and mastering reality; it can easily become a means of "thinking things through." Here we can see the close interdependence of fantasy and thinking. Thus, we can conceptualize two types of fantasy: *withdrawal fantasy*, in which frustration is defended

against by the creation of an imaginary substitute with pleasant emotional tones, and *creative fantasy*, in which reconstruction of one's experience, induced usually by some emotional stimulus, enables one to prepare more adequately for appropriate behavior. The latter type is a prelude to or is part of originality, inventiveness, and heightened activity. During the preschool years, when reality and unreality

Learning to pour water, and also learning the role of "host." (U. of Mich.)

are not always clearly distinguishable, it is easy for the child to use fantasy to replace reality. Often more than withdrawal from an unpleasant or misunderstood situation is involved; frequently, the child uses fantasy as a preparation for reality-oriented behavior. We saw how this operated in the child's play activities and we shall see how it operates in his intellectual behavior.

Because the young child is unable to distinguish clearly between the real and the imaginary (and because his conceptual ability is still primitive), he will often believe in the reality of his fantasies. He will play at imagining, but he will treat the products of his imaginings *as if* they were real. Adults, often failing to understand this, will rebuke the child for telling lies, when there is neither the intent nor consciousness on the child's part to deceive anyone. Even if the child is not rebuked, he may *experience rejection* when the adult fails to understand the vividness and the apparent reality the fantasy experience has for the child. Thus, the four-year-old, playing at make-believe, will pretend he is a giant, or a doctor, or mother or father, and the like, and will fail to understand why adults cannot understand that what he feels is therefore actually so. He will often believe he has a real companion (who is only an imaginary companion) and will talk with him, listen to him, and accompany him through various activities (56). Quite often, we can catch a glimpse of the developing superego (or conscience or morality) as the child plays with his sometimes approving, sometimes chastising imaginary companion.

By the time the child reaches the primary grades he will have learned to distinguish reality from fantasy on a fairly consistent basis. He will then give up his imaginary companions and will retreat into withdrawal fantasies only under relatively severe frustration. However, if his imagination has not been inhibited by overly severe rejection of his former attempts at fantasy, and if he is well adjusted, he will have learned to use fantasy

Fantasy is usually a very active ingredient of group play. (Merrill Palmer)

in the service of inventive thinking and originality.

Thus, we have seen how fantasy starts out as a reaction to unconscious wishes and their frustration in reality, how it is later substituted for reality at times but is also used in planning for more effective methods of coping with reality, and how it becomes the substratum of more mature thinking in later stages of childhood and adulthood. We can see how fantasy may be used in the process of learning about one's world, about one's identity, and finally of learning how to manage oneself in satisfying ways in the real world.

Intellectual development

Now we come to the highly complex problem of intellectual development. We propose to discuss this topic by considering, first, what intelligence is and how it develops and, then, by analyzing some important aspects of mental development, such as *concept formation* and *memory*. The experimental literature in these areas is quite extensive, and the interested reader who wishes to make a more intensive study of special problems will want to be alert to the selected references cited in the text.

What is intelligence? As one wag put it (the source has been lost in the course of endless repetitions and variations of the original formulation), "Intelligence is what intelligence tests test." This remark is more valid than its apparently facetious content would indicate. Despite many years of intensive research, authorities do not agree precisely on the exact nature of intelligence. Moreover, intelligence cannot be observed directly; it can only be

inferred from the behavior of the individual. We mean by this, quite simply, that intelligence is a *capacity* and that until this capacity is manifested in some overt act it cannot, so far as is known, be measured. It will be seen at once that an act of behavior is not likely to be a pure expression of the capacity of intelligence, but that it may be the admixture of many capacities. (Even abstract reasoning and conceptualization depend on such factors as knowledge, experience, previous motor experience, language development, and the like.) Moreover, behavior may be greatly influenced by emotional adjustment, by motivation for the task, and by many other factors. Hence it is not so naive to say that we should consider intelligence to be that which a *particular* intelligence test indicates for a *particular* individual at a *particular* time under *particular* circumstances. We may then wonder whether, with all these reservations, the concept of intelligence or a measure of intelligence is of any value. However, we shall see that despite important cautions that must be observed in evaluating the results of intelligence tests, the concepts of intelligence and its measurement are important and useful.

A great number of intelligence tests have been devised, but only a few have been widely accepted and used for individual testing purposes.* Some of these

* There are two general classes of intelligence tests: *individual* tests, designed to be administered to one person at a time, and *group* tests, designed to be administered to a group of persons at one time.

tests have a range of applicability from the preschool years through the adult years; others are designed for use with a restricted age range. We shall discuss briefly two of the most widely used individual intelligence tests in order to gain some idea of their content and of the types of measures they yield.

The New Revised Stanford-Binet Tests. This test consists of two alternate forms, Form L and Form M, which are based on an earlier form of the test, first published by Terman in 1916 (57). The present revision, published in 1937 (58) and carefully analyzed statistically in 1942 by McNemar (59), contains a total of 129 test items in each form, and extends from the two-year level to the adult level. The items are grouped by age levels and increase in difficulty and complexity with age. (See Table IV.) It will be observed that some items call for comprehension, some for memory, some for conceptual similarities, some for "reasoning," and so on. In the conventional method of administering this test, the subject is given items from several levels so that a *basal age* is established (the highest level in which he passes all the items), and a *maximal age is* established (the lowest level in which he fails all the items). All the test items of the intervening year levels are also administered. The test yields a *mental age* and an *intelligence quotient* is then calculated. The *mental age* is a score which indicates that the subject who earns it is comparable in mental level (for *that* test under the *par-*

ticular conditions in which the test was given) to average subjects of the given age. Thus, if a child earns a mental age (usually abbreviated as M.A.) of six years, it means that he is comparable in mental development, on that test, to average six-year-old children. In order to determine the degree of brightness, the *intelligence quotient* (I.Q.) is calculated. This is obtained by dividing the child's earned M.A. by his actual C.A. (chronological age) and multiplying the result by 100. (In practice the I.Q. may be obtained directly from tables provided in the manual for the test.) Thus, an average I.Q. score would be 100, and I.Q.'s above or below 100 would represent brightnesses above or below average, respectively. The I.Q. score tells us what the child's present rate of mental development is (again as measured under the given conditions)—this is useful for predictive purposes. If a child has an I.Q. of 130, for example, he is very bright; conversely, the child with an I.Q. of 70 is very inferior in brightness.

Reflection will indicate that two children who obtain the same score on such a test as this will not necessarily pass the same items; that is, two children may obtain the same M.A. by virtue of different combinations of items that are passed. Hence, for this reason alone the M.A.'s of any two children, even if equal, are not necessarily directly comparable. One child may have had a greater spread over a larger number of year-levels than the other; one child may have passed more memory items than the other; and so on. This serves to point up the fact that the M.A. is simply a *total* or *composite* of many different types of mental test items

Table IV. *Representative items of the Terman-Merrill Revision of the Stanford-Binet (Form L)*

Year level	Number of items	Credit for each item (mos.)	Representative item
II	6	1	A card with pictures of common objects is shown. The child is asked to identify the objects.
II–6	6	1	The child is asked to repeat a series of 2 digits.
III	6	1	The child is asked to copy a circle.
III–6	6	1	The child is asked to tell about a picture.
IV	6	1	The child is asked to complete a drawing of a man.
IV–6	6	1	The child is asked to identify the "prettier" of two pictures.
V	6	1	The child is asked to count a series of objects.
VI	6	2	The child is shown pictures of common objects with parts missing. He is asked to name the missing parts.
VII	6	2	The child is shown pictures depicting absurd situations. He is asked to recognize the absurdity.
VIII	6	2	The child is asked to define a series of words.
IX	6	2	A series of absurd situations are related, and the child asked to identify the absurdity.
X	6	2	The child is asked to repeat a series of 6 digits.
XI	6	2	The child is asked to define abstract words.
XII	6	2	The child is asked to repeat a series of digits backwards.
XIII	6	2	The child is asked to repeat a series of words.
XIV	6	2	The child is given an absurd picture and asked to spot the absurdity.
Average adult	8	2	The subject is asked to give the difference between pairs of abstract words.
Superior adult I	6	4	The subject is asked to give the similarity between pairs of words.
Superior adult II	6	5	The subject is asked to reconcile pairs of words that have opposite meanings.
Superior adult III	6	6	The subject is asked to repeat a series of 9 digits from memory.

and therefore merely represents the average level of performance on samples of items from a particular test. If the test contained different samples of items, the average would necessarily be derived from different types of intelligence test items. We shall have more to say about this problem shortly.

In using intelligence tests such as the Terman-Merrill, it is commonly assumed that the I.Q. remains constant throughout life. Such an assumption is a gross distortion of a scientifically more cautious and more reasonable assumption. Constancy may be assumed only if the I.Q. is obtained under favorable conditions by a competent examiner, and if the test is an appropriate one for the child (that is, if it is fair in that his opportunities for acquiring the information and skills upon which the items are based are comparable to those upon whom the test was originally developed or *standardized*). Further, it will remain *reasonably* constant for a short interval of time (approximately one or two years), *providing* the life conditions of the subject remain constant over this period of time. The latter type of assumption is noticeably more limited and is based upon considerable research evidence (60). Most careful workers in the field will agree to the validity of this more cautious assumption, and yet it is common experience to find many parents and even teachers who accept the I.Q. as an immutable, all-embracing evaluation of a youngster's mental capacity, even if the test upon which it was based was administered many years ago by some unknown examiner under unknown conditions of adequacy. One may commonly hear discussions at parent-teacher meetings and at meetings of staffs of school personnel in which the meaningless (and even dangerous) question is asked, without qualification, "What's his I.Q.?" It is *always* necessary to specify, at least, on what *test*, at what *time*, under what *conditions*. We shall have more to say about this matter later in this chapter and in later sections of this book.

The Wechsler-Bellevue Intelligence Scale for Children. As another example of an individual intelligence test for children, this modern scale, which differs in some important respects from the Stanford-Binet, will be discussed briefly. It is based in part upon an earlier test by Wechsler for adolescents and adults, published in 1949 (61). The test consists of two sections, a verbal section consisting of five subtests and an alternate subtest, and a performance section consisting of five subtests and an alternate subtest. The alternate tests provide for flexibility in administering the scale. For instance, if one of the subtests is inappropriate or has been invalidated for some special reason (as, for example, because the child was disturbed while taking this subtest), the alternate test may be used to replace it. The verbal section contains the following five regular subtests: general information, general comprehension, arithmetic, similarities, and vocabulary. The performance subtests are: picture completion, picture arrangement, block design, object assembly, and coding.

Unlike the Stanford-Binet, the items are not grouped by chronological age. Instead, the items are arranged within each subtest according to difficulty. Thus, regardless of the child's age, he starts with the items at the beginning of each subtest and continues with the increasingly more difficult items until he has made the designated number of failures. The score on each subtest is converted, by means of tables, into *weighted* scores (in which the difficulty level of the *raw* score is taken into account), the weighted scores for each section of the scale (verbal and performance) are totalled, and these weighted scores are converted directly, by means of tables, into verbal and performance I.Q.'s. Usually, a total I.Q. is obtained for the *full scale* from the total weighted score of ten subtests from both sections. If desired, separate I.Q. scores may be obtained for each subtest, and the pattern of I.Q.'s on the various subtests may be analyzed and evaluated for special clinical purposes.

In general, I.Q.'s from the Stanford-Binet and the Wechsler correlate fairly well, the product-moment correlation ratios usually being of the order of about .80 (62). It has been reported that the Stanford-Binet yields slightly higher I.Q.'s than the Wechsler. These results indicate, once again, that I.Q. results are specific to specific measuring instruments, at least to some extent.

We have discussed these two intelligence tests in order to give the reader some idea of the kinds of test items that go into such tests and of the fact that an I.Q. is always a composite score based upon a particular sampling of certain kinds of test items. Of course, tests for very young children differ both in content and in organization from those for

Mental examination of young children requires perception, comprehension, and use of simple materials. (U. of Mich.)

older children and, in turn, these differ from those for adults. An analysis of the results obtained with intelligence tests has led to a number of important conclusions, and we shall discuss some of these briefly.

The concept of intelligence. As we noted earlier, there is no common agreement with respect to the nature of intelligence. The theorists may be arranged on a scale according to the extent that they believe intelligence to be a *unitary phenomenon* or to be highly *specific.* Modern conceptions of the nature of intelligence are based, for the most part, on a statistical analysis of test results known as *factor analysis.* There are many methods of factor analysis but they have in common the aim of extracting from the data the least number of factors or variables necessary to account for the data. Although the technical aspects of factor analysis are highly complex and their discussion is beyond the province of this book, it may be said that no method of factor analysis can go beyond the data that are given, to begin with; that is, the analysis *starts* with the results from the specific tests that are thrown into the statistical hopper. From that point on, the statistical task is to account for the data in the most parsimonious manner.

At one extreme of the scale on which the theorists may be placed is Spearman (63). He believes that there is a *general factor* underlying all intelligent behavior; he calls this factor g. Individuals differ in the amount of g that they are born with, although g may be influenced by various factors in postnatal life. Different tests, and different behaviors, depend to different degrees upon the amount or proportion of g they involve. Individual differences in intelligence depend, then, in the main, on differences in g. In addition, they depend upon specific factors, called *s* (these are unique to each behavioral act), and upon *group factors* of personality and other nonintellectual traits like musical ability (called by various other letters, such as *w* for volition). The group factors are common to a number of activities but do not enter into all intelligent behavior, as does g. Spearman has defined g as that which leads to the "apprehension of one's own experience, the eduction of relations and the eduction of correlates."

At the other end of the scale is Thorndike who believes that intelligence is simply the aggregate of all the specific abilities that underlie all intelligent behavior (64). According to this view there is no such capacity as *general intelligence* but only *specific intelligences,* as numerous as different kinds of intelligent behavior. Whatever correlation is found among tests of intelligence is due, according to this view, to the commonality of specific intelligences underlying the responses to such tests and not to any general factor. However, Thorndike believed that, based on research evidence and because of usefulness for purposes of practical prediction, one could arbitrarily group intelligence factors into the three main categories of *abstract, mechanical,* and *social.* Within each of these three categories tests tend to correlate fairly highly but only because of the common elements that are involved. Tests of *abstract* intelligence have the highest correlation with certain kinds of behavior, such as performance in school subjects, particularly of an academic nature. Our culture, generally, favors people with high abstract intelligence, but in other cultures, and for certain kinds of situations, other types of intelligence may be more important.

Somewhere between these two extremes are proponents of a middle position, among whom Thurstone is very prominent. Thurstone's position is that there is no general factor but only *primary mental abilities.* Behavior, according to this view, is the resultant of the complex of *primary factors* which account for the given ability (65). Thus, there are neither specific factors nor any general factor, but only factors that are essentially independent of each other, and that operate in varying proportions in various mental tasks. Thurstone has identified twelve such primary factors, seven of which he has named as follows: verbal relations (V), perceptual abilities (P), spatial relations (S), words (W), memory (M), numerical abilities (N), and induction (I). He has been less certain in naming the other five primary abilities, but has tentatively identified them according to a common-sense description of their meaning. Like Thorndike, he has constructed a test based on his theory; he calls it *The Primary Abilities Test*. This test is now available for the range from the five-year level through the college level, and each of its subtests provides as pure a measure as is feasible to get for each of the primary factors. It does not provide a measure of general intelligence, but instead offers a profile of the individual's functioning on the primary factors—five at the lower levels and seven at the intermediate and upper levels (66, 67). Each of the several factors correlates differently with various aspects of behavior and achievement.

As we can see, the concept of intelligence is, in part, an arbitrary matter. We can conceptualize it as "the ability to learn or profit from experience," we can think of it as "abstract conceptual ability," or we can consider it to be an aggregate of a variety of factors. In each case, our measures of this "thing" we call intelligence will correlate differently with specified criteria. The most commonly used tests of "general intelligence" are heavily loaded with abilities of a verbal nature (especially from the primary school grades on up), and are composite measures of ability to learn, remember, and synthesize experience, all measured through tasks that have a marked com-

monality with school content, especially of the academic variety. As we have seen, tests at different age levels tend to involve different kinds of content and measure somewhat different abilities.

The growth of intelligence. The growth curve of intelligence will depend, among other things, on the type of measure of intelligence that is employed. Based, for the most part, on tests of general intelligence (composites of verbal skills), research evidence has indicated that the curve is a semi-parabola (see Figure 12). In this type of curve mental growth is pictured as developing rapidly during the periods of infancy and early childhood, then slowing up until the maximum, or *apogee*, is reached somewhere in the adult years. According to Thorndike this apogee occurs at about 21 years of age (64). There is then a *plateau* for quite a number of years until a gradual decrement appears during the middle years of life. The decrement becomes more marked during later years of life (*senescence*). This type of curve, which is most widely accepted by authorities today, displays the phenomenon of *negative acceleration* until the apogee is reached, that is, the rate of growth shows regular decrement. Some authorities, using more refined methods of scaling mental tests so as to achieve *equal units* of measurement, have arrived at a very similar type of curve, only its form is *logarithmic* rather than *parabolic* (65). The facts described by both types of curves are essentially the same, varying only in detail. Such curves reveal the interesting fact, rather startling at first acquaintance, that the midway point in mental growth is arrived at somewhere between three and five years of age. At the upper end of the scale, after the plateau period, intelligence, *as measured,* begins to taper off somewhere about 30 years of age. We emphasize *as measured* because most modern tests of intelli-

of this curve, some of the implications should be stressed. Of first order in importance is the finding that half of the final height, or *altitude,* is achieved during the preschool years. It is surprising to learn that children at this age can think so well and can learn so many complicated mental skills at such an early age. It is also interesting to note the similarity in the growth curves of intelligence and of weight of the brain. Both sets of findings indicate how important the early years are in making use of

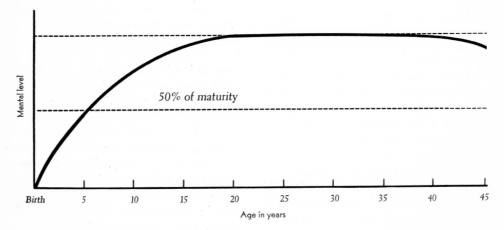

Figure 12. *Growth in intellectual ability, from birth to 45 years.*

gence place a premium on speed and on academic abilities and may thus characterize the upper end of the age range unfairly. Adults can continue to learn, even learn some things better than they could in younger years, and may be able to compensate for their loss in some functions by greater use of acquired knowledge and by greater sagacity as a consequence of this accumulated experience.

Turning, once again, to the early part

the intelligence that is already there and in helping children to acquire maximum use of their mentalities and to develop good habits of mental work. It is also worth noting that children of high-school age have sufficient intelligence to master most of the course content that is now taught at the college or post-graduate level. In view of world developments which have emphasized the values of early training in scientific skills and of the assumed comparative superiority in the science of high-school youth in some foreign countries, we should ponder long and well the remarkable assets for learning that high-school youth have and capitalize on their very high intellectual capacity.

Some workers believe that with adequate tests for infants and with adequate methods of sampling and measuring, the growth curve will resemble an *S-shaped* figure and not a semi-parabola. Courtis, who has studied many types of growth, believes that this type of curve more accurately describes mental increment (69). His curve indicates that increase in mental ability is slow during the first year or so, then gains momentum rapidly, and finally shows an increasing decrement in the rate of growth. This curve has two *inflection points* (points at which the curve changes direction), one in late infancy and another in the primary grades.

Most studies of mental growth have been based on *cross-sectional* studies, that is studies in which *different samples* from different age levels have been compared. This makes for difficulty in obtaining comparable samples. (For instance, because of drop-outs in school during the adolescent years it is difficult to get truly comparable samples at the several ages from 14 to 18. The difficulty is even greater in later years.) Moreover, as we have said, tests measure different functions at different ages, and this makes for questionable comparability of results. Infant tests are based on sensorimotor behavior, to a very large extent, tests for the school-age population depend heavily on verbal skills and school

information, and tests for adults may sample more of general information. Finally, the problem of deriving comparable units of measurement is a difficult one. Unless the units of measurement are comparable at all ages, the results may be suspect. These are some of the problems that modern researchers are trying to solve.

Factors influencing intellectual performance. It was once held that intelligence was a unitary trait and that it was entirely dependent upon hereditary factors, simply unfolding or maturing with the passage of time. It is now believed that intelligence is a highly complex phenomenon, its manifestations depending on a variety of cognitive, affective, and sociological phenomena (not to mention physical attributes), and that inheritance sets the limits very broadly for some functions and more narrowly for others. However, it is the interaction of heredity and environment that fianlly determines the degree of intelligence displayed.

We have seen how the child's adjustment may profoundly influence his mental development, either inhibiting it or facilitating it. Problems of the oedipal period are likely to be important to an unusual degree in the kinds and amount of intelligence developed. The fearful, insecure child learns to inhibit the free exercise of his intelligence as he withdraws from some aspects of troublesome living. The severely repressed child may show even more limitations in his use of intelligence, repressing not only the traumata that have disturbed him but the functioning of his needs to explore his world, to learn new experiences, and to integrate experience freely into a new conceptual framework. At the other extreme, a home atmosphere that encourages intellectual and emotional freedom, that places a premium on effective thinking, and that provides the raw materials of experience and learning opportunities to foster intellectual growth may accelerate mental development.

One of the unusual cases that came to our attention illustrates how significantly mental development (among other phenomena) may be impaired by unfortunate emotional experience.

Stan was a well developed, likable boy of almost 12 years who was doing very poorly in all his academic school subjects, and especially in reading. In the latter subject his reading level was about second grade and he was only slightly better in arithmetic, spelling, and composition. He was in the fifth grade largely because of his age, in a small school, with small classes. Almost all of his academic work was done individually. He seemed quite dull in other ways: his comprehension and common sense seemed definitely inferior, he was poorly oriented with respect to affairs in his community and in the world, he showed little curiosity about most educational matters. On the other hand he was a good athlete and got along well on class and school teams. He had been given a number of individual intelligence tests and his I.Q. was usually about 70, occasionally testing as low as 65 and sometimes going as high as 75 or 76. The school, his friends, and his parents believed he was dull; he had been diagnosed as borderline feebleminded. Stan was re-

ferred to a private clinical psychologist for evaluation of his potentialities, for educational guidance and for possible psychological help, if any seemed indicated.

The following facts were obtained in interviews with him, his mother, his regular classroom teacher, and his special teacher: Medical examination was essentially negative and had been for some years. At the age of 5 years he had been seriously ill with pneumonia. Shortly after his recovery from this illness his family sent him to live with relatives in Florida for about a year. When he returned he was entered in his present school. He had always seemed to try hard but had never been able to learn the work of his grade. When he failed to make any noticeable progress in reading he was given individual reading instruction and coaching by a remedial reading teacher; during some periods of his school career he received daily remedial reading instruction. He would seem to learn some things in reading and then forget or fail to retain what he had apparently learned. He had an older brother, 14 years of age, who attended the same school and who was doing above average work. Stan fought frequently with his brother; the two seemed to have little liking for each other. Stan's father was a successful businessman who was distant from the entire family. He had difficulty in expressing warm and positive emotional reactions. He was greatly disappointed in his younger son and let him know it in many ways. Stan's mother tried to help, but she was busy with many community projects and seemed unable to "reach" her son. Stan seemed fearful of all adults but was friendly with many boys of his own age.

Re-examination of this boy's intelligence and reading abilities confirmed the impression the school had given. During therapeutic interviews he gradually revealed many of his "frozen" emotional reactions and in play sessions was able to develop these more fully. It turned out that he had felt rejected by his family, and especially by his father, ever since his illness at the age of five years. He believed that he was

Large, light blocks can be used in many forms of play. (Merrill Palmer)

"like Knute Rockne" but he knew he could not succeed "because you have to go to college to become a football coach."

On the basis of these and other data, intensive psychotherapy was begun. It developed that Stan was severely repressed in many areas of his emotional life. After a few months he began to "warm up" to the male therapist and many of his feelings toward the members of his family were clarified and worked through. He recovered many memories of earlier years in which he re-experienced his disappointments and frustrations. With the help of the therapist, the family began to take more interest in Stan's ambitions in football and his father made some effort to get closer to him, even taking him to some college football games. During therapy, his remedial instruction was discontinued for about a half year until his resistance (on an unconscious level) was dissipated. Stan gradually began to blossom out, almost to "thaw out." At the end of a little more than twelve months of therapy, he was retested and he obtained an I.Q. of 128! He had begun to read on his own, and was then given remedial work when he asked for it. Within the same period he was able to progress to fourth-grade reading, with indications that his improvement in reading was progressing more rapidly than had been the case at the beginning. During the following year he had caught up to and surpassed his own age level in reading comprehension and his school work became progressively easier for him. He also learned to get along better with his brother who had developed some real admiration for his formerly "dull brother."

This admittedly exceptional case shows in bold relief how emotional disturbance may influence mental functioning along with total adjustment. In milder cases of frustration as well as in cases of emotion-

not wanted and that he would be sent away again some day. He had developed many fantasies in this area. He hated his brother who, he believed, had displaced him in his father's affections. He disliked his mother because he felt she pitied him and was dissatisfied with him. He had an intense ambition to become a football coach ally and intellectually stimulating environments, the decrement or increment to intellectual functioning may not be so great but may be significant, nevertheless.

A number of studies have attempted to determine whether the I.Q. can be raised by various types of environmental experiences. It is very difficult to design appropriate studies to test such a global hypothesis since it is not possible to manipulate human beings in all of the significant ways that might be experimentally desirable. Moreover, factors involving control, not only during the experimental period but for long periods after it, are almost impossible to deal with adequately. Wellman (70), as well as others, has attempted to assess the influence upon intelligence of attendance in nursery school. Her large number of cases, approximately 600, and her careful methodology require us to give considerable weight to her findings. She was able to show that nursery-school attendance did raise the I.Q. significantly, on the average, for her population of subjects. Of course, it may be argued that only the results on tests of intelligence were altered and not the ability to think. It is very difficult to separate some abstract conception of "innate intelligence" from intelligence as measured, and it is acknowledged that tests of intelligence do depend upon certain skills that are acquired as a result of experience. (There is no "pure" test of intelligence.) Nevertheless, Wellman's results were confirmed by follow-up analysis of the functioning of her children in school subjects and school situations. There did seem to be a "permanent" effect of nursery-school attendance when results were compared with those of apparently similar children who did not have the benefit of such experience. Some investigators, with smaller samples, have not been able to confirm the studies done by Wellman and others whose results were in agreement with hers.

However, there are ample data to indicate that personality in general, and specific aspects of personality such as stability, interpersonal relations, adjustment to school, and the like, may be favorably influenced by nursery-school attendance. (We shall presently discuss these findings further in the section on school adjustment.) Taken all together, research does indicate that a favorable and stimulating environment, including attendance at nursery school, does improve both learning and adjustment. We still do not know, unfortunately, precisely which experiences produce the changes under consideration.

Bearing on this question are the results of the classic study by Newman, Freeman, and Holzinger (71). Fifty pairs of identical twins who were reared together were compared with 19 pairs of identical twins who were reared apart. In comparing the relative differences in I.Q. of these two groups of twins one may gain some idea of how much effect, if any, differences in environment may have upon differences in I.Q. Of course, the problem is not that simple, for it is almost impossible to separate out the effect of heredity and environment by such an experimental procedure. One would have to be able to measure each of these complexes of factors with precision, to note the degree of similarities in hereditary and environmental factors, and evaluate the influence of the *time* of separation of the twins as well as the *length* of the separation, before one could conclude with any degree of precision what the results indicate. The findings are, nevertheless, suggestive. The twins who were reared together showed an average difference in I.Q. of 5.3 points, with a range from 0 to 20 points in I.Q. difference; those who were reared apart showed an average difference in I.Q. of 8.2 points, with a range of 1 to 24 points of difference. The difference in averages is statistically significant. We may conclude with Woodworth, in his very careful evaluation of this study and other related findings, that "radical differences in education can create substantial differences in intelligence," and that "differences . . . are not due mostly to differences in environment" (72). What is meant by these statements is that ordinarily large differences in I.Q. will not occur, but that small differences and *occasionally very large* differences may and do occur.

Finally, we wish to point out that the predictive value of intelligence tests is only relatively fair. The I.Q. does *not* remain absolutely constant over a period of time, even when the child remains in the same environment. On the average, differences between five and ten points in I.Q. may be expected when the same child is retested under similar circumstances within approximately one year. For some tests and for some children, the differences may be much smaller or much

larger. Looked at in another way, the correlations between I.Q.'s obtained on retesting within a reasonably short period during the preschool and primary school periods are relatively low. For example, Honzik, Macfarlane, and Allen demonstrated that the correlation coefficients obtained between intelligence test scores at two years, three years, and four years of age with scores obtained at ten years of age were, respectively: .37, .36, and .66 (73). These results, which are typical, indicate that intelligence varies somewhat and that intelligence tests furnish a measure of the child's functioning in one broad area at the *time of measurement only*; to predict to real-life situations or to predict to later periods of life, many other factors must be carefully considered.

Some important aspects of mental development. We shall select for discussion two aspects of intellectual development that are of great importance: *conceptual thinking* and *memory*. Our focus will be upon the preschool child, but of course we shall refer to developments before and after this period to make the discussion more meaningful.

Many authorities distinguish between concepts, as such, and thinking, as such. Although good justifications can be adduced for such a distinction, we believe it will be more meaningful to discuss the interrelated phenomenon of conceptual thinking especially because this type of process is characteristic of the preschool period. *Webster's Collegiate Dictionary* gives the following meaning of *concept*:

"A mental image of a thing formed by generalization from particulars; also, an idea of what a thing in general should be." It is possible in theory to distinguish between a *percept* and a *concept* and, at the adult stage of development, these phenomena are operationally readily distinguishable, but in early mental development the two products are essentially indistinguishable. Percept refers to an immediate experience that is simultaneously being recognized as such, i.e., interpreted. Concept refers to a mental image, or in other words an idea or a symbolic representation about the experience that one has had. One can think about a former percept, and in so doing one *conceptualizes* the percept. Thus, to have concepts one must have had (or be having) percepts which are represented by an idea or a name or some other form of symbol. Therefore, to have concepts implies, at least in the beginning, some thoughts about percepts or, in other words, to do some simple thinking, at least, about the percept.

We should emphasize, in the first place, that conceptual thinking is the product of a particular kind of socialization and does not mature automatically and inevitably irrespective of the social conditions of which it is a part. We have only to consider how greatly different is the conceptual thinking of primitive peoples from that of people in modern, complex society to see the relationship between the needs and organization of a society and the thinking of its members. Conceptual thinking arises, then, out of the necessities of social living, and mainly out of the discomforts and threats which have to be dealt with. It is motivated by the needs of social reality; the more complex the social organization, the more complex the concepts of its members. We have considerable experimental evidence to justify these sweeping conclusions. Bartlett's excellent studies and reviews of the research literature lead to the general conclusion that we attempt most intensely to *cognize* (think about) unfamiliar and dangerous situations (74). We give only passive attention, tend to think repetitiously and stereotypically about things and situations that are familiar and especially those that are nonthreatening.

The child's first concepts are based on the immediacies of his earliest percepts and these are inevitably bound up with his experiences with "mother" and later with other members of his family. These first concepts involve, essentially, the process of *naming* something. Naming becomes a method of holding in one's mind or recalling to one's mind a concrete, perceptual experience that is relevant for tension reduction. Thus the most primitive concepts of the child arise out of need-gratification (i.e., they are motivated) and involve a process of mental recognition. Persons and things, as we have seen, are very hazily perceived at first, and similarly early concepts are hazy and undifferentiated. They are hazy in two main ways: the infant has difficulty in differentiating between his internal world (his needs especially) and the external world; and the infant has difficulty in differentiating different things and events from each other in the external world. These characteristics are highly important, for they help us to understand how emotionally "loaded" are our original concepts. (Consider the emotional loadings in such adult concepts as "communism," "slavery," "patriotism," and "dictatorship.") They also help us to understand that concepts are simply ways of categorizing experience.

As the child develops, and as his life conditions require it, he begins to develop more *differentiated* concepts and more *functional* concepts. Differentiation involves the more accurate application of specific attributes to an appropriate object or situation, and later the recognition of similarities among objects. According to the findings of the Stanford-Binet Test, similarities in conceptual thinking can be first employed functionally at four years of age, and then in only the most elementary manner (58). The functional use of concepts which involves comparison among concepts (noting differences and similarities concerning the specific characteristics of pairs of concepts) develops later. The whole preschool period, in our modern culture, is spent in this process of differentiating more refined out of crude and primitive concepts. By seven years of age the child is able to compare and extract the similarities of such pairs of terms as "wood" and "coal," and of "apple" and "peach" (58).

During this process of concept development, thinking is markedly conditioned by needs and by language development. When necessity requires it we develop a concept to be able to deal more effectively with our environment. In order to be able to develop such concepts, we have to feel free to explore our environ-

ment and to feel free to manipulate it within safe limits. Hence, more than *threat* motivates conceptual development; basic emotional security in combination with moderately threatening situations fosters its maximum growth. It is also true that language is both a result of conceptual development and further conditions its growth. Words are labels for experiences—or concepts. The availability of appropriate words in our culture further conditions the types and refinements of our concepts. As an illustration, the word "stutter" does not occur among certain North American Indian tribes, or at least it did not until very recently (75). The lack of such a word reflected the lack of concern, or absence of the concept, of nonfluent speech, and in turn the lack of the word prevented the development of the concept itself. When the words "sputnik" and "missile" came into use with the threats of intercontinental warfare they conditioned our conceptual thinking beyond the levels to which we had been accustomed. Note that, in this process, our emotional reactions to the words and the things they were used to describe also influenced our conceptual movement at the same time.

The conceptual thinking of preschool children is largely concrete in nature and tends to have quite specific referents. During later stages of this period concepts become more *relative* and more *relational* (76, 77). As relative thinking develops, children begin to make active comparisons (all of the "why" questions!), their thinking becomes less *magi-*

cal and *animistic*, and the sense of time begins to become more meaningful. It is usually not before five years of age that children can tell how long it will be (in rough time units) until their next birthday and how old they will be then. *Relational* concepts involve ideas of causality, spatial relationships, and quantitative comparisons. Such concepts also include relative notions with respect to emotional state or condition. Although each of these and other types of relational concepts emerge during the preschool period it would be a serious mistake to think that children's concepts in these areas are similar to those of adults. Among children, such concepts still have a highly personal reference; that is, they cannot easily be divorced from immediate personal experience. Moreover, children are able to entertain simultaneously highly irreconcilable ideas with respect to causality, space, and quantity. Thus, preschool youngsters can believe that everything is due to what mother wants, and at the same time they can also believe, even with respect to the same event, that things must happen that way by themselves—as if by magic!

Memory. When we now turn our attention to the phenomenon of *memory* we meet some amazing findings. Perhaps of greatest interest is the fact that preschool children are avid memorizers. They seem to relish the "taking in" process which memorization involves and will therefore take delight and spend considerable time in saying things over and over again and memorizing them. In contrast to adolescents and adults, children love rote memory or at least resent it far less than older people. Growth in memory ability is very rapid during childhood, and some authorities believe that ability to memorize matures at about puberty, or about 12 years of age (79). However, specific motivational factors play an important part in whether one is able to memorize well at a given time. A concrete notion of how rapidly memory ability develops may be gained by an examination of the findings with the Stanford-Binet Test. The norms of this test indicate that at 2½ years children can repeat two digits (they will get one of three trials with two-digit series like "4, 7"), at three years of age they can repeat three digits, and at 4½ years of age they can repeat four digits. At the superior adult level the digit memory is only eight numbers, and the average 14-year-old can repeat only seven digits. Thus, memory ability, as exemplified in these findings, develops quite rapidly during early years. As the person grows older, he learns to retain more in proportion to the interest the material has for him; in the preschool and early primary grades, material that has less intrinsic interest is memorized quite readily, perhaps because the general motivation to "incorporate" one's environment is still so great and a sense of mastery and hence of self-esteem can thereby be fostered.

SCHOOL ADJUSTMENT

In large urban centers parents are more and more frequently sending their youngsters to nursery schools and kindergartens. Quite frequently, however, they are not fully aware of the functions and values of such educational programs, and sometimes they are unconcerned with these matters but conceive of placement in such schools as entirely a matter of convenience for the parent. The very term "preschool" seems to connote that this is not part of the educational program but is simply a superfluous experience for the child from which little should or can be expected. Moreover, schools, their staffs, and their facilities vary tremendously, both in urban and rural areas, so that attendance at one of such schools is no guarantee that any particular type of program or any particular type of objective will prevail.

As we shall see, evidence is accumulating that attendance in such schools, or in some of them, may provide very real gains for the child, some of them of a temporary nature and others of a fairly permanent nature. What, then, should the objectives be for a nursery school or a kindergarten class? These objectives will vary of necessity by virtue of the locale of the school and the needs of the community, of course, but there are several broad objectives that are common enough and important enough to be specified. The first and most important of these is to extend the social experience of the child: to enrich it and to stabilize it. There can be tremendously important increments in the child's social skills, in his perceptions of himself in terms of social interactions, and in his mastery of suitable habits of behavior. Such gains may be achieved even without attendance at such a school, but systematic provision for their attainment is likely to be much more difficult in the home situation

alone. Second in importance, perhaps, is familiarity with materials of the environment under guided conditions of learning, together with suitable mastery in methods of management of such materials. Third may be the acquisition of suitable conceptual tools involving language, methods of thinking, methods of learning and retaining, and the like. Finally, the beginning development of suitable habits of work, both alone and in cooperation with others, may be set as an appropriate goal. These and other educational goals—educational in the broadest and most profound sense—should be the objectives of such schools, rather than providing the parent with an interval of freedom from responsibility in supervising the youngster, or disciplining for poor behavior at home, or acquiring specific kinds of "knowledge." The importance of such goals at this stage of development can hardly be overemphasized. In addition, there are other values of preschool attendance which we shall point up in our subsequent discussion.

We may ask, "Should the goal be to send every preschool child to a nursery school?" We should like to reverse this implied proposition to: such schools should be available for every preschool child. Probably every normal or reasonably well adjusted child could profit from attendance in a preschool program. However, even for these children, the age of admission will necessarily vary with their readiness for this type of experience. Because of differences among familial patterns and across cultural patterns, some normal children may be ready for nursery school at three years of age whereas others may hardly be ready at four years. Then there are the children whose emotional and social development may be too immature or too aberrant to warrant introduction into even a well planned and well organ-ized preschool program. In addition, such factors as the child's physical condition (his health status, his susceptibility to infection, and the like), and the level of his mental development (a child may be too retarded in mental development, for example, to profit from the *usual* type of nursery-school program) may be contra-indicative of preschool attendance. The parent can make a wise decision in

The presence of an adult can offer emotional support and add enjoyment in physical activities that might otherwise be frightening. (Merrill Palmer)

such cases only if suitable guidance facilities are available. The family pediatrician, the child guidance clinic, the director of a well organized child center, and the head of the nursery school may be among the appropriate persons or agencies to consult in such matters (79).

The experience of going to nursery school can have profound implications for the child. Aside from his immediate family, and possibly his "sitter" or governess, he is not likely to have had the opportunity of making a *continuing* adjustment to a *highly important* adult: his teacher. The adjustment to the teacher is likely to be important and, if favorable, to have important, positive consequences to the child, for a number of reasons. The teacher will now become the supreme authority in the child's life for a number of hours each day for a whole semester, a year or two years. To the young child she seems indeed to be a "supreme authority." It is in her power to bestow special praise or criticism upon a child or a whole class; she introduces the child into a wonderful new world of play materials and school experiences; she seems to have endless knowledge and can answer all questions with superlative ease. To the youngster she is, indeed, a paragon of all important virtues (and when she is unkindly disposed, of evils). Hence the teacher becomes a significant model for identification to the child. He wishes to be liked by her, to become like her, and to be favored by her more than other members of the group. Thus, the youngster has to learn how to identify with her while retaining his identification with his mother at the same time. This is a conflict situation

and, with wise and patient guidance by *both* mother and teacher, will help the child in his continuing attempts at identification with other adults, and will therefore help him in his interpersonal adjustment and in the acquisition of a broader range of ego skills (through the learning of the skills of important and available models represented by these adults). On the other hand, some mothers feel unduly threatened when their child comes home from nursery school one day and blurts out quite unexpectedly, "My teacher is the smartest person in the world," or the even more devastating remark, "Gee, Mom, I wish you were as beautiful as Miss Smith!" Most mothers can recognize such behavior for what it is, and assume that the child is going through a process of identifying with other adults who *seem* (and for the time being are) more intelligent, or beautiful, and the like. It is well to recognize that there is some apparent threat to the mother's previously undisputed position as matriarch of the family, however.

Attendance at nursery school also provides for the experience of being away from home and mother for an extended period of time. This type of separation provokes some anxiety in some children (perhaps in all) and stimulates such frantic questionings as "Are you sure my Mom will come for me?" and "How long am I going to have to stay here?" Both mother and teacher will have to accept the quite natural anxiety about separation and permit the youngster to express it and work out the problem in his own way. In the process, not only is mastery of anxiety achieved, but the child also grows in feelings of independence and autonomy. The experience is likely to facilitate the important differentiation of the child from his mother and help *both* to develop a more mature pattern of adjustment to each other.

Preschool experience provides other kinds of useful social experiences. The child has an opportunity of playing with other children of about his own age. Too often, the child does not have suitable companionship of this type in his own neighborhood. Even when he does, interference from older children who are likely to push him around at times and provoke him in other ways may provide unusual difficulties. Moreover, he will have opportunities in school for playing with only one other child, with small groups of children, and with larger groups of children. All of these experiences will be embedded in situations in which the guidance of the teacher, the availability of suitable equipment, and a rich variety of experiences (such as group play, group rest, and visits to interesting places in the neighborhood) will be provided.

In this connection, a word should be said concerning the organization of the child's activities in the school program. As we have seen, the child has boundless energy and almost limitless interests. School will have to provide for a great variety of experiences with a great variety of materials (blocks, paints, sand, water, slides, stories, games, and the like). At the same time provision will have to be made for frequent shifts in activity to accommodate to the child's short attention span. Periods of group rest, periods of solitary play, and periods of group eating, for example, will also have to be provided. In all of these activities, the child will learn the meaning and importance of regularity and the meaning of cooperative use of both time and space. Perhaps above all else, he will learn to impose *limits* upon himself, as the teacher wisely permits both sufficient freedom for exploration and self-expression and limits to the degree and frequency when these may be expressed. From our previous discussions we can understand how traumatic harsh discipline can be, but on the other hand, undisciplined license will not result in maturity but only further rebellion and immaturity. In fact, it has been noted that the child needs and likes to have limits set for him, for he is unaware of his own limitations and gains in security when he knows that an understanding adult is there to protect him from pain and anguish. He thus learns to incorporate these limits within himself and make them part of his own flexible controls (80).

One of the uniquely important experiences of children in a group preschool situation is learning to go to the toilet or bathroom in strange surroundings. The sharing of these experiences with other children makes them less threatening and, at the same time, offers ample opportunity for nontraumatic questionings about daily biological processes, and about methods of self-care. Even the mastery of new types of bathroom equipment, or of familiar (but usually smaller equipment—since schools try to provide fixtures of the appropriate size for the age group) can be an important part of self-mastery and increased emotional security.

The qualifications of the teacher in a nursery school and kindergarten program are highly important. We shall not attempt to discuss these in detail since there are special books and technical articles available on the subject. The interested reader may wish to read Gardner's fascinating account in this regard (81). However we should like to point up two issues. One of these is that the nursery-school teacher should have special training in methods appropriate to preschool ages and in the very rich variety of materials necessary for the program with such children. Above and beyond this, and assuming a mature personality and a liking for children, the nursery-school teacher needs special training with respect to the personality characteristics of such young children. Knowledge of the psychology of childhood, in general, or of the primary grade level, in particular, is not enough. Familiarity with the specific adjustmental problems of preschool children, their unique needs, their physical attributes, and the like is also highly necessary and cannot be taken for granted.

A number of studies have shown that attendance in nursery schools has a beneficial effect upon personality development and upon subsequent learning capacity. Most of these studies were done in better schools; some of them in special experimental schools and in schools organized to provide training for preschool teachers. Hence it is likely that the results achieved by all nursery schools,

some of which are no more than day-homes for children or inferior caricatures of what a good nursery school should be like, are not as good. Moreover, it is difficult to separate out the biased sampling which is sometimes present when children who attend a nursery school are compared with those who do not. With these reservations in mind, some typical findings that have been confirmed in a number of studies with care for the methodological problems involved will be considered.

Nursery-school attendance fosters more mature patterns of social adjustment. In this pattern of improved behavior, ability to tolerate and deal with frustration is especially noticeable (82). This type of gain is significant directly in terms of the improved social adjustment it facilitates, and is important indirectly in fostering more independence, greater learning ability, and more pleasure in relating to people under various conditions of living. Other studies have confirmed similar types of gains in social adjustment. Among these additional findings we may note that children gain in degree of social participation, and in ability to make effective and cooperative use of the skills and resources of other persons in solving problems (83).

Aside from these types of global gains in social adjustment, nursery-school attendance helps to diminish or to eradicate maladaptive responses and poor habit patterns. Among the types of behaviors that are thus affected, as typical, are: decreased tension and "nervousness," *hyperkinesis* (overactivity), poor eating habits, failure to complete tasks, and decreased number of mannerisms (84). It should not be expected that nursery schools will be able to correct very serious problems of maladjustment, although they may be of some help in reducing the severity of some of these problems, but rather they can help to *improve* already good habit patterns, help to stabilize good social adjustment, and help to *prevent* the emergence of poor behavior responses and poor social adjustment. It is likely that such improvements will be long-lasting and have cumulatively beneficial effects on other aspects of behavior (85).

REACTIONS TO PHYSICAL INJURY AND DISEASE

In the course of the child's development he is likely to injure himself, have certain common or rare diseases, and possibly need some operative procedure. In all cases such conditions are likely to exaggerate, slightly or severely, the psychological problems peculiar to the period in which the affliction occurs or the personality patterns that the child has developed as part of his unique methods of adaptation. However, these reactions are not necessarily inevitable. In some instances the effects of the illness or the injury, per se, may produce concomitant psychological changes, but in most instances it is not the physical condition that accounts for the change but rather the ways in which the child and his family (and especially his mother) react to the condition. Even when the physical condition is highly important in its direct effect upon behavior, the emotional and social conditions affecting the child are also of considerable importance.

Any physical injury or disease tends to have some psychological effect upon the child. Not only is he incapacitated or impaired in physical functioning to some extent, but his concern over his "illness" causes him to focus more attention upon his own body. This has important psychological (and indirectly physical) advantages, since more energy is available for dealing with the body condition. It is quite natural then for the child to withdraw some of his attention and interest from the external world of affairs; he has less of it available for such purposes. He may also require or demand that mother give him more attention than she formerly did. All of this is to be expected and is part of the process of recovery and convalescence.

At times the youngster may become more, rather than less, active. We may think that he is being "cantankerous" or willful, but this may not be the case at all—at least not in the beginning. Such heightened irritability may not be the result of any physical illness in any direct sense, but it often is a defensive reaction of the ego to the threat which it perceives as a consequence of the physical illness. A *certain amount* of flexibility, even of yielding to the youngster's demands, may be helpful. He is trying to fight his reduced effectiveness as a total person, and needs some help through understanding and increased attention during this stage of the process.

To understand these alternate (and sometimes simultaneous) ways in which the child responds to injury or disease, we must understand the regressive process that accompanies such conditions (86). When the body is handicapped the person suffers some degree of trauma. In severe conditions the trauma may even precipitate castration anxiety; i.e., the child may feel that he is losing body intactness, that he may suffer catastrophe, or that he will remain forever incapacitated. It is difficult for the adult, who

has undergone many illness experiences, to understand why the child should expect never to recover even from a minor illness. A little reflection will show, however, that since the child has not had any, or has had very little, experience with recovery from illness, he has not yet learned to *anticipate* recovery. Often, too, the concern or overconcern of the parents with the illness may make it seem even more threatening in this respect. Since the child experiences trauma,

Convalescence may often be speeded up when the hospital ward offers diversions such as play activities, pets, or other interests. (U. of Mich.)

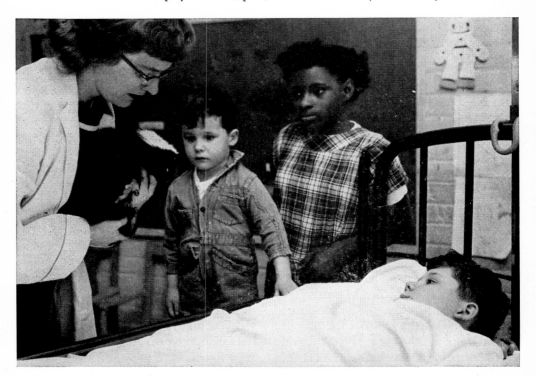

he responds as he responds to all trauma: he regresses slightly or even markedly. He tends to employ for a while mechanisms of behavior that formerly proved successful; that is, he retreats to former modes of defense. If the parent is unduly concerned with such temporary regressions (as is usually the case), then the regression tends to be reinforced.

Modern pediatricians recommend that some indulgence of the child during illness or in the recovery period after injury be tolerated. If the child refuses to remain in his bed, but wishes to wander around the room or play on the carpet, it is not essential, except during acute stages of the illness or when other factors definitely contra-indicate, to insist upon bed-rest (86). Special attention, opportunity to play with toys that were previously discarded, and permission to engage in some activities that have been outdated may be not only necessary but desirable. These serve the child's temporary regressive needs and provide avenues of tension-discharge that are important to the process of recovery.

There are two special problems that involve the parents. One of these is parental anxiety over the illness of the child. When such anxiety is neurotic in character (that is, when it is overdetermined by the inner needs of the parents), it is likely to be communicated to the child and increase his own anxiety. Although it is understandable for the parent to be concerned about the child's condition, it is also important to be objective and not become too involved emotionally.

Good care (familial, medical, and the like) is necessary, but overconcern solves nothing and only produces stronger regressive effects in the child. It is also worth emphasizing that there must be limits to the child's quest for special attention and indulgence. As far as possible, the usual routines should be maintained with respect to discipline and to interpersonal relations. A "softening" or relaxing rather than an abrogation of these controls is desirable. The usual controls help the child to retain or to recover more rapidly his own inner security and to prevent the exploitation of *secondary gains.*

Secondary gains refer to the indirect advantages an individual obtains from his symptoms or his illness. As a result of illness, the sufferer is given special attention and things are made somewhat easier for him. He is often relieved of his responsibilities and obligations, at least for a while. Thus the individual tends to want to hold on to the advantages he has gained through his illness. That is why it is so important to relax but not abrogate all controls or all discipline. Moreover, the positive gains from recovery, which are usually quite evident to the child, must be maximized as soon as it is possible to do so.

A special problem which confronts both parents and their children concerns hospitalization and surgery. When such procedures become necessary, the child's anxiety may become very marked (and so may the parents'). Separation from the anchorage of one's family is difficult enough under favorable circumstances, but separation when one is ill and incapacitated is doubly difficult. Hence separation anxiety under such circumstances is to be expected. Similarly, fear of mutilation or even death as a result of surgery may stimulate considerable castration anxiety. To a child, surgery is confusing, fearful, and foreboding. Tonsillectomies may precipitate fears of dying or losing one's physical capacities or even of losing one's penis, even when the doctor knows that the danger in a given case is very slight. In addition, the strange and restricting routines of the hospital, the new sleeping quarters, the absence of loved ones, the changes in routines, the sometime rough and even painful physical handling, the constant change in nurses-attendants-doctors-visitors—all of these are anxiety-inducing for a time. Recent studies of hospital procedures for children, and in particular of operative procedures for children, have led in many instances to radically revised procedures. In the first place, hospitalization is now more often avoided, and treatment given in the home (even when somewhat better facilities may be available for the condition in the hospital), in order to avoid the anxieties of hospitalization and thus to avoid delaying recovery. Then, it is often recommended that operative procedures be delayed until the child is emotionally ready or can be prepared for such a procedure (16). When hospitalization is necessary or cannot be delayed, emotional preparation for the hospital visit (by someone who is not himself or herself emotionally upset at such a prospect), involving discussion of its purposes, what is likely to happen, how beneficial (although painful) the procedure may be, and the like—all of this can be quite helpful. Some hospitals now ask that a parent (usually the mother) accompany the child not only to the hospital but also to the operating room; some permit or encourage the parent to stay or sleep in the same room with the child. Contrary to previous beliefs, parents do not, as a rule, interfere with hospital procedures, and, on the contrary, can assist the hard-pressed staff and greatly aid the child in recovery from the traumata of hospitalization and recovery from operative conditions. In the hospital, as in the home, the emotional anchorage of the mother offers many assets for recovery from trauma and for healthy emotional growth.

The case of Harold, previously discussed in Chapter 1, illustrates some of the principles we have been discussing. Harold showed regression in many aspects of his behavior when he had his tonsillectomy at the hospital. He suffered from both separation anxiety (since he was removed from his home and could see his mother only in the evenings) and castration anxiety (although some attempt had been made to prepare him for his operation). His anxieties precipitated his regression and made his convalescence during and after hospitalization more difficult and prolonged than it might have been. In Harold's case, the practice of the hospital in advising his parents not to remain with him before and after the operation literally severed him from the anchorage he so desperately needed during his emotionally traumatic experience.

GENERAL READINGS

1. Berne, E., *The Mind in Action*. New York: Simon and Schuster, 1947.
2. Child Study Association of America, *Facts of Life for Children*. New York: Bobbs-Merrill, 1954.
3. Josselyn, I., *The Happy Child*. New York: Random House, 1955.
4. Murphy, L. B., *Personality in Young Children*, 2 vols. New York: Basic Books, 1956.
5. Valentine, C. W., *The Normal Child and Some of His Abnormalities.* Baltimore: Penguin, 1957.
6. Wolff, W., *The Personality of the Preschool Child*. New York: Grune & Stratton, 1946.

SELECTED BIBLIOGRAPHY

7. Katcher, A., "The discrimination of sex differences by young children," *J. Genet. Psychol.*, 1955, 87, 131-143.
8. Hattendorf, K. W., "A study of the questions of young children concerning sex: A phase of an experimental approach to parental education," *J. Soc. Psychol.*, 1932, 3, 37-65.
9. Kinsey, A. C., *et al.*, *Sexual Behavior in the Human Female*. Philadelphia: Saunders, 1953.
10. Huschka, M., "The incidence and character of masturbation threats in a group of problem children," *Psychoanal. Quart.*, 1938, 7, 338-356.
11. Rabban, M., "Sex-role identification in young children in two diverse social groups," *Genet. Psychol. Monogr.*, 1950, 42, 81-158.
12. Schilder, P., *Mind*. New York: Columbia University, 1942.
13. Horowitz, R. E., "Spatial localization of the self," *J. Soc. Psychol.*, 1935, 6, 379-387.
14. Schilder, P., *The Image and Appearance of the Human Body*. London: Paul Kegan, Trench, Trubner, 1935.
15. Dillon, M. S., "Attitudes of children toward their own bodies and those of other children," *Child Develpm.*, 1935, 5, 165-176.
16. Jessner, L., Blom, G. E., and Waldfogel, S., "Emotional implications of tonsillectomy and adenoidectomy on children," in *The Psychoanalytic Study of the Child*, Vol. VII. New York: International Universities Press, 1952.
17. Erikson, E. H., *Childhood and Society*. New York: Norton, 1950.
18. Fisher, S., and Cleveland, S. E., *Body Image and Personality*. Princeton, New Jersey: Van Nostrand, 1958.

19. Baldwin, A. L., "The effect of home environment on nursery-school behavior," *Child Develpm.*, 1949, 20, 49-61.
20. Olson, W. C., *Child Development.* Boston: Heath, 1949.
21. Mechem, E., "Affectivity and growth in children," *Child Develpm.*, 1943, 14, 91-115.
22. Hutt, M. L., and Gibby, R. G., *Patterns of Abnormal Behavior.* Boston: Allyn and Bacon, 1957.
23. Hebb, D. O., *The Organization of Behavior.* New York: Wiley, 1949.
24. Macfarlane, J. W., Allen, L., and Honzik, M. P., "A developmental study of the behavior problems of normal children between twenty-one months and fourteen years," *Univer. Calif. Publ. Child Develpm.*, 1954, No. 2.
25. Harris, D. B., Gough, H. G., and Martin, W. E., "Children's ethnic attitudes: II. Relationship to parental beliefs concerning child training," *Child Develpm.*, 1950, 21, 169-181.
26. Sewall, M., "Two studies in sibling rivalry: I. Some causes of jealousy in young children," *Smith College Stud. Soc. Work*, 1930, 1, 6-22.
27. Bossard, J. H. S., and Sanger, M., "The large family," *Amer. Sociol. Rev.*, 1952, 17, 3-9.
28. Challman, R. C., "Factors influencing friendships among preschool children," *Child Develpm.*, 1932, 3, 146-158.
29. Radke, M. J., "The relation of parental authority to children's behavior attitudes," *Univer. Minn. Child Welf. Monogr.*, 1946, No. 22.
30. Murphy, L. B., *Social Behavior and Child Personality.* New York: Columbia University, 1937.
31. Honigmann, J. J., *Culture and Personality.* New York: Harper, 1954.
32. Sontag, L. W., *The Fels Research Institute for the Study of Human Development.* Yellow Springs, Ohio: Antioch College, 1946.
33. Wegeman, M. E., "Using today's resources for your child's health," in Gruenberg, S. M. (ed.), *Encyclopedia of Child Care and Guidance.* Garden City, New York: Doubleday, 1954.
34. Gesell, A., and Ilg, F. L., *Child Development.* New York: Harper, 1949.
35. Collins, S. D., "The incidence and causes of illness at specific ages," *Milbank Memorial Fund Quart.*, 1935, 13, 320-338.
36. Mowrer, O. H., *Learning Theory and Personality Dynamics.* New York: Ronald, 1950.
37. McCarthy, D., "Language development in children," in Carmichael, L. (ed.), *Manual of Child Psychology.* New York: Wiley, 1954.
38. Goldfarb, W., "Psychological privation in infancy and subsequent adjustment," *Amer. J. Orthopsychiat.*, 1945, 15, 247-255.

39. English, O. S., and Pearson, G. H. J., *Emotional Problems of Living.* New York: Norton, 1945.

40. Fenichel, O., *The Psychoanalytic Theory of Neuroses.* New York: Norton, 1945.

41. Rugg, H., Krueger, L., and Sondergaard, A., "Studies in child personality. I. A study of the language of kindergarten children," *J. Educ. Psychol.*, 1929, 20, 1-18.

42. Smith, M. E., "A study of five bilingual children from the same family," *Child Develpm.*, 1931, 2, 184-187.

43. Hayakawa, S. I., *Language in Action.* New York: Harcourt, Brace, 1939.

44. Smith, M. E., "An investigation of the development of the sentence and extent of vocabulary in young children," *Univer. Iowa Stud. Child Welf.*, 1926, No. 5.

45. Nice, M. M., "Length of sentences as a criterion of child's progress in speech," *J. Educ. Psychol.*, 1925, 16, 370-379.

46. Nice, M. M., "An analysis of the conversation of children and adults," *Child Develpm.*, 1932, 3, 204-236.

47. Wellman, B. L., *et al.*, "Speech sounds of young children," *Univer. Iowa Stud. Child Welf.*, 1931, No. 2.

48. Mead, M., *Sex and Temperament.* New York: Mentor Books, 1950.

49. Kidd, D., *Savage Childhood: A Study of Kafir Children.* London: Black, 1906.

50. Van Alstyne, D., *Play Materials and the Choice of Play Materials of Preschool Children.* Chicago: University of Chicago, 1932.

51. Freud, A., *Introduction to the Technique of Child Analysis.* New York: Nervous and Mental Disease Publishing Co., 1926.

52. Axline, V. M., *Play Therapy.* Boston: Houghton Mifflin, 1947.

53. Cockrell, D. L., "A study of the play of children of preschool age by an unobserved observer," *Genet. Psychol. Monogr.*, 1935, 17, 377-469.

54. Murphy, L. B., *Social Behavior and Child Personality.* New York: Columbia University, 1937.

55. Rapaport, D. (ed.), *Organization and Pathology of Thought.* New York: Columbia University, 1951.

56. Ames, L. B., and Learned, J., "Imaginary companions and related phenomena," *J. Genet. Psychol.*, 1946, 69, 147-167.

57. Terman, L. M., *The Measurement of Intelligence.* Boston: Houghton Mifflin, 1916.

58. Terman, L. M., and Merrill, M. A., *Measuring Intelligence.* Boston: Houghton Mifflin, 1937.

59. McNemar, Q., *The Revision of the Stanford-Binet Scale: An Analysis of the Standardization Data.* Boston: Houghton Mifflin, 1942.

60. Goodenough, F. L., "The measurement of mental growth in childhood," in Carmichael, L. (ed.), *Manual of Child Psychology*, 2nd ed. New York: Wiley, 1954.

61. Wechsler, D., *Wechsler Intelligence Scale for Children*. New York: Psychological Corporation, 1949.

62. Krugman, J. I., Justman, J., Wrightstone, J. W., and Krugman, M., "Pupil functioning on the Stanford-Binet and the Wechsler Intelligence Scale for Children," *J. Consult. Psychol.*, 1951, 15, 475-483.

63. Spearman, C., *The Abilities of Man*. New York: Macmillan, 1927.

64. Thorndike, E. L., *et al.*, *The Measurement of Intelligence*. New York: Teachers College, Columbia University, 1926.

65. Thurstone, L. L., *The Vectors of the Mind: Multiple-Factor Analysis for the Isolation of Primary Traits*. Chicago: University of Chicago, 1935.

66. Thurstone, L. L., and Thurstone, T. G., "Factorial studies of intellegence," *Psychometr. Monogr.*, 1941, No. 2.

67. Thurstone, L. L., *Tests of Primary Mental Abilities for Ages 5 and 6*. Chicago: Science Research Associates, 1946.

68. Heinis, H., "A personal constant," *J. Educ. Psychol.*, 1926, 17, 163-186.

69. Courtis, S. A., *The Measurement of Growth*. Detroit: Mimeographed and published by the author.

70. Wellman, B. L., "Some new bases for interpretation of the I.Q.," *J. Genet. Psychol.*, 1932, 41, 116-126.

71. Newman, H. H., Freeman, F. N., and Holzinger, K. J., *Twins: A Study of Heredity and Environment*. Chicago: University of Chicago, 1937.

72. Woodworth, R. S., *Heredity and Environment: A Critical Survey of Recently Published Material on Twins and Foster Children*. New York: Social Science Research Council, 1941.

73. Honzik, M. P., Macfarlane, J. W., and Allen, L., "The stability of mental test performance between two and eighteen years," *J. Exp. Educ.*, 1948, 17, 309-324.

74. Bartlett, F. C., *Remembering*. Cambridge, England: Cambridge University, 1932.

75. Johnson, W., *People in Quandries*. New York: Harper, 1946.

76. Springer, D., "Development in young children of an understanding of time and the clock," *J. Genet. Psychol.*, 1952, 80, 83-96.

77. Ames, L. B., "The development of the sense of time in the young child," *J. Genet. Psychol.*, 1946, 68, 97-125.

78. Jones, H. E., and Conrad, H. S., "The growth and decline of intelligence," *Genet. Psychol. Monogr.*, 1933, No. 3.

79. Read, K., *The Nursery School*. Philadelphia: Saunders, 1950.

80. Redl, F., and Wineman, D., *Controls from Within*. Glencoe, Illinois: Free Press, 1952.

81. Gardner, D. E. M., *Education in Nursery Schools*. London: Methuen, 1951.

82. Keister, M. E., "The behavior of young children in failure," *Univer. Iowa Stud. Child Welf.*, 1938, 14, 27-82.

83. Jersild, A. T., and Fite, D. M., "The influence of nursery-school experience on children's social adjustments," *Child Develpm. Monogr.*, 1939, No. 25.

84. Hattwick, B. W., "The influence of nursery-school attendance upon the behavior and personality of the preschool child," *J. Exp. Educ.*, 1936, 5, 180-190.

85. Van Alstyne, D., and Hattwick, L. A., "A follow-up study of the behavior of nursery-school children," *Child Develpm.*, 1939, 19, 43-72.

86. Freud, A., "The role of bodily illness in the mental life of children," in *The Psychoanalytic Study of the Child*, Vol. VII. New York: International Universities Press, 1952.

7

Early school years —socialization away from home

THE PERIOD FROM six years to about thirteen years is commonly referred to as the *middle school years*, in contrast to the immediately preceding period of the *preschool* years. We shall discuss the development of the child during this span of eight years in two sections; the first, which we shall call the *early school years*, will be treated in this chapter; the second, which we shall call the *intermediate school years*, will be presented in the next chapter.

Like all divisions into periods or stages this division is somewhat arbitrary, and is made for convenience of study. As we have learned, growth is continuous although it is accented by spurts and lags, and transition between successive stages of growth is inconspicuous for the most part. Nevertheless, each period in life has certain outstanding characteristics which differentiate it, as a total period, from all others, even though the boundary lines between successive periods are obscure. The early school years, by which we refer to the period from six to ten years of age inclusive, differ in some important respects from the subsequent period, which ends in puberty and adolescence. They are the years when family ties are broken for the first time, when the child may even "forsake" his family for his gang, and when socialization away from the family becomes highly important. In contrast, the intermediate school years are marked by a more accurate and more objective self-appraisal, when moral standards have some degree of flexibility in contrast to the rigidities of the earlier period, and when prepubertal spurts in physical growth begin to usher in the turbulent changes of puberty.

Both periods, the early and the intermediate school years, comprise the psychosexual stage that the psychoanalysts have described as the *latency period*. Both periods are marked by the comparative slowing down in the rate of growth from that of the preceding years and by the acquisition and integration of complex social and intellectual skills. Thus the two school periods from six years to thirteen years have much in common. As we have suggested, however, their differences are sufficiently important to warrant separate consideration of at least selected aspects. The general phenomena of latency and of personality development will be discussed in this chapter, inasmuch as these apply equally well to both periods.

PERSONALITY DEVELOPMENT IN THE LATENCY PERIOD

Latency is the period when the child's interests turn to reality, and when he begins to give up the imaginative fantasies of the preceding epoch for more realistic and more objective types of activities. According to the psychoanalytic view, partly because of intense anxieties stemming from the castration fears of the oedipal situation, with reinforcement having its source in social-sexual taboos, the individual shows a marked reduction in his sexual interests in the parent of the opposite sex. There is decreased overt sexual behavior, in general, and the begin-

ning of *sublimation* through which sexual drives are channeled into socially approved, nonsexual activities. In this view, there is a period of sexual quiescence lasting until puberty ushers in a new phase of highly intense sexual strivings and conflicts. However it should be noted that Freud did *not* suggest that: (a) all of the phenomena of latency were uniformly present in all persons, or that (b) all sexual interests and activities were eliminated. This point is emphasized because so many writers who have commented on Freud's formulations assumed that this is just what was stated and have then proceeded to demonstrate its invalidity on this basis.

The traditional psychoanalytic view postulates only that the oedipal phases of sexuality are repressed and that with this repression a considerable portion of the sexual drives are deflected from obvious sexual objects and interests. Where cultural practices have previously instilled considerable guilt and anxiety about sexual drives and where sexual behavior has been strongly disapproved, repression is more severe and the latency phenomena are more pronounced (10). It would be expected that where these conditions did not obtain, latency would be less severe or perhaps not present at all.

It is clear from relatively recent research that sexual interests do not disappear during the latency period (11). Children continue to engage in masturbatory activity and to show exploratory interests in each others' bodies. It is also clear that the extent of such activities and interests varies with social class and with social practice (12). In some primitive societies in which the overt expression of sexual drives is not discouraged there may even be a continuing and increasing amount of heterosexual activity (12). All of these findings do not negate the Freudian hypothesis although they may lead to some modification of it and to more rigorous statements of its operation.

Repression of oedipal sexuality is accompanied by repression of some aspects of fantasy, sublimation into intellectual pursuits in which imagination plays a relatively minor role, reduction of emotionality and of spontaneity in emotional life, and increased needs for conformity and ritual. As Susan Isaacs has put it, "The fantasy life as a whole *gradually* [italics ours] tends to become repressed, and the child begins to concern himself much more with what is real and true." (13) Repression is supported by the defense mechanisms of *reaction formation* and to a lesser extent by *denial*. As we have said, through sublimation the child shows an increased interest in "taking in" and making realistic use of the methods and goals of his environment. Reaction formation may be observed fairly directly during this period in the child's needs to be a "goody-goody," in his great willingness to conform, and in the upsurge of morality (superego). When the phenomena of latency are very marked the behavior of the child becomes excessively rigid and the symptoms of *compulsion neurosis* may become evident. This psychoneurosis is marked by a strong, impelling need to engage in endlessly repetitive and apparently irrational behavior with marked anxiety when such behavior is restricted or prohibited. In the American culture, especially among the middle

class, even among normal children there is some increase in compulsivity which may be observed in the repetitive chants that children love to say over and over, in preoccupation with magic and ritual, or in the secret and symbolic ceremonial of childhood gangs and groups.

The phenomena of latency increase until about ten years of age, when they are at their height, and then remain at this level until puberty begins. Some writers suggest that latency reaches its peak at about eight years (14). Freud believed that latency was an essential part of civilization and was *inevitable in this kind of society* (10). The discouragement or deflection of sexual impulses at a time when the zones are changing (due to biological development) and when procreative ability is not yet present permits a period of integration in behavior to take place and encourages the internalization of social mores. Such a period is therefore preparatory for the assumption of later, adult responsibility. The increase in realistic interests fosters mastery of the world of real people and real objects. The work of sublimation is helpful in increasing the extension of intellectual interests and mental growth of certain kinds.

The hazards of latency are that excessive repression leads to severe inhibition of emotional behavior and imagination, produces overconformity at the expense of vital spontaneity and growth, and even fosters the emergence of neurotic behavior. Gurin has shown that even within the "normal range" of school children latency tends to produce excessive and harmful stereotypy and conformity. She also demonstrated experimentally that, in comparison with adolescents, children in the primary grades and adolescents who have not emerged from their latency are lacking in imagination, spontaneity, and freedom from intellectual inhibition (15). In our society, which tends to be highly ambivalent about sexual matters (note the "double standard," or the norm which permits men to enjoy vulgar stories openly while women must be more "lady-like" in this respect), and which augments anxiety by inconsistent attitudes and excessively moralistic attitudes toward childhood sex, children may seek psychological refuge in excessively severe repression and excessive latency. Modern parents are unnecessarily shocked when they discover that their children may have had what the adult would regard as "homosexual experience," but which may be a perfectly normal, temporary increase in nonheterosexual interests.

During this period children interiorize the code of the gang. More and more time is spent away from home and much of it is spent in gang activities (16). We shall have more to say about the formation and characteristics of such gangs in a later section of this chapter, but at this point we wish to emphasize that such activity encourages the assumption by the child of his gang's values, quite often in conflict with those of the home. Through the gang he learns to assume new roles for identification. Now his idols are the kinds of people who show good mastery of the world—often they are people of abnormal strength, skill or mental capacity. These new idols gradually become more important during the latter phases of the early school years as the relationship to the parents is loosened and, at times, strongly defied. The assumption of new sex roles or of further differentiation in sex roles, and the evolution of a more mature morality also occur during this period. In all of this, the foundations laid in the home, the earlier characteristics of the personality structure, the nature of the continuing home conditions, and the characteristics of the child's physical development influence the course of further personality development. In the following sections we shall examine each of these and related factors in turn.

Sex roles and sexual identification

We have repeatedly stressed the point in preceding chapters that many, if not all, aspects of sex roles as they are manifested in social interactions are clearly related to cultural practices. Whatever may be the proclivity for certain kinds of social behavior that is founded on biological differences between male and female, the actual behavior of the sexes is markedly influenced by the roles assigned to them by society. Nevertheless, psychoanalytic theory indicates that the problems of the sexes are different in many respects because of the differences in the process of identification. Both boys and girls initially, in our culture, identify with their mother. During the oedipal period both experience conflict because of the opposing pull of attraction toward the father, and both experience threat because they find it difficult to reconcile these opposing drives toward father and mother. In the case of the boy, castration fears, with focus on fear of bodily damage or pain, arise as he finds his father a rival for his mother's affection. He then, in order to resolve this threat, moves in the direction of identifying with his father, who is biologically a more similar model to himself than his mother. Once he has begun to identify with this new role, his problem is to learn it thoroughly, and to learn to integrate all of his behavior around this nucleus. During the latency period he can proceed toward this uninterrupted goal as he learns to assume the appropriate (for our culture) models of active, striving, aggressive maleness, until finally he can assume the adult role of a procreator and breadwinner. On the other hand the girl has a more complicated route, as we have pointed out previously. She has to learn to shift her identification from her mother to her father, and then to *shift back again* to a re-identification with her mother (and women) in order to find her mature role as a woman, a wife, and a homemaker (in our culture), as well as that of a mother in a biological sense. Her psychological route is longer and more complicated than that of the boy. On the basis of this theory, we would expect more complications and difficulties in her course of psychosexual development as well as a slower rate of identification with the appropriate sex-role. As we shall see, research as well as clinical evidence favors these predictions.

There is considerable evidence that girls are more prone to develop neurotic traits than are boys (and that boys develop aggressive conduct problems more

frequently). The evidence shows that girls score higher on tests involving anxiety, depression, seclusiveness, and emotionality (unstable emotional behavior) than do boys of a comparable age (17). It is true that our culture emphasizes certain personality characteristics for girls, such as passivity, dependence, and inhibition of aggressive, outgoing behavior. These culturally fostered traits increase the difficulties of the emotional adjustment of girls, since they cannot as easily direct their impulses outward in aggressive acts (and they thus learn to inhibit the *direct*, behavioral expressions of their frustrations). Hence, this finding alone (that girls tend to be neurotic more often than boys) cannot be taken as confirmation of Freudian theory. We can only say that it is consistent with it. Boys are more frequently referred to clinics for aggressive and antisocial behavior, for hyperactivity and motor symptoms, and for academic difficulties (18). This is also what we should expect in view of both culture-bound practices and psychoanalytic theory. Boys may, however, be referred to clinics more frequently than girls not only because their behavior is, in fact, more unruly, but because cultural expectations are such that it is easier to refer a boy for such a problem than a girl. On the whole, however, it is clear that boys "act up" more often but have less frequent and less intense emotional or neurotic maladjustment. One possible exception to this general conclusion is that boys stutter more frequently—and stuttering often reflects an underlying emotional disturbance. However, the pattern of hyperactivity and motor behavior we have already discussed as prevalent for boys in our culture may foster this problem in boys more often as part of their development of greater hostile drives and aggressive behavior. It may thus lay the basis for this form of "oral aggression" in their case.

More directly pertinent to the general hypothesis of slower and more complicated sex identification for girls is the finding that girls do, in fact, learn their sex identity at a later age (19). Boys show clearer awareness of sex-appropriate behavior when they are given a free choice with toys, and they show this awareness at an earlier age. They prefer to play with and are more interested in such "masculine" toys as a fire-truck, a cement mixer, and the like while disdaining toys related to female interests. Girls' interests are more indecisive and become sex-oriented at a later age (after eight years). On personality tests, too, girls and boys showed significant differences in terms of sexual identification (20). Even when economic factors were controlled, there was evidence "for the assumption of greater prestige value in the male as compared to the female role in young children" (ages 5 years 4 months to 6 years 4 months). Again, it is difficult to separate out the effects of culture practice, but the kinds of findings we have been summarizing have been confirmed in widely varying cultures by anthropologists (12). They are certainly consistent with the general thesis that girls have a

longer period of learning identifications appropriate to their sex. As we shall see later, such factors as class status and class practice influence identification in a significant manner. It is only toward the end of the early school years that most children have developed unequivocal sex identifications.

When children first attend the primary grades there is little differentiation between the sexes in the composition of play groups. Boys and girls at the age of six years play together freely and spontaneously. There are some activities that boys prefer, usually those involving more muscular activity and more "rough-house," but at this stage such differentiations are not the rule. By the age of ten years, however, the differences in patterns of play activity between the sexes are quite marked. At this stage, boys strongly prefer to play with boys, and girls with girls, and separate gangs as well as play groups have been developed. It is interesting to note how much easier it is for girls to resent being kept out of boys' games than the other way around. Again, this is an interesting commentary on our culture values. For some girls, being shut out of the games and activities of boys is a serious problem. Many of these "tomboys" hold on as long as they can to the myth that they are not different from boys. There are many reasons for this state of affairs, but one of the most common configurations of determining factors has to do with the status that "maleness" has in the home. When high male status is reinforced by a strong *electra complex* in the girl or when the parents have clearly expressed preferences for boys, the girl may have great difficulty in accepting her feminine role—sometimes with grave personality consequences.

There is a parallel development of the differentiation of play groups and the development of substitute models for identification outside the home. At six years of age the idol of the boy is the father while the idol of the girl is the mother (under usual circumstances). Gradually these parental idols are replaced not only by the idols taken from stories, radio, television, and movies, but also by idols from the play group or gang. As we shall see, this shifting in models for identification frequently causes clashes with parental authority, for the out-of-family idols seem to have special virtues and strong characteristics to the child. They tend to be idealized images—projections of the still somewhat magical wishes of the child upon his idol, or they tend to have much more salience for the child than the parent—for being like the leader of the gang or being accepted by the gang becomes a matter of psychological life-or-death while the child is away from home. Even more than this, the shifts in identification are a necessary testing out of one's mastery of reality and of the integration of new roles for oneself—and during the process, while this integration is taking place and still is precarious, the youngster over-reacts by rejecting familial values at times (or so it seems to the parents). Tolerance for these needs and consequent behaviors of the child, together with faith in the adequacy of the foundation for character laid in the home, may help to tide a parent over during this transitional, and occasionally rebellious or defiant, period.

Along with these changing identifications, the interests and abilities of youngsters change rapidly. We have already indicated some of the differences in sex-related interests. In our culture, and during the present epoch, boys show greater interests in tools, machines, space ships, antiaircraft missiles (and guns of all kinds), and science, while girls show greater interests in dolls, cooking, sewing, and dancing (21). These differences are not universal, however, even in our own culture. They vary greatly from country to country and from family to family within the culture. The interests of girls in the Soviet Union are far different from those of girls in this country; the differences in interests between boys and girls in the southern states are quite different from those in the northern states; and the interests of both boys and girls are quite different in a family of the lower class.

During the early school years girls not only do better academic work (they remain superior in school work and grades through the high-school level) but they perform better on the verbal subtests of intelligence scales. What causes this type of difference is an open question. Here again, culture and constitution may interact in very complex ways so that it is difficult to distinguish native capacity from acquired talent and interest (22). Boys, on the other hand, perform better on tests and functions requiring mathematical abilities and scientific skills. Boys excel on abstract thinking as well as on tasks requiring rational, objective orientation—they seem to have more practical common sense, while girls are more likely to be more emotional, more unstable, and more idealistic. Once again we must caution that these sex-linked characteristics are *not necessarily* biologically linked; it is likely that cultural practices and not original human nature play a decisive role in producing the obtained differences.

Our review of the evidence concerning sex roles and sexual identification has uncovered considerable differences in the paths and characteristics of the two sexes. These differences must be taken into account in understanding a particular child, in planning the educational program for children, and in preventive or therapeutic mental hygiene measures. The differences are not inevitable in all cultural conditions nor in the life of a particular child. Nevertheless, a child's deviation in the pattern of sex-role or of sex-interest contributes to his difficulty in adapting and making further progress toward maturity.

Influence of home conditions on development

The period of the early school years marks the impact of community influences upon the child—the children of the neighborhood, the environment of the school, and the experiences of the church. We shall try to assess the ways in which these cultural forces outside of the home affect the child's behavior, but first we must consider the still central role of the home itself. For the home is the crucible in which personality development began, and throughout childhood it will continue to exercise the critical influence on its further development. The home is the place in which the culture of the community is reflected and through which its meaning is interpreted during the entire period of childhood.

During this period the child needs the security and understanding that a good home environment can give him. He may defy his mother or father, as he "tests out his wings" in extrafamilial identifications, but he still has to be able to fall back to his home with the firm assurance that he is liked and respected. Even his transgressions are understood in such a home as beginning attempts to find himself—that is to establish a new identity for himself away from home. This does not mean that he is given license to behave in any way that he sees fit; but it does not mean that his growing individuation, his faltering if rebellious attempts at asserting himself in terms of his gang, will be punished for fear that he is becoming bad or is willful or is trying to deny parental authority. The secure and understanding parent will enjoy seeing him test out his new sense of independence, not taking it too literally, and seeing it as evidence of growth toward maturity. He will not relinquish discipline in the home, only modify it to accord with the changing needs of the youngster, and only be more tolerant of his necessary "transgressions" as part of the pattern of maturing development. For the child will continue to need the models of his parents as mature people who are *different* from his own peers, who can restrain him when he impulsively wishes to go too far, and who can protect him against his own mistakes. He will also need them to punish him when punishment is called for—for moderate punishment that is just and appropriate serves to allay guilt over one's own insufficiently controllable impulses and sometimes dangerous tendencies. The control of the home affords the child limits against which he can and has to test out his own judgments and expectations. Parental patterns of guidance and discipline can vary tremendously within this general framework, but they must provide affection, understanding, and encouragement of the tendencies toward self-expression and individuality. The parents must welcome the child's growing uniqueness not as evidence of their own failure but as evidence of the child's movement away from his infantile dependence upon the home and toward his own separateness.

One of the best ways to demonstrate the influence of a "good" home is to contrast its consequences with those of a "poor" home. One could say, in general, that a poor home is one that retards the child in achieving independence, due to any factors in the parents such as over-concern about the child, neuroticism of the parents, overprotection of the child, inconsistency in general attitudes of the parents toward discipline, marital discord, and the like. Looked at from a positive view, one could say that the healthiest parents are those who make themselves as dispensable as possible to their children as quickly as their children's maturity will permit. There is ample evidence that overprotectiveness by the parents, particularly by the mother, dur-

ing the child's early formative years retards the child's emotional growth and makes him unduly dependent or even maladjusted (23). Symond's excellent, recent studies in this area offer specific types of evidence of this kind which we shall shortly review (24). The clearest general contrasts, however, may be derived by comparing the children of neurotic parents with those of well adjusted parents. One of the most comprehensive of these types of studies was that reported by Hardy (25). In this study two groups of children, from the third through the junior-high-school grades, who differed in respect to general adjustment, were compared in terms of the adjustment of their parents. The two groups were selected so that other relevant background factors of the parents were equated: factors such as social status, economic status, country of birth, permanence of residence, and the like. It was not possible to control for all relevant factors, but these were then considered in relationship to the patterns of findings. There were 144 poorly adjusted children and 110 well adjusted children, so judged mainly on the basis of psychological interviews conducted annually. It was found that the poorly adjusted children came much more frequently from disturbed homes. These were homes in which parent incompatibility, family tensions, and "complicating situations to wholesome development" were present. These differences were obtained even when the groups of parents were still further selected in terms of educational level and absence of "obvious forms of mental instabilities." It was further learned that most often maladjustment in the child was related to the "combinations of two or more complicating situations." This finding was based on the analysis of daily experiences of the children and showed that it was not single or infrequent disturbances in the home that resulted in the child's maladjustment, but rather it was the repetitive occurrences of such experiences that were significant. It may be heartening to parents who are apprehensive that occasional tensions in the home may unduly affect their children to learn that in these cases of maladjusted children four or more daily occurrences of complicating disturbances were the rule.

Experience in child guidance clinics and in psychiatric clinics bears out the conclusions of the Hardy study. (Indeed this study was derived in part from reports of such experience.) Maladjusted children typically come from broken homes, homes with intense marital discord, homes in which rejection of children is the rule, and homes with highly anxious parents (often guilt-ridden and highly insecure emotionally). Symonds has furnished us with experimental verification of some of these findings.

Symonds' studies are reported in his book, *The Psychology of Parent-Child Relationships* (24). In a series of researches, children coming from contrasting types of familial backgrounds were compared with respect to personality adjustment and social adjustment. The essential data consisted of ratings of parents and children made by carefully trained observers in terms of empirically derived check lists. We shall summarize the findings of two studies. In one on the effects of *rejection* of children by their parents, two matched groups of children (31 in each group) came respectively from homes in which they were accepted and rejected. The children were equated in terms of age, sex, socioeconomic status, intellectual ability, and school grade. In contrast to the children who came from homes in which they were accepted, the rejected children tended to be antisocial, rebellious against authority, and delinquent; they were emotionally insecure and showed many indications of underlying anxiety. The rejected group could be characterized as maladjusted with poor superego development. In this study no attempt was made to differentiate the specific patterns of rejection; indeed the small number of cases would render such a task very difficult. Moreover, some of the ratings of rejection–acceptance could have been biased since the raters were familiar with both children and their parents. However, the over-all differences were so significant and so consistent with intensive findings from clinical studies that they may be regarded as reliable. It is clear that the unfortunate consequences of a rejecting home atmosphere involve basic aspects of personality maladjustment.

In the other study reported in the same volume children coming from homes with *dominating* parents were compared with those coming from *submissive* parents. Unlike the previous study, in this case both sets of parental groups were deviant. The dominant parents could also be characterized as *overprotective*, although they did more than overprotect their children. They not only tended to control their children's daily routines to an unnecessary extent, but they were overprotective in such ways as giving them unnecessary special privileges (that is, preventing them from exercising initiative and independence); they were also overly critical and overly punitive. The *submissive* parents were dominated by their children: being too indulgent, and too permissive (that is, acceding unnecessarily to their wishes). This was a mixed group of parents, in the writers' opinion, since some of these parents were also neglectful or even deserted the child when the parent was needed. Unfortunately, this may mean that the two sets of parents were not consistently differentiated on the same variable of dominance-submission. Nevertheless, the findings for the two groups of children are illuminating. (There were 28 children in each group.) Children in the dominant group, in comparison with those in the submissive group, were unable to express themselves readily, inhibited, overly polite, retiring, and shy. On the other hand they were honest and dependable. In contrast the children from the submissive group were generally rebellious, irresponsible, stubborn, and careless. They were also rated as self-confident and capable of forming friendships outside of the home. We may note that both groups showed unfavorable personality characteristics and that both groups showed some positive personality traits. It might be worth asking whether the price in personality maladjustment was worth the gain of the positive personality traits under these

circumstances. One further point might be worth recording. The children in both groups had a considerable range in age: from the primary-grade level through the late adolescent level, with an average age approximating puberty. It would be interesting to know how variable the results would be for each separate age group; that is, *when* the effects of a particular home atmosphere become evident, and *what* these specific effects look like at each stage. Our previous analysis, in Chapters 4 and 5, has indicated that severe rejection or overproduction during the early years is likely to have even more profound consequences for general personality development.

Another, more recent study focuses upon an even more general issue; namely, the effects of extremes in strict and permissive home disciplines. Watson compared the personality characteristics of two groups of children coming from extremes on the variable of strict versus permissive home discipline (26). After extensive searching, and with the cooperation of parents, teachers, and social workers, 78 children in the first six grades of elementary school were selected for further study. All of these children came from "good" homes, that is, they came from homes in which they "were wanted, loved, and well cared for." The sample was drawn on the basis of a specially devised questionnaire, submitted to the mothers, in which home disciplinary practices in such common situations as those concerned with eating, sleeping, toilet-training, and caring for toys was evaluated. Watson discovered that it was *extremely difficult to find cases at the extreme in home permissiveness in discipline*. His sample consisted of only 34 such cases. He was much more easily able to secure cases from homes with extremely strict discipline: he used 44 cases of this kind. He commented that he was surprised at his difficulty, but in retrospect should not have been since it has been noted that of 47 cultures reported on by Whiting and Child *none* was evaluated as being less permissive than typical middle-class, white American families (27). All of these children, living in the eastern portion of Westchester county, New York, were brought voluntarily to the Guidance Center for psychological evaluation on the basis of a free-play period, Rorschach and Thematic Aperception tests, a figure-drawing test (all designed to get at personality characteristics of the children) and the Alexander Passalong performance test (to assess reaction to frustration).

In reviewing Watson's results it must be remembered that these children came from homes at the extremes in discipline. It was found that "no clear personality advantages (were) associated in general with strict discipline in a good home." Moreover, on four of the most reliably rated personality characteristics, the differences that were found were clearly in favor of the children who came from permissive homes. As a group, such children were found to be better socialized and cooperative, showed more initiative and independence, had less inner hostil-

ity and more friendly feelings toward others, and had a higher level of spontaneity, originality, and creativity. Watson is very cautious in interpreting these results, pointing out that it is difficult to establish a causal basis in a study that is essentially correlational in character. Nevertheless, these findings, supported as they are by many other related research studies, point up the highly important, favorable outcomes of permissive as opposed to strict home discipline. The bugaboo that many people append to permissiveness in the home is simply not supported by the evidence. We should note, further, that it is probably true that we are attacking a "straw man" when we complain of too much permissiveness in American homes; the facts indicate that just the opposite is true—we tend to be an inordinately strict type of culture in comparison with other cultures that have been studied.

One other general point should be made. We have said that some degree of rebelliousness on the part of children should be expected as part of the normal developmental pattern during the middle school years. At first this rebellion occurs without much conscious awareness on the part of the children; later they become conscious of it and are able to verbalize and report it. Indeed, such types of verbalized and reported expression of conflict tend to increase until sometime after puberty—probably until about 15 years, on the average (28, 29).

Social class and personality

We have seen in previous chapters how membership in a social class may influence child-rearing practices (Chapter 2), and how it may affect child-parent inter-actions (Chapters 4 and 5). Of particular importance in the middle years is the influence of class membership upon the extrafamilial experiences of the child, the kinds of playmates he has and their values and behavior, the kinds of schools he attends and their philosophies, goals and methods, and the like. Class membership is also related, of course, to the kinds of home conditions to which the child is exposed.

It must be clearly understood that it is not class membership, as such, which defines the variety of experiences a child has; it is, rather, the kinds of conditions and practices prevalent in that class in a particular community during a particular period of time. In some of the discussions of class and personality we find an assumption that certain characteristics are an inevitable part of class membership. Class membership, on the contrary, is only the vehicle that carries the contemporary practices of a particular community. The features of that vehicle are different in the same class (or even subdivisions of a class) in different parts of the country, in different countries, and at different times. Moreover, the relations of any class to another class are not fixed and immutable. Such relationships also vary widely depending on the characteristics of the adjacent classes which have a functional proximity to the class under consideration—and these relationships differ in different sections of the world, as well as within a given country. Finally, there is no constancy in the influence that membership in a class has upon all members of that class. Some people are deeply and continuously involved in and

influenced by the activities and experiences of their own class whereas others are only marginally affected, or even not affected at all by some or all of these phenomena.

The problem is even more complicated than this. The definition of a class is an arbitrary matter and one upon which sociologists are not in agreement. Some maintain that the primary basis of a class is the economic factor; others suggest that it is social practice, prestige value, and still other things. Some classes are highly *mobile* during certain epochs and under certain conditions—which means that membership in the class is fluid and that individuals can shift from one class to another without too much difficulty. Moreover, there are profound differences within the class in terms of the organization of the members of that class in vocational life or in community life. For example, some members of the middle class may be in a small business for themselves and as a consequence tend to associate with and be influenced by different selections of people than other members of the same class who work in a large industrial organization. (See Chapter 8 for further discussion of this problem.) The extent to which the parents of that class are able to or wish to participate in community activities which bring them into close relationships with members of other classes varies greatly in different types of communities.

These briefly stated considerations will caution the reader to evaluate the findings in this and other chapters in which class influence is discussed with considerable care. After all, the concept of class, although a useful one, is an abstraction to assist in cataloguing and evaluating certain kinds of societal experiences. Like all abstractions, the conclusions obtained in a study of a class are limited generalizations—which can only be applied properly to other samples if the conditions are replicated. In the end we have to know what *specific factors* associated with membership in a class, rather than the mere fact of class per se, contribute to the findings.

A number of studies have indicated that there are significant differences in adjustment of different classes. On the whole, it seems that middle-class parents tend, as a group, to be more accepting of their youngsters and more understanding and tolerant of their behavior than parents of the lower class (30). It used to be thought that the cause of this difference lay essentially in the economic differences of the two classes. It seemed reasonable to assume that economic privation fostered familial tension and so contributed directly to increased difficulties of parents in accepting their children —some even argued in understanding them. There is no gainsaying the fact that economic difficulty may be associated with some of these conditions in the parents, but one might still wonder whether the economic status was not determined, at least in part, by the personality and capability of the individual. This should not be taken to mean that the writers

have a "Voltairian notion" that in this "best of all possible worlds" anyone can become anything if only he wants to. However, it is reasonable to assume, we believe, that under modern conditions in our country many people can significantly influence their own economic destiny to some degree, and that therefore at least some of the individuals of the lower class were tense or maladjusted not as a result of their economic condition, but their economic status was influenced by their difficulty in adjustment and also *subsequently* contributed to their poor adjustment. One intensive and interesting study sheds some light on this complex problem.

Francis made a study by means of psychiatric interviews with 30 families to evaluate the relation between economic factors and parental attitudes, on the one hand, and the personality adjustment of their children, on the other (31). The families came from two different types of neighborhoods, one a poverty-stricken lower-class neighborhood and the other an average, substantial, middle-class neighborhood. It was found that whereas parental attitudes and behaviors were significantly related to children's adjustment, the physical and material aspects of the environment were not. Lack of money, lack of recreational facilities, and type of neighborhood did not relate to degree of adjustment but parental behaviors and attitudes such as interest in the activities of the children, upkeep of the home, interest in their childrens' school work, and tolerance of and encouragement of children's activities outside the home did have a significant bearing on the personality of children. The study

Learning about some of the social roles of the community. (U. of Mich.)

concluded that economic conditions, broken homes, foreign-born parentage and even physical sickness, which the investigator originally thought might be related to the adjustment of the children, were not so related.

Allison Davis has pointed out that lower-class and middle-class families have different kinds and different degrees of fears and tensions (32). They differ in their attitudes toward housing, activities carried on in the home, the importance placed on school work, attitudes about aggression, attitudes related to sex behavior and many other salient features of adjustment. In turn, these kinds of class differences, in anxieties and attitudes, affect the personality development of the children. Moreover, it has been noted by others that most American schools foster middle-class values, and hence lower-class children have greater difficulty in adjusting to such values (33, for example). Such children find it harder to progress in their academic work in the beginning, find less acceptance in school by predominantly middle-class teachers, and find it necessary to "go back" to their lower-class identifications and friends for support. These and other conditions of lower-class children lead them and their parents, in Davis' view, to acceptance of the unabashed use of•aggression as a mode of behavior, not only toward their peers but even toward their parents. However, although Davis and others believe that the economic factor is all-pervasive in generating such behavior, we have tried to show that both economic status and such behavior may be more significantly related to underlying personality configurations in the family (the parents, especially) and that although they are class-linked there is no inevitability about the relationships.

Another important issue related to class status is that of minority-group membership. Membership in such a group predisposes the individual to certain kinds of personality-forming experiences. It goes without saying that the qualifications we suggested about class status and personality apply to this problem as well. However, minority-group membership imposes an unusual burden, except in the ideal community in which there is true and full democracy in the practices of majority-group members toward the minority. For when parents or children feel defensive about their status in society, when they are denied opportunities for education, work and social participation because of minority-group membership, and when their group membership is difficult to reconcile with their

psychological needs, conflict and difficulty in personality adjustment, among other things, are more likely to ensue. There is nothing "innate" in any of these conditions. Children tend to be consciously unaware of their minority-group memberships until about five or six years of age, although the effects of such membership may have been present previously and they were cognizant of some of its aspects. By the age of six years, certainly, such awareness has begun to be conscious and identification with the group has become manifest. For example, in one study in which Negro children were asked to select which of two dolls, one a white one and the other a Negro doll, "looks like a Negro doll," most of the six-year-old children selected the Negro doll but at earlier levels they were unable to make such a choice. Such evidence merely points to an acknowledgment of the similarity in an aspect of appearance to one's color-group membership. Other studies have shown that it is much later when awareness of some of the cultural characteristics becomes manifest (34). It is not until about puberty that defensive reactions of minority group members become well established as "out-group" members of the society. At about this period, such children, even when well adjusted in other respects, have overt and latent hostility, regard the environment as generally unfriendly, and have well developed awareness of prejudices operating against them. Here is a prime example of how special subgroup status may influence the behavior of a group in subtle as well as gross ways. Research evidence points up the general conclusion that specific cultural factors, and not factors indigenous to race or group members *as group members*, are responsible for these deviant behaviors we sometimes call "natural" or "human nature" when we see them in the adult.

Physique and personality

Physical growth slows up during the early school years. Height and weight progress at rates of increase of about 5 and 10 per cent per year, respectively. By the time of puberty, at about an average age of 11 years for girls and 13 years for boys, height will have reached 5 feet on the average. Although girls reach a higher stature for a while than boys (and then boys overtake the girls), boys show a greater increase in muscular strength—possibly on the basis, in part, of different and more vigorous kinds of muscular activity. There is wide variability in the rates of growth among children, and although most of this variability is presumably re-

lated to constitutional factors, there is evidence that diet, emotional state, and cultural practices influence the rate and extent of growth. We have emphasized the fact previously that different children have different curves of growth—a fact that was largely obscured until longitudinal studies made this clear. Some individuals have a slow rate of growth for a while, then speed up during later childhood and adolescence, sometimes overtaking and exceeding those whose earlier pace of development was more rapid. Proportions of the body begin to approximate the proportions of the adult increasingly as the child moves through childhood to puberty.

One of the striking and significant features of physical growth during this period is the change in the structure of

Daytime naps are routine practice for many first-grade children. (U. of Mich.)

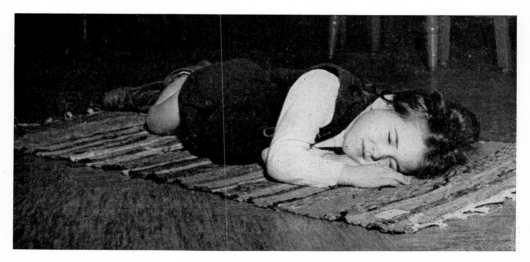

the face. Not only does the face begin to look more slim and lean during the early school years because of the change in the amount and distribution of fatty tissue in the face, but the proportions of the face and of the head gradually approach those that will be attained in adolescence. The forehead and the skull, however, assume a disproportionate amount of the area of the head during the early school years and the child appears to be a bit top-heavy. At about six years, too, the permanent teeth begin to make their appearance. As the baby teeth drop out and the larger permanent teeth appear the mouth takes on a "toothy" appearance, sometimes with large gaps where no replacements have developed. Some children seem to be wearing a perpetual grin! Often they look comical and charming at the same time.

Childhood illnesses and injuries take their toll during this period. There has been a remarkable drop in some causes of death due to considerable advances in medical care and in diet (35). The three leading causes of death up to and including the beginning of puberty are accidents, cancer, and poliomyelitis. Of these, accidents are about four times as frequently a cause of death as are the nearest competitive causes, and poliomyelitis is rapidly diminishing as a cause of death in recent years due to new preventive measures. Other causes of death have declined more than 90 per cent over the past 15 years—causes such as communicable diseases, rheumatic fever, and tuberculosis (36).

It seems clear that general bodily health as well as body type exert some influence on the course of personality development. We shall review the findings of two major studies to highlight this relationship. However, we must be cautious in interpreting the results of studies that show some degree of correlation between physical status and personality. In the first place, it is often difficult to say which came first: the physical condition or the personality characteristic. It is quite possible for disposition or the patterns of living to influence diet, metabolism, and growth. Then, the way in which the individual and others around him react to his difference in physical status or capacity will influence the significance of that factor in terms of personality reactions. When parents are overprotective or overconcerned about a child's physical condition (often because of unconscious anxieties of their own), or when playmates or siblings are inconsiderate of the differences in physical status or exaggerate their importance for their own amusement or defense, or when the child learns to overvalue physical attributes in relation to all other attributes, these secondary factors, rather than the specific physical condition itself, may produce the deleterious effect. Finally, the relationship of the child's chronological age to his physical deviation must be taken into account. In general, the closer to puberty the child is the more significant his physical status is likely to be in terms of his adjustment. This relationship is largely the result of the growing importance of adequacy in stamina, coordination, and size in the daily activities of children in our culture.

This is particularly true for boys to whom athletic prowess is important because of the significance for them of physical skills in many aspects of social interaction.

H. E. Jones studied a group of 78 boys over a six-year period, from age 11 years to age 17 years. From this group the ten boys rating highest on total strength, as measured by a battery of tests, were compared with the ten boys rating lowest on the same index (37). Comparison was made at each of the ages by a group of trained raters in terms of personality traits as observed during free play and in terms of personality measures derived from a personality inventory. At the earlier age, there was some difference in favor of the "strong" boys on emotional buoyancy and family adjustment, the other differences being very slight. By the later age, the "strong boys" were superior in every respect, and the differences in almost all personality factors between "weak" and "strong" subjects had become more pronounced. These differences involved, besides the two factors already noted, four additional factors: social adjustment, freedom from tensions, freedom from inferiority, and popularity.

Another study on a small group of subjects was made by Sanford (38). Again personality tests and ratings of personality were utilized, supplemented by teacher ratings and composites of ratings by experts. A total of 48 pupils from a private school was used in this research. Seven personality clusters or *syndromes* were first isolated, clusters such as *structured personality* (including such traits as orderliness, cooperativeness, and self-

sufficiency), *timidity* (including passivity, dependence, and the like), and *activity* (including playfulness, liveliness, talkativeness, and productivity). It was found that there was a reliable tendency for five of the clusters of personality characteristics to be associated with certain physical conditions. For example, *structured personality* was associated with good diet, better developed parasympathetic responses (like ease of perspiring), and lower muscular and verbal activity. The *timid* group tended to be small, poorly nourished, poorly coordinated,

Imitative activity. (Merrill Palmer)

weak, and apathetic. The *active child* had better coordination, strength and energy, superior bone development, and a higher metabolic rate. Our sampling of the findings is suggestive of the general conclusion—that certain types of personality responses tend to be related to certain physical indices. As we pointed out earlier, whether there is a specific cause-and-effect relationship cannot be determined from these data alone. The small number of cases and the highly select sampling also make generalization hazardous. Nevertheless, the phenomena of relatedness of physique and personality, supported as it is by other more extensive studies of body build and physical attributes in relation to personality for adolescents and adults, seems reasonably well established.

CHILD MORALITY—
SUPEREGO DEVELOPMENT

The concepts of morality are the handiwork of civilization. Until people lived in groups, morality was quite primitive and was probably quite absolute; conduct was governed by the absolute needs of survival and the rules of conduct were both simple and highly explicit. As social organization gradually became more complex and the varieties of individual and group interactions became more complicated, so too did the system of moral values. Not merely the act, but the nature of the situation in which it was performed and the intentions of the performer were to be evaluated in terms of the morality or immorality of behavior. The rise of religion and of moral theology contributed enormously to the types of present-day morality. Different groups have different, even though complex, views about the nature of morality. Compare, for example, the morality of Middle Eastern people with that of the American population, or the morality of a communistic society with that of a democratic society. The differences are vast indeed, and the people who adhere to one moral position will often give their lives to defend it from attack.

The nuances within a given society with respect to moral judgments are quite marked. Consider, for example, the kinds of judgments people of the twentieth century, living in the United States, would make for the following crimes, and try to imagine how people in the nineteenth century would judge the same acts: a group of soldiers pillage a town during a stormy battle; a hungry and destitute man robs a bakery for a loaf of bread to feed his children; an obviously disturbed man suffering from *kleptomania* (a neurotic compulsion to steal) steals a watch from a jewelry store. In different epochs the same crime may be judged quite differently as features of the situation and the nature of the motivations are taken into account.

These considerations are presented to point up the fact that children have to learn to understand and to act on the basis of codes of morality they did not create. They are expected to learn to be moral, yet we have relatively little evidence that tells us in adequate detail how this learning proceeds and how it is best facilitated. We can, however, say that most children, in their own moral growth, *tend to recapitulate the history of the growth of morality through the various stages of civilization*. Before the age of six children are essentially amoral; they act in terms of impulse and habit and have little, if any, real awareness of the moral meaning of their behavior. They may transgress *adult* moral codes but they do so without either *intent* or even *awareness*. In the life of children, true morality begins in the early school years. At this time theirs is a *morality of reality*. Piaget's work with French and Swiss school children showed that children during this stage behave in the ways that their parents behave or approve; their morality is "unilateral"—that is, it

is an uncritical acceptance of what is good or proper in terms of parental authority (39). Gradually, "moral reality" gives way to "moral relativism," a morality in which the rules of conduct are guided by "reciprocity" so that the mutual needs of the interacting parties are considered. Piaget divided the growth of morality of children into three periods on the basis of his studies: (a) a period up to about 7-8 years in which justice depends upon adult authority; (b) a period from 8-11 years in which equalitarian justice prevails—in which the rights and needs of others are considered; and (c)

Boxing lessons teach motor skills and develop self-confidence. (U. of Mich.)

a period beginning at 11-12 years in which equalitarian morality is modified by "considerations of equity." During the first stage children will regard the deliberate or accidental destruction of a single dish or of many dishes as worthy of equal punishment. Piaget demonstrated that about 95 per cent of the solutions of six-year-old children to the problem of the source of morality were "obedience to parental authority," whereas none of the twelve-year-old children gave this solution. (The specific problem posed by Piaget was to solve a story situation in which there was a conflict between parental authority and a sense of justice.) These findings of Piaget's study have been corroborated by others (40, 41).

If this is the usual course of moral growth in children, what influences it and what happens under abnormal circumstances? It appears that morality is learned, in the first instance, through identification. As the child identifies with each parent he interiorizes the moral values and behaviors of each parent. Most of this learning is, at first, quite unconscious. The child is anxious to please his parents because he loves them and he needs their support. He behaves as "if they were inside him" even when they are not present, and he feels that he is behaving that way because he wants to do so. To misbehave is to risk punishment or withdrawal of support, or worse. Finally, to misbehave arouses *guilt*—that is, anxiety derived from the internalized superego—the internalized prohibitions. Under normal circumstances, the child

will gradually give up the overly rigid requirements of his infantile and strict superego as he matures. He will have many other models for identification: his siblings, his relatives, his playmates, his teachers, and many other adults. The differences in the moral values of these different models, together with the development of critical thinking and better control over impulses, will motivate reassessment of morality and superego values. The child who is secure in his affectional relationships with his parents and who has gradually been encouraged to express himself and differentiate himself from others will solve the problem of conflicting identifications by testing himself out, integrating attitudes, and finally establishing a mature and more flexible superego or conscience. In this long-term process of learning, the understanding parent will recognize the child's occasional impishness or even rebelliousness as part of the pattern of healthy growth and he will both tolerate and limit it according to the child's growing maturity.

When parents have been unduly strict, harsh, or inconsistent, the problems of moral and superego development are greatly complicated. In many of these situations the child will either develop a very strict or absolute superego (when prohibitions are too rigid) or will develop an inadequate superego (especially when parents have been grossly inconsistent). In the latter case, the child has difficulty learning any consistent model of moral values and is thus likely to become delinquent or yield to impulses without proper restraint. Broken homes and homes with intense marital discord are likely incubating grounds for this type of character development because of the inconsistent learning models that result (42).

During the early school years children will shift their loyalties (and their models) from the parents to peer groups and to adults outside of the home (especially teachers). They will continue to rely upon parental values for moral problems for a few years, but they will also spasmodically resent parental authority and parental justice. The need for belonging to the peer group ("the gang") will create new loyalties. Children will show resentment of parental discipline and parental judgment when there is a conflict with the group's norms. We have tried to explain the nature of these conflicting behaviors of the child. Because no parent is entirely consistent in his application of moral values and because children are so realistic morally, the child will constantly be ready to pounce on an inconsistency of the parent. He will sometimes behave as if he doubted his parent's honesty, often accusing him of being unfair. Often this will be the result of some parental inconsistency of which the parent is entirely unaware. Sometimes the child will seem spiteful, as, for instance, when he is told not to take things from the refrigerator, and having been found out because he stuffed himself and developed indigestion, he will righteously explain, "But I didn't *take* anything from the refrigerator; Bobby was here and *he* took the stuff out for me." It may be difficult for the parent who has reached a state of mature morality to comprehend the literalness of his child's morality. A good sense of humor, the ability to view events in perspective, and security in the

basic pattern of child-parent relations (which at this time means security on the part of the parent) will be a great help. Above all else, maturation and many new models for identification will enable the youngster to build on the good moral base implicit in his early home experiences to a more "civilized" morality "with equity."

SOCIAL SKILLS AND PEER GROUPS

We have already indicated how important for the child are his experiences outside of the home, and we should now like to examine these influences more carefully. Between the ages of six and ten, the child becomes more and more involved with and a *participant* in social groups, at school and in the neighborhood. In the beginning these groups are highly *informal*, the groupings depending on matters of physical contiguity and age, but being largely uninfluenced by sex cleavages. They are also highly *transient,* so that it is sometimes difficult for an observer to tell when a group activity or organization has begun and when it has ended. Children who happen to be near each other tend to play and interact with each other, but the entry of a new child on the scene or the development of a new activity is likely to draw a child out of one group and one activity into another group and another activity (43). By the age of ten, groups have a more formal structure and tend to be much more *persistent*. Now children have *mu-*

tual friends, the *gang*, as it is called, has a definite identity, leaders and followers and their roles are well defined, and the *rituals* and responsibilities of group membership are clearly demarcated. Above all, perhaps, the group or gang at this stage has a high interest in the importance and *literalness* of the organization and its activities.

If we were to observe a group of six-year-olds, we would find the members fluidly shifting from one set of activities into another, and we would find that the grouping of the participants was in an almost constant state of flux. The ten-year-olds would, however, know to which groups they belonged, what the specific roles of each member were, and would have learned to subsume their own role

to that of the group's goals. The following illustration of a "game" (quite an unusual one in terms of content) of ten-year-olds will concretize these characteristics.

Nine boys were engaged in a highly complex game, each one intent on playing his specific and literal role. The game started when one youngster, clearly the leader, suggested that it begin. The others immediately acquiesced, seeming to be ready to begin and only waiting the signal of the leader. At once the total group split up into sections. As they now moved about the street, one could easily note seven subgroupings. Each subgroup seemed to be engaged in peculiar movements and contortions, each seemed to be carrying on its part in some degree of independence of the others, yet all were clearly part of the total game. The observer walked over to the first subgroup of two boys who were jumping up and down together as they moved forward and asked them what they were doing.

Listening to stories—a first-grade group experience. (U. of Mich.)

Without interrupting their activity they responded by saying that they were playing "automobile" and that they were the front bumpers of the car. The observer moved to the second subgroup of two boys and asked them what they were doing. They explained, while twisting from one side to the other, that they were the headlights and were shining their lights in all directions to make sure there was not going to be a collision. Following them was one lad who kept jumping up and down emitting groans and grunts all the while. He said he was the motor. Behind him was the boy who was the obvious leader of the group. It was clear from his semi-squatting position and his pantomimic use of his hands that he was the driver who was agilely steering the vehicle through some very difficult terrain. The next boy told the observer that he was the car seat. Following him was a lad who explained that he was the rear bumper. Some distance to the rear was still another boy, holding his nose and moving one arm up and down. The observer asked him, with some querulousness, what he was doing, and he proudly answered, "I'm the bad smell that comes after the car."

Such a highly organized and complicated game may be unusual, but it demonstrates a good deal of the structure of the gang of the older age period of the early school years. There was a clearly designated leader, there were major and subordinate roles for group members, there was a "scapegoat" (the "bad smell" was played by a boy whom the gang fondly called "Stinky" and who was usually the ambivalent butt of the group), and there was a definite and literal purpose of the game—the explicit and involved production of playing "automobile." Piaget found, for example, that during these years the rules children used for games were "realistic" and were taken

by the members as immutable and "right" (39).

In their group activities children not only learn new roles and new models for identification, but they gain the strength to move away from complete dependence upon the home and parental authority. During this breakaway process, when they are testing out their social wings, it is understandable why they should over-react, at times, to parental wishes by rebellion. Not only do they have to compensate for their insecurity in the separation process, but they have to feel an intense loyalty to their new gang. It comes to mean so much to them during a significant portion of their daily lives, when they are out of the protective support of the home and when acceptance or rejection by one's peers can seem to be a matter of life or death. The varying models of behavior of these peers, the variability in ethnic background, the varieties of skills of the group members serve to provide for rich social learning. As these new experiences are assimilated the child's ego is broadened and strengthened. The child learns to be sensitive to and to understand the roles of others, he learns skills in social interaction, and thus he is implicitly preparing for his mature role as a social participant and as an adult member of society.

We have said that the social group outside of the home helps the child to develop toward social maturity. We may also say that as chronological age increases the structure of the social group more closely approximates that of adult society. Thus, there is an interactive process: the maturing child becomes more capable of an interest in broader patterns of social interaction; in turn, these broader patterns of social interaction facilitate more mature social behavior. Just as the child had to learn, in the home, to regulate his behavior in a manner that was mutually compatible with his own needs and those of his parents, so the child now has to learn patterns of mutual relationships in the social group. At the beginning of the early school period, when groups are fluid and transient, the degree of truly reciprocal relationships between members of a group is minimal. Such children interact, they may be imitative, they may alternately dominate and be submissive, but they are not capable of truly cooperative and mutually considerate behavior. Frequent flare-ups between children, if they have not been overtrained to avoid expression of their needs (i.e., severely repressed), take the form of pushing, punching, and wrestling. A few moments later, seeming to have forgotten the "violent" quarrel that has hardly ended, the same children are playing together again. This kind of behavior is preliminary to socially cooperative behavior. Near the end of the early school period, when formal groups have developed, children regularly assume cooperative relationships with each other, although some may tend to be dominant while others are submissive. During the school years children have to learn how to regulate their needs in terms of the group's *without*

losing their own individuality, their spontaneity, or their regard for others (44). Even at the adult level, however, a group will not be, or be experienced as, productive unless the members of the group have learned to reconcile their own needs (their "self-oriented needs"—to use a term conceptualized by Hutt) with those of the group's needs and the group's goals (45). This intricate balancing of individual and social need requires many years of learning, and the gang of childhood is an important part of this learning experience.

We have noted that, at first, children are unaware of ethnic identifications and that they respond to each other in terms of nonprejudice and nonsnobbishness—as judged by adult standards. Children seem to choose their playmates pretty much without regard to sex, and more in terms of age and size—during the early primary grades (46). Differences in intelligence are not particularly important at this stage. As children mature, they begin to respond more to prejudice (reflected from their respective home atmospheres), physical agility, and leadership qualities. By the end of the early school years, too great differences are not tolerated within the group, and leaders are most likely to be individuals with intelligence that is near the top of the group or only *slightly superior* to the group. Usually, the leader is a child having aggressive qualities of behavior, at least moderately dominant, and possessing some unusual skill. Academic superiority is not, however, an important qualification for group leadership in the gang-life of this period.

Children are frequently very severe in their criticism of each other and have little guilt about rejecting someone as a member of their group. Such criticism or rejection may be unusually harsh on an individual, but the experience of being rejected and learning how to accept it and overcome it is helpful in the process of social maturation. It is probably best for adults not to intervene in such matters unless the particular child is characteristically rejected and is persistently disturbed by the experience. In such cases, the child (or his parents) may need help in making a better adjustment to himself and his peers (or he may need psychotherapy), but the group should not be dealt with directly. The exception to this general principle would be the case in which a more or less formal group, with an adult leader or advisor, could benefit from the model presented by the adult's behavior or by his leadership in discussions with the group about their behavior.

One of the special problems which has been investigated with respect to group behavior, and its influence on its members, is that of the phenomena of *contagion*, or more generally of the *dynamics of power*. In studies of disturbed and normal children, and children varying in socioeconomic status, it was found by Lippitt, Redl, and others that group members were more likely to be influenced by individuals in the group (that is, group contagion of the influence would appear) when those individuals had a high power status in the group (47). Children in the group were able to agree with respect to who was dominant in their group. Such dominant individuals were seen by other children as having more physical prowess and were better liked by the group than others. (See

Chapter 8 for a discussion of children's sociometric choices.) They led by directive, not permissive, behavior and were, in turn, responded to with deference and permissiveness by the others. This study also found that intelligence was not highly related to dominance or group leadership.

LEARNING TO LEARN— SCHOOL ADJUSTMENT

Although increasingly greater numbers of children are attending nursery school and kindergarten in this country, attendance at school from the age of six years until some later point is well-nigh universal. Children were sent to school to "learn the 3 R's" in the early days of our country's history, but now they are expected to learn much more. Not only are they supposed to learn social studies, manual arts, physical fitness, science, and art, to name some of the more commonly accepted curriculum areas in the elementary grades, but they are supposed to learn social adjustment, ethical conduct, principles of leadership, civic pride, citizenship, and much more. The diversification of the goals of high-school and college or technical-school curricula are even more extensive. Many educators, as well as parents and interested citizens, are asking that we "go back to fundamentals," while others are demanding that the schools expand the areas of their instruction. Whatever the future holds in store for the appropriate role of the school, it may seriously be questioned whether schools are not already being asked to do too much and to assume a responsibility for some things that belong elsewhere. In any case, whatever it is that schools set out to do, one thing is certain: they are supposed to teach, and pupils are supposed to learn.

Since learning is the fundamental experience of going to school, this seems to be a good point at which to introduce some formal consideration of the problems of learning. It is clear that although every child has been learning at least from a short time after birth, and that there is a strong likelihood that every organism engaged in some learning even during the prenatal period (see Chapter 2), formal learning of school subjects begins for most children when they enter school at about six years of age. The learning of many social skills in a systematic way also begins at this time. Hence, we shall examine some of the more important principles of learning. Our discussion of this highly complex area, and indeed of this controversial arena in which opposing "schools of learning" are arrayed against each other, must necessarily be both brief and introductory, but we hope that it will highlight some important generalizations. Following this general discussion of learning we shall turn our attention to some of the more specific problems of school adjustment.

First, let us try to make clear what is meant by the term *learning*. It is usually contrasted with the concept of *maturation* (as we have done in previous chapters), in which maturation is seen as a gradual unfolding of innate potentialities with the passage of time. Learning, however, requires specific training, that is, it involves the acquisition of skill or ability of some kind through practice in the use of the skill or ability. The practice may occur accidentally through fortuitous experience or it may be carefully designed and controlled to maximize the acquisition of the desired behavior. As we have seen, however, maturation does not occur in a vacuum; it is hindered or facilitated by external conditions of the organism. Similarly, learning is not independent of the maturity of the organism; in fact, it depends upon it. Hence when we refer to learning, we are emphasizing that part of the total process of behavorial change which depends upon specific kinds of experiences or training. We should be clear at the outset, however, that some behavorial change may occur because of maturation, without learning, and that learning and maturation are interdependent to some extent.

We should also be aware that learning may occur either at the conscious or unconscious level. When we deliberately set out to change our behavior or acquire some skill we are trying to do so consciously. But we learn many things, some of them of crucial importance to our way of life, without any intent to do so and without any awareness that a learning process is taking place. The learning of many attitudes, or prejudices, or fears, and of likes and dislikes quite commonly occurs unconsciously. Sometimes, as we have seen, such unconscious learning results in behavior that people then assume is "human nature." Thus, the submissiveness of some cultures and the aggression of others was thought for a long time to be due to human nature and was attributed to *racial differences* in temperament or nature, until it was learned through research (mainly anthropological and sociological) that the experiences of the culture, and not innate tendencies within the individual, were responsible for the final product.

Closely related to the degree of conscious awareness in learning is that of *explicit* versus *incidental* learning. We may make the meaning of these two terms clear by citing an all too common example in which both types of learning occur. In some schools and for some teachers, the teaching of arithmetic results not only in an increment in arithmetical ability but also in an aversion to arithmetic. (In this type of situation, many pupils will even fail to learn arithmetic or will learn very little of it.) In this example, we do not have to examine the specific conditions that give rise to the twofold result, for we wish to focus our attention, for the moment, on the nature of incidental learning. We may simply assume that some condition, such as poor teaching methods, poor motivation of the pupils, or inadequate readiness on the part of the pupils for arithmetic, fosters the development of unfavorable attitudes toward this subject and even of fears or phobias in relation to it. The explicit instructional goal may be the learning of arithmetic skills; the incidental result of the teaching may be the acquisition by the children of certain attitudes. It is probably true that in all learning, or at least in most, some incidental learning is taking place. These side-effects may be favorable as well as

unfavorable, of course, and their total effect may be more important than the explicit results of the learning experience. Often, however, they are not considered and not evaluated in analyzing the effects of learning.

Principles of learning

Most modern psychologists agree that a great deal of learning may be explained by the principle of *reinforcement* (48). In this type of explanation of learning, it is believed that when an individual has a *drive* to do something (due to some tension), and when there is an appropriate *stimulus* (or stimulus situation) which triggers a response (which may be overt or covert), that the response which is made will be learned if it is *reinforced* in some manner as soon as it is made. In this explanation of learning, reinforcement refers to the *reward* that is given for the correct response. Reinforcement may be increased if the correct response is rewarded in some manner that is satisfying to the individual and the incorrect response is punished in some way. Such selective rewarding and punishing helps the individual to discriminate the correct response with a greater degree of accuracy. Let us illustrate this basic principle with two simple examples.

A child has a drive to learn to read. His teacher stimulates him to read a word or a phrase in a particular way. She then gives her approval (reward) when he reads the material correctly. He also is gratified when his peers and his parents find out that he can read. His errors in reading are punished by disapproval, by being made to try again, and even by being prevented from making the wrong response. Or take another example. A child has a drive to eat because he is hungry. He is given some bread and jam to eat and shown how to ask for the bread, how to hold it, and the like. The eating of the food reinforces the act (called the *instrumental act*) of eating the food in the appropriate manner while it serves to *reduce* the drive. The act rewards the eater, and the approval of the child for his manner of eating reinforces through this reward the appropriate method of eating. In both of these very simplified illustrations we are emphasizing the general principle of reinforcement, which involves four elements: (a) a drive or need or impulse (some kind of motivation); (b) a stimulus (or cue or model); (c) an instrumental act which reduces the drive; and (d) some kind of reward or rewards.

The adherents of the principle of reinforcement are not, however, agreed on all the conditions of reinforcement or on the extent of its applicability (49). Despite these differences the principle is helpful and serves to explain much of learning. There are a number of conditions and subordinate principles that are important to any discussion of reinforcement. One of these is that the sooner the reinforcement is given after the response occurs, the more likely it is that the response will be learned (learned more quickly or more strongly). This has been termed the *gradient of reinforcement*. Another stresses the importance of *motiva-*

Visual aids can be very helpful in reinforcing verbal learning. (U. of Mich.)

tion to learning. For anything to be learned, the organism must be in a state of *drive arousal*. This means that the drive or the appropriate drives must be operating if reinforcement is to occur. The mere contiguity of stimulus and response will not guarantee that learning will occur; that is, many repetitions of the correct response to a stimulus will not of themselves insure learning of the connection between stimulus and response.

In recent years, psychologists concerned with the processes involved in *perceptual learning* discovered that one of the special motivators for learning was *curiosity*. It was found that when subjects were required to learn such perceptual skills as the more accurate and more rapid perceptual discrimination of visual and auditory stimuli, those who were higher in the factor of curiosity showed superior learning (50). Curiosity is, however, nothing that is entirely new in considerations of learning. Psychoanalysts have long emphasized the general readiness of some individuals to learn and the lack of readiness of others. It is true that psychoanalysts talked of repression, referring mainly to the negative effects of this defense on all learning and adjustment, and that they failed to make explicit (or *operational*, as modern scientists term it) the processes and conditions by which this factor operates. Nevertheless, modern pedagogues have stressed for some time the importance of motivating the child and of insuring his readiness for the learning situation. Psychoanalytic theory has been accused of being responsible for "sugar-coating" educational methods. Whether education is "sugar-coated" is entirely unrelated to psychoanalytic theory, however. This theory simply elucidates the importance of motivation (both conscious and unconscious) and emphasizes that repression (which interferes with learning) may be discouraged by discouraging guilt and frustration.

Another principle closely related to motivation is that of *feedback* (51). This principle has also been called *hypothesis behavior*. In the earlier days of learning theory, Thorndike, emphasizing the trial-and-error of much of learning (and learning of animals in the laboratory did seem to involve much of trial-and-error), suggested that correct responses were learned through the *law of effect*. This meant that a correct response made by accident was learned or stamped in by the reward at-tending it. However, much behavior and much learning involve *anticipation* of the possible results of many kinds of solutions to a problem or conflict situation. The individual does not simply try one response after another until he hits upon a solution. He has some hypothesis or hypotheses which provisionally guide him in selecting possible responses. Then as the appropriate clues become clearer, he is able to make more precise and accurate responses. In other words, through feedback of past learning situations the individual is able to make an intelligent choice in his behavior. This principle may be helpful in understanding solutions to many kinds of cognitive and social learning situations. The person not only learns specific responses to specific situations; he also acquires a general fund of information and certain kinds of hypotheses or expectancies which guide him in similar or related situations.

Another closely related principle is that of *generalization*. Whereas feedback emphasizes the ways in which a person learns to use cues to guide his behavior, generalization refers to the spread or transfer of a learned response to other situations. The former refers to *anticipatory behavior potentials*, that is, learning to anticipate a response to an old situation through more and more accurate discrimination of relevant cues. The latter refers to the spread of the response itself to other situations. Both principles involve ways of broadening the base of our learned behavior. In generalization, a response given in one situation is later given to another situation—at first, probably automatically. Thus after a child has learned to call his mother "Mama" he may call other people (males as well as females) "Mama." The generalization is checked, in time, in which case it is applied with discrimination to appropriate situations, or it may not be checked, in which case false generalizations may occur and be stamped in.

Two special conditions of learning should be emphasized. One of these is that the *ability* (or, more generally, the *intelligence*) of the learner will influence his speed and quality of learning. As any teacher knows, two different individuals exposed to the same learning situation will learn at different rates. The specific ability or combination of abilities that affect the learning curve varies, of course, for different kinds of learning. The other condition to which we wish to refer is that of *specific readiness* for the learning task. Thus, the former condition refers to a capacity for learning of the type under consideration, whereas the latter refers to the specific background in appropriate experience for the task. As an example of this condition, we may note that in order to be ready to learn to read, the child must have sufficient verbal language skills, a need to communicate, and social skills appropriate to the communicative process involved in reading. Of course, these are not the only conditions necessary for learning to read, but they are used as illustrations because they appear to be so critical for this type of learning situation. Unless the child has this

kind of specific readiness for reading, even though his intelligence is superior and his teacher's pedagogical techniques skillful, he may have difficulty in learning to read or else be saddled with many unfavorable incidental effects of the experience.

It is well known that when a child *overlearns* some skill, he will tend to retain it longer and will forget it less quickly. (Overlearning means learning that proceeds beyond the point at which a 100 per cent, correct response could first be made. If, for example, a child practices the memorization of a poem, he will gradually learn more and more of it. When he continues to practice beyond the point at which he has just learned to repeat it without error, he begins to overlearn.) Usually, overlearning is more efficacious for motor than other types of skills—as for example, in learning how to ride a bicycle, in which a relatively small degree of overlearning will reduce forgetting to a very small amount. It is also well established that when the child learns through *distributed practice*, his learning is likely to be more efficient than when he learns through *massed practice*. Put another way, the same amount of learning time and effort, distributed over a larger number of learning periods (appropriate units being learned in each trial, of course), will produce more efficient learning than highly intense practice over a shorter period of time.

Finally, we cannot leave our discussion of the general principles of learning without calling attention to one of the great problems, or *paradoxes*, as Mowrer calls it, of learning theory (52). It seems clear that although motivation and drive arousal are necessary for learning, too intense motivation may interfere with learning. Learning theorists have been struggling with this problem for some time, and no easy solution seems to be available. The fact is that intense drives often do interfere with learning. The writers would suggest that, in their view, such conditions are those in which not merely a drive has been aroused but, more specifically, a condition of anxiety has been created. As the writers have pointed out, *high degrees of anxiety* interfere with both adjustment and learning (53). The intense arousal of a drive may create so much undischarged tension (that is, it cannot be reduced rapidly enough by instrumental acts) that the individual's general anxiety state is increased. When the anxiety level then becomes very high, it serves to disrupt learning. Conversely, a small amount of anxiety, which alerts the individual into a state of readiness, may and, in fact, does improve learning (54). These generalizations should be accepted for what they are—tentative formulations—and not as an attempt to solve all the difficulties of the paradox.

School adjustment

The child's experiences in school are of great importance in three major ways, especially during the early school years. They will determine *what he will learn* of the academic and nonacademic content, and *how he will learn it.* They will contribute to his *social skills* and to the character of his *social adjustment.* And they will be responsible for his *attitudes toward learning,* not only of school sub-

Children combine use of various sense modalities in learning. (Merrill Palmer)

jects but also of experiences outside of school. Of course, as research evidence strongly indicates, the nature of the child's personality as already shaped in the home and the immediate community will tend to be perpetuated and reinforced by his school experiences (55). School will not produce a new personality; it may strengthen trends that already exist and weaken others. Nevertheless, its potential influence is enormous, and the subsequent effects upon the society of which these children will be a part, as well as upon the child himself, are of no little importance.

In many ways schools are a reflection of the values and organization of society (see Chapter 8). Although the responsibilities for determining methods and content, in our country, are largely vested in the superintendent of schools and school administrators, these individuals inevitably reflect the characteristics of the society of which they are a part. The teacher has relatively little influence in determining curriculum and objectives, but is seen in our culture as an agent,

259

specially trained, to do society's bidding. Schools represent, therefore, a miniature cosmos, but a cosmos that accurately reflects the features of the society of which it is a part. By and large, the features that are emphasized in schools are those that represent the wishes and even the practices of the middle-class portion of our society (56). (Of course, private schools and parochial schools may furnish some striking examples of exceptions to this generalization, but even such schools tend to follow middle-class values as a general rule.) Thus schools are supposed to assist in the socializing process in terms of conformity to society's goals. It is in this sense that they are a miniature society with special advantages adapted to transmitting the culture unharmed and essentially unmodified.

Schools of the past tended to emphasize adult values as well as middle-class values, and the goal was to *prepare children for their adult status*, rather than to assist them in their *current problems*. This older orientation contributed to the teaching of content that was ill adapted to the contemporary characteristics of the growing child, and to teaching methods that were logically appropriate to these long-term goals but psychologically inappropriate to the personality and needs of the youngster. When the influences of such leaders of thought as Dewey and Freud permeated the school structure and organization, the pendulum swung all the way over to a focus upon the child's orientation rather than the adult's. In the process, the error was made of indulging the child and "sugar-coating" educational methods in the mistaken belief that such was the implication of the newer psychology. Gradually, schools corrected this error as they planned their curricula and methods on the basis of the contemporary needs, interests, and developing abilities of the youngster, while requiring that the child move toward the societal goal of adapting to the current adult way of life. Modern schools, then, attempt to use the child's own motivations and his own experiences in helping him to learn. "Readiness of the child" became a catch-phrase in designing curricula, although rigorous learning experiences might be required. The schools also reflected society's growing concern with social adjustment by making this a major aim of the educational process. (In some schools this led to de-emphasis upon academic content, to the unfortunate detriment of the child who was poorly prepared in the "fundamentals" as a result.) The *guidance role* of the school came to be recognized quite widely, sometimes more as a means of getting the child to develop effective spontaneity and mature skills and social responsibility. In these and many other ways, schools reflected and are reflecting what we adults want them to do. Only as we are able to envision broader horizons than those we have been acquainted with, and only as we learn to tolerate constructive nonconformity, will the schools become *architects of the future instead of museums of our past*.

In this connection it is well to emphasize that many of society's current dissatisfactions with the schools (much stimulated by our own insecurities in the face of uncertain and rapidly moving current events in the world) are, in effect, criticisms more of ourselves than of the school system. If the schools do not accomplish what they should, it is largely because this is what we have required them to do. The educational system becomes the easy "whipping boy" to relieve our anxieties as well as to express realistic concern with a less than satisfactory product. School personnel are, on the whole, far better prepared than many members of other professional groups, and yet their prestige position and their economic status are markedly inferior. Although school staffs may be poorly prepared to carry out certain functions, and their training should be improved in such respects, they are doing a remarkably effective job. If improvement is needed, the rewards that are offered to school staffs should be commensurate with the requirements that are made of them.

We have emphasized the middle-class values of the educational system because this fact explains some of the difficulties encountered by large groups of children in their early experiences in school (57). (See also Chapter 3.) Lower-class children and foreign-born children are likely to have or to develop negative attitudes toward school for a number of reasons. In the first place, the attitudes of their parents are more likely to be either unfavorable or neutral about school (56). Hence, such children have less interest than others in the academic, ethical, and social values of school experience. This does not mean that all such children, or all of their parents, may be characterized in this way, of course; there are notable

exceptions. In the second place, the prior life-experiences of such children have not equipped them as well as others for the content of school experience. As a frequent consequence, they have more difficulty, experience more frustration and rejection, and engage in behavior that brings punitive or critical reaction from school authorities. Unless schools make special provision not only in the revision of curricula but also in learning how to understand and accept these children, such a consequence is even more likely to follow. Finally, it must not be forgotten that teachers and school administrators are commonly drawn from the middle class, so that they are likely to reflect the prejudices and misunderstandings of this class, even when they consciously try not to, in regard to lower-class children.

None of these likely conditions needs to exist. Recognition of the condition is the beginning of possibilities for constructive preventive and remedial programs. As an example of what can be done, we can cite the case of a school in New York City that was "plagued" by school disabilities, conduct problems, truancy, and disinterested or even more negative parental attitudes. The school was located in a poor section of the city with a high proportion of foreign-born parents; the predominant groups were Italian and Puerto Rican. There was considerable unemployment among the parents. Children typically were unable to speak much English when they started school. They were poorly clothed and often poorly fed. Their intellectual experiences in general,

The nine-year-old already has all the basic human motor skills. (U. of Mich.)

and their linguistic skills in particular, were atypical and inferior. Yet the school had the same type of curriculum and same type of organization as other schools in the city whose populations were predominantly middle-class, American-born individuals. Children coming to this school had the experience, for them, of coming into a foreign atmosphere. They had difficulty in understanding and in learning the materials they were offered by way of instruction. They met failure and frustration. Their parents seemed uninterested in the school program and resented the criticisms that were directed at them by the school. Teachers resented teaching in this dif-

ficult school, were themselves frustrated in their attempts to teach the subjects they were supposed to teach, and were uncomfortable in the unfriendly atmosphere of the school and its neighborhood. The children showed a very high proportion of disabilities in school subjects, particularly in reading, and there was a high proportion of delinquency cases.

When the total program of this school and its relation to the community were changed things began to happen. A new principal, some new teachers who accepted the challenge of the situation sympathetically, and a greatly revised curriculum accomplished "wonders." The school arranged meetings with parents, not to discuss educational policy, but to discuss employment problems and to provide assistance along the lines of training and employment techniques. Reading was delayed until the third grade and a program of studies substituted which was based on the past experiences of the children and their current needs. The cooperation of social agencies—Y.M.C.A., psychological clinics, churches, and the like—was solicited and obtained, and a common program of assisting the parents and their children was organized. As a result, the whole complexion of the school's meaning and the relevance of its activities changed for both parents and their children. Learning and adjustment of the pupils showed remarkable improvement. The attitudes of school personnel, in turn, became much more favorable.

This illustration highlights another important factor that affects learning in all schools and in all classes: *the atmosphere of the school class.* There has been some research on the effects of such factors as class organization, teacher attitudes, teacher behavior, and the like, on the adjustment and learning of pupils. The general conclusion is that the general factor of *atmosphere* greatly influences the learning situation. Let us look at some important examples of such research. A classic in the field, although not focused on the specific problem of school adjustment, is the study by Lewin, Lippitt, and White (58, 59, 60). This study was concerned with the influence of the role of group leaders and group organization upon child behavior. The subjects were 10- to 11-year-old boys. Each of five groups was composed of five children,

and each group was subjected to three different and carefully defined group atmospheres, with an experimental plan for rotation through these experiences to give each of the "atmospheres" an equal chance to function. The three atmospheres were: *democratic* (in which the leader, an adult, acted in a responsible adult fashion but was responsive to the requests and needs of the group members and maintained a distinct leadership role); *authoritarian* (in which the leader dictated the activities of the group, offered impersonal and severe criticism, and clearly dominated the group); and *laissez-faire* (in which the group was permitted to make its own decisions and the leader was entirely passive). The distinction between the democratic and laissez-faire groups is particularly significant. The latter represents *some* teachers' conceptions of extreme, progressive methods of education which, in practice, permit or encourage children to do what they wish, in the name of spontaneity, and abrogate the important role of responsibility of the teacher. Each leader "played" each of the three roles with different groups so as to control for the possible contributions the unique personality of the leader might have upon the experimental results. The behavior of the children was recorded by a group of trained observers and some of the sessions were photographed to insure objective analysis of the data. The groups were equated for intelligence, physical activity, and various aspects of social behavior.

A host of findings were reported for these studies. The most important of these, for our purposes, will be summarized. In the first place, the democratic groups showed more *cohesiveness* or *solidarity;* that is, they felt and acted in terms of common group goals and were more satisfied with their productions. They were more friendly and showed less "scapegoating." The democratic groups were able to continue with productive activity when the leader was absent and could continue as a group after the experiment was over. Although the autocratic and democratic groups showed about equal total productivity, the latter group showed superior results qualitatively and were more satisfied with their work. Productivity of the laissez-faire group was low. The autocratic group became apathetic and indifferent toward its tasks and had a persistent need for "scapegoating." In both the laissez-faire and autocratic groups, irritation with other members of the groups appeared, and in the latter groups resentment was developed. In general, the autocratic groups developed more aggression and less goal-oriented behavior. All of these results are of considerable significance in pointing up the effect of atmosphere upon learning—in this case learning of a recreational type, but learning nevertheless. The study did not attempt to evaluate the effect of the background of these children upon the effectiveness of the several group climates, and we may wonder how different groups, with perhaps less experience in democratic atmosphere,

would react to the experimental conditions. Nevertheless, the significance of the experimental condition was demonstrated convincingly.

A series of studies has investigated the effects of teacher behavior or teacher personality upon pupil behavior. Anderson and his co-workers evaluated the relative effects of *integrative* and *dominating* behavior in preschool, school, and experimental play situations (61). In one of these researches, the comparative reactions of two groups of second-grade children, promoted on a chance basis into each of two different classes with teachers who were, respectively, dominating and integrative in their usual behavior, were investigated (62). By dominant behavior was meant punitiveness, use of force, insensitivity to pupil needs, cooerciveness, and the like. In contrast, integrative behavior meant responsiveness to the pupil's needs, cooperative relationships, reciprocity in teacher-pupil interactions, use of approval. The two groups of pupils were presumed to be equivalent at the start of the experiment in the second grade. As a consequence of their experience with these two teachers, the group with the integrative teacher became spontaneous, more socially cooperative, and showed more initiative. The other pupils, with the dominant teacher, became more rebellious, showed less harmony in classroom behavior, and were more readily distracted. A follow-up study of these same children one year later, after they had been placed with new teachers, indicated that the behavior of the children shifted in accordance with the differing personalities of the new teachers (63). On the other hand, the original teachers, who were also followed up, showed consistent types of behavior: the dominant teacher remained dominant and the integrative teacher remained integrative.

The evidence from such studies as these is quite convincing. The teacher who can provide a favorable classroom climate, using her role as a teacher in a spirit of firm but democratic leadership, strongly encourages healthy growth in personality, appropriate spontaneity, better group membership and productivity, less frustration and aggression. It seems reasonable to assume that the behavior of the teacher is closely dependent upon her personality, and that the punitive teacher, who tries to force conformity, is

emotionally less secure than the democratic teacher, and uses autocratic methods largely because of her own personality needs. Lack of responsiveness to the needs of children produces, in the end, more nonconforming behavior and more problem behavior—the opposite of what the punitive teacher, herself, desires. Although the effect of any single teacher is likely to have only temporary results upon the pupils (since evidence indicates

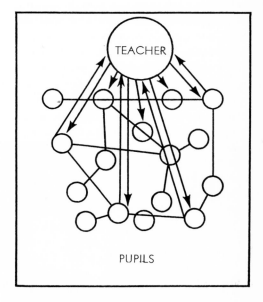

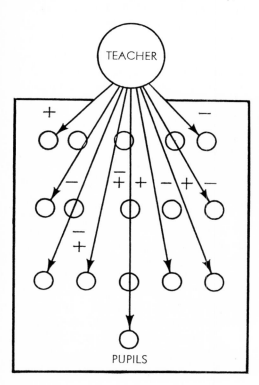

Figure 13. *Two patterns of teacher-pupil interactions in the classroom. At left, the pattern is one of dominating and autocratic interactions, with the teacher "above," and largely apart from and unresponsive to, the pupils. At right, the pattern is democratic and integrative. Pupils interact, and the teacher is responsive to and offers leadership while interacting with members of the class.*

that pupils continue to change with changes in teacher behavior), the cumulative effect of unfavorable teacher behavior can be devastating, and in exceptional cases, a single teacher can have extremely signficant effects upon a child or even upon a whole class.

In view of what we have seen concerning the identification process during the early school years, the role of the teacher's personality during this phase of school experience becomes even more important. The child is eagerly looking for new models with which to identify. He uses not only the models of peers and peer groups, but also those of the teachers to differentiate himself still further

from his parents. The important role of the teacher in encouraging personality trends that are either constructive or adjustive can hardly be overemphasized. In the ideal school, the selection of teachers must be guided to a considerable extent by evaluation of their personality characteristics. In addition, such a school will place emphasis upon training methods for teachers, preprofessionally as well as professionally, that will assist them in understanding, being sensitive to the need for, and being effectively democratic in providing strong but democratic leadership in the classroom.

This is not the place to discuss in any detail the specific pedagogical problems and techniques that confront teachers of the early school grades. However, several significant principles based upon the

A daily physical check-up is an important part of school routine. (U. of Mich.)

psychology of child development are relevant. We have already alluded, in this section, to the importance of "learning readiness." Our principles of learning showed us that there must be an interest (*drive arousal*) if learning through reinforcement is to take place. But readiness implies much more. As Strang points out, the preparatory experiences and the specific preparatory skills must be appropriate for efficient learning (64). For example, learning to read depends upon a general need for communication, a desire for interpersonal relations (and an absence of fear of exploration and of curiosity), familiarity with a wide variety of objects (perceptual skills and conceptual development), a sufficient language base (including vocabulary, sentence experience, and the like), and a felt need for discovering and using printed words. Beyond this, an adequate general level of intellectual development, absence of sensory defects or correction or attention for them, and ease of adjustment to social situations (which school learning always involves) are some of the other necessary preconditions. If any of these is lacking, motivation or special preparatory experience should first be provided. On such a basis, good teaching methods will have an opportunity of being truly effective. Evaluation of such factors assumes formal methods of gauging such abilities, informal observations of pupil skills and interests, physical examination, and the like. These, and other measures, are not luxury procedures to be applied when ample funds are available, but are *requisites* for an efficiently planned and properly organized school program. Frustration and failure in early

school experience may otherwise have far-reaching and unfortunate effects on the total learning process.

CONCEPTUAL DEVELOPMENT

In the previous chapter we discussed some of the characteristics of intellectual development during childhood. At this time, we wish to accent some of the special features that distinguish the early school years. We should note that these features are not absent in other periods but are more prominent during this phase of development.

We have said that the latency period is marked by a "turning toward reality." Children become preoccupied— one might say obsessed—with mastery of their real world. This shift of orientation and interest either causes or is part of some of the major characteristics of mental development in the primary grades. One of the findings that has been well established is that *variability* in mental abilities among six-year-old children is lower than it was during the immediately preceding years and than it will be for some years to come. The fact is that when measured by means of standardized intelligence tests or when measured by means of other kinds of mental tests, the contraction in mental abilities of the six-year-old group is noticeable (65). By eleven years of age, variability becomes very marked again. One might suppose that prior to age six children varied greatly as they mature and as they learn to interiorize the familial and related environment—some progressing rapidly and others slowly. By about six years of age, with a turn toward literalness and with the new, away-from-home environment just beginning to affect their growth, variability in functioning is reduced. However, the preoccupation with mastery of the new environment soon leads to increased variability. Thus, the onset of latency is accompanied by an impression of children's increasing "sameness in mental ability"—a fact that is confirmed by research investigation.

Another general feature of intellectual functioning during this period is the great frequency of *eidetic imagery*. Eidetic imagery refers to the ability to reproduce a visual memory as if the stimulus were still present for visual inspection. Thus, in trying to remember what one had for breakfast, the child with eidetic imagery will be able to call up a vivid mental picture of the breakfast table, and remember in detail just how it actually looked—and then "read off" from this photographic image the details of its contents. This type of imagery is far less frequent among older children and adults—just why is not really known—but it is a commonplace in the early school years (66). Again we may suspect that the literalness of the child's experiences produces a much more vivid sensory impression upon him than upon an adult, but here we are in the realm of supposition. At any rate this explanation is consistent with both the psychoanalytic explanation of mental development and with the research evidence that young children are unable to abstract or deal readily with symbols. As the latter forms of mental ability develop one tends to remember by means of generalizations and other abstract qualities, forgetting or hardly noticing the minor details of the experience from which these memories were derived.

Unless repression is severe, children will learn readily during the early school years—in fact learn an amazing quantity of things. During this period children are eager to explore their world and to believe in it. Reading becomes a means of gaining further information and understanding about this world, but here too, children are wont (like some immature adults) to believe everything they read as literally true. Reading is also one of the first forms of symbolic thinking—despite the literalness of the words and the whole

Art and craft work builds creatively and fine motor coordination. (U. of Mich.)

reading experience for the child. So too, learning numbers is a fascinating game for youngsters who are eager to master the meanings of addition and multiplication; such learning also proceeds best when it is anchored in concrete illustrations. Every teacher of the primary grades knows that one has to teach that two sticks plus two sticks equals four sticks even though the child is quite confident that two apples plus two apples is four apples. The abstract generalization that two plus two equals four comes slowly, and only after it has been reinforced many times with examples from concrete experience.

For similar reasons, children are more easily able to see differences between things than similarities. The differences may be visualized directly, or experienced directly, but the similarities must result from abstracted generalization of each of the elements of the comparison. The literalness of children's thinking at this stage of development is exemplified by the joke reportedly told by a school superintendent who, while visiting a third-grade class, asked the question, "If each of three clocks in the hallway tells the time as 3 o'clock, what time is it really?" Reputedly, the answer he was given, and one might well expect such an answer, was, "It's 9 o'clock." All experience tends to be referred to the immediate; all rules are taken literally and concretely. It is only slowly that the ability to separate oneself from the present, and take a more conceptual framework, develops. By the ninth year, however, these capacities for abstraction and conceptualization can be noted in children's thinking and in their games, although it will be another few

years before such types of thinking are as well developed as they will be at the adult level.

Nevertheless, children are eager for explanations. They want to know the reason for everything that happens, but, of course, are interested in a practical and immediate explanation, not a generalization about general factors. They want to know what makes the sun come up, why people sleep, why married people have babies, why there are traffic lights, and so on *ad infinitum*. By the same token, they are interested in explanations that they "can see"; i.e., that they can apply immediately. It is only on the basis of probably many thousands of experiences of this kind that they have a sufficient base and, equally important, sufficient confidence to begin venturing to accept more generalized explanations. The first beginnings of truly conceptual thinking— thinking that involves categorization in terms of abstract and general concepts— may begin with the preschool years, but they achieve maturity only some years later. In the early school years symbols have direct reference to reality. Even the symbols used in rituals or in games are anchored in concrete experience, and hence have to be adhered to very literally. Hence the need for mastery of experience during latency retards, as it were, more abstract mental development, but it also provides for the ingestion of considerable quantities of basic information and basic learning of skills and attitudes that accelerate such thinking when it first makes its appearance.

PROBLEM BEHAVIOR

If by problem behavior we mean behavior that is nonconforming, then it is probably safe to say that all normal children show problem behavior during the primary grades. It is only the "goody-goody," who is far from normal or well adjusted, who shows no signs of rebellion, defiance of rules, resistive conduct, tantrum spells, "naughtiness," aggressive behavior, inability to remain quiet for long periods, food fads, screaming, or one of the many other types of normal problem behavior during this period. However, in most well adjusted children, who display such behavior on occasion (sometimes for no apparent reason), the problem quickly dissipates itself, reversion to form occurs again (although sometimes for only a relatively short period), and basic relationships with peers and adults remain within reasonably comfortable limits.

A more appropriate conception of problem behavior would involve some consideration of the extent to which *the ego of the individual has been impaired.* In such an approach it is not the problem behavior or the symptomatology of the child that is crucial but the extent to which it is a reflection of underlying difficulties that affect, in some continuing way, the adjustmental capacities. Many types, if not all types, of problem behavior may occur in connection with temporary stresses associated with normal growth, with new or changed situations, with difficulties in educational learning, with adjustment to cultural change, and with new problems in relationships with peers and authority figures. Some types of problems occur in conjunction with physical disease or organic damage. These transient difficulties—which many of them are—do not constitute problem behavior in the psychological or psychiatric sense—although they may present problems to the parent or teacher who fails to understand them. On the other hand, persistent or progressive difficulties in adaptation, based on disturbances of the ego—in which failure to resolve conflict has resulted in inappropriate defense mechanisms, undue anxiety, and impaired effectiveness in meeting the daily problems of living—constitute true psychological maladaptation, even when overt symptoms are minimal or absent. For example, a child may be quiet, well behaved, cooperative in class, and the like, and yet be unhappy, unable to relate effectively to people, indulge in excessive daydreaming, or have persistent difficulties in sleeping—and from our point of view be seriously maladjusted. The point we are making, then, is that it is only when we evaluate the underlying dynamics of the behavior that we can say with some assurance whether or not an individual is maladjusted. The presence or absence of symptoms, by itself, is not an adequate criterion.

A fourfold classification

Elsewhere we have introduced a method of classifying childhood deviations in behavior and discussed the rationale and empirical data on which it is based (53). We shall summarize this scheme of classification briefly to provide one example of modern attempts to deal with this problem. In our presentation, we divide problems in behavior into four main categories. The first of these is called *transient adaptive problems*. This group of problems includes those temporary disturbances, such as common habit and conduct problems, that are associated with normal problems of growth, physical illness, culture change, and exceptional ability. Children showing these problems may have symptoms but they are *relevant* to the traumata or stresses they are experiencing. Once the situation is changed, or once they have had an opportunity to work through the new problems, they are able to make a good adjustment again and their symptoms, if any, subside. No impairment in ego-functioning, except temporarily, has occurred. When the situation is normal once again, whatever anxiety may have been experienced is no longer felt. This type of reaction may be conceived of as an emergency reaction in which the individual is temporarily subjected to increased stress and in which he experiences some temporary disturbance.

A second category is called *persistent non-adaptive problems* (or *persistent maladjustment*). These are behaviors in which the capacity of the ego to tolerate anxiety and to deal with conflict has been more or less permanently impaired. Such children use inappropriate defense mechanisms, may experience anxiety when the objective situation should not elicit it, show symptoms, and are unable to function effectively in intra- or interpersonal situations. Due to severe trauma when the ego was unable to deal with it, these

children learned maladaptive methods of coping with conflict, experience conflict even when the objective situation does not warrant it, manifest rigidity in their methods of dealing with difficulties, and, above all else, are not able to work up to their potentialities. Some examples of such types of problems are: persistent regression in behavior, such psychoneurotic difficulties as anxiety states and severe compulsivity, or such other psychoneurotic reactions as bronchial asthma when the physical basis for this condition is absent or minimal, or persistent distortion in traits (character traits) like marked aggressiveness or excessive dependency which operate even when the situation does not call for such traits of behavior. Persistent non-adaptive behavior usually requires psychotherapy or some other intensive form of treatment for its correction. Harsh discipline or punitive measures not only fail to correct the problem but even exaggerate it.

A third category is called *extreme persistent non-adaptive problems*. In these instances, anxiety is so severe and conflict so great that the ego loses its capacity for harmonious and integrated functioning. In older parlance, such children were called *psychotic* or insane. Due to extreme stress when the ego is unable to tolerate it, the ego becomes *fragmented*; that is, it loses the capacity to coordinate stimulus and response. Hence, such individuals would show bizarre and inexplicable changes in mood, their thoughts or ideation would be inconsistent with their feelings, their cognition would be disturbed so that they developed delusions or other kinds of peculiar thinking, or their physiological responses would become highly erratic so that they would show inexplicable changes in temperature, be unable to ingest food, and the like. This category of disturbance indicates a profound dislocation in the self-image, and an inability to perceive and relate accurately to internal sensation as well as to external events. In common language, such cases "have lost touch with reality." There is some question whether all such cases have some constitutional predisposition (not hereditary predisposition, necessarily), but in many instances, at least, the difficulty can be

An oral examination is an important part of speech diagnosis. (U. of Mich.)

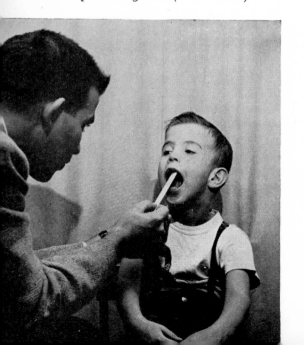

traced to severe anxiety during early stages of development. The correction of such conditions is very difficult, but they are no longer considered hopeless. Modern methods of treatment are often surprisingly effective. Usually, intensive treatment by psychotherapy, often in a hospital setting, is required.

The fourth category of problems is called *constitutional problems*. These are problems in behavior that are primarily due to physical factors present at birth or occurring after birth. Severe inadequacies in neural or cortical development, neurological diseases or accidents, specific brain diseases, and other physical conditions that affect the integrative functioning of the nervous system may contribute directly to mild or severe disturbance in behavior. Even in such conditions it is not the constitutional factor alone that determines the behavorial reaction, for the total personality of the individual still determines how he will react to his condition. This principle holds even in cases of highly localized brain damage. Nevertheless, in such cases the constitutional factor is the principal determinant of the problem. Examples of such conditions (in each of which the personality reactions vary considerably) are: *encephalitis lethargica* (or "sleeping sickness"), *cretinism* (dwarfism due to insufficient thyroid secretion from birth or shortly after), *polioencephalitis,* and *convulsive disorders* (or epileptic reaction). Such conditions require expert medical diagnosis and treatment, but often they also require appropriate psychological treatment—and some guidance for the parents is also advisable.

All children will show problem behavior, to some degree, during phases of their development when they are under undue and temporary stress. When these are transient, adaptive responses to stress, it may be expected that the child will recover his typical adjustment within a short time as the stress subsides or as he learns to adjust to it. Problems of physical growth, adjustment to new peer relationships, adjustment to the school situation and all of the elements in it—all of these and other situations create temporary disturbances as part of the normal process of adjustment. Parents and teachers should be able to deal with these problems as they arise. A safe rule to follow is to assume an attitude of "watchful waiting" without alarming the child and without becoming anxious about the condition, meanwhile trying to evaluate the factors that may have contributed to the child's stress and anxiety. The healthy child will often learn to master the situation by himself if only we permit him to do so and do not interfere unnecessarily. Our emotional support and understanding will prove to be of great help to him. Calling undue attention to the problem, or worse, forbidding its manifestation, is likely to aggravate the difficulty since such procedures serve either to conceal the cause or to increase the tension or both. Often, however, alleviation or modification of the stress situation will speed up the process of recovery from the trauma and assist the child in reasserting his normal methods of coping with problems. It is in this connection that psycho-logical insight on the part of the parent or teacher can be extremely helpful. Two basic questions that should always be kept in mind are: (a) what condition or conditions have given rise to the reaction, and (b) what purpose is the child's reaction accomplishing for him? If we can learn to understand the *goals* of the child's behavior (and therefore what is motivating him to behave as he does), and what specific difficulties are contributing to the problem, common-sense guidance can then be extremely useful. In particular, the teacher who is sensitive in such ways can be a great asset to the child. She should be able to understand the individual's needs, his methods of adaptation, and his immediate goals in behavior (since she is presumed to be a professionally trained expert in matters of child development and guidance). Through her understanding of the behavior (and not simply concern with the symptoms), she can communicate her understanding to the child, and assist him in adapting to the stresses so as to maintain appropriate goals while at the same time reducing his tensions. (Of course, she may also be able to relieve the stress situation.) Unfortunately, it is probably true that most present-day teachers who have taken courses in mental hygiene only know the principles of mental hygiene as intellectualizations but are unable to apply them to concrete situations with any adequate degree of competency (4). Teachers, particularly (and parents, too, if the situation were ideal), should obtain specific training in evaluating children's behavior from observation of their reactions and in making appropriate inferences from such observations.

Problems falling in the category of persistent, non-adaptive reactions require expert diagnosis and treatment by competently trained specialists: psychiatrists, neurologists, school psychologists, school counselors, and the like. In the following paragraphs we should like to sample some of the more frequently occurring types of problems and discuss them briefly. The objective is to gain some preliminary appreciation of their nature and their development, but we must leave for more technical texts on this subject detailed consideration of etiology, manifestation, and treatment (53, 67).

We may begin by pointing out that many types of physical factors may be associated with maladjustment. Although, unlike conditions of the fourth category we have described above, these do not, of themselves, cause the maladjustment, they may *contribute* to problem behavior and poor learning ability. We have seen (in Chapter 6) that there is a general tendency for the organism to act as a whole, to go up or down in total adjustment as a total unit. Organismic age is correlated with mental development, with personal adjustment, and with achievement (68).

Thompson has reported an interesting study in which the relations between marked differences in diet and school achievement were studied (69). In this study, two groups of children, matched with respect to such variables as age, intelligence, and educational achievement, were given two different kinds of nutrition for one year. One group received tablets of vitamin B-1 every day while the other group was given similar-looking tablets of no nutritional value. None of the children knew the content of the tablets they were getting. The diet of the two groups was similar in other respects since all of the children were in an orphanage and this factor could be controlled experimentally. At the end of the research period the group receiving the vitamins was significantly superior in a variety of measures of specific and general school achievement. This study is particularly important because it was possible to control for social class and general environmental conditions which, in other studies, varied along with differences in physical nutrition and thus contaminated the results. Other studies have shown that visual defects, hearing difficulties, physical stamina, and other physical conditions affect both adjustment and achievement. When such conditions contribute to severe maladjustment their removal will not automatically produce a state of good adjustment, but treatment or correction may alleviate the problem.

We have already referred to Gilbert's analysis of types of referral problems seen in child guidance clinics in New York City (18). Although the frequency of referral is not necessarily commensurate with the actual occurrence of problem behavior, this study furnishes a good guide with respect to the relative frequency of types of problems which are seen by the school as in need of some form of psychological attention. For children of all school ages up to 18, the most frequent referrals were for academic difficulties (45 per cent), aggressive and antisocial behavior (30 per cent), passive and social behavior (33 per cent), emotional instability and anxiety (23 per cent), and hyperactivity and motor disturbances (14 per cent). (It is also interesting to note that 27 per cent of the referrals were for mental retardation with which a variety of other problems was associated).* During the early school grades these problems were also very high in relative frequency, but the proportions changed from this period to the next school phase (10 to 14 years of age). For example, academic difficulty changed from a relative frequency of 43 per cent to 52 per cent, a gain of 9 percentage points, while both anxiety and hyperactivity decreased in percentage from the early to the later school period (from 26 to 18 per cent for anxiety, and from 17 to 11 per cent for hyperactivity). The possible reasons for these shifts are unclear, but the data seem to support at least three generalizations: (a) Academic problems are not only generally highest in frequency among school adjustment difficulties but such problems tend to increase as children get older. (b) Problems of emotional insecurity (represented by anxiety and hyperactivity) are relatively more frequent in the early school years, when children are first attempting to adjust to the new school environment, than during later school years. And, (c) contrary to popular belief (especially beliefs emphasized by somewhat sensational journalism in re-

* These percentages add up to more than 100 per cent since some children were referred for more than one condition.

cent years) problems of aggression do *not* increase during the later elementary school years.

Among academic difficulties, *reading disability* occupies a prominent place both because of its frequency and because of its impact on all other school learning (and therefore on adjustment). Disability in reading, by which is meant an inability to read at a level commensurate with the individual's level of mental development, may be due to one or a combination of many factors. It may be related to problems of sensory impairment or physical deficiency, although such causes are far less important than is commonly supposed (53). It may be due to specific learning difficulties such as frequent change in methods of instruction, poor teaching methods, insufficient practice in fundamental reading skills, and the like. Or it may be symptomatic of an underlying emotional maladjustment which interferes with the capacity to utilize one's native ability. The last type of cause, emotional maladjustment, is very often responsible for serious cases of reading disability (53). In such cases, remedial reading instruction, by itself, may be insufficient to correct the difficulty, or may even aggravate the problem. In these instances, careful diagnostic appraisal, by appropriate child-guidance specialists, is necessary before an appropriate remedial and therapeutic approach can be planned.

We have noted that rebelliousness may be expected as a normal phenomenon during the early school years. How-

An audiometer test. (U. of Mich.)

ever, aggression on a chronic basis and with persistent severity is another matter. The typical tantrums of preschool children become less frequent with age, and more mature forms of aggressively independent behavior begin to emerge during the primary grades (70). It is the extremes of the latter condition that are our present concern. They often represent the symptomatic expression of underlying maladjustment. Various clinical and research studies have shown that deprivation, especially emotional deprivation, and frustration in the satisfaction of basic needs can produce chronically aggressive behavior (71, 72). The external sources of such deprivation or frustration have to be removed, or at least alleviated, and the child may need psychotherapy to learn how to deal with his aggressive drives in a more suitable manner. Physical punishment my be helpful in sharply calling attention to an infrequent transgression in behavior, but persistent use of such punishment only serves to suppress the overt expression of the aggressive drives, and drives them

deeper into the unconscious, producing more difficulty in time (61). Repressed hostility together with strong needs for dependence are the breeding conditions of some forms of *bronchial asthma* in children, and even of *ulcerative colitis* (53).

Problems involving severe anxiety, passivity, and their motoric expression in hyperactivity may be even more serious in the long run. By anxiety we mean a general state of uneasiness or apprehension (which may become *latent*, that is concealed from conscious awareness) from sources unknown to the individual. It may be distinguished from *fear* in which the apprehension is clearly related to some specific and external stimulus. We have previously discussed the internal sources of anxiety as stemming from separation and castration types of experiences and in which the individual felt helpless in resolving internal conflicts. Anxiety in severe form, and present from an early age, may produce grave alterations in the ego, leading in some cases to schizophrenia. In less severe form, and occurring at later stages, particularly during or after the oedipal period of development, it may give rise to psychoneurosis and other forms of problem behavior of a persistent kind. Thus, excessive anxiety is at the root of many kinds and degrees of personality disturbance.

In the early school grades children may suffer from *anxiety states* in which there is a chronic and overt expression of the anxiety: general apprehension, fear of people and many kinds of situations, and various kinds of physiological reactions such as rapid pulse, excessive perspiration, rapid heart beat, heightened metabolic rate, and the like. Gradually this rather direct expression of anxiety is changed into other forms of behavior. These may vary greatly in type, depending on many other conditions of the individual. There may be persistent and terrible *nightmares* (different from the occasional nightmare of a child after a frightening experience), *tics* (localized, involuntary twitchings of a group of muscles), chronic *nail-biting* (often a sign of internalized tension), *memory difficulties, phobias* (displaced fears based on some unconscious anxiety), and many more. Anxiety states and their derivatives are found most frequently in homes in which there is considerable tension, with rejection of children as a consequence (18). Such conditions warrant immediate and careful attention from child-guidance specialists. The teacher may be most helpful by being emotionally warm, accepting, and furnishing emotional support in other ways to the anxious child, permitting him to ventilate his feelings and discharge some of his tension in discussions and in rewarding types of tension-reducing activities such as play, art work, and successful social participation. It should not be expected that the teacher can correct the condition, although she can do much to maintain it at a low level of intensity and can provide a climate of acceptance in which the child can be helped to secure more emotional stability. In this connection it seems well worth pointing out that criticism of the mother (with the intent of getting her to change her behavior at home) may contribute

to the mother's already intense feelings of insecurity and hostility and so increase the child's difficulties as a consequence. Rather, a sympathetic attitude toward the mother's difficulties, even to the extent of helping her to see the value of possible psychotherapy for herself, may accomplish much more for both mother and child.

We have said that anxiety tends to be transformed into many forms of symptomatic disturbance and noted a few of these symptom clusters or *syndromes*. It is not as frequently recognized as it should be that many forms of passivity or asocial conduct and many forms of hyperactivity are symptomatic derivatives of anxiety. In the former case, the child withdraws from social contact as the main mode of defense. In the latter, there is an attempt to discharge the anxiety through motor release.

The teacher should recognize her limitations as well as her assets in dealing with problem behavior in children. She can help most in a preventive and constructive sense by providing a warm, accepting, and understanding climate in the classroom in which the children can adjust and learn. She can be helpful in spotting problem cases and assisting in the evaluative process that is necessary. In cases with mild difficulties she may become the main therapeutic agent. In more serious cases she needs competent and available professional help.

GENERAL READINGS

1. Baruch, D., *One Little Boy*. New York: Julian Press, 1952.
2. Bowlby, J., *Child Care and the Growth of Love*. London: Pelican, 1953.
3. Child Study Association of America, *Facts of Life for Children*. New York: Bobbs-Merrill, 1954.
4. Dreikurs, R., *Psychology in the Classroom*. New York: Harper, 1957.
5. English, O. S., and Foster, C. J., *Fathers are Parents Too*. London: G. Allen, 1953.
6. Jersild, A. T., *Child Psychology*, 4th ed. Englewood Cliffs, N. J.: Prentice-Hall, 1954.
7. Murphy, L. B., *et al.*, *Personality in Young Children*, Vol. I. New York: Basic Books, 1956.
8. U.S. Children's Bureau, *Your Child from Six to Twelve*. Washington: U.S. Government Printing Office, issued periodically.
9. Valentine, C. W., *The Normal Child: And Some of His Abnormalities*. Baltimore: Penguin, 1956.

SELECTED BIBLIOGRAPHY

10. Freud, S., *An Outline of Psychoanalysis*. New York: Norton, 1949.
11. Campbell, E. H., "The social-sex development of children," *Genet. Psychol. Monogr.*, 1939, 21, 461-552.
12. Mead, M., and MacGregor, F. C., *Growth and Culture*. New York: Putnam, 1951.
13. Isaacs, S., *Social Development in Young Children*. London: Routledge, 1946.
14. Bornstein, B., "On latency," in *Psychoanalytic Study of the Child*, Vol. VI. New York: International Universities Press, 1951.
15. Gurin, M. G., "Differences in psychological characteristics of latency and adolescence: A test of relevant psychoanalytic propositions, utilizing projective material," Unpublished Ph.D. dissertation, University of Michigan, 1953.
16. Wright, H. F., "Psychological development in Midwest," *Child Develpm.*, 1956, 27, 265-286.
17. Bonney, M. E., "Sex differences in social success and personality traits," *Child Develpm.*, 1944, 15, 63-79.
18. Gilbert, G. M., "A survey of referral problems in metropolitan child guidance clinics," *J. Clin. Psychol.*, 1957, 13, 37-42.

19. Rabban, M., "Sex-role identification in young children in two diverse social groups," *Genet. Psychol. Monogr.*, 1950, 42, 81-158.

20. England, A. O., "Cultural milieu and parental identification," *Nerv. Child*, 1947, 6, 301-305.

21. Terman, L. M., *et al.*, *Genetic Studies of Genius*, Vol. I. Stanford: Stanford University, 1925.

22. Terman, L. M., and Tyler, L. E., "Psychological sex differences," in Carmichael, L. (ed.), *Manual of Child Psychology*, 2nd ed. New York: Wiley, 1954.

23. Levy, D. M., *Maternal Overprotection*. New York: Columbia University, 1943.

24. Symonds, P. M., *The Psychology of Parent-Child Relationships*. New York: Appleton, 1939.

25. Hardy, M. C., "Aspects of home environment in relation to behavior at the elementary school age," *J. Juv. Res.*, 1937, 21, 206-225.

26. Watson, G., "Some personality differences in children related to strict or permissive parental discipline," *J. Psychol.*, 1957, 44, 227-249.

27. Whiting, J. W. M., and Child, I. L., *Child Training and Personality*. New Haven: Yale University, 1953.

28. Liccione, J. V., "The changing family relationships of adolescent girls," Unpublished Ph.D. dissertation, Syracuse University, 1954.

29. Tryon, C. M., *University of California Inventory. I: Social and Emotional Adjustment. Inst. Child Welfare.* Berkeley: University of California, 1939.

30. Honigmann, J. J., *Culture and Personality*. New York: Harper, 1954.

31. Francis, K. V., and Fillmore, E. A., "The influence of the environment upon the personality of children," *Univer. Iowa Stud. Child Welf.*, 1934, Vol. 7, No. 2.

32. Davis, A., *Social Class Influences upon Learning*. Cambridge: Harvard University, 1948.

33. Weckler, L., "Social class and school adjustment in relation to character formation," in Havighurst, R. J., and Taba, H. (eds.). *Adolescent Character and Personality*. New York: Wiley, 1949.

34. Mussen, P. H., "Differences between the TAT responses of Negro and white boys," *J. Consult. Psychol.*, 1953, 17, 373-376.

35. Data published by the National Safety Council, National Office of Vital Statistics, Washington, D.C., 1949.

36. Wheatley, G. M., and Hallock, G. T., *Health Observations of School Children*. New York: McGraw-Hill, 1951.

37. Jones, H. E., *Motor Performance and Growth*. Berkeley: University of California, 1949.

38. Sanford, R. N., *et al.*, "Physique, personality and scholarship: A co-

operative study of school children," *Monogr. Soc. Res. Child Develpm.*, 1943, No. 1.

39. Piaget, J., *The Moral Judgment of the Child.* New York: Harcourt, Brace, 1932; Piaget, J., *The Construction of Reality in the Child.* New York: Basic Books, 1954.

40. Lerner, E., "The problem of perspective in moral reasoning," *Amer. J. Sociol.*, 1937, 43, 249-269.

41. MacRae, D., "A test of Piaget's theories of moral development," *J. Abnorm. Soc. Psychol.*, 1954, 49, 14-18.

42. Glueck, S., and Glueck, F. T., *Unraveling Juvenile Delinquency.* Cambridge: Harvard University, 1950.

43. Harley, R. E., Frank, L. K., and Goldenson, R. M., *Understanding Children's Play.* New York: Columbia University, 1952.

44. Anderson, H. H., and Anderson, G. L., "Social development," in Carmichael, L. (ed.), *Manual of Child Psychology*, 2nd ed. New York: Wiley, 1954.

45. Fouriezos, N. T., Hutt, M. L., and Guetzkow, H., "Self-oriented needs in discussion groups," in Cartwright, D., and Zander, A. (eds.), *Group Dynamics, Research and Theory.* Evanston: Row, Peterson, 1953.

46. Newcomb, T. M., *Social Psychology.* New York: Dryden, 1950.

47. Polansky, N., Lippitt, R., and Redl, F., "An investigation of behavioral contagion in groups," *Human Relations*, 1950, 3, 319-348; and Lippitt, R., Polansky, N., Redl, F., and Rosen, S., "The dynamics of power," in Cartwright, D., and Zander, A., (eds.), *Group Dynamics, Research and Theory.* Evanston: Row, Peterson, 1953.

48. Skinner, B. F., *Science and Human Behavior.* New York: Macmillan, 1953.

49. Hilgard, E. R., *Theories of Learning*, 2nd ed. New York: Appleton, 1956.

50. Butler, R. A., "Incentive conditions which influence visual exploration," *J. Exp. Psychol.*, 1954, 48, 19-23.

51. Kretch, D., "Dynamic systems, psychological fields, and hypothetical constructs," *Psychol. Rev.*, 1950, 57, 283-290.

52. Mowrer, O. H., "Two-factor learning theory: summary and comment," *Psychol. Rev.*, 1951, 58, 350-354.

53. Hutt, M. L., and Gibby, R. G., *Patterns of Abnormal Behavior.* Boston: Allyn and Bacon, 1957.

54. Ericksen, C. W., Defense against ego-threat in memory and perception," *J. Abnormal Soc. Psychol.*, 1952, 47, 230-235.

55. Snyder, W. U., "Do teachers cause maladjustment?" *J. Except. Child.*, 1947, 14, 40-46.

56. Hollingshead, A. B., *Elmstown's Youth.* New York: Wiley, 1949.

57. Warner, W. L., Meeker, M., and Eells, K., *Social Class in America.* Chicago: Science Research Associates, 1949.

58. Lewin, K., Lippitt, R., and White, R. K., "Patterns of aggressive behavior in experimentally created 'social climates,'" *J. Soc. Psychol.*, 1939, 10, 271-299.

59. Lippitt, R., "An experimental study of the effect of democratic and authoritarian group atmosphere," *Univ. Iowa Stud. Child Welf.*, 1940, No. 3.

60. Lippitt, R., and White, R. K., "An experimental study of leadership and group life," in Newcomb, T. M., and Hartley, E. L. (eds.), *Readings in Social Psychology.* New York: Holt, 1947.

61. Anderson, H. H., and Brewer, J. E., "Studies of teachers' classroom personalities: I. Dominative and socially integrative behavior of kindergarten teachers," *Appl. Psychol. Monogr.*, 1945, No. 6.

62. Anderson, H. H., and Brewer, J. E., "Studies of teachers' classroom personalities: II. Effects of teachers' dominative and integrative contacts on children's classroom behavior," *Appl. Psychol. Monogr.*, 1946, No. 8.

63. Anderson, H. H., Brewer, J. E., and Reed, M. F., "Studies of teachers' classroom personalities: III. Follow-up studies of the effects of dominative and integrative contacts on children's behavior," *Appl. Psychol. Monogr.*, 1946, No. 11.

64. Strang, R., *An Introduction to Child Study* (rev. ed.). New York: Macmillan, 1938.

65. Dearborn, W. F., and Rothney, J. W., *Predicting the Child's Development.* Cambridge: Science Arts Pub., 1941.

66. Kanner, L., and Schilder, P., "Movement in optic imagery," *J. Nerv. Ment. Dis.*, 1930, 72, 489-517.

67. Caplan, G. (ed.), *Emotional Problems of Early Childhood.* New York: Basic Books, 1955.

68. Olsen, W. C., and Hughes, B. O., "Growth of the child as a whole," in Barker, R. G., *et al.* (eds.), *Child Behavior and Development.* New York: McGraw-Hill, 1943.

69. Thompson, G. G., *Child Psychology: Growth Trends in Psychological Adjustment.* Boston: Houghton Mifflin, 1952.

70. Kanner, L., *Child Psychiatry* (2nd ed.). Springfield, Illinois: Thomas, 1948.

71. Bender, L., *Aggression, Hostility and Anxiety in Children.* Springfield, Illinois: Thomas, 1953.

72. Dollard, J., Doob, L. W., Miller, N. E., Mowrer, O. H., and Sears, R. R., *Frustration and Aggression.* New Haven: Yale University, 1939.

8

Intermediate school years—integration and stabilization

WE SHALL NOW DISCUSS some of the features of child development occurring roughly in the period from ten years to the beginning of puberty. Some aspects of development during this period were treated in the previous chapter where they seemed more pertinent, such as various conditions of personality development and some aspects of physical growth. We shall defer until the next chapter most of the specific characteristics of puberty. This will leave us free to concentrate our attention on the unique conditions of growth that are manifest during the intermediate school years.

EXPANDING HORIZONS

The maturity of the organism during this period is such that it can devote itself to new tasks and to new skills in a wide variety of ways. Physical growth is slow and steady for most children until the beginning of the pre-adolescent spurt, so that by 12 years of age children are about 58 inches tall, on the average, and the large muscles of the body are able to do everything the adult muscles can do except that they do not have as much strength (5). Physical health tends to be very good since the organism is well stabilized, and immunities to most childhood diseases have already been developed. Basic skills in thinking and in the academic subjects have been mastered, and the child is well aware of reality and of his own assets and limitations. The support derived from association with one's peers and from integration into peer

Boating can provide a whole new range of learning experiences. (U. of Mich.)

groups has led to personal feelings of adequacy and independence (if not adventurousness). The time is therefore eminently suited for expansion—for broadening one's base of operations, for ingesting the content of new subjects, and for trying oneself out in all types of new "field operations."

The base of operations that is most important to children in the intermediate years is the *gang*, or the *group*. Unlike the informal groupings of the primary grades, the gang of this period is likely to be more structured. Each child knows who the leader is, the nature of the major roles and contributions of each member of the gang, and what sort of goals the gang has. This structuring of the group is more implicit than explicit, and

it is more a matter of daily happenstance than of planned intent. The most common gang is likely to be that of the neighborhood, and even more specifically that of the block or the street. Children tend to organize into such neighborhood groups on the basis of geography rather than on the basis of any real community of interests, to begin with. The gang simply exists because the children happen to be together. Gradually, its routines emerge and communal interests and patterns of behavior develop. There are other gangs than those of the neighborhood. There is the clique in the classroom or in the school which tends to stick together in play and athletic activities, unless prevented from doing so by the teacher. There is the church gang, the Boy Scout gang, the summer camp gang, and so on. Unlike the gangs of the earlier period, these tend to persist (despite acrimonious arguments and fights at times), but individual members may be added and subtracted as children move into or out of the neighborhood, or as new children attend or leave community or camp groups. Moreover, such gangs are restricted to members of the same sex. Play and other interests dictate that boys play with boys and girls play with girls. The gang has a deep emotional meaning for the child because it is the focus of his growing independence from home and the bulwark of his support in doing daring, adventurous deeds. Although some of the gang's activities may be open to inspection by all, there are some that are reserved for "members only." Groups during this period love their rituals, their secret codes, their special methods of greeting, and their secret places of meeting. (One may note certain similarities of type of activity, if not of degree of sophistication, with adult groups such as fraternal orders, leagues, and the like.) Members of the group have an intense loyalty to it and are willing to defend it at the slightest provocation. Indeed, the gang has become a "home away from home" and its mores and values are at least as important as those of the real home. The gang offers support to the ego of each member, so that patterns of unique difference from the behavior in the home can be more easily tolerated. It is the source of one's first adventures with cigarettes, of "hitching rides" on the back of moving vehicles, of camping out at night, of stealing something for the sheer joy of showing one's cunning and skill, and the like. We shall have more to say about the values and disadvantages of these and other experiences shortly.

Group membership

First, let us consider the general advantages of group membership. We have already indicated that growth in independence requires opportunity for some degree of rebellion against the home and some degree of self-assertion in new modes of activity. The gang furnishes opportunities for such developments. It supports the individual's early attempts at independence and individuation when he is not strong enough to engage in

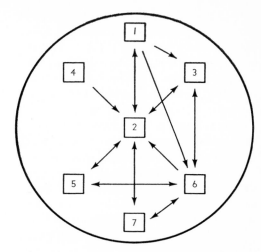

Figure 14. *Sociometric diagram of the "likings" within a peer group. The arrows indicate the direction of preferences. Individual 2 is the leader and is liked by all six other members of the group; but he likes only four of the others. Individual 4 is an "isolate" and is liked by no one, although he likes the leader. Individual 6 is a "sub-leader" and is liked by four members of the group.*

such departures from parental requirements by himself. Further, the gang offers opportunity for experiences in group interaction under conditions of self- or group-directed participation. In contrast, groups directed by an adult, as in the school or in a community center, offer other kinds of group participation, valuable in their own way, but different from those of the self-led group. Participation in groups, both adult-led and self-led, offers opportunity for assuming various roles in group membership and gaining appropriate experience in them, such as the role of the leader, the role of the follower, the role of the organizer, the role of the propitiator, and so on. Participation in groups allows for joint planning and execution of activities of many kinds, thereby fostering the development of many new interests and skills. Finally, group experience furnishes the sometimes satisfying and sometimes frustrating experiences of being liked or being rejected. Children have to learn how to adapt to such experiences and how to behave to avoid isolation from social participation.

During the intermediate school years the stability of individual and group friendships increases gradually (6). The trend toward stability in this respect will increase through the adolescent years. In turn, this increasing stability permits the child to learn to depend more on, and establish more intense mutual interdependencies with, other children. It is interesting to note that this need to depend on others in the group fosters

the separation of the sexes during this period. Children are eager to learn about sex information and sex practices but are fearful of utilizing these increments in knowledge. Biologically and socially, they are learning to repress and work through the sexual conflicts of the oedipal period. They are neither ready nor sufficiently aroused biologically to engage in heterosexual experience, and so they are fearful of interacting with members of the opposite sex. The gang assists in fostering the advantages of being with children of the same sex, and supports the separation of the sexes in many ways. Research studies have indicated that children learn to choose not only persons of the same sex but persons who are

Group hikes offer much emotional and intellectual stimulation. (U. of Mich.)

similar in needs and in other personality characteristics during this period (7). The total group may be composed of some individuals who differ markedly from each other, but mutual friends tend to be pretty much alike in personality features. When the correlation coefficients are computed for traits in pairs of mutual friends they turn out not only to be positive, but are typically fairly pronounced (on the average, they are of the order of 0.2 to 0.4). Thus, it appears that for children opposites do not attract each other.

Moreover, the interests and activities of boys and girls become quite well differentiated during these years. Studies by Lehman and Witty indicate clearly that games and other activities become sex-linked after about nine years (8). Boys become interested in activities emphasizing athletic skill and adventure while girls become involved in nonaggressive pursuits and domestic types of play (9). Similarly, reading interests diverge, boys like stories about adventure and biographies of great men, while girls prefer romantic stories and fairy tales. Recent studies of the kinds of interest children show in response to radio and television programs as well as in their reading interests confirm these differences between the sexes at this phase of development (10). One can now speak of masculine as opposed to feminine interests since the patterns of identification of each sex with its respective role are fairly well established.

It is also important to point out that children perceive each other—their assets, their special characteristics, and the like—differently from the ways that adults perceive them. In studies comparing children's judgments of each other with adults' judgments of children's likes and dislikes, it is found that these sets of judgments do not agree. This was not the case in the primary grades or in the preschool period. The fact that adults are unable to judge accurately how children feel about each other is one additional reason for permitting children to determine their own friendships. Wisdom suggests that parents can be helpful in *encouraging* the formation of other and perhaps more desirable friendships (rather than in discouraging what may seem to be undesirable friendships) by providing opportunities for these children to meet and work or play together under favorable auspices.

We noted (in Chapter 7) that children begin to show awareness of sex-national-and-race prejudice by about the primary-school grades. By the time of the intermediate grades, these prejudices are well evident in the behavior of children. It has been learned that such biases are the results, in the main, of contagion from adults who already have such biases (12). Generally speaking, lower-class children tend to develop such biases earlier than do other classes, possibly because adults in these strata are more insecure and more hostile (13). In any case it seems clear that segregation, practiced by adults and then imitated by children, leads to further prejudice and to inaccurate information about the "other groups." On the contrary, experiences with "other groups" lead to clearer and more complete perceptions of their roles and behavior and to a decrease in prejudice (14).

We have noted that there are some disadvantages in group experiences, not necessarily an inevitable part of such experiences but a likely by-product of them under contemporary cultural conditions. Children may associate with "bad" companions and so imitate "bad" practices. This danger is probably far less serious than one would at first suspect, since the basic adjustment of the child will determine how he reacts to such experiences and how he makes use of them. (See the section on delinquency in this chapter, and also Chapter 9.) Although it is true that disturbed children will be likely to identify with the "bad" models of contemporaries in their effort to develop some compensatory defenses, and although such models may contribute to the antisocial behavior of some who would otherwise use different methods of behavior, the well adjusted child will soon revert to more satisfactory methods of attaining personal gratification. For such a child, experience with some unfavorable social behaviors may actually increase his discrimination of better from poorer models of behavior. Parents and teachers can be constructively helpful by providing opportunities for meeting with and having social relationships with suitable individuals and groups, and by encouraging suitable behavior (rather than discouraging unsuitable behavior).

Competitive behavior in groups

One of the more serious and unfavorable consequences of participation in group behavior is a reflection of the culture-

values emphasized by the group. Both in school groups and in neighborhood and community groups, our culture tends to foster an overemphasis on *competitive behavior.* Excessive stress on competition together with inadequate integration of such behavior with cooperative behavior can have far-reaching and unfortunate results. Let us look first at the ways in which competition is fostered. In the schools, the emphasis on grades, the mania for "ranking people," the stress on being "top man on the totem pole"— all of these reflections, to some extent, of the competitiveness prevalent in the business world, and a carry-over from the "dog-eat-dog" spirit of pioneer days in this country, mean that most pupils are constantly meeting failure experiences. After all, only one child can be best, and

Planning and cooperation. (U. of Mich.)

all others are relative failures when emphasis is placed on being first. Moreover, such competitiveness is not integrated with cooperative needs in which the goals of the group are kept foremost in mind. As a consequence of both of these failures in our social teaching in schools (to which school personnel are themselves strongly subjected), pupils tend to generalize feelings of inadequacy, worthlessness, and failure. In their school subjects, in school sports, and in many other areas of school activity, being *first* assumes an importance far out of proportion to its effectiveness in encouraging individual growth. Pleasure and confidence in making the most use of one's own talents for one's own growth, satisfaction in the process of *doing* rather than solely in the rank one attains by doing it, and realistic acceptance of one's variability in assets are neglected as a consequence. Insufficient attention is frequently given to learning to work together, to contribute one's share for the common good, and in learning to assume differentiated roles in accordance with reality factors. Both competitive and cooperative trends should be fostered, and even more important, these trends should be reconciled. All of this requires specific kinds of experiences, specific kinds of teachings, and specific kinds of cooperative programs in which group rewards are emphasized.

The same patterns of overemphasis on competition and "getting there first" may be seen operating in the home and in the community. This is all the more reason why such trends should be counteracted by school experiences of another kind. Our culture seems to take exceptional pride in offering prizes and rewards for excellence for its own sake—for being first even if this does not contribute maximally to individual development or group achievement. The overemphasis upon winning (note the grandiose scale that this has reached in college sports), and the acclaim for the winner and the neglect for all the effort and contribution of the loser are evident everywhere. All other virtues tend to be minimized. Our criterion tends to become, not how valuable something is or how useful it is, but how much bigger, stronger, faster, more expensive, or more sumptuous it is.

We have been discussing the problem of competition in groups mainly because it indicates that many types of group experience precipitate feelings of failure. We have considerable evidence that the accumulation of such failure experiences unfavorably modifies the self-image and undermines and distorts perceptions of reality. For example, Sears' study showed how even a minimal amount of failure experience contributed to such difficulties (15). In one part of her study, she evaluated the effect of failure experience versus success experience upon subsequent performance. Her subjects consisted of 18 school children who were given speed tests of reading and arithmetic. Under failure conditions, the subjects who had taken the tests previously under neutral conditions (that is, being given the tests without any comment about them or any special expectations for them) were told how poorly they had done previously, and were asked to predict how well they would now be able to do on the next succession of trials. Under success conditions, the reverse type of evaluation was made, and children were told, after the neutral trials, that they had done well; they were then asked to predict how well they would now do on the following trials. (This type of study is usually called a study of *aspiration level,* to determine how the goals of the subject fluctuate under normal or under experimental condition, with respect to degree of success.) Sears found that failure conditions *decreased* the accurate or realistic prediction of subsequent achievement, whereas success conditions tended to *increase* it. In other words, failure tends to impair one's effectiveness in judging realistically what one's actual capabilities are; it impairs the accuracy of one's self-image. Sears also studied the influence of each child's

Art and craft activities invite both individual and group work. (U. of Mich.)

previous success or failure (before the experiment), in reading and arithmetic upon the accuracy of prediction of subsequent achievement. Since some subjects had been successful with both subjects and others had met failure in both subjects or had failure in arithmetic but not in reading (Sears therefore was able to organize her subjects into three groups), she was able to evaluate the effect of this differential pattern of former success or failure upon the accuracy of aspiration level. It was found that results similar to those reported above were obtained: success resulted in more realistic and more accurate self-appraisal (it also encouraged appropriate effort with accompanying improvement), whereas failure had the opposite influence.

Maller has investigated this problem from another viewpoint (16). In a series of studies involving over 1500 children from the intermediate and upper elementary school grades, he focused his inquiry on the general question: Under what conditions of self or group participation have children *already learned* to do the best work? He measured the ability to perform under varying conditions of working for oneself and in various types of group conditions. It was found that when children worked by and for themselves (they were given individual rewards for achievement on an arithmetic test), they did better than when working with and for a group (with group prizes). Not only was their achievement better under individual, competitive conditions, but they also preferred such conditions of work; i.e., *they had learned to like individual competition better than group participation!*

These studies reinforce the comments we have been making concerning some possible disadvantages of group experience. We should emphasize, once again, that unfavorable consequences are not inevitable. It is only when the group, formal or informal, reflects or exaggerates tendencies of an unfavorable kind that are already present in the culture that the results are unfortunate.

Ability and individual differences

Another general aspect of the expanding horizons of children in the intermediate grades is that of the ingestion of large quantities of information and skills. We use the term *ingestion* advisedly for pupils "take in" a great deal of their ever-changing kaleidoscope of life experiences, and many years are required before they have fully evaluated these events. As a matter of fact it will not be until middle or late adolescence that they have developed a mature perspective on all that they have experienced. Many of the complex skills that children develop are based on their play and recreational activities. New integrations of motor skills and the development of the finer muscular coordinations develop not as an explicit goal of such activities but as a byproduct of them. Moreover, experiences of being popular and of being a leader clearly become evident during this time. In this respect, it has been demonstrated that physical prowess and athletic ability are impor-

tantly related to popularity and to being chosen as leader for boys, whereas for girls the qualities that prove to be popular are docility, nonassertiveness, and linguistic rather than physical abilities (17).

School curricula are designed to take advantage of the child's growing interest in his community, his country, his nation, and the world. Emphasis upon social studies in which history, geography, current events, and scientific developments are stressed enables the child to see himself and his family in ever-widening perspectives. The skillful teacher tries to relate such learning to the child's immediate interests and environment, knowing that such anchorage gives the new learning a greater hold. For similar reasons, learning that is highly dramatic is likely to be more effective than the mere recital of facts, and teachers use projects, contests, public demonstration, and the like to help dramatize the material of school learning. As a consequence of such varied types of learning of different

"Ingesting" reading skills. (U. of Mich.)

kinds of subjects, as well as directly as a function of the classes in English, children expand their vocabularies very rapidly, some studies showing that the increase, for example, in total vocabulary from the fourth to the eighth grades is about 60 per cent (18). Not only total vocabulary increases; the increase in the understanding and use of abstract words is also marked and indicates, in turn, children's growing conceptions and ability to make generalizations. This finding, that vocabulary and language usage are related to many types of subjects, indicates the value of providing for integration in curriculum-building. In our example, for instance, the learning of new words and new ways of phrasing things should not be the exclusive function of the English class, but should be one of the goals of *all* school classes and subjects. The same may be said for the learning of social attitudes and social behavior.

There is considerable evidence that *individual differences* increase markedly during the school years. Not only do the differences in mental ability become more marked with age, but the differences in scholastic abilities also increase. With respect to the former point, consider the mental ages of two children at chronological ages 6 and 12. Suppose the I.Q. score remains constant for these children, but that one has an I.Q. of 100 and the other has an I.Q. of 130. The first child's mental age at 6 years is 6 years, and at 12 years his mental age is also 12 years. However, the second child's mental age at 6 years is 7.8 years, and at 12 years of age it is 15.6 years. During the 6-year span the original difference in mental

age of 1.8 years increased to 3.6 years— a difference reflecting a considerable divergence in mental maturity. Similarly, the spread in educational abilities increases markedly. Both the differences in brightness and the related differences in ingestion of experience assist the brighter child, when the educational environment is stimulating, to improve relatively more than the average child, and still more than the below-average child. By the end of the elementary-school grades, individual differences among school children have become very pronounced, indeed, in all academic school subjects and in all school-related abilities.

The increase of differences in individual abilities which we have been discussing relates to differences in level of abilities among different children. Another phenomenon is the increase of *intra-individual* differences, in contrast to *inter-individual* differences. As children develop, their patterns of individual abilities and interests become more differentiated and diverse. While bright pupils tend to be relatively superior in most activities involving mental capacity, and dull pupils tend to be relatively inferior in most activities, the diversification of interests and abilities of each of these groups becomes more and more pronounced and, as a consequence, considerable overlapping in levels occurs among children. The evidence shows that with increasing age the correlations among mental abilities and skills *within* the child decreases, that is, greater diversification occurs. At the beginning of the elementary-school grades, tests of such mental abilities as memory, numerical ability, and verbal ability show a correlation within the child, on the average, in the order or magnitude of about .50. By 9 years of age the intercorrelation among these abilities has been reduced to about .30, and by 15 years of age the intercorrelation averages about .18 for boys and .10 for girls (19). These findings point to the possibility of providing more and more differentiated programs of studies for children with differing patterns of interests and abilities.

In Chapter 7 we summarized some of the more important general trends in personality development during the whole latency period and discussed the importance of personality factors in adjustment and learning. At this point, we wish to highlight two types of findings that are especially relevant for school learning. Every teacher knows that some pupils are characterized as *underachievers*, that is, they achieve, on the average, less than

Differentiation of interests and activities can readily be seen. (U. of Mich.)

their mental ability would warrant. Probably the most important single fact accounting for underachievement in school children is poor personality adjustment, although other factors such as physical handicap and poor learning opportunities may be important in individual cases (20). Many of these underachievers are only moderately disturbed in adjustment and do not necessarily need extensive counseling or psychotherapy. In turn, their pattern of failure has further reduced their motivation for learning and contributes to still more underachievement. Providing more and more remedial instruction does not necessarily help such children, because the difficulty they are having is not so much one of specific disabilities as one of emotional conflict. There is impressive evidence that considerable help can be given such children by group programs providing for discussion of their problems, *ventilation* (or verbalization) of their feelings, and emotional support in correcting their self-distorted self-images. In one study in which such an opportunity was provided for underachievers, there was considerable change, in comparison with a control group of underachievers who did not have this opportunity, in attitudes toward school work, in study habits, and in types of self-insight achieved (20). Unfortunately, this study by Sanford did not continue the discussions for a sufficiently long period, and there has as yet been no follow-up, so that the possible long-term effects on attitude and achievement cannot be evaluated. Nevertheless the fact that some important and statistically significant changes did occur in directly relevant areas of habits and attitudes is

indicative of the possible values of appropriate group guidance.

The other type of finding that is worth emphasizing is that the general level of the pupil's anxiety is related to effectiveness of learning experience. Clinical evidence is far more impressive on this score than is experimental evidence. Many clinical studies have shown how markedly the level of mental functioning and degree of learning can be retarded by severe anxiety. When anxiety has reached such extreme levels, some form of intensive psychotherapy is usually necessary. Recently, however, research evidence has shown that even milder degrees of anxiety are related to mental effectiveness. For example, McCandless and others have shown that even manifest (that is, directly observable and reportable) anxiety is moderately related to school achievement in sixth-grade pupils (21). The consensus of research studies has indicated that small degrees of overt anxiety may act as spurs to learning, whereas extreme degrees of anxiety may have profound and unfavorable effects upon memory, learning of new and especially complex skills, and upon complicated motor behavior (22). In school, as in life, it is helpful to keep anxiety within easily tolerated limits, if maximum growth and learning are to be achieved.

MECHANISMS OF DEFENSE AND STYLES OF BEHAVIOR

As we have pointed out, the incubation period in personality development may be considered to occur during infancy and the preschool years. It is during this total period that the child learns methods of resolving conflicts and acquires certain basic personality characteristics. We have cited both theory and research to indicate the vast differences that exist in personality manifestations as a result of differing experiences in the preschool period. Our review of the evidence has indicated that class membership and cultural factors markedly influence the ways in which personality developed, and we have emphasized the ways in which these factors are transmitted, in the first instance, by the home, and subsequently reinforced or modified by experiences in the school and in peer groups.

Psychologists have long been interested in two specific questions related to personality development: How are the various mechanisms of defense learned? What are the over-all styles of behavior that emerge as a consequence? Clinical and anthropological evidence has shown that different classes and different cultures show different proclivities toward different types of maladjustment or of psychopathology (23). For example, the relative frequencies of depression, suicide, schizophrenia, and manic-depressive psychosis have been shown to differ according to variability in class and culture. Although studies of co-variations in environmental and personality maladjustments have been extremely valuable, they have had two severe limitations. On the one hand, they have been concerned with the *extremes* in psychopathology found among adults. On the other hand, and even more pertinent, they have failed to provide much light on the *specific ways* in which these characteristics were acquired. Of crucial importance to our understanding of personality development is greater awareness of the specific ways in which the mechanisms of defense are learned during childhood by the wide range of normal and fairly normal individuals. Also of importance is an understanding of the ways in which the patterns of defense differ among individuals of fairly normal adjustment. We need to know, too, how defenses of the normal group differ from those of the extreme psychopathological group.

We have seen how child-rearing practices produce considerable differences in general ways of responding and in general levels of adjustment. The studies by Brody and by Sears and co-workers discussed in Chapter 3 are examples of recent research in this area. In Chapters 5, 6, and 7 we summarized the effects upon personality development of the emotional climate of the home, group membership in the community and in the school, and the atmosphere of the classroom and the personality of the teacher. We have seen that many conditions exert their influence upon the personality development of the child, although the central importance of home conditions is clearly evident. Now we should like to take a closer look at the effects of class and social status upon the development of specific mechanisms of adjustment. The intermediate school years offer us a particularly opportune time to do this, since personality mechanisms have become well stabilized by this time, and it is possible, therefore, to subject children of this age to a variety of examination procedures that were unavailable for such purposes or were less reliable during previous periods. We have learned that at this time in their lives children are able to describe themselves and their peers with considerable accuracy, and that they are able to respond more adequately to psychological testing procedures and so to provide the investi-

gator with more relevant and more reliable information.

We have chosen to focus our attention upon the methods and findings of a series of extensive research studies carried out by Miller, Swanson, and their associates (24). These studies are specifically concerned with the relationships of certain social-class and child-rearing variables to

Plays provide "role" experiences and encourage socialization. (U. of Mich.)

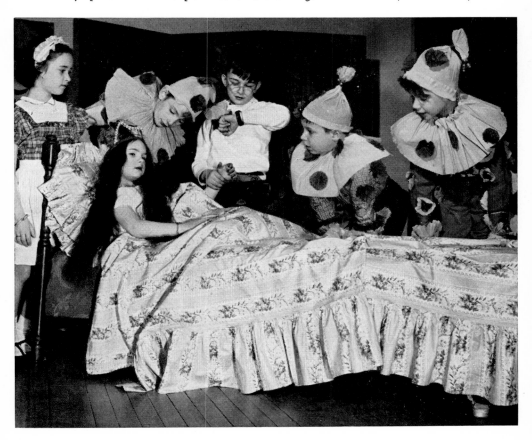

the mechanisms of adjustment and the styles of expressive behavior (on which we shall presently comment) of boys from the seventh, eighth, and ninth grades. In order to control for the possible effect of extraneous factors upon their findings, only white Christian children were studied. These children, who were attending the public schools of Detroit, presumably were not retarded in intelligence, were not severely disturbed emotionally, were born north of the Mason-Dixon line in the United States, and were descended from immigrants from the northwestern part of Europe. In selecting the sample for study, the mothers of prospective research subjects were interviewed, comments were obtained from their school teachers (particularly to eliminate disturbed children), and their school records were examined for various types of relevant data. The first major sample in 1951 consisted of 185 mothers (of whom only 120 were left after refusals and eliminations because of incomplete or inadequate interview data). The second sample in 1952-53 consisted of 245 mothers (of whom only 145 were left). (Thus, both samples furnished a total, after eliminations, of 265 boys.) The number of boys used in each specific research subproject varied as the different types of criteria deemed relevant for specific research problems varied.

The general question posed by these studies was whether differences in class and social status were associated with differences in personality variables. The parents of the children were divided into four subgroups in terms of criteria of socioeconomic status: upper-middle, lower-middle, upper-working, and lower-working classes. The families of the boys used in the studies were further classified into two groups on the basis of what Miller and Swanson call *"integration."* This variable is based on data about the fathers having to do with the type of economic mobility, the nature of occupational interpersonal relationships, and the power position of the job or occupation. On the basis of these criteria, two categories of *integration* are distinguished. One category is known as *bureaucratic.* In this type of integration, the individual works in an organization in which the employee is responsible for only a small part of the total functions of the organization, is subject to a hierarchical arrangement in which he is supervised and directed by others, and his status within the organization is relatively well defined and circumscribed. In contrast to this, the other integration category is called *entrepreneurial.* In this type, the occupational experience involves a high degree of self-directedness and individual responsibility. It is the type of experience a person working for himself, or as the owner of a small business, is likely to have. For example, a person is placed in the entreprenurial category if he meets one of five criteria: (a) was born on a farm, (b) was born outside the United States, (c) is self-employed, (d) gains at least half of his income from profits, fees, or commissions, or (e) works in an organization having no more than two levels of supervision. These categories were employed because it was believed that each category tended to result in different kinds of life styles of behavior of the parents, and that these would then be reflected in the types of defense mechanisms and life styles learned by the children.

One of the general problems in this research was whether *expressive style* of behavior was related to factors in the social class and to social experience. By expressive style is meant the pattern of behavior by which an individual communicates his needs and tensions. McNeil, who studied this problem, conceptualized two general, expressive styles: *motoric* and *conceptual*. The first involves relatively pronounced use by the individual of the voluntary and large muscle groups in communicating his needs and feelings. We can think of examples of such people, whose motoric methods of expression are clearly excessive. The person who expresses his rage quite openly, using violent movements of the arms and body, making flourishing gestures, and the like, illustrates the use of a motoric style. Similarly, the person who expresses grief by wringing his hands, crying out loudly, having convulsions of the body, and the like, manifests marked motoric expressiveness. The second style, the conceptual mode, involves "the manipulation of ideas." Such a person may feel as much as persons in the first category, but he conceptualizes more, verbalizes more easily. He uses less motoric behavior to convey his feelings. McNeil employed a number of tests to get measures of preference for motoric or conceptual style. In one test, the subjects were asked to play "statues," expressing by pose and gesture each of four emo-

tional states: happiness, fear, anger, and sorrow. They were then rated for the degree of motoric expressiveness they employed. In another test, they were asked to use paints to convey the same four emotions communicated in the game of "statues." In still another, a modified form of the Carl Hollow Square Test was employed. The problem was to fit irregular forms into a square frame. The subjects were also asked about their preferences for hobbies.

On the basis of all of the results, it was found that children tended to have a general expressive style over the whole range of activities and interests that were observed. Some showed a preference for motoric while others showed a preference for conceptual modes of expression. Working-class boys tended to express themselves motorically more often than middle-class boys. The difference between boys whose parents were engaged in entrepreneurial occupations and those whose parents were engaged in bureaucratic occupations was even more marked, the former group showing an even greater tendency toward the use of motoric modes of expression. Analysis of the child-rearing practices of the families of these boys revealed that motoric expression in children is more characteristically related to practices in the home favoring the use of corporal discipline, concrete rather than symbolic rewards for good behavior, and loss of emotional control by the mother. Thus, *both* class status and organization, on the one hand, and methods of child-rearing, on the other, are associated with the type of expressive style that is learned.

An analysis of the data seems to indicate that it is not class, per se, that produces the differences in expressive style. Class does contribute to these differences, but it is only as the cultural practices happen to be associated with class that the influence is manifest. What this means is that different cultures may assign different functions to the same class at various times. The class then becomes the mechanism through which these experiences are transmitted.

Another part of the research focused on methods by which anger is expressed. Beverly B. Allinsmith sought to determine whether such methods were related to social class and to methods of home discipline. Projective tests and interviews with the subjects were the chief means of obtaining data on the ways in which aggression was expressed. It was found that the most direct forms of expressing aggression, namely through flight or through fight, are significantly related to social class. On the other hand, it was found that less direct forms of aggression are not so related. This study, like that of McNeil, also found that methods of home discipline were related to methods of expressing anger. Children whose mothers use corporal punishment, for example, express their own anger in both real-life situations and in projective tests in a direct rather than an indirect manner. Moreover, the children state that they would favor the use of corporal punishment in the rearing of their own children. Taken together with the findings on expressive style, we can see that characteristic methods of personality expression and of resolution of conflict are the result of the interrelationships of specific types of learning experiences in the home, and factors in the social class and general social organization. This means that it is not any single factor, taken by itself, that produces the effect, but rather the combination of factors, acting together, that causes the final behavior.

In another part of this study, Betty J. Beardslee considered the problem of the nature of the defenses that were employed by boys in dealing with a conflict situation. Conflict was aroused (and later resolved by discussion and explanation) by reporting to the subjects some of the negative feelings mothers had about boys. Before and after such arousal, the subjects were given stories which they were asked to complete. The story-completion technique was used as a projective device to obtain evidence concerning the methods by which boys defended themselves against the conflict: arousal of aggression and the need to maintain accustomed attitudes of morality involving mothers. The story endings were scored to determine the extent to which the boys used defense mechanisms to distort the ways they really felt (i.e., angry and troubled). It was found that there is a significant tendency for boys in the middle class to make increasing use of defense mechanisms while boys from the working class do not show this tendency to a significant degree. (The defense mechanisms that were measured are called *second-order defenses* since needs, and *not* reality, were being distorted when conflict was aroused.) Thus, social class is associated with capacity to *shift* mechanisms of defense. This study is particularly important in that it focuses on the malleability of defense—appropriate shift from characteristic defense under neutral conditions to other, more suitable defenses under conflict arousal. It is interesting that individual methods of child-rearing, in this part of the study, were *not* related to *shifts* in defense, although combinations or patterns of methods of child-rearing, taken together, did predict such shifts. We have seen that some individual factors in child-rearing, and particularly total patterns of child-rearing, are related to the defense mechanisms that are learned, that is, to the choice of defense mechanisms. We have also summarized, in previous chapters of this book, how level of adjustment and general patterns of adjustment are related to social class and to cultural practices. Now, we have the added fact that at least some types of shift in defenses are more easily possible for individuals reared under certain conditions than under other conditions.

If we attempt to integrate the findings of the studies we have just summarized with other clinical and research evidence that is now available to us, we can come to the generalization that not only level of adjustment but also *potential for adaptation to changing circumstances* is related to those cultural conditions that are modal for a given society. It appears that when children have been reared under conditions that are most clearly appropriate to the usual conditions of a particular society, and when these con-

ditions involve acceptance, warmth, and some degree of permissiveness, they are most likely to develop *healthy and adaptable* personality characteristics. Middle-class conditions in our own society probably represent such modal features. Hence, we can hazard the generalization that children from this class, when the other criteria of healthy child-rearing which we have noted are present, should be the ones most likely to make effective and healthy personality adjustments.

DELINQUENCY DURING PREADOLESCENCE

During periods of social or economic upheaval society often becomes keenly aware of the problem of juvenile delinquency. Children are found to be breaking the laws with markedly increasing frequency during such transitional periods. They manifest such types of delinquency as stealing, burglarizing automobiles, attacking men and women, engaging in intensified "gang warfare," and even committing murder. Certain cities and sections within the cities suddenly become designated as "delinquency areas." Examples of this phenomenon of an apparent outcropping of delinquency may be found in any postwar period, during periods of economic recession, and during periods of rapid social change. Delinquency is present, however, during all periods in modern society. Although it may, in fact, increase in frequency during times of uncertainty (but really adequate data on this problem are rarely available for reasons that we shall soon see), it is best to recognize the fact that delinquency is an ever-present phenomenon.

To understand this last statement it is necessary to realize that delinquency is simply a particular form of *reactive behavior*. It is basically a legal concept: delinquency is a violation of the laws for which the child has been apprehended by the authorities. Many children engage in similar types of behavior but their offenses may be milder, less frequent, and they are not apprehended. Thus delinquency has much in common with other forms of hostile, reactive behavior—which usually results from some type of frustration. Aggression is a common reaction to frustration, but we do not consider all aggressive children to be delinquents. It is only when the aggressive behavior constitutes a violation of the law and when the individual is apprehended for the violation that it is technically known as delinquency. From these considerations we can infer that delinquent behavior may have much in common with other, nondelinquent forms of behavior; and indeed this turns out to be the case.

It may now also be more understandable why delinquency appears to be, or in fact is, more common during periods of rapid social change. During such periods conflicting values and changing ideals become more prominent. Uncertainties, both economic and social, contribute still further to feelings of insecurity and to frustration. Adults are often the first to

feel the effects of these factors: in the home, in terms of economic distress; in the political arena, in which claims and counterclaims are likely to be bandied about in extreme form; and even in the sphere of social relations, in which societal turmoil is often reflected. These same factors are likely to affect the youngsters. Some of this effect may be direct, since the youngsters may experience changes in their economic status, in the adequacy of school programs (note how often school programs are curtailed in times of economic distress), and in the availability of social and recreational programs in the community. Moreover, youngsters are likely to experience the effects of the frustrations of their elders who, because they are troubled, displace some of their feelings on their own and other children. Finally, it is easy for children to become the "scapegoats" for the problems of their elders, who then tend to over-react to the very conditions for which they were in part, at least, responsible. Thus there may be a real as well as an apparent increase in delinquency during periods of uncertainty.

What produces delinquency in the first place? Several investigations have shown that delinquency is related to broken home conditions, emotional rejection of children by their parents, and substandard economic conditions (25, 26). Yet these conditions by themselves do not lead inevitably toward delinquency; they may precipitate other forms of maladjustment, including withdrawal tendencies, severe anxiety, and even psychotic behavior. When delinquency occurs it is because, for some reasons, the child has learned to discharge his tensions in a hostile manner. In other words, delinquency often represents a specific form of maladjustment, the effects of which are increased by any conditions that produce conflict, and in which aggressive behavior has been learned as the typical means of discharging tensions.

𝕣As we shall see in Chapter 9, delinquents come from all levels of society, from all the ranges of intelligence, and from all ethnic groups. However, delinquency is most frequent in those areas in which emotionally insecure home conditions are frequent and in which children have frequent examples in the community of antisocial behavior. In the latter case, delinquent behavior may be largely or simply a reflection of the mores of the culture which provides the child with frequent examples of antisocial behavior. In such an event the delinquent child may not be profoundly disturbed emotionally, but rather behaves in ways similar to those of his contemporaries. (This is one of the main reasons for helping youths to maintain groups under favorable community auspices with good adult leaders and guides. They may thus be rewarded for learning good models of social behavior—and as a result learn to express their aggressions in socially desirable forms—rather than be punished for acts of transgression against society.) Some delinquency is largely, or entirely, a reaction to specific conditions of frustration or deprivation. Part of the "cure" then lies in a correction of these conditions. By far the largest percentage of delinquent children, however, are individuals with personality disturbances for whom aggressive modes of behavior have become habitual; in one study it was esti-

mated that this group constituted 91 per cent of the population of delinquents (25).

One of the puzzling questions that is often asked is why the same family, with presumably similar or identical conditions for all the children, will sometimes have one child who is delinquent while another is not. A number of studies have concentrated their attention on this problem (25, 26, 27). In some studies like those by Healy and Bronner, and those by the Gluecks, siblings were paired, one being the delinquent and the other not, or controls for the delinquents were matched with them for family, age, intelligence, and socioeconomic condition. It was found that the delinquent group, in contrast to the nondelinquent group with the same type of background, is far more insecure, far more maladjusted, and expresses far more feelings of hostility. Closer examination of the data reveals that the nondelinquent child, for example, did not have exactly the same home conditions as his delinquent brother. The former was able to feel accepted, feel more secure emotionally, and had different modes of discharging his tensions. In turn, these differences were related to *differences within the family*, so that there was a close emotional attachment to a parent (usually of the same sex). On the other hand, the delinquent brother did not have an opportunity for such an attachment or was rejected, or development in his personality was not stabilized *before* home conditions or economic factors became

Learning to swim is of great help in developing self-confidence. (U. of Mich.)

disturbed. The major point is that parents do react differentially to their children. It is also clear that changing circumstances in the home may differentially affect different children who are at different stages of development.

Another factor that may help to explain why some siblings become delinquent and others do not, and which may contribute in general to the causation of delinquency, is the *constitutional* condition of the individual. In Chapters 2 and 4 we discussed constitutional factors

302

and their relationship to personality. We learned that children are born with different physical capacities and different autonomic excitabilities. Some of these differences are related to heredity; others are attributable to prenatal and congenital influences. At any rate, the child at birth is endowed with certain constitutional characteristics, one of which is body build. Sheldon and his co-workers have been investigating for some time the relations between body build and personality characteristics (28). Unfortunately, for our purposes, almost all of this work has been done on adults, and, as we pointed out in another connection, no adequate norms are available for typing the body build of children. Recently the Gluecks, in the third volume of their studies on delinquency, did an analysis of the body build of 500 delinquents and of their controls (29). The results of this study are quite pertinent to our problem. Three well trained judges rated the body build of the Gluecks' subjects (they determined the *somatotype*) according to Sheldon's criteria, dividing the cases into 13 categories. When the delinquents were compared with the nondelinquents for somatotype it was found, as might be expected, that the nondelinquents were well distributed in the three major categories (*mesomorph, ectomorph,* and *endomorph*), with a small percentage showing what is termed a *balanced* somatotype. In contrast, although delinquents were also found in all major categories of somatotype, they came predominantly from the mesomorphic category. Moreover, there was a significant difference in the frequency of mesomorphism between delinquent and nondelinquent groups (about twice as many). The Gluecks did *not* conclude that there is an inevitable relationship between body build and tendency toward delinquency, but did believe that it is a relevant factor. We must note that Sheldon found that mesomorphs tend to show "vital energy, love of risk, lust for power, physical courage . . ." and that therefore individuals with such a body build would be expected to be more likely to engage in outgoing, aggressive types of behavior when frustrated (30).

We may agree that body build and tendency toward delinquency are correlated but the question concerning the precise nature of the causation remains an open one. We have previously noted that body build is variable during the childhood years. We have also learned that the type of daily activity and particularly the type of nutrition have an influence upon the body build of children. Hence it may be that body build contributes to the general type of behavioral reaction, but it is equally possible that other factors influence the development of body build in the first instance. There may very well be a circular relationship between body build and personality, and it is hard to say, in a given case, which came first. Nevertheless, the high frequency of mesomorphism among delinquents is an important finding, and no matter how the condition of mesomorphism came about it appears to be statistically, if not causally, related to delinquency.

We have been discussing delinquency in connection with the intermediate school period because most cases of delinquent behavior begin before puberty, although apprehension (and delinquency technically) usually occurs after puberty (26). Hostile acting-out is common during this period of integration and stabilization of the personality precisely because maturity is still in the offing and needs for independence and group imitation (*contagion*) are prominent. If careful investigation were made of the nature and causation (and the meaning) of antisocial behavior when it occurs during this period, and if preventive or corrective action were taken for the child or the family at this time, when it is necessary, the incidence and severity of delinquency during adolescence would be far less striking.

GENERAL READINGS

1. Hechinger, F. M., *An Adventure in Education*. New York: Macmillan, 1956.
2. Jersild, A. T., *Child Psychology*, 4th ed. Englewood Cliffs, N. J.: Prentice-Hall, 1954.
3. Thompson, G. G., *Child Psychology: Growth Trends in Psychological Adjustment*. Boston: Houghton Mifflin, 1952.
4. Valentine, C. W., *The Normal Child: And Some of His Abnormalities*. Baltimore: Penguin, 1956.

SELECTED BIBLIOGRAPHY

5. Baldwin, B. T., and Wood, T. D., "Weight-height-age tables for boys and girls of school age," in Strang, R., *An Introduction to Child Study*. New York: Macmillan, 1938.
6. Thompson, G. G., and Horrocks J. E., "A study of the friendship fluctuations of boys and girls," *J. Genet. Psychol.*, 1947, 70, 53-63.
7. Bonney, M. E., Hoblit, R. E., and Dreyer, A. H., "A study of some factors related to socioeconomic status in a man's dormitory," *Sociol.*, 1953, 16, 287-301.
8. Lehman, H. C., and Witty, P. A., *The Psychology of Play Activities*. New York: Barnes, 1927.
9. Campbell, E. H., "The social-sex development of the child," *Genet. Psychol. Monogr.*, 1939, No. 4.
10. Lyness, P. I., "The place of the mass media in the lives of boys and girls," *Journ. Quart.*, 1952, 29, 43-54.
11. Radke, M., Trager, H. G., and Davis, H., "Social perceptions and attitudes of children," *Genet. Psychol. Monogr.*, 1949, 40, 327-447.
12. Bonney, M. E., "Relationships between social success, family size, socioeconomic home background, and intelligence among school children in grades III and IV," *Sociol.*, 1944, 7, 26-39.
13. Bird, C., Monachesi, E. D., and Burdick, H., "Infiltration and the attitudes of white and Negro parents and children," *J. Abnorm. Soc. Psychol.*, 1952, 47, 688-699.
14. Mussen, P. H., "Some personality and social factors related to changes in children's attitudes toward Negroes," *J. Abnorm. Soc. Psychol.*, 1959, 45, 423-441.

15. Sears, P. S., "Levels of aspiration in academically successful and unsuccessful children," *J. Abnorm. Soc. Psychol.*, 1940, 35, 498-536.

16. Maller, J. B., "Cooperation and competition: An experimental study in motivation," *Teachers Coll. Contr. Educ.*, 1929.

17. Jennings, H. J., *Leadership and Isolation*. New York: Longmans, Green, 1943.

18. Cuff, N. B., "Vocabulary tests," *J. Educ. Psychol.*, 1930, 21, 212-220.

19. Garrett, H. E., "A developmental theory of intelligence," *Amer. Psychol.*, 1946, 1, 372-378.

20. Sanford, H., "An evaluation of group guidance utilizing a projective technique with twelve underachieving adolescent boys," Unpublished doctoral dissertation, University of Michigan, 1958.

21. McCandless, B. R., and Castenada, A., "Anxiety in children, school achievement, and intelligence," *Child Develpm.*, 1956, 27, 379-382.

22. Hoch, P. A., and Zubin, J., *Anxiety*. New York: Grune & Stratton, 1950.

23. Hutt, M. L., and Miller, D. R., "Social values and personality development," *J. Soc. Issues*, 1949, 5, No. 4.

24. Miller, D. R., Swanson, G. E., *et al.*, *Inner Conflict and Defense*. New York: Holt, 1958.

25. Healy, W., and Bronner, A. F., *New Light on Delinquency and Its Treatment*. New Haven: Yale University, 1936.

26. Glueck, S., and Glueck, E. T., *Unraveling Juvenile Delinquency*. Cambridge: Harvard University, 1950.

27. Bovet, L., *Psychiatric Aspects of Juvenile Delinquency*. Geneva: World Health Organization Monograph Series, 1951.

28. Sheldon, W. H., *The Varieties of Temperament*. New York: Harper, 1942.

29. Glueck, S., and Glueck, E. T., *Physique and Delinquency*. New York: Harper, 1956.

30. Sheldon, W. H., "Mesomorphs in mischief," *Contemp. Psychol.*, 1957, 2, 125-126.

9 | *The crisis of puberty*

IN THIS CHAPTER we shall deal with the intricate problems and adjustments of adolescence. This period begins with puberty and may be said to continue for many years until adult maturity is established. We shall devote our attention to the beginning years of this period, and focus our major interest on the so-called period of puberty, the early phase of adolescence, when its major stresses are first experienced.

SOME GENERAL FEATURES

There is considerable confusion as to the meaning of "adolescence," and it is very difficult to define precisely. Rubé has commented, and in our opinion quite rightly, that we have paid much more attention to adolescents in primitive cultures than to those in our own (11). We often become concerned with the adolescent youngster when he gets into trouble of some sort, and give relatively little study to normal adolescent development and characteristics.

There is no precise time at which adolescence either begins or ends in our society, even though it is true that legislation has often attempted to set such limits. For example, according to the laws in some states an individual is not a child but an adolescent after the age of 12; he is considered to be an adult at the age of 21. In England, the legal definition of puberty places its beginning as 12 years for girls and 14 years for boys. Such legal definitions are arbitrary, of course, and are designed to meet practical exigencies. They do not conform to what we already know about adolescence.

The term *adolescence* refers to the whole range of characteristics, biological and psychological, covering all the periods from prepubescence to maturity. It is the reflection of the total process of maturation of the individual. It is a period of *gradual developmental change,* although, at times, it appears to be abrupt. Crow and Crow feel that adolescence is the period during which the individual moves away from dependence upon adult direction and protection toward self-dependence and self-determination (12). They feel that in our culture this period is bracketed roughly between ages 13 and 19, but they emphasize the fact that tremendous differences exist among individuals as to when the period begins and ends.

Some writers distinguish three periods: (a) *prepubescence,* the period of the rapid spurt when physical changes preparing for puberty occur; (b) *puberty,* when biological changes have produced evident manifestations of primary sexual characteristics (for example, menstruation in girls, and the production of spermatazoa and the appearance of pubic hair in boys); and (c) *maturity,* when the biological growth phenomena have completed their cycle. The onset of prepubescence and puberty vary widely both within a culture and across cultures. Within our own culture, for example, the onset of menarche commonly varies about four years (some girls manifest menarche at four years of age, and others at eighteen); and puberty in boys shows almost as wide variation. Not only is

there such wide variability in physical time of change, but the social and psychological characteristics of the individual *do not necessarily coincide with this change.*

We have noted that there is a tendency to confuse adolescence with the biological maturation of sexual characteristics. Although it is a fact that primary and secondary sexual characteristics mature during the adolescent period, merely because an individual has the capacity for biological reproduction or manifests other adult sexual characteristics does not mean that he has reached an adolescent stage in his development. Bernard points out that a distinction should be made between puberty and adolescence (13). *Puberty* refers essentially to the maturation of the physical aspects of sexual organs, and so may be rather narrowly defined with considerable validity. *Adolescence* more properly refers to the total process of growing up, and is a product of the era and culture in which the particular individual lives. Bernard states that adolescence, which begins with puberty and ends with maturity, is difficult to define because maturity itself is difficult to define. Within our culture some persons may not be mature until relatively late in life (for example, a professional person who undergoes a long period of training), whereas others mature relatively early (for example, the teenager in the armed forces who does a "man's" job).

Greulich cites a case of a sexually precocious girl who attained puberty at the age of 3 years and 11 months (14). When she was one year old it was observed that her breasts were quite large, and at the age of 3 years and 7 months she menstruated. *Sexual precocity* is not unusual, although the age of the girl in this case is admittedly extreme. Greulich's case is cited to illustrate the fact that puberty and adolescence are *not* synonymous terms.

Rubé has attempted to define what is meant by adolescence (11). He conceives of adolescence as a definite break in the growth process. There are *two new factors* present during adolescence which are not found in either childhood or adulthood. One is puberty and the other is the break made by the child with the parental milieu. However, Rubé scoffs at the usual definition of adolescence as "an age of transition." He states that this is a cliché that adds nothing to our knowledge, in that it is equally true of every other period of life, and that life itself is a transition between birth and death. Since life is not a harmonious process of growth followed by a regression leading to death, we cannot consider adolescence in terms of childhood and adulthood transition.

The adolescent cycle is similar to the cycle that starts at conception and ends at birth. At conception the infant intrudes into the parental milieu following the "dramatic breaking of the physiological egg (birth)." Similarly, as Rubé points out, the parental milieu is a kind of "social egg" which has to be broken when the adolescent intrudes upon the wider world. The analogy may not be exact, but the point emphasized in each case is the new *type* of separation and individuation of the person. The time, duration, and characteristics of the "breaking-out" process vary tremendously among individuals, since the rhythm of the biological process is not the same for all people, and since psychological maturity is reached at different times and in different ways by different people.

Rubé views adolescence as a "second birth," and we will see later that this view is expressed symbolically in the puberty rites of primitive cultures. He compares adolescence to the birth of the butterfly, which breaks out of its cocoon after first being a caterpillar. Childhood would correspond to the worm stage, adolescence to the cocoon stage, and adulthood to the butterfly stage. During the cocoon phase (adolescence) there are great changes in physical and psychological characteristics. These bring the individual to the point where he can achieve emotional independence from his parents, and his interests shift from his family group to wider social circles. In the process the adolescent learns to give up his narcissistic orientation and to develop adult reciprocity in which he can *give* at least as much as he *receives*.

Adolescence may be viewed as a period involving "rebirth" of the individual, and is based, in part, on the new physiological processes and social and cultural forces. This is a nonemotional, intellectual definition of adolescence. But how does society generally regard this period? Its reaction is often *not* one of equanimity and acceptance. The younger generation is frequently characterized as "no-good" and sometimes as "going to hell in a basket." Some years ago the models of scorn and ridicule were the "coonskin" college boy and the "flapper." Today we focus our hostilities upon the "teenager," and ascribe all forms of crime, wantonness, and irresponsibility to him. He is often regarded automatically with negative feelings just because he is between the ages of 13 and 19 (the "teen" years). Newspapers feature law infractions of the "teenager" but less often report on his positive qualities and achievements. Such reports are often biased by strong hostilities and demand strong penalties and retaliatory actions for the alleged waywardness of "our youth."

The adolescent is often a misunderstood individual. There are a number of reasons for this. In part, this misperception of the adolescent may be attributed to a lack of understanding of the numerous forces at work within and outside him and of his consequent problems. But there are deeper reasons for some of society's reactions to adolescence. To understand these we must know more about the "problem" of adolescence. We have to be certain, indeed, that there really is such a problem.

We have noted that the adolescent processes (physiological and psychological) drive the child toward the assumption of more adult roles within his culture. Adults tend to prevent the youngster from assuming an adult status, however; they may even drive him away from the world of adults. Rubé feels that this conflict between the adult and the adolescent is based upon a rebellion by adults against a biological phenomenon they

do not understand, and that the so-called rebellion of the adolescent is a justified reaction on his part to the rebellion of the parents (11). We shall have more to say about this in our later discussion of the puberty rites of adolescence.

Let us look briefly at some of the unfavorable phenomena of adolescence. Frank points out that in our culture the period from 10 to 15 years of age has the lowest death rate of all age periods from infancy to senility (15). *During the period 15 to 19 years, however, the death rate increases nearly 100 per cent.* The chief causes are accidents, tuberculosis, heart diseases, pneumonia-influenza, and appendicitis. The rate of first admissions of children to state hospitals in the age span of 10 to 14 years is very low. In New York state, for which Frank reports these figures, it is 4.3 per 100,000 children; but, for ages 15 to 19, the rate jumps to 40.3 per 100,000, *a tenfold increase.* It is also reported that the cases of suicide, vagrancy, delinquency, alcoholism, drug addiction, and related maladaptive behavior increase at an appalling rate during adolescence. All of these facts point to a callous waste of human resources. In addition to these misfortunes of adolescence, the adolescent suffers emotionally—and frequently unnecessarily.

These are only a few of the serious problems of adolescence. On the positive side, there are many advantages to being adolescent. We shall examine these in the following sections.

PHYSICAL DEVELOPMENT AND SEQUENCES

Numerous physiological and physical changes occur during puberty. It may appear that they occur "all of a sudden," but in reality they develop gradually. Further, we are more likely to notice the external changes in appearance than the far more basic physiological changes. For example, we are aware of the development of external sexual characteristics such as pubic hair and breasts, but we may fail to understand the significance of marked *internal* changes in glands and in metabolism which are of profound importance.

Glandular changes

Remarkable changes occur in the endocrine gland system as the child approaches puberty. Studies have shown that sex hormones (known as *androgens* in the male, and *estrogens* in the female) are eliminated from the body in the urine (16). Boys and girls secrete both androgens and estrogens prior to the onset of puberty, but at about age nine there is a change in the ratio of these hormones secreted by each sex. In the boy, the proportion of androgens over estrogens increases, and in the girl the reverse is true. The presence of these hormones is closely related to the development of masculine and feminine characteristics. Sollenberger compared boys having a high male hormone output with those having a low one, and found that the high group had more interest in

heterosexual activities and strenuous sports (17). In girls, there is a cyclical secretion of estrogens for approximately a period of 18 months prior to the first menstrual period (the *menarche*).

During puberty the pituitary gland becomes more active, and produces two types of hormones that greatly influence the physical development of the individual: one stimulates the growth of the gonads (the *gonadtropic* hormones) and the other controls bodily growth. The development of the mature testes of the male and of the ovaries of the female is dependent on gonadtropic stimulation. If the amount of these hormones is not sufficient, the reproductive organs will not mature fully. As the gonads mature they produce, in turn, other hormones which stimulate the maturation of sexual characteristics, such as the mammary glands, breasts, uterus, and vagina of the female, and the penis, prostate gland, and the development of facial as well as pubic hair, of the male. In addition, the gonadtropic hormones regulate the production of the growth hormones by the pituitary gland. If the growth hormones are produced too early the child will usually be unusually short in stature; if they are unduly delayed, the body structure will be large and gross, and similar to that of a *eunuch* (a castrated male). If their production is deficient in general, bodily growth does not occur, and the individual is short (*dwarfism*). If their production is excessive, bodily growth is accelerated, and the individual becomes excessively tall (*giantism*).

We have pointed out that puberty need not immediately precede adolescence, and cited a case to illustrate this.

However, puberty normally initiates the adolescent period. Jersild has summarized the ages at which boys and girls attain puberty (18). The criterion for boys was the development of characteristics associated with the production of pubic hair. He found that at approximately 13 years of age, 18 per cent of boys have attained puberty; at age 14, 46 per cent; at age 15, 70 per cent; and at age 16, 93 per cent. The criterion for the attainment of puberty in girls was the menarche. (It should be observed that regular menstrual periods need not always follow the menarche.) According to Jersild's data the "average" American girl reaches menarche at about 12½ years of age, but there is considerable variation from girl

to girl: 3.2 per cent of 10-year-old girls reach the menarche; 12.1 per cent of 11-year-olds; 33.5 per cent of 12-year-olds; 36.3 per cent of 13-year-olds; 3.2 per cent of 15-year-olds; and .8 per cent of 16-year-olds. Thus, by the age of 13, 48.8 per cent, by the age of 14, 85.1 per cent, and by the age of 15, 95.6 per cent of girls have attained menarche. However, as Jersild points out, the attainment of menarche does not necessarily mean that the girl is capable of reproduction. This is borne out by many other studies. Ford and Beach report that menstruation in the girl does not necessarily mean that

Figure 15. *Physical developments in adolescence.*

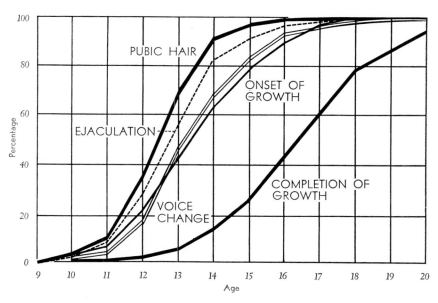

From Kinsey, A. C., Pomeroy, W. B., and Martin, C. E., *Sexual Behavior in the Human Male.* Philadelphia: Saunders, 1948.

the ovaries produce mature eggs capable of being fertilized (19). Further, they found that often both menstruation and mature egg production may start before the uterus is capable of supporting the fetus. Their findings indicate that regardless of the age of menarche, only a small proportion of girls are capable of bearing a child prior to the age of 15, although numerous case histories indicate that it is certainly possible. Kinsey has summarized some of the physical characteristics of adolescent boys (20). These are presented in Figure 15, which shows the development of pubic hair, ejaculation, voice change, onset of growth, and completion of growth.

Basal metabolism

There is a significant change in the basal metabolic rate of both boys and girls during adolescence. Basal metabolism represents the energy that the individual expends in order to maintain life. It refers to the minimal heat produced by a person 14 to 18 hours after eating. This is measured when the person is at rest, but not asleep, by means of an instrument known as a *calorimeter*. It is expressed in calories produced per hour per square meter of body surface. In both sexes the rate declines very sharply at puberty, but the drop is greater for girls than it is for boys, although it continues longer for boys than for girls.

According to the data reported by Shock, the male adolescents he studied dropped from a production of 45 calories per square meter per hour at age 12 to about 42 at age 12½ years (21). The girls dropped from the production of 41 calories per square meter per hour at age 12 to 33 at age 12½. However, as in the case of all physiological processes studied, there is considerable variation from one person to another. These lowered metabolic rates result in the temporarily reduced physical activities of the adolescent, for a time.

Other physiological changes

Garrison has summarized some other changes in the internal organs and systems that occur during puberty (22). During early childhood boys' hearts are usually larger than girls', but at puberty the size of the heart in both boys and girls doubles. At age 9 or 10 to age 13 or 14, girls' hearts are larger than those of boys, but after age 13 boys' hearts grow at a much more rapid rate than do those of girls. The growth-pattern rate of the arteries and veins is the reverse of that of the heart. In childhood they grow rapidly, while the heart grows slowly. In adolescence the veins and arteries grow slowly, while the heart, comparatively, grows much more rapidly. These developmental factors are reflected in changes in blood pressure in both boys and girls. There is little difference between blood pressure of boys and girls during childhood, but between the ages of 10 and 13 blood pressure is higher in girls than it is in boys. After the age of 13, the blood pressure of boys exceeds that of girls, and the difference between them tends to increase with age. In girls, blood pressure tends to decrease after age 16.

There are also many changes in gastrointestinal functions. In general, the stomach increases in size, and as the parents of adolescent children know, they are "always hungry" and ready for a "snack" (which often turns out to be a full-sized meal!). The rapid growth pattern of the adolescent demands an increased food intake (for example, he needs three times as much protein as does the adult, and his other nutritional demands are proportionately increased).

Physical characteristics and appearance

We are all familiar with the striking changes in the physical characteristics and appearance of the adolescent. Perhaps the most pronounced of these are

the increases in weight and height. Here again, as we have noted in the development of other physiological characteristics, we find significant differences between the sexes. The adolescent spurt in rate of growth occurs earlier in the case of girls than it does in boys. For example, it has been found that the age at which the largest increase in height occurs is for girls 11.5 years, whereas for boys it is 13.8 years (23). The gain in weight by both sexes parallels that of height. When we compare the growth curves of boys and girls for height, we find that at first

Figure 16. *Average weight of boys and girls, from birth to 18 years.*

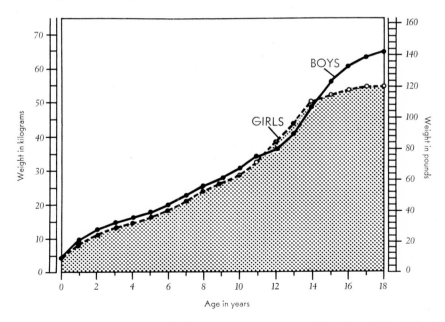

From Stephens, J. M., *Educational Psychology,* rev. New York: Henry Holt, 1958; based on data from studies by Baldwin and by Shuttleworth.

the adolescent girls tend to be a little taller than boys of similar age. However, the boys soon catch up with the girls and on the average are taller at maturity. This is also true for weight: the girls first exceed the boys, but the boys continue to increase in weight beyond the age when girls do, and so boys are heavier at maturity. The growth curves of weight for boys and girls are illustrated in Figure 16.

Each individual's unique pattern of growth is maintained through the adolescent period. Stolz and Stolz studied the relationship between the height of boys at the begininng and at the end of the pubertal period (24). They found that boys tended to remain either short or tall as compared with their own age group, and reported the high correlation of .82 between height at onset and termination of puberty. The same principle of constancy of pattern of growth during this period also holds true for girls who reach the menarche at the same age. The relative positions in weight are not as closely maintained for girls reaching the menarche at different ages. The principle is apparently more accurate for boys than it is for girls.

The increase in skeletal growth, as reflected in the over-all increase in height, produces some disproportionate growth in various bodily areas: the arms and legs grow longer, the hands and feet become bigger. We often refer to the adolescent as "awkward and gangly" because of these phenomena. In the boy, the width of the shoulders increases, and in the girl the hips broaden. Of interest is the find-

ing by Bayley that early-maturing boys have broad hips and narrow shoulders, while late-maturing boys have thin hips and long legs (25). Late-maturing girls tend to have broad shoulders. He points out that the early-maturing boy tends to have the characteristic body build of girls, while the late-maturing girl tends to have the body build characteristic of boys. Bayley states, however, that these physical characteristics are not necessarily reflected in personality. We may note that the major bodily growth occurring in the extremities of boys and girls illustrates two of the principles of growth that we discussed in Chapter 4: growth proceeds in *cephalo-caudal* and *proximo-distal* directions.

We should like to re-emphasize the fact that each individual has his own growth curve, and that the tables of norms in height and weight are not particularly helpful in evaluating an individual's growth. One limitation of these tables is that they do not take into account the specific body build of the child. Another factor is the tremendous variability in growth of adolescents. These principles are well illustrated by the results of a study conducted at the University of Chicago (26). Growth data on 1,817 girls between the ages of 6 and 17, and on 1,884 boys between the ages of 6 and 18, were analyzed. In summary, it was concluded on the basis of the results that differences in the height-weight relationships indicate the importance of body build as a determining factor. The study also indicates that boys who mature prior to age 14 are heavier than those who mature later, and that those who mature between 14 and 15 are heavier at all ages

The trampoline is excellent for developing mature body control. (U. of Mich.)

than those who mature after the age of 15. Girls maturing before 13 years of age are heavier at all ages from 6 to 17 than those who mature later. Those girls who mature between 13 and 14 are heavier at all ages than those who mature after age 14. This study indicates that the maturational characteristics as well as the general body build of the individual (unique to each child) are important variables in the height and weight curves showing accelerated growth at puberty.

At the same time that skeletal and weight changes occur, there is a change in the amount and distribution of body fat. There is a rather steady increase in the amount of fat for girls between ages 6

and 13, at which time it takes a sudden spurt up to about age 18. Boys show a steady increase up to age 13, then show a marked decline (27). Factors related to the types of physical activity of the child may account for this, at least in part.

The skin texture of the adolescent becomes thicker and coarser, and the pores of the skin become enlarged. Activities of the skin glands increase: the *merocrine* sweat glands (which are scattered over the body) and the *apocrine* sweat glands (located under the armpits) both become more active, and their secretion has a decided odor which is often worrisome to the adolescent; the *sebaceous* glands (the oil-producing glands) are also more active and, due to the fact that their secretions are not readily drained, hard masses are often formed in the pores, blocking the secretion. This results in the formation of what are commonly known as "blackheads." All of us are acquainted with the concern of the adolescent over his "pimply complexion," and the irrational fears he may have on this account.

We are familiar, too, with the new growth of hair in various areas of the body during puberty. In the male, hair appears on the face, limbs, pubic areas, and chest. In the girl, it develops on the limbs and pubic areas. The hairline of the head changes, with two recesses appearing, one on each side of the forehead.

One of the most prominent physical changes in the girl during the adolescent period is the development of the *mammary* glands (the breasts). According to

Stratz, in early childhood the girl has a small *papilla* (nipple), which is just slightly elevated above the surrounding dark area known as the *areola* (18). In the 10th year, on the average, there is a slight swelling, which is known as the "bud" stage. This is essentially a swelling of the areola. Next, due to increase in the amount of fat underneath the papilla and areola, the "primary" breast develops. Finally, the mature or "secondary" breast is formed. However, as Stratz points out, many girls never develop this final, mature breast; their breasts remain in the "primary" stage, *but function as efficiently as the secondary breast.* Usually we do not think that the boy also has a mammary development, but he does develop rudimentary mammary glands. Due to hormonal action, they sometimes become enlarged during adolescence, and this may embarrass him. Such a condition is known as *mastitis adolescentium.* It is *not* pathological, but is rather a "reflection of a normal state associated with puberty and beginning sexual development" (14). However, there is a *different* and pathological condition known as *Frölich's Syndrome,* due to malfunctioning of the endocrine glands (particularly underfunctioning of the pituitary glands), in which there is underdevelopment of the genitals, enlarged breasts, and a female hair distribution.

We have seen that a great number of physiological and anatomical changes occur during puberty. These tend to follow similar, general patterns. At first, the rate of growth is slow, but then during puberty a cycle, first of rapid acceleration of growth, and then rapid deceleration, occurs. Finally, the rate of increase in growth diminishes to the vanishing point. As has been pointed out, the patterns for body dimensions, organ dimensions, and physical functions all follow what Harris and others call a general curve of growth (19). The specific characteristics of the curve vary for specific body tissues. The rate of growth of genital tissues differs significantly from all others during the pubertal period. It far exceeds the rate of growth for all other tissues, and highlights the changes that take place during puberty. The four basic curves of growth of body tissues are illustrated in Figure 5 (p. 106). Note the spurt in rate of growth of the testes reaching its peak at about age 12, while shortly prior to this the rate of growth of the lymphoid structures decreases quite significantly.

The bodily changes that occur during puberty are quite striking and important in themselves, but we should not forget that they do not occur in isolation. They are related to the total development of the individual, and in particular are associated with the psychological characteristics of the adolescent. We shall discuss this relationship in a later section.

PUBERTY IN VARIOUS CULTURES

There comes a time when it is recognized by society that the child is no longer a child, but that he is approaching the status of adulthood. As we have seen, the maturation of the person is evidenced in many ways: by an accelerated development of biological characteristics (many centering around procreative functions); by the changed perceptions by the individual of the world and his society which result in changed behavior; and by significantly altered perceptions by society of the child which also result in changes in his behavior. All societies and all cultures recognize the changing status of the child, but they do so in quite different ways. We shall examine some of the widely varying cultural attitudes so as to shed some additional light on the ways such factors influence the development of personality in general, and of adolescents in particular. Adolescence does not develop as an abstraction, but rather occurs to a particular individual who lives in a specific culture, and who is subjected to all the forces and learning experiences indigenous to that culture. These influences determine, to a large extent, the nature of adolescent experience and the consequent development of personality.

Margaret Mead has clearly pointed out that the strains and stresses that are characteristic of adolescents in our culture need not be a function purely of "being adolescent," but rather are due to "being adolescent in America" (30). In order to see how adolescent experiences differ from one culture to another, let us first look at Mead's description of the pubertal rites for the girls and boys in the Manus tribe (a tribe in Samoa). She states that the onset of puberty in the Manus girl is marked by public ceremony. The father initiates this at the time of her first menses by throwing cocoanuts into the sea, and the news rapidly spreads throughout the village. The girl is then placed by her family in a special cubicle in the center of her home, and she has to remain within it, without leaving, for five days. She is visited by the villagers who bring food and gifts, but is not permitted to commune with them. At the end of the five-day period a large feast is held in the evening and the girl is finally permitted to leave the cubicle. However, she is not permitted to walk about the village or leave her home while the sun is shining, and she is denied any experiences with males. Seven days later a second feast is held, and five days following this, a third. The girl is not finally freed from her taboos until the day preceding her marriage, which is arranged for her by her family. From puberty until marriage the girl does not take part actively in her village life, but, as Mead points out, is essentially an observer of the culture, "an inhibited spectator to life." Her adolescent years are one of waiting, years in which she has no active heterosexual relationships or even any close relationships with other girls. She waits passively for her husband, who is found for her.

Mead states that the first formal recognition of puberty in the boy (among the Manus) is the "ear-piercing" ceremony. The boy's family prepares a large feast, and he is dressed in his best clothes. Only adults and very young children are present at the ceremony; his peers are not permitted to attend. The boy's ears are pierced by sharpened hard wood splints, and the holes are then plugged with pieces of soft wood. He is then placed under a number of taboos: he may not cut anything with a knife, light a fire, or bathe for five days, after which he is allowed to move around and wash. The other taboos hold until his mother's relatives prepare a large feast for the relatives of his father. The boy is then finally freed from all his taboos, and no new duties are required of him. The only change in his freedom is that he is not permitted to play or to associate with girls of his own age. In the olden days it was the custom that the various youths, denied heterosexual relationships with girls of their own tribe, formed a raiding party and captured a woman of another tribe. They brought her back to their village, where she was successively raped by every man in the village, regardless of his age. The youths always kept their captive woman with them, and took her with them everywhere they went, sometimes selling her services to men in friendly villages. As Mead points out, men often displaced their hatred of women, which was often related to the frigidity of their wives and to the economic exactions imposed upon them by matrimony, on the prostitute. For similar reasons, the Manus youth displaced their dammed-up sexual energies upon some other woman or person. The boys were not required to do any work, and had no responsibilities until they married. In Mead's words they were a "group of arrogant, roistering blades." (Today they leave the village and work for the white man, finding sexual relief with prostitutes or in homosexual relationships. After about a period of three years they return to their village, where they are feasted and blessed.)

For contrast, let us look at the practices of some other cultures. Rust has described in detail the pubertal rites for the Mission Indian girls of southern California (31). This ceremony has been called the "roasting of girls," and its object is to prepare them for matrimony. A fire is lit in a large pit and is covered with green herbs, through which steam from the wet soil rises. The adolescent girls are then placed upon these herbs, and covered with blankets for the duration of the ceremony.

Howitt has described the pubertal rites which he observed for an Australian boy (22). The boy was blindfolded, and then was surrounded by many dancing men. One of them seized him, and forcibly pressed one of the boy's front teeth upwards with one of his own. He then placed a chisel against the boy's tooth, and struck it with a hammer. The blows were repeated until the tooth was driven from its socket. The boy was required to accept this torture in a stoical manner, and could not make any outcry, although Howitt noted many signs of severe pain and stress.

A large number of such additional primitive rites could be cited, many of them dealing with severe physical ordeals, such as circumcision, cruel beatings, deprivation of food and water for long periods of time, and various bodily mutilations. As societies became less primitive, the pubertal rites began to change in character. They tended to deemphasize physical ordeals and cruel punishments, and became more symbolic in character. It was not that the ceremonials and practices of primitive societies lacked symbolism altogether, but that the symbolic character of the ceremonials of ancient but more civilized cultures became more clearly symbolic and less extreme, physically. Let us look at some of these less primitive types of adolescent experience.

In ancient Greece the male adolescent had little opportunity for knowing and interacting with girls. It was felt that this would be harmful to him, and so he spent his adolescent years in close relationship with an older man, with whom he often engaged in homosexual practices. When he married, he had very little in common with his wife (and she usually had little to offer him). He received his intellectual companionship from the socalled Hetairai, his mistress, and satisfied his sexual needs through the services of prostitutes. The lower limits of adolescence in ancient Rome were fixed by law: age 12 for girls and age 14 for boys. However, the time at which the child actually engaged in puberty rites was fixed by the father. At that time the boy formally took off the clothes symbolic of childhood, and was ceremonially clad in the white garments of manhood. His childhood clothing was hung over the family hearth as an offering to the gods. He was taken to the Forum and Capitol, where he offered up sacrifices, and his name was formally added to the list of citizens of the Roman state. He was then considered a full adult, with all adult responsibilities and privileges.

These rites of puberty of primitives and ancients did not arise by chance, but rather they served definite purposes. In his detailed discussion of the underlying meaning of the puberty ceremonies of savages, Reik points out that there is one major theme which runs through the puberty rites of almost all primitive cultures (33). This theme centers around the symbolic death and subsequent resurrection of the adolescent, the child is "killed" and then is "reborn" as a new person. Reik feels that this recurrent theme is a function of the deeply repressed fears of the father, in whom still lives the unconscious memory of the incestuous and hostile wishes of his own childhood, which were directed at his own parents. He fears injury at the hands of his own child in the event that these desires would be realized. Reik summarizes the symbolic meaning of the recurring death and resurrection theme by stating that through the symbolism of the ceremony the fathers point out to the adolescents that they are ready to receive them as adults, but only upon the basic condition that the youths give up their own incestuous and hostile wishes. This condition is imposed upon the adolescent by the threat of death, and originally in the early history of man this threat was frequently carried out. As Reik stresses, the ritual services serve, in effect, to tell the youth: "We love you but we must rid you of your infantilisms." The youth must relinquish his incestuous desires. Freud also felt that society had extreme needs to erect a barrier against incest during adolescence, in order to promote the establishment of higher social units outside the family, and so used every means to break the family ties of earlier childhood.

Whether or not we accept the psychoanalytic interpretation of ancient and primitive puberty rites, certain facts are significant. The formal ceremony recognizing the adolescent status of youth has tremendous significance for both the adolescent and his parents. It marks the transition of youth from childhood into the more responsible status of adulthood. It marks a change in the attitude of the parents and society toward the youth. Through the pubertal ceremony the taboos, prohibitions, and customs of the society are preserved, and the authority of the older members of the society is maintained. Such ceremonies tend to inhibit the adolescent from usurping the powers of his elders, and aspiring to overthrow the existing order of things.

When we take a rather close look at our contemporary American culture we are struck by the fact that we have very few formal pubertal rites. There are some remnants, however, of older customs. One of these is the traditional "coming-out" party for the debutante, the formal announcement of the fact that the girl has reached a marriageable age. Then, of course, there are various religious rites followed by religious groups, but these have lost much of their relevance for adolescence, as such. Coming of age in our society is by and large a matter of legal definition, which varies from one section of the country to another. A child is *presumed* to have full adult responsibilities from a legal point of view at the age of 21, in most instances. Prior to this time, he usually is unable to vote (although there has been agitation in some states to reduce the age to 18), he may not purchase whiskey, and in many states may not legally own an automobile. Possibly one of the first recognitions by society of the adolescent's changing status is the granting of a driver's license, even though legal ownership of the automobile may be denied him. When he receives his driver's license he is then accorded some of the status of the adult—the right to control a powerful object which permits him greater mobility and freedom of action. This is one of the reasons for his frequent preoccupation with automobiles, motorcycles, and other motor-driven vehicles.

Great emphasis is currently placed upon graduation from high school, and this may, in fact, be regarded as a formalized adolescent rite. Yet the high-school graduate is far from being regarded as a responsible adult. It appears that in our culture the adolescent period is being continually prolonged. The lengthening period of formal education tends to perpetuate the adolescent features of the individual, and to delay his assumption of more adult roles and responsibilities. Frequently, our youth is not in a self-supporting situation for many years, and in fact is not encouraged to such status for some time after high-school graduation. This is particularly true of those who aspire to enter professions that require, in some instances, a minimum of eight years of college and university training. By the time the individual completes his training he is often well into the third decade of life, but is still in an "adolescent" status.

The absence in our society of clearly evident pubertal ceremonies leads us to consider some of the implications. Clearly visible initiation ceremonies of this kind assist in resolving some of the conflicts of both the adolescent and his parents. The absence of such highly visible signs of the onset of adolescence, and of society's recognition of the new role and new status of the individual, increases the adolescent's confusion regarding his role and aggravates the conflicts of the period. Further, we really have very few universal cultural taboos. What is accepted by one subculture is rejected by another, and even within a particular subculture there are differing beliefs. Then too, even within a family unit there are differing points of view: father might be accepting of sexual activities on the part of the adolescent, and mother might be quite opposed to their gratification. For such reasons our adolescents have very few "anchors" (from a cultural point of view) around which they can stabilize their behavior. In turn, this increases the needs of adolescents to

Group participation in "cook-outs" fosters a mature outlook. (U. of Mich.)

formulate their own code of behavior, which they do without exception. They compensate for these "lacks" in society by formulating their own intricate, and often highly rebellious, codes to afford them some degree of security and acceptance. In times of economic or cultural changes (especially following wars, or during recessions and depressions), adolescents tend to become more insecure, more rebellious—and hence sometimes highly delinquent.

Another example of the drive for adult status is the current trend toward "monogamous" sexual relationships in dating practices. The adolescent youth of today relates to one person of the opposite sex at a time. Complicated symbolic codes have grown up around these practices. For example, if the buckle strap in the back of the boy's trousers is unbuckled, he is free and not "going steady;" if it is buckled he is "going steady," and is not to be poached upon by other girls. When a boy takes a girl to a dance, she remains with him, and usually does not dance with other boys. She is regarded as "his property." This has led to the practice of "going steady," and eventually to earlier marriages.

As we have indicated, the absence of a formalized code of behavior provided for adolescents by society, and the lack of specific pubertal rites, has made it much easier for the adolescent to rebel against "adult domination" by his parents and by other authority figures in our culture. This is not as likely in primitive societies in which the adolescent and his parents have fewer and less intense conflicts in this area. Our society of today has failed to solve the problems that the amorphous, undefined roles for adolescents have created. We shall have to formulate some provision for the vacuum that has been created, for otherwise our intense adolescent crises will remain with us.

We have seen in the examples presented how societies vary in their recognition of the adolescent status of their youth and we have raised, *not solved,* many questions that stem from the changed status of adolescents in modern society. One thing is clear: many of these conflicts are *not inherent conflicts of adolescence itself.* Many of them are the direct results of the social forces which impinge upon youth during the period of adolescence, and of the way in which adolescents are recognized and treated by their societies.

INTERACTIONS OF PHYSICAL AND PSYCHOLOGICAL PROBLEMS

The adolescent individual responds *in toto* to the physiological changes that take place during puberty. As we pointed out earlier, such bodily changes do not occur in a vacuum, but are associated with marked changes in the psychological spheres. Perhaps the most significant of these occurs in the adolescent's self-image. We have seen how the child develops a self-image, and have noted how important this is in the development of the total personality. (See Chapter 4.) The concept of the self is not static and fixed, but rather is dynamic and is constantly being modified as a result of inner and outer forces. However, despite these changes, there is a central core that is relatively constant, and around which the modifications of the self-concept are organized. The somatic changes of adolescence serve to disrupt the previously established self-image of childhood and instigate a reformulation of the basic self-picture. We have already discussed the tremendous physical and physiological changes that occur in adolescence. In particular, the increased surge of sexual drives, and in fact of all psychic energies, stimulates a reorganization of the self-image.

The changing proportions and sizes of bodily structures and contours are accompanied by changing perceptions of the body and of feelings about the body. The adolescent actually "feels" different. This is due in part to the new sensory stimulations from the newly developing sex organs. It is no wonder that the adolescent sees himself as a different person!

The adolescent's preoccupation about the changing appearance of his body and its functions is a source of many anxieties and conflicts. The increased glandular functions, other than the sexual ones per se, create psychological problems. For example the increased activities of the sweat glands bring concern with bodily odors, and resulting emphasis upon cleanliness. In our society bodily odors are regarded with disfavor, and these attitudes are reinforced by the plethora of commercial advertisements extolling the virtues of cleanliness and the social rejection that might result from "B.O." A recent survey by Remmers and Radler of the problems of adolescents indicates the extent and nature of their concerns in this regard (34). This study of several thousand teenage boys and girls revealed that they were greatly troubled about their bodies. It was found that 52 per cent of the sampled population expressed a want either to gain or lose weight; 37 per cent were concerned about their body posture; 13 per cent complained of getting tired too easily; 12 per cent suffered from frequent headaches; and 24 per cent were concerned about pimples. Many had severe problems that centered around inabilities to coordinate their gangly limbs. In general *more than half* of the teenagers had problems that were related to the changed appearance or feelings of their bodies.

The changing attitudes of the adolescent toward his body and his new self are related to cultural factors. As Stolz and Stolz point out, the changing body is a symbol of a new attitude toward the self, others, and life in general (24). The ways in which cultural forces influence these new perceptions, for example, are related to how the culture emphasizes cleanliness, neatness, exposure of parts of the body, the uses or restrictions in the use of parts of the body, the meaning of some bodily functions, and the like. These cultural attitudes, and not the biological changes alone, affect the adolescent's perception. In turn, the new perceptions are integrated into the new self-image—the result being an admixture of new identifications, rejections, and of pride, embarrassment, and over- or underconcern.

Rubé has made some interesting observations about the changing percep-

The preadolescent very often has difficulty overcoming shyness. (U. of Mich.)

tions and self-image of the adolescent (35). He points out that the adolescent's daydreams or fantasies are different from those of the younger child. The "instinctual" drives of puberty are very strong, so strong in fact that they cannot be repressed. They find expression through the adolescent's daydreams which serve to "store" the drives. Moreover, the heightened sensitivity of the senses to such stimuli as color, sound, smell, and touch is transferred to the inner world. Thus, the external world loses some of its appeal and the adolescent tends to lose touch with reality, for a brief period of time. Rubé views the self-image as a "psychic somatic complex," which undergoes severe alteration during puberty, due to altered physiological functions. The adolescent daydream is the process through which the self-image is reorganized and re-evaluated. Further, the reorganization of the self is accompanied by a weaken-

323

ing of some ego characteristics. This is of particular importance because the destruction of the self-image of childhood leads to the development of strong anxieties. The adolescent then, according to Rubé, responds in one of three ways: (a) depressive reactions, sometimes quite severe, may occur; (b) strong hostilities may be directed outward toward the external world; or (c) healthy aggression may occur which helps the adolescent to overcome his anxieties.

Josselyn has summarized the psychoanalytic position regarding the characteristics of the adolescent's ego (36). The behavioral reactions of the adolescent are typical of those individuals who have not developed an adequate integrative pattern. In the same way as is true of psychotic and neurotic reactions, adolescence is characterized by a relative failure of the ego to cope with the stresses placed upon it. As a result of glandular developments, bodily sensations are different, and feelings are more acutely experienced. Further, not only does the adolescent need to adjust to the psychological stimulation stemming from the reproductive glands, but he also has to adjust to the constant changes in the balance of these secretions. In other words, he needs not only to adjust to an established stimulus but to a constantly changing one. The adolescent is much more sensitive to stimuli, not because his reality world has changed, but because he becomes much more sensitive to it. Josselyn points out that the pre-adolescent is like a violin made by string-

ing catgut over a cigar box, but that the adolescent is like a Stradivarius, in that he is sensitive to innumerable emotional overtones. The increased demands are simply more than the ego can handle and, as a result, the previously established patterns of the individual for dealing with his problems fail (this also is typical of neurotic reactions). Josselyn feels that the characteristic syndrome of the adolescent results from an exhaustion of the ego. The strains and stresses that create this condition are many, and, as she points out, are related to modifications in the adolescent's social milieu as well as to the biological and physiological changes that take place. There is, however, a large difference between the neurosis of the adult and the exhaustion of the ego of the adolescent. The adolescent tries out many different kinds of defenses and ways of behaving in order to cope with his problem, and, in the normal course of events, tends to remain fluid rather than fixing upon one particular kind of defense as does the adult neurotic. Josselyn feels that this fluidity is again an indication of the exhaustion of the ego, and thus many spontaneous changes may be expected in the adolescent's behavior.*

The superego as well as the ego of the adolescent is overwhelmed by the innate

* We should like to point out, even more carefully, that the similarities of adolescents' reactions to those of neurotics and psychotics do not mean that all adolescents are either neurotic or psychotic. Like the latter, the adolescent is undergoing stress and his ego is temporarily weakened. Unlike the latter, the *healthy* adolescent's ego is basically sound and spontaneously learns to adapt, in time, in an integrated, constructive, and appropriate manner.

instinctual demands resulting from increased hormonal production, as Wittenberg points out (37). This means that the individual superego values (his conscience) no longer seem relevant for the changing needs of the adolescent—at least temporarily. The adolescent tends, therefore, to reject his previous moral values and attitudes, but through the continuing process of re-identification with new peer and adult models, finally establishes a "new" superego—a moral value system that is both more mature and more appropriate.

Sometimes the changed bodily sensations and reactions are not perceived by the adolescent for what they are—as processes arising from normal growth—but instead serve as a source of anxiety. Under such circumstances, the adolescent tends to believe that he is ill, and develops *hypochondriacal* reactions.

Adolescents wish to be like others of their age-group, and any physical characteristic that singles them out from the group often proves to be a disturbing factor. Common examples of such differentiating factors are: excessive height or shortness, over- or underweight, unusual facial characteristics, or any significant alterations in bodily proportions. As Stolz and Stolz quite rightly emphasize, there is a very important factor underlying the adolescent's concern about his bodily proportions: he is concerned essentially with his "sex-appropriateness." Even though he appears to be concerned over a particular factor, such as height, or breast development, what is really bothering him is the total pattern of his development and the basic problem of fulfilling the appropriate sexual role.

RE-IDENTIFICATION— NEW SOCIAL ROLES FOR OLD

We have seen how the ego of the adolescent is subjected to very severe strains, and is temporarily disturbed by the new flood of stimuli. One of the major tech· niques of adapting to these exigencies is the mechanism of identification. During adolescence the ego frequently uses identification, a method of dealing with problems which proved to be helpful in early childhood. Wittenberg states that identification becomes the chief mode of relating for adolescents (37). There is, however, a significant difference between the identifications of the adolescent and those of the young child. The younger child identifies first and primarily with his parents, but the adolescent shuns identifications with parental figures, and even tends to make relatively little use of adult figures close to him. The reasons for differences in the use of models for identification are discussed in the following paragraphs.

During adolescence there is a marked increase in drives toward maturity, and the individual is forced to abandon the dependent anchorages of childhood (38). Josselyn points out that the exploratory drives of the adolescent increase, and he is consequently exposed to situations that are beyond his experience and his knowledge (36). Until the adolescent period the child's parents provided protection and dependence to a large degree, but the adolescent striving for independence and individuation is no longer willing to accept their protective role. His rejection of his parents' protection leads him into new conflict situations which he is not yet able to handle, but he continues to reject the help of the parents. As a result, he is continually threatened with failure, lowered self-esteem, and loss of self-confidence. At the same time, his sexual drives are experienced more and more intensely, and he is simultaneously subjected to the prohibitions and taboos of society insofar as gratification of these drives is concerned. Moreover, his oedipal conflicts are reactivated during adolescence and operate in opposition to sexual gratification. All of this contributes additional burdens to the ego. The reactivation of oedipal conflicts serves to cause the adolescent to reject the parent of the opposite sex, i.e., to act independent and self-assertive. Finally, he abandons both parents psychologically. As Josselyn stresses, to be like the parent of the same sex is a cause for self-depreciation, since it is perceived as an imitation of the parent and therefore as a loss of individuality. The adolescent needs to be a person in his own right, he has to be self-sufficient, and he needs to establish a new self (as we pointed out earlier in detail). Also, however, he badly needs emotional support, and since the revolt against the parents makes identification with them impossible, he seeks other figures with whom to identify. This

"Facing an audience" can contribute greatly to ego skills. (U. of Mich.)

need is filled by his peers, who give him the support that he needs, and fosters identification with them.

The adolescent has markedly narcissistic needs, reactivated from early childhood. These needs are projected on his peer group, which is able to offer him a sense of belonging, emotional support, and even extravagant approval.

The resulting identifications with the peer group are very strong, and the adolescent tries to conform as closely as possible to their mores and beliefs. The adolescent often insists on dressing exactly like his companions, he cuts his hair the same way, he likes the same music, he talks the same way, and develops the same mannerisms. Sometimes the fad is *not* to shine one's shoes, or *not* to cut one's hair for long periods, and the like. These conforming and yet rebellious fads serve to make the adolescent feel more powerful, and set him dramatically apart from the younger generation—"those kids!" Despite this high degree of peer-group conformity, he needs to be an individual, to be a person in his own right, and to be unique. This drive for self-identity (and for self-realization) is normally achieved within the framework of the peer-group structure. His identifications enable the adolescent to feel more certain of his sex and status roles. Further, these identifications with the peer group serve to erect a strong barrier against the intrusion of the adult.

Only in recent years have we *begun* to understand something of the nature and processes of peer-group relationships of adolescents, or of the actual organization and structure of such groups. Moreno conducted an experiment that illustrates how little adults know about adolescents' preferences (39). He asked children from the kindergarten through the eighth grade to select the two classmates whom they would prefer to sit on each side of them (their *sociometric* choices). At the same time he asked the children's teachers to predict what these choices would be. The results were quite interesting. Moreno found that kindergarten and first-grade teachers did fairly well (their judgments were 65 per cent accurate), but that, as the grade level increased, the judgments of the teachers' predictions were less and less accurate. In the eighth grade there was only 25 per cent agreement between teachers' judgments and children's choices.

We have seen that peer-group identifications are of great importance in the development of the adolescent. The group itself classifies its members and the classification is often brutally frank. For example, McGuire found the following classifications within adolescent groups: "wheels," "brains," "quiet ones," "outsiders," "drips," "dopes," and "wild ones" (40). He also found that as the adolescent grew older, his relative status and acceptance within his age group influenced his educational and vocational aspirations. The peer group serves to influence the social mobility of the adolescent, often in an upward direction. McGuire found that lower-class adolescents with a high peer status remained within the adolescent school society, they broke from home and learned new values and ways of living that were different from those of their parents and friends' families. He found that adolescent group identifications were the springboard for upward social mobility for about 40 per cent of the lower-class children in his study.

In addition to identifications with peer groups, adolescents also avidly seek to form identification with single figures, resulting in the so-called "hero-worship" of the adolescent. Adolescents often idolize particular figures. They seek to find in the hero the traits that they would like to have for themselves. Often it is *not* the whole adult who is identified with, but rather just those particular (and distortedly exaggerated) traits that adolescents need. Thus, for example, a criminal figure is idolized, not because of his criminal activities per se, but because of some special qualities, such as notoriety, strength, agility, hostility, defiance, and the like. In these identifications with idolized figures—outside the home, and often with nonconforming heroes—the approval of the peer group is most important.

Identifications, both peer group and individual, are of great importance to the adolescent. They serve to give him the protection and support that he needs. He experiments continuously until he finds the figures, outside his immediate family group, who gratify the greatest number of his psychological needs. Through his identifications he comes to have a clear knowledge of self and his new role in society, and he reaches a greater acceptance of his new status. He becomes, *in reality*, a person in his own right, and ultimately enters true adulthood.

SEX REARS ITS HEAD

During puberty the sexual drives of the adolescent are reinforced, and he is faced with many intensified sexual problems and anxieties. We have seen that sexual drives were present from birth on, reaching an apogee for the first time during the oedipal period, and now once again becoming intensified. During puberty there is more stimulation from these drives and more satisfaction in the genital organs and genital area; interest in general heterosexual relationships also increases. Further, the sexual drives, problems, and behavior of the adolescent more closely resemble those of the adult, and, therefore, are more readily recognized and responded to by adults. Hence, they are, also, more anxiety-provoking to the adult. There is no change in the basic nature of the adolescent's sexual drives. It is in the *intensity* of the drives and in the ways in which they may be *gratified* that significant changes occur from childhood to adolescence.

The sexuality of the adolescent, then, does not occur "all at once." It does not make its appearance "magically." Rather, it is the result of maturation and of the experiences of the total life history of the individual. In our discussions of the sexual maturation of the individual we have seen how sexual gratifications are achieved at each of the preceding psychosexual stages. Puberty is simply a continuation of the developmental process that originated at birth. The intensity and the manner in which sexual drives are experienced and gratified depend upon such factors as the adolescent's current and past relationships with his parents, his feelings of "goodness" and "badness," the ways in which he dealt with his childhood sexual drives and fantasies, his identifications with masculine and feminine figures, the level and degree of psychosexual fixations, and his total psychosexual development in general (41).

As we have seen, during the latency period of early childhood, sexual fantasies were repressed. Sexual drives were sublimated and a period of relative quiescence set in. This period of calmness is abruptly shattered during puberty. The changing biological development initiates new physical processes, centering around the genital organs. The boy, for example, learns that he has many involuntary erections of his penis which may be produced by his fantasies as well as by external stimulation. Following the initial seminal emission he begins to have fairly frequent nocturnal emissions ("wet dreams"). These are sometimes accompanied by vivid sexual dreams. During this period masturbation is almost universally practiced, usually being accompanied by sexual fantasies (20). It is important that the adolescent understand what is happening, and that he learn to deal in a wholesome manner with his increased sexual drives, since the particular patterns that he develops for handling the release of his sexual tensions will tend to persist throughout his adult life. The girl, on the other hand, does not experience like orgasmic discharges. Rather, as we have seen, physically her pubertal sexuality is marked by the occurrence of the menar-

che. Her sexual drives, like those of the boy, are similarly intensified. Unlike the boy, however, her patterns of sexual release during adolescence do not persist as inflexibly as those of the boy. She is not as aware of her sexual drives; they are present, of course, but are deeply repressed.

What, in particular, is so different about the sexual problems of the adolescent? Puberty is a highly critical time because it presents the problem of how to master the rapidly maturing sexual impulses in a manner that is consistent with

The adolescent soon grows to enjoy heterosexual experiences. (U. of Mich.)

the needs of *both* the individual and his society. Heterosexual relationships have to be established, and adequate adult patterns for the release of sexual drives need to be developed. Williams has suggested that the four or five years of adolescence hold the only chance that the average boy and girl will have to establish heterosexuality (42). He states that if heterosexuality is prevented from being established at this time, that it can never come *naturally* and *normally* to the individual again. Of course, difficulties and blocks to true heterosexual relationships may be removed later in life through psychotherapy or through other special procedures, but it is only in adolescence that they can be established as part of the normal developmental pattern.

The crucial problem of the adolescent, as far as sexuality is concerned, is learning an appropriate sexual role. (We may recall that this problem was at the base of the adolescent's worries over physical attributes.) This means that he must learn to integrate his past experiences not only with his new somatic impulses, but also with the prohibitions, customs, and taboos of his culture. The sexual role assigned to him (or her) by society must be understood and interiorized. This has some important implications. As Tryon points out, the adolescent must learn about his own sexual role, but he must also learn about the role of the opposite sex (43). Further, he must learn to appreciate the nature of the relationship between the two. The sexual problems of the adolescent are not only a function of

his own psychological and somatic processes, but are also a function of his social and cultural matrix. Learning to adapt to all of these internal and external needs presents a very complex problem indeed.

It is probably true that many, if not most, people in modern society are confused about the relative sexual roles of the male and female. Typically the male is thought of as necessarily the dominant individual in the family, as the one who makes the decisions, as the "boss," and as the one who "provides for" and "takes care of" his wife. He is supposed to be aggressive and self-sufficient. He "makes the living." The female on the other hand is seen as more passive and dependent, the follower rather than the leader, the one who is "provided for" and who is "taken care of." Her role is that of mother and homemaker; it is a family-centered one. In fact, we know this hypothetical picture of the roles of the male and female has been greatly modified in the course of civilization's program. During the past two decades many men in our American society have been assuming more feminine roles, while many women have been assuming more masculine ones. With the advance of modern technology and the equalitarian roles assumed by women, the relative roles of the male and the female have become increasingly difficult to distinguish. As a consequence of this overlap of roles, the adolescent has found his problem of assuming an appropriate adult sexual role much more complex.

However, despite these trends in our culture, the boy, on psychobiological grounds, has a greater adaptation to make in the assumption of his sexual role than does the girl. Tryon points out that although both boys and girls tend to assume a more passive, dependent, and compliant role during childhood, the girl may perpetuate this type of role more readily than the boy (43). The boy has to overcome his dependency patterns and become more "masculine"; that is, more assertive. It is true, on the other hand, that the boy has more opportunity in current society to clarify his sexual role than does the girl. Society makes it easier for him to discuss his sexual organs, functions, and needs in "gutter" language than for the girl. Boys are also more free to relieve their sexual tensions through crude jokes about sex in ways that girls are unable to. Adolescent boys are usually far less concerned about modesty, and are not unduly embarrassed about nudity in the presence of other boys and men in such places as dressing and shower rooms. Girls more often have reactions of modesty, often excessively, and attempt to cover up their nudity in the presence of other girls and women. Tryon believes that they try to deny the physical aspects of their sexual role in this way. These complex considerations indicate that: (a) when society expects the adolescent male to become assertive and independent, but does not expect the adolescent female to do so to the same extent, the boy has a more difficult problem of transition from childhood dependency; and (b) in our culture boys are more free to discharge sexual tensions without society's disapproval.

On biological grounds, the normal adolescent is impelled toward a love object of the opposite sex through whom he seeks heterosexual gratification. These impulses seek direct gratification, but society prohibits such behavior. These prohibitory attitudes, taboos, and legal restrictions, embedded deeply in our societal structure, are also deeply engraved upon the child from an early age. We must emphasize that the taboos against certain kinds of sexuality are not imposed for the first time at adolescence, but rather they acquire new valences to the individual at that time. He has known about the "badness" of sex for some time, and has already developed many conscious and unconscious attitudes about his sexual drives. In fact, some adolescents are so fearful of their sexuality that they need to deny it completely, and as a result shun all heterosexual contacts. It is as if they are attempting to maintain the comparative peace of the latency period. This is achieved only at the cost of psychological immaturity and, as far as society is concerned, the drive in the adolescent toward adult sexual gratification is recognized, but its expression is condemned and labeled as "bad." The adolescent is keenly sensitive to the attitudes of society, yet in spite of this many adolescents clandestinely engaged in sexual relationships (20). The "normal" adolescent tends to *sublimate* some of his sexual drives; that is, he transfers them to socially useful activities. He has numerous heterosexual contacts, often engages in "petting" activities, but infrequently engages in sexual intercourse. He takes part in the great national game of "dating," which in our culture has developed several unique characteristics.

Margaret Mead has discussed some of the characteristics of dating in some detail, and we feel that they are of sufficient importance to warrant summarization (34). Mead feels that dating is a competitive game, which must be conducted in such a way that the peer group is aware that dating is taking place. It thus serves to give the participants prestige and status. Frequently, adolescents decide to "go steady," and Mead attributes this to one of two causes: they may be genuinely in love, or they may be dependent on each other for protection—as in the case of unpopular boys and girls who seek to cover up their unpopularity by pretending to prefer each other. Frequently, adolescents who date do not really desire the companionship of the person of the other sex, but rather date because of the need to be popular, to "rate" in the group, to succeed socially. This sometimes gives the observer a faulty picture in that it *seems* as if adolescents are constantly preoccupied with sex, whereas in reality they are concerned with social values. Mead is quite critical of our culturally determined attitudes toward the sexual behavior of our adolescents. She points out that we have tended to abandon chaperons, and permit and even encourage situations in which adolescents feel that they can engage in any sexual behavior they wish. For example, we disapprove of extramarital pregnancy, and of abortion, but we do not disseminate birth-control information. In general, we provide our young people settings for the very behavior for which they are punished. Mead feels that our society has placed the controls for sexual behavior in the hands of the girl. The boy asks for as much as possible, the girl yields as little as possible, and the boy expects her to behave in such a way. The girl on the other hand expects the boy to accept her denial. The attitudes of society structure the sexual roles that our adolescents are required to play, and later create difficult problems for them to manage. The *more* successfully they deal with the problems of dating, the *less* prepared they are to meet sex adjustments in marriage, which requires a totally different set of rules and different roles.

Frequently, the adolescent will develop a very intense emotional relationship with a member of the opposite sex. Such an association has been called by various terms, such as "puppy love" or "crush." The intensity of this emotional relationship cannot be overestimated, and when for some reason it is broken, the pain and suffering of the adolescent is acute. At the basis of the relationship is a desire to possess the loved one exclusively; no one else may share her. The boy says in effect: "If you go with me, you can't go with anyone else. You belong entirely to me." Such relationships (and their disruption) are part of the growth experiences of the adolescent. They are probably experienced by almost all adolescents. Through such experiences adolescents learn to structure their sexual roles and to tolerate many types of emotional relationships.

One point is central to this whole exposition of the psychosexual development of the adolescent. His growth in this area is not simply a function of the maturation of physiological functions, but rather it is a complex process of *physiological-psychological-social-sexual development.*

SCHOOL ADJUSTMENT PROBLEMS

The adolescent has numerous problems in school adjustment. This fact is assuming more and more importance as the number of adolescents in our public schools increases. According to Garrison, there were approximately 8.5 million children between the ages of 14 and 17 in school in 1954, 8.8 million in 1955, 9.3 million in 1956, 9.9 million in 1957, and 10.3 million in 1958 (22). He estimates that there will be 11.0 million adolescents in school in 1960, and 13.6 million in 1965. Not only has the total *number* of adolescents in school increased, but the percentage of adolescents in the total school population has shown radical change. In 1900, only 5 per cent of all school children were between the ages of 13 and 17; presently about 25 per cent are in this age range. The problems in school adjustment of the adolescent are thus of increasing importance.

Adolescents themselves are aware of their school adjustment problems. This is borne out in two studies of Remmers in which adolescents were given an opportunity to detail their difficulties (34, 45). Remmers found that 50 per cent of the adolescents studied had doubt as to which of their high-school courses would be of value to them in later life, while 35 per cent indicated that they would like to study courses not offered in their schools. They apparently were dissatisfied with the school curriculum: 33 per cent stated that they would like to take more vocational courses, and 21 per cent doubted

the value of the courses they had studied. Apparently there was a feeling that the school offerings were removed from actual life situations: 49 per cent wished for some type of practical work experience, and 10 per cent stated that the courses they took were too far removed from their life situations. The need for guidance was also indicated: 25 per cent of the group of adolescents felt that they needed more advice in choosing their high-school courses.

Many other similar studies substantiate the fact that serious problems in this area do exist. Very few, however, are concerned with the reasons that underlie this finding. One study concerned with such underlying factors is that by Norton who studied the problems of adolescents as they were perceived by the teachers (46). He found that 35.8 per cent of the problems of adolescents were due directly to conditions at school, 38.9 per cent were due to conditions outside the school, and 25.3 per cent were due to postschool problems. Problems relating directly to the school included those of school citizenship, choice of study, difficulties in learning subject matter, and extracurricular activities. Those not due directly to the school were related to problems of the adolescent with his parents, family, friends, family condition, and health. The postschool problems involved vocational choice and further schooling.

Such a division of adjustment difficulties is of value in specifying the types of problems of the adolescent. It serves to emphasize a very important fact, that the adolescent, *in* school, is not a different person from the adolescent *outside* of school. Since he is the same person, he takes his problems with him wherever he goes. If he has considerable difficulty in his outside-of-school adjustment, then it is quite probable that he will also have difficulties in school. It is understandable why school problems are so important to him, since he spends a large portion of his waking hours in school, and it is the major social force affecting him. The school is a *social institution*, with many complex social and psychological forces to which the child reacts in terms of his own unique personality. The same forces that prove disturbing to the child outside the school prove equally disturbing within. The school is the world in miniature—and to the adolescent it is a critical part of the world of reality. Too often we fail to perceive the implications of this basic fact. For example, when a child has severe problems in relating to an autocratic, dominant, and hostile parent, he has precisely the same problem in relating to a teacher with similar personality characteristics. If a child has severe problems with his siblings, then he will probably have severe problems with his classmates. These examples are merely illustrations of the relation of adjustment in the school to those outside.

Educational stresses

We can see that, usually, it is not the school per se which produces the adolescent's problems; rather, they are the product of the interaction of the forces of the school with a particular adolescent personality. Although the school does produce some unique stresses, school adjustment should be analyzed in terms of this relationship to other factors in the individual's life. Let us examine briefly some representative examples of this relationship.

As we have seen from the survey by Remmers, the school often seems to be too far removed from the adolescent's world of reality, according to his perceptions of the problem. Frequently the adolescent does not understand its purpose. Bell points out that often schools are organized in such a way that adolescents need to go through the whole school program before they begin to see any value in it (47). He feels that this lack of perception of the values of the educational experience tends to create a sense of inadequacy in the adolescent. As a consequence, he may then drop out of school before completion of the high-school program, even though he has the intellectual ability to complete it successfully. Bell feels that the school should be geared more closely to reality, so as to make each school year an end in itself, rather than a transitional means to a remote end. This principle is in accord with what we know of the ego development of the individual. As the person matures he gradually acquires the capacity to plan ahead, to seek goals distant in time, and to delay the need for immediate gratification in order to secure additional gains in the future. The adolescent *has not fully attained this status*, and it is difficult for him to forego present needs for future goals. Education has been in part defined as "preparation for life," but living is a daily affair, especially for the adolescent, and it cannot be postponed to a few years hence.

Often, schools have not been sufficiently aware of the needs of the adolescent child. As early as 1939 Witty and Skinner discussed this shortcoming in detail (48). They pointed out that frequently schools tended to ignore the fact that the individual is constantly changing and that he acquires new orientations and attitudes as a consequence. This growth process is particularly evident in the significant changes in attitude that occur in the child between elementary and junior high-school grades, and later between junior and senior high-school levels. These changes of interests are manifested in many areas: sexual, social, and the like. One of the most striking shifts in orientation is the extreme concern shown by many adolescents about their vocational goals. This common and important concern is a function of many factors. (We may recall that the Remmers survey indicated that 33 per cent of the adolescents studied desired more vocational courses, and that 49 per cent wished for some practical type of work experience.) The adolescent is concerned with "what I'm going to be," and frequently he tries to attain more immediate adult status by getting and holding a job. He yearns for economic self-sufficiency, so that he can be "a man," and be freed of his dependence upon his parents. Further, the choice of a vocation or profession involves strong emotional problems. For some adolescents the attainment of a higher vocational level than that of the father seems dangerous since it may seem to be deprecating to

the father and thus invite his hostility. For others, the aspirations their parents have for them may seem threatening, and may be unattainable because of limited capacity or ability. Still other adolescents are conflicted in their choice of a vocational goal, not knowing whether to choose one having high prestige value in our society, or one with lower prestige that is more readily attainable. These and other problems related to vocational choice arouse serious emotional complications.

A study by Doane investigated the curriculum choice of adolescent high-school boys and girls (49). He gave them an inventory listing 19 different possible choices of action related to the school curriculum. The pupils were required to select the five *most* and five *least* desirable courses of action that they would like to follow. That of vocational choice and placement was selected as most desirable by both the girls and the boys. Doane also found that children of all levels of intelligence showed a major interest in the problem of choice of a vocation.

Acting out behavior in school

In the foregoing material, our interest was *not* in evaluating current educational practices. Rather, our focus has been on the stresses in adolescents induced by school experience. We have emphasized the principle that it is *the interaction of the type of school experience with the particular adolescent personality that is important*. On the other hand, it should be clear that the adolescent's personality characteristics present special problems for both himself and the school. It is to the latter problem that we now turn our attention.

As we have seen earlier in this chapter, the ego of the adolescent is overwhelmed, at times, by many forces brought to bear upon it. His strong internal conflicts are resolved by some defense mechanism that he, himself, has learned to employ. Although such conflicts cannot be *resolved* by another person, their resolution may be *facilitated* by appropriate assistance of some other individual. To the degree that such help is not available, the adolescent *acts out* his conflicts in a rather immature way, and at times his behavior is severely regressive. As Kirkpatrick points out, this acting out, which eventually leads to the personal and social maturation of the child, really should take place within the home (50). Parents are in a position to set limits, when necessary, on the undesirable behavioral reactions of the adolescent. Such actions of the parent are more readily accepted by the adolescent than similar restrictions imposed by other persons. To aid in promoting optimal emotional growth, the feelings of the adolescent should be fully accepted by the parents. This does *not* mean that the parents accept the behavior and its goals as necessarily appropriate; but it *does* mean that parents must be prepared to understand and view sympathetically the meaning of such behavior. When the necessary amount of freedom is not provided within the home

for the acting out behavior of the child, there are then only three possible avenues of adjustment, according to Kirkpatrick. These are: (a) repression of the feelings, with resultant hostility, (b) acceptance of the reality situation with consequent integration of the emotions, or (c) acting out of the forbidden impulses elsewhere. It is probable that, in any case, acting-out will frequently occur in the school situation, and Kirkpatrick feels that much of adolescent misbehavior in school stems from this cause.

Adolescents frequently lose interest in school work, and their grades often drop abruptly. They seem suddenly to have "lost all ambition," and to appear lethargic. This lack of interest is most commonly due to the unconscious hostilities that adolescents have in regard to domination by the parents. It is an unconscious expression of their resistance against parental wishes, but is one that is expressed in a more passive rather than active manner.

Many adolescents do not finish high school because of the severity of their adjustment problems. They often leave to take a job. Some, of course, do not have the intellectual capacity to complete the usual high school program, and others have physical disabilities to which they react in a way that seriously handicaps them in school. It has been estimated that approximately one per cent of adolescents are so seriously handicapped mentally or physically that they are not educable in the usual high school (51). These account for a very small number of adolescents who drop out of school. In fact most drop-outs are due to other and avoidable causes. As Allen found, most adolescents who drop out of school are *definitely educable,* and could profit from further education (52). The subjects of Allen's study were *not* mentally retarded by any means, even though they tended to score slightly below average on group intelligence tests and had frequently repeated subjects or grades. An important finding was that 69 per cent of the boys and 75 per cent of the girls who dropped out of school came from laboring-class families.

In another report, Barnes states that most adolescents who drop out of school perceive themselves as having been thwarted in their role (53). He feels that part of the reason for this is that adult supports of children are removed too early. He describes such children as being impulsive and having little insight, having little feeling of responsibility toward others, lowered self-image, and lacking in social conscience. He calls them "egoless" children. (It would seem preferable to designate such a child as having an *inadequate* or *weak* ego development.) Studies such as these indicate that our high schools do not meet the needs of all our youth. They point to the need for more highly differentiated high-school curricula to meet the increasingly varied needs of adolescents.

The school's responsibility

If schools do not provide adequately for adolescents, we should ask: What is the responsibility of the school for the adolescent? As we have said, the school is a social institution whose role is a reflection of that of society. This was clearly evidenced by the increased concern of the public with the educational system

following the successful launching of the Russian "sputnik." At that time considerable dissatisfaction was expressed with the policies and practices of our educational institutions at all levels. For example, the Virginia legislature, in 1958, enacted a bill that provided for a drastic cut in the number of professional educational courses required of teachers in order to qualify for a teacher's certificate

Through helping others, the adolescent attains individuality. (U. of Mich.)

in Virginia! Public concern at that time was also expressed over such a formerly sacrosanct matter as the school curriculum in general, and the "softness" of school programs was debated throughout the country. These examples illustrate the oft-forgotten fact that the school system is an institution of society, and reflects its attitudes and customs. If the school perceives itself as a social agency, it should be more fully aware of its impact upon adolescents of widely varying cultural backgrounds. It must be cognizant of the different personality needs, attitudes, abilities, aptitudes, and aspirational levels of its youth, of how these are related to the culture in general and, more specifically, how they are related to the cultural background of a given adolescent.

McKenzie has dealt extensively with the responsibilities of the school toward the adolescent (54). He points out that the school should aid the adolescent to attain individuality and move toward an organized personality pattern. This means that the school should encourage the development of an emergent philosophy of life, which stresses values, desirable behavior, and a realization by the adolescent of his place in society. It should also assist the adolescent in acquiring a better understanding of his personal assets and liabilities, and encourage him to develop and implement mature plans for his future. The school should also aid the adolescent to adjust to the rapid changes resulting from his physical maturation, and to secure satisfying relationships with his peers of both sexes. McKenzie also feels that the school should help the adolescent to establish his independence from his family, and to attain adult status through the development of vocational plans and more adequate family and social relationships. Above all, it is the feeling of the authors of this book that the school, in addition to perceiving its role as a social institution, should perceive the adolescent as an individual, and help him to attain the maturity toward which he is striving in terms of his own unique needs. This implies that the school should provide highly developed programs of assessment and counseling, and implement them through differentiated curricula. Such a program is not a luxury or a "frill," but constitutes part of the very core of the high school's function.

PERSISTENT NON-ADAPTATION

As we have pointed out, the adolescent has many severe conflicts. He wishes to be free and independent of adult control, yet at the same time he fears such freedom and independence. He rebels against authority, yet desires its imposition. He has strong hostilities which he fears to express openly lest he lose the supports that he needs—and he pretends that he needs no supports. His sexual excitements are strong, and he has difficulty in the control of sexual impulses. We have also seen that the ego of the adolescent is not strong enough to cope readily with the frequent surges of sexual impulses, and that the superego is frequently too rigid and quite punitive. Since the relative strength of the ego as compared with the superego tends to be weak, severe emotional reactions are frequently precipitated and are manifested in erratic forms of behavior. Due to the intensity of the energies that flood the adolescent, it is difficult for him to maintain repressions. As a result, regressive reactions occur and periods of "acting-out" are common.

It is therefore not surprising that many forms of maladaptive behavior develop during adolescence. The adolescent may show all of the disturbances of younger children, in addition to those usually shown by adults. However, we shall limit the present discussion to problems that are relatively more specific to the adolescent period.

The fact that adolescents have many serious adjustmental problems and numerous strong emotional reactions has been known for some time. In 1904 the classic two volumes of G. Stanley Hall, entitled *Adolescence,* were published, and his scholarly discussion of many characteristics of adolescent development increased our knowledge in this area and, even more important, stimulated considerable research activity (55). Hall attempted to formalize the then existing knowledge of adolescence, and stressed the finding that the typical emotional life of the adolescent was one of *Sturm und Drang* (storm and stress). In accordance with the existing philosophy of the early twentieth century, Hall felt that the upheaval of the adolescent was due to the increase in glandular and somatic activities, to the physiological sexual developments, and to the generalized state of bodily imbalance that resulted. We cannot agree with this aspect of Hall's conception of adolescence. As we have repeatedly pointed out in our previous discussions, it is not such changes as these that are important, in themselves, in the production of undesirable emotional reactions, but rather it is the *individual's reactions to them* that are of prime importance. As we have seen these reactions are determined by many cultural and social factors. From Hall's point of view all adolescents are seen as inevitably suffering from strong emotional disturb-

ances, as would be expected *if* the physical changes alone were responsible for their production. We know, however, that *many adolescents do not show any severe emotional disturbances.* Hall's concept of the underlying reasons for the storm and stress of adolescence therefore needs to be revised in terms of the more recent knowledge concerning the dynamics of adolescent adjustment.

The likelihood that an adolescent will suffer from severe emotional disturbances depends mainly upon the *personality characteristics* with which he enters the adolescent period. If there are few serious conflicts, at that time, and if his previous emotional development has been adequate, then it is not probable that any serious problems will occur during adolescence. In fact if the adolescent develops maladaptive behavior it is likely that the personality characteristics developed during early childhood and his early relationships with his parents were disturbed (56). As Luchins suggests, emotional instability may be manifested at any age, but it is particularly probable when reality is not clearly structured and when there are wide gaps between levels of aspiration and capacities for achievement (57). These factors are certainly present during the period of adolescence.

Sexual adjustment

Many severe conflicts of adolescents are related to their increased sexual drives. Such conflicts are, to a large extent, a result of the attitudes of the culture toward sexual functions. If the conflicts are sufficiently severe, then persistent mal-adaptive behavior may result. Girls more frequently have conflicts in the sexual area than do boys. The reason for this difference in the frequency of sexual con-flicts, according to More, is that girls use different defenses than boys in attempt-ing to resolve such difficulties (58). Girls usually handle the upsurge of sexuality in adolescence through a *denial* of the drive, and a displacement of it into social activities.

To understand the different patterns of defenses employed by the different sexes we should note, first, that the sexes differed in their psychosexual develop-ment in prior years. We will recall (from our discussion in Chapter 6 particularly) that the psychosexual development of the girl is slower and more complicated than that of the boy. It was also learned that girls more frequently display emo-tional maladjustment (see Chapter 7). These prior learning experiences set the stage for the problems of adolescence. Girls are more mature in their psycho-sexual development and enter adoles-cence at an earlier period than boys. At the same time, they are able to repress sexuality more readily (on both biological and sociocultural grounds). They are, in fact, encouraged, in our culture, to be "ladylike," to repress overt interest in and expression of sexuality. They are more mature, therefore, but more re-repressed than boys, and *feel* their sexual drives less acutely. They may even, in extreme instances, become frigid, sexu-ally. On the other hand, boys are aware of their sexual drives, have many more culturally approved ways of displacing or satisfying them, and only have to face the problem of avoiding too open and too antisocial expression of these im-pulses.

This does not mean that all girls re-press their sexual drives completely. The frequency of sexual delinquency among girls is an indication that repression sometimes fails. Edwards states that if a girl has not developed an appreciation of her femininity, then she may either be sexually promiscuous or be sexually un-responsive or frigid (59). Sometimes, girls engage in sexual intercourse in order to express symbolically their hostility to-ward their parents.

We may conceptualize three major types of undesirable reactions of the ado-lescent to increased sexual drives (60). These are: (a) diminished sexual activi-ties, (b) increased sexual activities, and (c) manifestation of infantile ways of sexual gratification (*perversion*). We shall discuss each of these briefly in turn.

Diminished sexual drives usually occur in adolescents whose sexual interests and behavior have been severely repressed (60). Their previous development is usu-ally characterized by excessive conform-ity to parental demands, restriction of spontaneity, reaction formation against the expression of any hostile trends, and consequent excessive "goodness," cleanli-ness, and orderliness. Their sexual curi-osity is usually at a very low level, and attempts at masturbation are usually sup-pressed, even though they may mastur-bate occasionally. The emergence of in-creased sexual drives at puberty creates tremendous anxiety in such adolescents, and these reactions are further reinforced by feelings of revulsion, shame, and remorse about all aspects of sexuality. As a result, adolescents who have diminished sexual drives become severely introverted, and tend to withdraw from social contacts. They very carefully avoid all types of contacts that might lead to sexual temptation, but merely staying away from girls is not a solution to the problem, since going out only with boys serves to increase the possibility of homosexual temptation. As time goes on, they show more social withdrawal, increased asceticism, and they frequently become preoccupied with intellectual, moral, or spiritual problems. More infantile defenses such as denial, repression, isolation, reaction formation and projection tend to be used. Diminished sexual drive does not completely solve the problem, of course. It means only that the sexual conflicts have been displaced to another level and *not* that they have been resolved.

Increased sexual drives and activities are characteristic of adolescents in all cultures in which sexual activities are not severely discouraged. Within our culture such an increase may be regarded as a "carrier" of other problems; that is, other conflicts are displaced to the sexual sphere and are more readily expressed in this area. Often increased sexual drives are the expression of the defiance of the adolescent against what he perceives as excessive parental restrictions. Moreover, sexual behavior is often accompanied by aggressive drives. In part, this is due to the fact that the solution to unconscious oedipal problems requires sexual union with a partner through whom the hostile

feelings toward the parent of the same sex can be indirectly discharged. Further, the hostile and competitive feelings toward the parent indirectly lead to the same end; as he attempts to become "more adequate" than his parent, he also becomes more aggressive. Thus increased sexual drives may serve to express the generalized hostility of the adolescent. Often the basis of the increased drive stems from fears of one's inadequacy, and may be viewed as an attempt, through compensation, to reduce fear or to "prove oneself." Again, the adolescent who has been denied closeness by the parents will seek to gratify his needs by seeking close heterosexual relationships. As in the case of diminished sexual drive, markedly increased sexual drives do not solve the problem, but rather may indicate the presence of deep and unresolved conflicts.

If the adolescent has been severely fixated at early psychosexual levels, *perverse sexual activities* may result from the increased pubertal drives. The term "perverse" connotes sexual behavior in which the *main* pleasure is derived from a *partial* aspect of the sexual act rather than from true genital pleasure. Such activities are commonly used by normal individuals in the forepleasure that precedes sexual intercourse and true genital satisfaction. The criteria for distinction between a pervert and a nonpervert is that the former seeks the forepleasure as the main goal, whereas the latter may use the forepleasures as part of the movement toward the achievement of genital primacy, and a more mature interpersonal relationship. There are many forms of perverse sexual behavior. The more common among these include: *homosexuality* (sexual gratification from a person of the same sex); *fetishism* (deriving sexual pleasure from some part of the body, or from some object such as shoes, stockings, underwear, etc.); *voyeurism* (looking at sexual areas of the body); *exhibitionism* (exposing the genital organs to others); *sexual sadism* (inflicting pain on the sexual partner); *sexual masochism* (having pain inflicted by the sexual partner); *fellatio* (use of the mouth for sexual gratification). We wish to emphasize that when such types of behavior occur as part of the total act of emotional relationship and of sexual intercourse, they are *not* perversions. There are other forms of perverse behavior, but all have in common the fact that they are not engaged in by deliberate or conscious choice and are compulsive in nature. Perversions are really infantile ways of gaining sexual satisfactions, and when utilized indicate an immature psychosexual development of the individual (60).

Aggressive behavior

As we have seen the period of adolescence brings, in addition to the sexual problems discussed, many other conflicts —all of which are frustrating to the individual. Since the usual human reaction to frustration is aggression, it is not surprising to find that many adolescents show hostile and aggressive behavioral reactions. In fact *almost all* adolescents show some form of rebellious and hostile behavior at one time or another. Further, factors in the social pathology of the community contribute to the personal disorganization, counteraggression, or the delinquency of the adolescent (61). Since aggression is therefore *not* pathological in itself, but is frequently an overt indication of the adolescent's attempt to develop independence and to free himself from adult controls, it is manifested in much of his behavior. For example, we have noted the need of the adolescent to belong to a peer group. As Escalona states, the mere fact of belonging to such a group has a defiant quality in itself (62). When the adolescent identifies strongly with a group of his own age, he is pointing out that he is not like other people and does not need to follow adult standards. Such an identification permits him to make a defiant assertion of his own individuality. As Escalona indicates, boys tend to discharge their hostility through athletic games which are often outlets for aggressive tensions, and they invest intense emotional energy in such activities. Girls do not express their hostility as openly as do boys through physical activities, but rather tend to express hostility more through words than through actions. We find that teenage groups of girls "have secrets," whisper to each other, form "cliques" within the group, and tend toward exclusiveness. Apart from such "normal" aggressive behavior, which is to be expected, some adolescents develop a pattern of hostile and aggressive reactions so severe as to constitute serious adjustment problems both to themselves and to society. When such a pattern of behavior takes extreme form, or persists in spite of other, more effective ways of coping with problems, then it is probably psychopathological in nature. When it results in the breaking of law and in arrest by the police and conviction by the court, it is called *delinquency.*

⌐ In the past delinquency was frequently regarded as a "disease," which was attributed to some specific condition such as "moral imbecility," brain injury, or "ethical degeneration." Today we regard delinquency as a hostile form of *antisocial behavior* in violation of some particular law. It is perceived as being a form of *reactive behavior* on the part of the individual. We no longer believe that delinquents are born feebleminded, or that they possess physical characteristics that set them apart from other people. Delinquents do not all have below-average intelligence, but rather are found in all the ranges of intelligence. It has also been found that delinquents as a group are found more frequently in slum or transition areas, but again the individual delinquent may come from any type of environment. Modern research indicates that there are many complex causes of delinquent behavior of the adolescent (63).

It is customary to group the types of reactions represented by delinquency into three main categories: (a) delinquency that is a reflection of the sociocultural patterns of a particular neighborhood or group (*sociopathic*), (b) delinquency that is a reaction against deprivation and frustration, and (c) delinquency that is the expression of a personality disturbance. A mixture of these three types is frequently found in any given case of delinquent behavior.

Delinquent behavior should be related to the dynamic personality factors of the individual who engages in such behavior. Delinquency should be regarded as a form of *maladaptive behavior,* and hence the personality difficulties of the particular delinquent need to be understood. There are many dynamic factors leading to the production of delinquent behavior. For example, the parents of delinquents are found frequently to be either very rigid disciplinarians or, on the other hand, very overindulgent parents. Also, the parents of some delinquent adolescents have inconsistent but perfectionistic standards for their children. When such types of parental behaviors are present, the child then shows both poor ego and poor superego development (64). It is also possible that a delinquent may be either a *schizoid* or a *psychotic* personality. Again, the delinquency may be related to reactions of the individual to physical injury or disease, or to a particular social condition of his cultural background.

Havighurst and Taba found that the overly aggressive adolescent is openly hostile toward society, does very poor school work, refuses to conform to the usual demands of society, and frequently discharges his hostility through destruction of property (65). He does not adjust too well in his peer group, and tends to blame society for his failures. These researchers state that the early experiences of the overly rebellious adolescent are characterized by neglect and frustration. Their personality needs, in general, are not satisfied, they fail to incorporate the ideals and values of society, and as a result tend to be aggressively selfish and self-centered.

In contrast to the aggressive behavior discussed in the foregoing paragraph, the severely disturbed adolescent sometimes reacts to his frustrations and conflicts through the development of *overly submissive* reactions. Such behavior is characterized by a lack of spontaneity on the part of the individual. He does not tend to initiate many actions by himself, and shows no *overt* aggressive reactions toward other people or objects. (Strong, unconscious, hostile needs may underlie his passivity.) He wishes to be told exactly what to do by others, and is loathe to undertake any action without explicit instructions to do so. As Havighurst and Taba point out, the submissive adolescent passively accepts the domination of other people, he lacks self-confidence, and so attempts to gain inner security through conforming to the demands of more aggressive personalities (65). He is not a leader within his group, avoids all leadership responsibilities, and tends to be a follower. One of his chief aims is to avoid conflict, and he takes great pains to avoid involvement in conflict situations. His peers tend to see him as a nonentity and as a friendless person. Such an adolescent is without close friends, not because he wishes to be unfriendly, but rather because he does not wish to draw attention to himself, pre-ferring to be inconspicuous within the group. Havighurst and Taba point out further that the submissive adolescent is a person who has a very strong superego structure, has accepted the imposition of external authority, and so cannot exercise independent judgment. His ego structure is relatively undeveloped, and he has little capacity for creativity or a sense of freedom. The development of such a submissive pattern of behavior on the part of some adolescents is encouraged by excessive domination by parents, other aggressive persons, or social-cultural agencies.

Psychopathological behavior

Occasionally very severe psychopathological reactions, such as *psychoneuroses* and *psychoses*, are manifested by adolescents. We shall review some of the major characteristics of these conditions in the following paragraphs, but shall not discuss the specific syndromes of the numerous types of each. For a full discussion, the reader is referred to a text on abnormal behavior (60).

In the *psychoneuroses*, there is a basic conflict between the id and the superego, with the ego being the site of the conflict. The ego itself in the psychoneuroses is relatively intact, perception of reality is essentially maintained, and the individual is able to function effectively in many areas (see Chapter 7). However, the individual is under considerable tension, and there is significant impairment in some areas of the personality. This impairment is manifested by the *neurotic symptoms* which the individual develops. A psychoneurosis may be defined as a continuing disturbance in the integration of the personality resulting from the conflict of drives within the individual, which manifests itself in tension states, impaired functioning, and specific symptomatology. The formative years of the individual are crucial in determining whether a psychoneurosis will develop in the adolescent period. These early disturbances in personality development produce an imbalance between the drives (id) and the forces that serve to prevent their free expression (ego and superego). Conflicts then occur, and the neurotic personality develops patterns of defenses (defense mechanisms) to cope with the anxiety and conflict. In particular, the usual defenses employed in a psychoneuroses are: repression, displacement, reaction formation, and rationalization. Such defenses as these permit a partial discharge of the drives, and thus a partial amount of gratification, but the discharge is insufficient and so tension continues to mount in the individual. A *vicious circle* is thus instituted: (a) the primary conflicts lead to defensive behavior; (b) this does not permit adequate discharge; (c) the inadequate discharge reactivates the conflict; (d) the defenses are elaborated to cope with the increasing tension; and (e) the heightened tension breaks forth in symptom behavior.

The authors have developed the following criteria for the presence of a psychoneurosis (60):

(1) There is an inadequate resolution of basic and conflicting drives. This is manifested either as anxiety or as some persistent tension condition.
(2) The symptoms erupt on a functional basis.
(3) Inappropriate defenses are utilized to deal with the conflicts. These permit only *partial* discharge of the drives.
(4) There is reduced effectiveness and impairment of some functions.
(5) There is a high degree of irrational repetitiveness in the pattern of behavior shown, even when it is clearly inappropriate to the situation.
(6) The individual lacks insight into the causes of his condition.

There are many types of psychoneurotic conditions. Examples of these are: conversion hysteria, obsessive-compulsive and phobic disturbances, psychophysiological disorders, anxiety neuroses, and traumatic reactions. Regardless of the specific form of psychoneurosis that develops, there are three major types of psychoneurotic personality patterns. These differ essentially in the nature of the ego boundaries. The basic patterns of the ego structures in psychoneuroses are represented in Figure 17 (page 346).

In part "A" of Figure 17 the ego boundaries are such that the internal and external worlds of the individual are effectively differentiated from each other. Many internal drives can reach consciousness, but many others are repressed. Also, external stimuli can have a real impact upon the personality reaction of the individual. It will be noted that the drive direction *shifts* as it passes through the ego boundary, due to the operation of the particular defense mechanism. This type of ego structure is representative of the usual *psychoneurotic* condition (often called "classical neurosis").

In part "B," the ego boundary is represented as a sieve. The internal impulses of the individual are acted upon *without* any mediation by the ego. The individual has an impulse, and he acts directly upon it. Since the ego has inadequate inhibitory and integrative characteristics, the individual does not have adequate control over his impulses. An example of a psychoneurotic condition of this type is that known as *psychopathic personality.*

The ego, as represented in part "C," is so rigid that an individual does not experience his internal impulses. As a result, he often feels "this is the way I am." He tends to respond as a whole, that is, as a total character rather than to a specific drive. Outer stimuli do not really intrude upon the basic core of the personality; they are warded off by the rigid ego structure. An individual with an ego such as this does not usually experience much anxiety or tension, but instead

feels that the world should adapt to his way of life. A *character disorder* is an example of this type of psychoneurosis.

Adolescents may have any of the above types of ego structure, and may develop any of the major types of psychoneurotic reactions. However, it is very rare that we find any "pure" type of reaction shown. Clinically, the picture presented is usually that of a mixed psychoneurosis, with the features of one type predominating.

Occasionally, the adolescent is faced with so severe a threat that the integration of the ego structure is not maintained as it is in the psychoneuroses. In such instances the ego is overwhelmed and cannot function in a mature and integrated fashion. As a result of severe stress, especially during the formative years, the ego structure is destroyed. The individual then is said to be *psychotic.* There are many specific forms of psychoses: schizophrenia, manic-depressive psychosis, senile psychosis, and the like. Schizophrenia is the most common form

Figure 17. *Stimulus-response patterns in three categories of neurosis.*

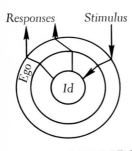

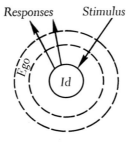

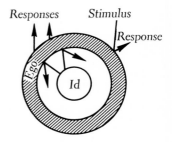

A. PSYCHONEUROTIC   B. "PSYCHOPATHIC"   C. CHARACTER NEUROTIC

From Hutt, M. L., and Gibby, R. G., *Patterns of Abnormal Behavior.* Boston: Allyn and Bacon, 1957.

of psychosis in adolescence. In fact, the older name for schizophrenia was *dementia praecox,* or "insanity of the young." We know now that schizophrenia may make its appearance at any age, although the incidence of schizophrenia does rise sharply during the adolescent period.

The psychotic individual usually shows severe regression—regressing to infantile modes of adaptation; that is, he uses behavioral patterns similar to those employed in infancy and early childhood. Such modes were appropriate during the infantile phases of his development, but are quite inappropriate when utilized by the adolescent. Moreover, the psychotic person is usually unable to test reality; that is, his perception of reality is highly inaccurate. Often, he shows decreased effectiveness in mental functioning. For example, judgment and memory are often severely impaired. Bizarre speech, severe disturbances in mobility, extreme rigidity of behavior, hallucinations, delusions, extreme withdrawal, and other types of symptoms may be present. Such psychotic disturbances are very difficult to treat, but many psychotic adolescents do profit from skilled and intensive psychotherapy.

In our review of the varied types of emotional disturbances of adolescence, we have seen that all the forms of maladjustment may occur during this period, from mild, transient disturbances through severe disturbances of the psychotic form. Since adolescence is a period of stress, readjustment, and emancipation from childhood dependencies, disturbances are more likely to occur as a consequence. Understanding of the adolescent, and specific psychotherapeutic help or some form of guidance or counseling, can be very helpful. For just as the adolescent is prone to instabilities, so his drive toward maturity is of assistance in recovery from such disturbances.

GENERAL READINGS

1. Ausubel, D. P., *Theory and Problems of Adolescent Development.* New York: Grune & Stratton, 1954.
2. Davis, A., and Dollard, J., *Children of Bondage.* Washington: American Council on Education, 1940.
3. Hollingshead, A. B., *Elmtown's Youth.* New York: Wiley, 1949.
4. Kuhlen, R. G., *The Psychology of Adolescent Development.* New York: Harper, 1952.
5. Landis, P. H., *Adolescence and Youth.* New York: McGraw-Hill, 1952.
6. Malm, M., and Jamison, O. G., *Adolescence.* New York: McGraw-Hill, 1952.
7. Mead, G. H., *Mind, Self, and Society.* Chicago: University of Chicago, 1934.
8. Seidman, J. M. (ed.), *The Adolescent: A Book of Readings.* New York: Dryden, 1953.

9. Wattenberg, W. W., *The Adolescent Years.* New York: Harcourt, Brace, 1955.

10. Willoughby, R. R., "Sexuality in the second decade," *Monogr. Soc. Res. Child Developm.*, 1937, 2, 1-57.

SELECTED BIBLIOGRAPHY

11. Rubé, P., "Is there a problem of adolescence?" *Am. J. Psychotherapy*, 1955, 9, 503-509.

12. Crow, L. D., and Crow, A., *Adolescent Development and Adjustment.* New York: McGraw-Hill, 1956.

13. Bernard, H. W., *Adolescent Development in American Culture.* Yonkers, N. Y.: World Book, 1957.

14. Greulich, W. W., "Physical changes in adolescence," in *The Forty-Third Yearbook of the National Society for the Study of Education: Part I, Adolescence* (N. B. Henry, ed.). Chicago: Dept. of Educ., University of Chicago, 1944, pp. 8-32.

15. Frank, L. K., "Introduction: Adolescence as a period of transition," in *The Forty-Third Yearbook of the National Society for the Study of Education: Part I, Adolescence* (N. B. Henry, ed.). Chicago: Dept. of Educ., University of Chicago, 1944, pp. 1-7.

16. Nathanson, I. I., Towne, L., and Aub, J. C., "Urinary sex hormone studies," in *Physique, Personality and Scholarship* (R. N. Sanford, ed.). *Monogr. Soc. Res. Child Developm.*, 1943, 8, 70-81.

17. Sollenberger, R. I., "Some relationships between the urinary excretion of male hormones by maturing boys and girls and their expressed interests and attitudes," *J. Psychol.*, 1940, 9, 179-189.

18. Jersild, A. T., *The Psychology of Adolescence.* New York: Macmillan, 1957.

19. Ford, C. S., and Beach, F. A., *Patterns of Sexual Behavior.* New York: Harper, 1951.

20. Kinsey, A. C., Pomeroy, W. B., and Martin, C. E., *Sexual Behavior in the Human Male.* Philadelphia: Saunders, 1948, p. 130.

21. Shock, N. W., "Physiological changes in adolescence," in *The Forty-Third Yearbook of the National Society for the Study of Education: Part I, Adolescence* (N. B. Henry, ed.). Chicago: Dept. of Educ., University of Chicago, 1944, pp. 56-79.

22. Garrison, K. C., *Psychology of Adolescence*, 5th ed. Englewood Cliffs, N. J.: Prentice-Hall, 1956.

23. Nicholson, A., and Hanley, C., "Indices of physiological maturity; derivation and interrelationships," *Child Developm.*, 1953, 24, 3-38.

24. Stolz, H. R., and Stolz, L. M., *Somatic Development of Adolescent Boys.* New York: Macmillan, 1951.
25. Bayley, N., "Skeletal maturing in adolescence as a basis for determining percentage of completed growth," *Child Developm.,* 1943, 14, 1-46.
26. Reynolds, E. L., "The distribution of subcutaneous fat in childhood and adolescence," *Monogr. Soc. Res. Child Developm.,* 1950, 15, 1-189.
27. Richey, H. G., "The relation of accelerated, normal and retarded puberty to the height and weight of school children," *Monogr. Soc. Res. Child Developm.,* 1937, 2, 1-67.
28. Stratz, C. H., *Der Körper des Kindes und seine Pflege.* Stuttgart: Enke, 1909.
29. Harris, J. A., Jackson, C. M., Patterson, D. G., and Scammon, R. E., *The Measurement of Man.* Minneapolis: University of Minnesota, 1930.
30. Mead, M., "Coming of Age in Samoa," in *From the South Seas.* New York: Morrow, 1939.
31. Rust, H. N., "A puberty ceremony of the Mission Indians," *Amer. Anthro.* (New Series) 1906, 8, 28 ff.
32. Howill, A. W., *Native Tribes of South-East Australia.* London: Macmillan, 1904.
33. Reik, T., "The puberty rites of savages," in *The Psychological Problems of Religion: I. Ritual, Psychoanalytic Studies.* New York: Farrar, Straus, 1946.
34. Remmers, H. H., and Radler, D. H., *The American Teenager.* Indianapolis: Bobbs-Merrill, 1957.
35. Rubé, P., "The inner world of adolescence," *Am. J. Psychotherapy,* 1955, 9, 673-691.
36. Josselyn, I., "The ego in adolescence," *Amer. J. Orthopsychiat.,* 1954, 24, 223-227.
37. Wittenberg, R., "On the superego in adolescence," *Psychoanal. Rev.,* 1955, 42, 271-279.
38. Deutsch, H., *The Psychology of Women,* Vol. 1. New York: Grune & Stratton, 1944.
39. Moreno, J. L., *Who Shall Survive?* Washington: Nervous and Mental Disease Pub. Co., 1934.
40. McGuire, C., "Adolescent society and social mobility." Unpublished dissertation, University of Chicago, 1949.
41. Blos, P., *The Adolescent Personality: A Study of Individual Behavior.* New York: Appleton, 1941.
42. Williams, F. E., *Adolescence: Studies in Mental Hygiene.* New York: Farrar and Rinehart, 1930.
43. Tryon, C. M., "The adolescent peer culture," in *The Forty-Third*

Yearbook of the National Society for the Study of Education: Part I, Adolescence (N. B. Henry, ed.). Chicago: Dept. of Educ., University of Chicago, 1944.

44. Mead, M., *Male and Female*. New York: Morrow, 1949.

45. Remmers, H. H., and Shimberg, B., "Problems of high school youth," *Purdue Opinion Poll for Young People*, Report No. 21. Lafayette: Purdue University Press, 1949.

46. Norton, S. K., "Student problems met by the teacher," *School Rev.*, 1948, 51, 404 ff.

47. Bell, H. M., *Youth Tell Their Story*. Washington: American Council on Education, 1938.

48. Witty, P. A., and Skinner, L., *Mental Hygiene in Modern Education*. New York: Farrar and Rinehart, 1939.

49. Doane, D. C., "The needs of youth: An evaluation for curriculum purposes," New York: Teach. Coll., Columbia University, *Contributions to Education*, No. 848, 1942.

50. Kirkpatrick, M. E., "The mental hygiene of adolescence in the Anglo-American culture," *Proceedings* of the 4th Int. Cong. Ment. Health, 1951, 273-280.

51. Gaumnitz, W. M., and Tompkins, E. E., *Holding Power and Size of High School*. Washington: U.S. Office of Education, Federal Security Agency, Circular 322, 1950.

52. Allen, C. M., "What have our drop-outs learned?" *Educational Leadership*, 1953, 10, 347-350.

53. Barnes, M. W., "The nature and nurture of early adolescents," *Teach. Coll. Rec.*, 1956, 57, 513-521.

54. McKenzie, G., "Implications for teachers and counselors," in *The Forty-Third Yearbook of the National Society for the Study of Education: Part I, Adolescence* (N. B. Henry, ed.). Chicago: Dept. of Educ., University of Chicago, 1944.

55. Hall, G. S., *Adolescence*. New York: Appleton, 1904.

56. Jones, H., "Maintenance of mental health," *Mental Health*, 1951, 10, 40-42.

57. Luchins, A. S., "On the theories and problems of adolescence," *Journ. Genetic Psychol.*, 1954, 85, 47-63.

58. More, D., "Developmental concordance and discordance during puberty and early adolescence," *Monogr. Soc. Res. Child Developm.*, 1953, 18, 1-127.

59. Edwards, V. C., "The adolescent girl," *Journ. Hum. Rel.*, 1955, 3, 26-40.

60. Hutt, M. L., and Gibby, R. G., *Patterns of Abnormal Behavior*. Boston: Allyn and Bacon, 1957.

61. Shaw, C. R., and McKay, H. P., *Juvenile Delinquency and Urban Areas*. Chicago: University of Chicago, 1942.

62. Escalona, S., *Understanding Hostility in Children*. Chicago: Science Research Associates, Inc., 1954.

63. Kuhlen, R. G., and Thompson, G. C., *Psychological Studies of Human Development*. New York: Appleton, 1952.

64. Bovet, L., *Psychiatric Aspects of Juvenile Delinquency*. Geneva: World Health Organization Monograph Series, 1951.

65. Havighurst, R. J., and Taba, H., *Adolescent Character and Personality*. New York: Wiley, 1949.

10 | *Childhood disturbances —prevention, correction, and treatment*

WE HOPE THAT the reader has, by this point, obtained a comprehensive view of the nature and course of child development. In the course of our presentation we have discussed general principles of child development, the nature of hereditary and prenatal influences, the effect of social and cultural factors, the specific importance of family constellation and home atmosphere, the influence of the school climate and the personality of the teacher, the effect of membership in peer groups, and the relevance of social and cultural change. We have examined aspects of physical development, of the growth of communication skills, the nature of emotional development, the process of socialization, and the over-all maturation of the personality. On occasion we had need to evaluate disturbances or abnormalities in development, to inquire into their causation, and to wonder about methods for alleviating or eliminating them. We found that all children go through periods of stress and discomfiture, develop some anxiety, and even show unusual symptoms. Some children become very severely disturbed and may develop the characteristic features of psychoneurosis or psychosis. Moreover, many children may become temporarily or more persistently disturbed because of their reactions to physical illness or accident, excessive environmental stress, and because of the anxieties which both adults and children often develop in reaction to such conditions. Because disturbance in development, mild or severe, is commonplace, and because an understanding of methods of dealing with such disturbances is needed by everyone who has any important relationship with children—and few of us can be excluded from this category—we feel it is important to present an overview of the problems of prevention and correction of such phenomena. We should thus be better able to cope with such problems, and be in a better position to make use of our capacities for helping others, and of recognizing our limitations and the need for specialized assistance when this is required. It is to these matters that we now turn our attention.

AN OUNCE OF PREVENTION

The old saying has it that "an ounce of prevention is worth a pound of cure." It certainly is far better not only to prevent the occurrence of some abnormal condition which may then lead to secondary complications, but also to provide a healthy environment for maximal growth and development. Although we still have much to learn concerning the specific characteristics of "the healthy environment," we have noted that those conditions which foster emotional security in infancy are conducive to the development of a sense of *basic trust* in oneself, and that, in turn, the development of basic trust fosters good physical and psychological development. Another factor that fosters healthy development is the understanding by the adult of the child's needs, for only then can the adult respond properly to gratify these needs. Directly related to this last factor is the important principle of *pacing*, by which is meant providing stimulation for the child's growth that is appropriate to his particular developmental level. We have

seen how the infant's oral needs have to be gratified during this period, and that gradually, as he moves into the anal phase of his development, he has to be encouraged to give up some of his oral gratifications (a *normally frustrating* type of experience) so that he can learn to move on to the next and more mature phase of his development. Thus, pacing provides some frustration but it is mild enough so that it provides encouragement to change to a more mature form of behavior—and one that provides, consequently, richer rewards than the previous and less mature form of behavior. Finally, we have learned that normal growth is characterized by periods of progression, integration, and regression. Thus, healthy growth and adjustment do not consist of constant and continuing movement upward; there are also periods in which reversion to more immature modes of behavior occurs for a short time, or in which unobservable growth during plateau periods occurs. Prevention of abnormal growth involves the maximal use of these related principles of child development.

Prevention means much more than simply providing a good environment for growth, however. Even the best planned environment cannot prevent entirely some difficulties in growth and adjustment. There is therefore a second set of precepts with which we must become familiar. These precepts involve *preventing a mild upset or a mild disturbance from becoming a major one*. The crucial question here is how one deals with mild difficulties when they inevitably occur. One of the preliminary questions to which we must first direct attention is how to distinguish a mild disturbance in growth and adjustment from a more serious one. Then, assuming that we can answer this question satisfactorily, we wish to know what, if anything, we should do about it.

The first of these problems does not usually involve detecting a very serious disturbance, for such conditions usually have their own special characteristics. The more serious disturbances may be recognized, in the first instance, by the *degree* of the deviation from the average or normal. Deviation of a mild degree is normal, as we have learned, and should not alarm us unless we have unnecessarily strong (and neurotic) needs for conformity per se. Extreme deviations, however, are immediately suspect, and, although not necessarily abnormal, call for examination and evaluation by the appropriate expert in the particular field of abnormality. Moreover, serious disturbances tend to persist and become aggravated, and in this respect they differ significantly from milder degrees of disturbance. An important implication of this statement is that one of the criteria for mild disturbance is the transitory character of its manifestation. Thus, if a child seems unduly upset but is not disturbed in any fundamental or basic sense, the changing scene will of itself enable him to correct his adjustment and return to more adequate means of behaving. This phenomenon of self-correction or self-adaptation of the normal or near-normal personality may be thought of as its *autoplastic* characteristic. Individuals who show this characteristic, that is who are able to adapt, in time, to frustration and revert to appropriate modes of behavior or move on to improved modes of adaptation, will make use of frustrations by changing themselves as circumstances warrant. They have the capacity for growth and for adaptation (10). All of this means that one of the criteria of severe maladjustment is the inability, in time, of the individual to correct or adjust his behavior to changing circumstances. This leads us to consider another characteristic of the severely disturbed person, namely, the extreme degree of *rigidity* in his personality make-up. Evidence of this rigidity is the habitual use of repetitive, unchanging modes of behavior, even when stress is minimal, in a wide variety of environmental circumstances. The extreme form of such rigidity in a severely neurotic personality is known as *obsessive-compulsive* neurosis, but it is characteristic of all severely disturbed individuals (6). Finally, severely disturbed people show some significant impairment of their capacities, so that they may be chronically fatigued due to the need of exerting extreme effort when it is not really necessary, or so that they regularly function below their former level of efficiency, or so that they have persistent difficulty in interpersonal relationships.

One can therefore say that one can distinguish a mild degree of disturbance by differentiating it from the condition of a severe disturbance. Having done so, we wish to know what, if anything, we should do about it—and this constitutes the core of the "ounce of prevention." The first implication of all that we have been saying in this book is that the observer (parent, teacher, or supervisor) should learn to tolerate and to accept transitory manifestations of disturbance. If time or changing circumstances do not readily lead to a progressive change in behavior, then simple preventive steps should be taken. These are far short of those we shall presently describe in later sections of this chapter.

Toleration of some degree of deviation, thus enabling the child to express and work through his frustration, assumes that the adult is not himself a very anxious, highly conforming person. (It does *not* mean that he will tolerate rebelliousness for the sake of rebelliousness or that he will refuse to set realistic and appropriate limits which the child needs for his own safety and security.) Toleration also implies the positive act of accepting the child emotionally—respecting his integrity and communicating this acceptance in some manner. It also implies that the adult will try to, or in fact does, understand the child, that is, he will try to understand the motivations that cause this child to seek the particular goals in his behavior. (We pointed out in Chapter 8, as well as in other chapters, how even the sensitive parent or teacher could benefit from some training along these lines.)

A next step in prevention is to try to provide the kind of environment that will enable the child to satisfy his needs in a constructive sense. These needs are constantly changing, and therefore what may once have been a very favorable en-

vironment may, by virtue of failure to provide for the constantly changing requirements of the child, become a less favorable situation. We saw an example of this type of problem in connection with our presentation of Harold's case in Chapter 1. Harold led a very sheltered but secure life in the country with his parents. He had little opportunity during his second and third years for continuing interpersonal contacts with other children of his own age or even with adults, other than his parents. Largely as a consequence of his severe restriction in his social experiences he was unable to learn to tolerate separation from home and from parents. Then when he suffered the trauma of hospitalization and tonsillectomy, his adjustment suffered severely. We wish to emphasize that his home environment had been appropriate to his developmental needs during his infancy, but thereafter this very fine home was no longer able to supply gratification of his emerging social needs. Harold's case illustrates the special problems of the preschool child, but we can think of other situations in which a formerly appropriate environment subsequently fails to provide for the emerging needs of the child because of changes within him. Thus, opportunity for some degree of independence of home authority becomes more necessary during early childhood (the primary-school period) than it was during previous periods, and new recreational outlets and group participation become more relevant. Similarly, opportunity for some kinds of heterosexual experience becomes quite important during adolescence whereas the provision for such opportunities was not as crucial before puberty. There are many other kinds of changing opportunities needed by the growing child, involving such things as: opportunities for physical activity, opportunities for expressing aggression in socially desirable forms, opportunities for relating to an adult of the same sex to provide more firm anchorage in one's identification, and opportunities for mastering the appropriate social skills necessary for effective social intercourse. These additional opportunities insure more adequate provision for new needs that can no longer, or not as easily, be provided in the former environment.

One of the highly important means of preventing minor difficulties from becoming major ones is that of *cathartic experiences* (6). All of us become tense at times, unnecessarily confused at others—adults as well as children—and we need some means for "letting off steam." Catharsis involves discharging the heightened emotional components of an experience in some effective manner. Of critical importance in such cathartic measures is "talking oneself out." Other means are also helpful, such as discharging tension through play and recreation, using hobbies for this purpose, and the like, but talking things out has special virtues. In the first place, it enables the individual to gain some insight into his difficulties, because as he talks things over he becomes aware of elements in the situation or in himself that were not directly in the center of conscious attention; thus, he can integrate these elements into his solution to the difficulty. Moreover, if the listening participant (the parent, the teacher, or some friend), really listens and is *accepting* (thereby respecting the integrity of the person in trouble), guilt is lessened because there has been a sharing of the unpleasant (and often hostile) feelings. In this sharing process one's "evil" thoughts lose some of their sting—especially if the listener does not act as a moral judge but mainly as a sympathetic and understanding friend. If the guilt is not lessened through some procedure such as this, it may become oppressive and may accumulate, thus producing increasingly corrosive influence. Further, catharsis of the kind we have been discussing takes place in an interpersonal setting and thereby offers emotional support for the troubled individual. As we have seen in previous chapters, emotional support furnishes a climate for effective working through of one's difficulties. It supports the temporarily disturbed ego in tolerating the stress and of finding ways of meeting or avoiding it.

We may have noted that our discussion of catharsis said nothing concerning the *giving* of advice or the *giving* of insight. It seems to be far better for the individual to find his own unique solutions to his problems, for in the process he not only obtains a good solution but also learns how to go about getting solutions and increases his confidence in his own ability to do so. This is not to say that advice or suggestion is not sometimes helpful, or even sometimes necessary. For the objective observer, and especially the older and wiser observer, may be able to see issues and possibilities that the troubled individual is unable to see or even guess. Such advice should first be sought for by the troubled person, however, and even then it should only be offered as a suggestion to be worked through by the individual himself. For although advice or imperative command may occasionally be necessary in emergency situations or under extreme circumstances, it serves best when it is provided as a *tentative model for a solution* which the individual can do with as he needs to. Otherwise, it is likely to be conceived of as interference, it may create further hostility and confusion, and may prevent the individual from learning to use his own resources maximally in working things out. It might be observed parenthetically that we are often driven to offer advice because of our own inability to tolerate the tension we see in others rather than because it is really called for. In the process we may relieve our own anxiety or our own frustration, and we may feel more potent or even omniscient because of the apparent wisdom of our judgment, but we are not helping the other person to work out his own problems.

Parents who are able to provide a home atmosphere in which children can easily come to them just to talk things over can provide inestimable help along these lines. If the child knows that he can talk things over with Mom or Dad, *when he feels like it,* he will have a very useful means for ventilation of his feelings and learning to deal with them more effectively. The wise parent, though, is more often a listener than an adviser, in

the literal meaning of the latter term. Nevertheless, the child may experience the situation as one in which his parent was "very wise." For the child will be able to incorporate the wisdom of his parent in the subtle interactive process of talking things out, rather than by being told what to do—in which case his own inadequacy may seem even more striking. As a very wise clergyman said in a recent interview, he lights a pipe when his parishoners come to him to ask his advice, and smokes while he listens. When he finds that his pipe has gone out, he becomes aware that he has been talking too much and listening too little!

It should not be expected that the child will always run eagerly to his parent for a "talk session" whenever he is troubled, and the parent should not feel troubled if his expert wisdom is not always eagerly sought. It will suffice if the parent is available and the child often comes to him. There are times when the child feels too guilty about what he has done or wishes to do, or too uncertain of possible reactions by his parent to share his troubles with someone else. It is probably best to "wait out" such situations rather than to try to force a cathartic session. The child is also entitled to his own secrets and his own feelings of guilt! Perhaps after he has made some amends or after he has worked some of his problems through, he will still come to talk things over.

The teacher (or the wise group leader) can also be of inestimable value in making available the opportunity for im-

promptu "talk sessions." It is highly useful to have even a few moments' chat
about something when the situation is
immediately relevant, and when emotional tension can be directly dissipated.
Many frustrating situations occur in
school or in club groups in which discharge of tension before it mounts to
high levels can be effectively growth-in-
ducing. Moreover, since the teacher has
different responsibilities from those of
the parent (and hence has different types
of emotional involvement in the child)
he can sometimes be effective when the
parent could not. The parent is often so
emotionally involved in helping the child
progress toward a specific goal that he
may be unable to take an objective and
uninvolved attitude in some situations in
which the teacher can do so. (The reverse is also sometimes true, of course.)
The teacher and parent can thus be sup-
plementary in providing opportunities of
somewhat different kinds for the child to
talk and reason things out. Under some
circumstances, as we shall see, group
"talk sessions" (more commonly called
group guidance sessions) may be organized, and these in turn may provide still
additional means of helping the child to
grow in emotional and social stature. But
the short, informal, and individual conference whenever the situation is ripe for
it has a unique value of its own.

INDIVIDUAL AND GROUP NEEDS

A healthy environment for the individual
is also a healthy environment for the

society—and when society has a healthy
environment it may be said to be a
healthy society. Yet today we have ample
evidence that in many ways some aspects
of our society are somewhat unhealthy.
Evidence for this may be found all
around us. The National Association for
Mental Health has estimated that well
over 10,000,000 people in the United
States are suffering from various forms of
emotional disturbance serious enough to
require hospital or out-patient psychiatric treatment. It has been estimated
that at least 10 per cent of our school
population is seriously maladjusted, and
it is well known that school guidance
clinics, community child-guidance agencies, and state mental-hygiene clinics
are unable to keep up with the heavy
load of referrals. During the early part of
1958 the Board of Education in New
York City, during an acute outbreak of
widespread delinquency in that city, had
to set up two different types of correc-
tional schools for such youngsters and
enlist the police force in an attempt to
cope with the problem. During World
War II more than 17 per cent of all
draftees were rejected for psychiatric reasons. During 1946 the combined rate of
homicidal and suicidal acts per 100,000
of the adult population was 24.02 in this
country (3). Facts such as these indicate
that a very large segment of our population is severely disturbed emotionally.
We cannot attribute these facts to any
innate "sickness" in the population.
Rather we must attribute them to emotionally disturbing conditions in society.
When a society thus provides the breeding ground for emotional disturbance
even the most prophylactic home en-

vironment is not immune to its influence.

The condition is not confined to the United States; it is worldwide. The rate of psychiatric illness is high throughout most of the civilized world, although it varies considerably from one country to another. Referring again to the combined rate for homicide and suicide, the rate per 100,000 of the population in some representative countries is as follows: for Denmark, 35.76; for France, 16.36; for Canada, 13.07. It is comparatively and noteworthily low for the Republic of Ireland, in which the rate is 4.24, but this figure is still high in absolute terms (11). We could illustrate the worldwide nature of this problem by citing other statistics, but it suffices to say that the problem is quite apparent whether we consider psychoneurosis, or alcoholism, or drug addiction, or criminal behavior, including juvenile delinquency.

The figures we have just offered refer to a particular year in the history of modern civilization, and they vary from year to year, depending on social and economic factors, among other things. Even more important is the fact that the figures are on the increase. Some of this increase may reflect society's growing awareness of many forms of emotional disturbance it formerly failed to recognize. Some of it may reflect better methods of detection and greater provision for treatment, with the consequence that more and more people are seeking help. It is highly probable that there is, in fact, an actual increase in the rate of the combined total of all forms of emotional difficulties. It is also safe to conclude that this increase in rate is due to conflicting

values in the needs of the individual and those of society.

As society has become ever more complex and as the pace of change has quickened, it is, perhaps, inevitable that conflicts between the needs of the individual and the group should become more severe. We have paid considerable attention to advances in technology and the physical sciences but have paid far less attention to the scientific study of human needs and methods of satisfying them. The individual, and therefore in the end even his society, has lost sight of the central fact that advances in the physical and scientific fields can have meaning and value only as they are put to use by individuals and by society, and this means learning how all advances affect persons, and then providing appropriate means for gratifying their needs. Thus far in our history, society and the individual have been left to shift for themselves. We have not yet learned how to reconcile all of our conflicting needs and how to adapt to uncertainties on a global scale or to very rapid rates of change. As a consequence we are ill equipped to plan our society to make effective and productive use of our technical know-how in the physical sciences.

Here in this volume we are concerned, primarily, with the growing child. As we have seen, he lives not only in the society of adults, but he also lives in a society (or many societies) of children. Although we may be unable to do as much for him in the over-all planning of society as we might like, there is much we can do for him in providing, at least, a more healthy society of children. Even the most aggressive children learn to adjust better when they have a well planned society of children, although they are still subject to the unfavorable influences of their particular adult society (12).

Starting as early, at least, as the stage of toddlerhood, careful provision should be made for healthy group experiences for the youngsters. Good nursery schools can provide a large part of the answer to this problem. As we pointed out in Chapter 5, the chief goals of nursery education should center on the socialization of the child away from home. The school can provide a secure environment in which, under guidance and with proper pacing, youngsters can learn to adapt to each other, interdepend on each other, learn to tolerate mild frustrations, develop a sense of belonging in the group, and have varied opportunities for disciplined work and spontaneous expression. Such an environment can also provide the materials and equipment that will supplement those available in the home so that the child can learn to experience and get to know more of the world around him. Above all, it is in meeting more kinds of children, and in having the mature and emotionally accepting support of a warm teacher while doing so, that such a society of toddlers and other preschool children can be most helpful.

There are, of course, other aspects of community resources that could be dis-

cussed, such as the church group and the neighborhood group, but we wish only to illustrate our general thesis that a planned and mentally healthy society for children can be highly beneficial. We shall illustrate this thesis with examples at two other levels of development.

During the early school years, the needs of children change gradually and adaptations in the nature of their society have to be made. Children are able to participate in larger groups and are able to form their own, informal peer groups. They need more opportunity for independent and even some rebellious activity, and they need much more freedom to move about and explore their environment—hence the desirability of all kinds of physical facilities appropriate to this age, and of excursions to different parts of the city and country. They also need to learn the cognitive skills with which to communicate more effectively, argue and sustain their rights more convinc-

Learning need not stop because of confinement to a hospital. (U. of Mich.)

ingly, and begin to ingest more of the knowledge relevant to their immediate world. Trained leadership is vitally needed to protect (but not overprotect) children during this adventurous period of their lives, to stimulate (but not over-stimulate them, to understand and tolerate their needs for spontaneity and aggression, and to furnish inspiring models for identification. Good teachers and good group leaders who have well-balanced personalities and who are challenged by and interested in their work are very important, basic ingredients (not window dressing) during these experiences (2).

We should like to illustrate our thesis of a more adequately planned society for children with some remarks about the adolescent period—a period that is marked by many opportunities for further healthy development, and by many possible pitfalls as well. Perhaps the most focal theme for this whole period is the establishment of reasonably mature patterns of heterosexual adjustment. This means learning to get along with both sexes, beginning to point to vocational goals, beginning to assume mature responsibility, and having some freedom to get into "little jams" and work them out on the basis of one's own resources. The leadership required during this period should involve, above all, a deep understanding of adolescent phenomena, and a *respect for them*. Intellectually and emotionally children are now prepared to begin to assume adult roles, but they have not yet acquired the skills appropriate to handle such roles with ease (and society is not yet ready to grant them either economic or social independence). The

leader must feel a responsibility to accept the mature needs of the youngster without abrogating his right to offer wise guidance and needed restraining influence. Children need help to get over their own awkwardness in heterosexual experiences. They also need opportunity for gaining a sense of maturity and responsibility in making decisions, in planning their own programs, and for *jointly* participating with adults in carrying out such programs. Since they also vary widely in interests and capabilities, they need guidance in overcoming frustrations which may seem to them to be insuperable, and in chanelling their capacities along the lines of their greatest talents. They also need opportunities for making mistakes (and for avoiding the most serious ones) so that they can learn to profit from mistakes and to experience a wide variety of exploratory phenomena. The adult hand must be ever-present, but never oppressively felt—present to provide resource capabilities and wise guidance and rarely felt as a punitive influence. Such a society can do much to prevent excessive or prolonged regression to more infantile modes of behavior, on the one hand, and violent, antisocial acting out, on the other.

MENTAL HYGIENE IN EDUCATION

Good education is good mental hygiene. The program for mental hygiene in the schools should not be separate and apart from other programs, but should consist of good mental hygiene practices as part of all of them. As we shall see, special provision needs to be made for exceptional cases and for extreme circumstances, but the mental hygiene program should basically be good educational practice alert to the emotional needs of children.

Mental hygiene in the school starts with the school staff. Unless the staff, in its own organization and functioning, practices good mental hygiene it will be unable to provide maximal opportunity for healthy personality development of children. Hence, from this viewpoint, it is important that the organizational and functional characteristics of the school staff be hygienically sound. Hutt and Miller have expressed part of this viewpoint as follows (13):

> The school is a miniature society which helps to democratize its individual members to the extent that it embodies sound educational practice.
>
> In the study of this microcosm, there are two aspects of the teacher's influence which merit special attention. The first concerns the teacher's conscious awareness of democratic objectives, procedures and organization. *The teacher must actively assist in the formulation of educational policy of the school.* Only thus can she fully appreciate the meaning of the democratic attitude that she is then supposed to convey to her pupils. Only thus can she develop that respect for differences among the personnel who are unified with respect to their basic goals. . . .
>
> It is necessary that the teachers accept common goals if they are to attain true respect for the individuality of the students. Children can then view differences among teachers in the light of these goals. In fact,

the expression by teachers of differences in their points of view can then be encouraged.

A good school staff, then, is one in which the structure is *clearly visible* to all its members, and in which different members of the staff have well defined and acceptable positions in the total structure. Teachers must be full participants in the functioning of this structure, although their functions will necessarily differ from those of the principal and the superintendent. Their individual contributions, their viewpoints, and their criticisms must be utilized in the formulation and carrying out of policy decisions so that each member feels a full sense of participation and assumes an appropriate degree of responsibility in daily operations.

We would place next in importance the mental health of the teacher. Since she serves as a model for identification, and since she has to deal with all kinds of personality characteristics in her children, the teacher should be free of gross emotional disturbances in herself and should be emotionally mature enough to tolerate and to accept the emotional differences of her pupils from herself. Most schools today make little or no effort to evaluate the personality disturbances of their staffs or provide opportunity for their staffs to obtain mental hygiene assistance when it is desirable. (We believe the day will come when such procedures and opportunities will be routinely available.) Selection of teachers should be based not only on technical competence and preparation but also on, at least, the absence of seriously undesirable personality characteristics.

The content of the school curriculum should also be considered in terms of its mental-hygiene aspects. Schoolwork should simultaneously provide for preparation for later life and be intimately related to the emerging interests and abilities of the youngsters. This type of balance is easier to suggest than prescribe, and considerable thought must be given to meeting both these requirements. Moreover, the school curriculum must be related to the specific backgrounds and to the actual levels of abilities of the pupils with adequate provision for differences among pupils. Children need to be motivated to work to the maximum of their capacities but they should not experience too frequent or too severe failure. An appropriate curriculum is one that combines these characteristics so that growth is encouraged in attaining individual and maximum skill through many success experiences.

There is also need for consideration of the emotional climate of the classroom. (See Chapter 7, particularly.) A relaxed but not unstimulating atmosphere with provision for individual contact and interaction between pupils and teacher is necessary. A tense classroom with frequent turmoil is neither a good place in which to learn nor to grow emotionally. The child needs to feel accepted as part of his group and to develop a sense of making important contributions to the work of the group. Group-oriented goals, and group as well as individual competition, need to be fostered. Above all, the teacher has to have sufficient time to learn to know something of the individual needs and other characteristics of each child, and to offer individual discus-

sions at appropriate times. Some opportunity is also necessary for individual and informal tutoring when the child needs special assistance.

We cannot leave this discussion of the mental hygiene of the school without a word about the need of *significant* cumulative records of the child's developing personality characteristics. Too often schools provide only for notations of the unfavorable personality characteristics of their children, or else simply rate pupils on aspects of social adjustment. Much more, and much more positive, information needs to be accumulated. How is the child best motivated? Is he growing in assuming responsible social characteristics? Under what circumstances can he be expected to provide group leadership? How does he relate to others? How does he respond to criticism and to reward? What kinds of things disturb him? Does he need special provision to meet his individual needs? These are some of the kinds of questions for which a cumulative record would prove to be most helpful to successive teachers who deal with the child. And these are the kinds of things that can be *constructively reviewed*, in a mutual attempt at helping, with the mother or father.

THE THREE R'S VERSUS THE CHILD

For many years people have been increasingly debating the general issue of the place of "character development" in education and its relation to more formal, "academic" education. The cry has gone up for more emphasis by schools on "tough courses," and especially on scientific education. Programs that assist in personality development for children have received much criticism. It has been claimed that too little attention is given to "fundamentals" and that the school program has too much "fluff." Some critics have gone so far as to say that our schools have pampered our children and that we ought to "go back" to the old days when the "three R's" were given central if not primary importance.

We do not wish to enter into the heart of this controversy except to point out that occasionally the chief issues have been confused and that there has been a search for a "scapegoat." Surely no one would advocate seriously that we should neglect to provide proper conditions for suitable personality development as part of the ongoing process of education. The real issue is not "the three R's versus the child," as the title of this section might suggest, but how to provide adequate learning of academic and other scholastic skills while at the same time insuring good, sound conditions of education for personality adjustment. There is no necessary conflict between these goals. On the contrary, they can and should be integrated as part of sound educational practice.

We have seen that the school is a microcosm of society and that it is entrusted with the job of helping to transmit the values of our culture. We can have a great deal of healthy debate on which values are most important, but it should be obvious that *some* values will necessarily be transmitted, with high or with low levels of efficiency. The question is not whether we shall have character education but rather what kind of character education we deem to be desirable. Whether we agree to give 90 per cent or 50 per cent, for example, of school time to the learning of fundamental academic skills, the educational program should assist in fostering good habits of learning, a high degree of appropriate skills and the important by-product of effective personality which can utilize these skills properly.

If mental hygiene, and if guidance, are integral parts of the total program of education, then the very ways in which the academic program is implemented will have favorable effects upon personality development. The maladjusted child is not only maladjusted but he is also unable to learn efficiently and he cannot utilize effectively what he does learn. The climate of the classroom and the personality of the teacher are indispensable parts of a good learning environment, therefore. Attention to individual needs by the teacher is designed to increase the effectiveness of both learning and adjustment so that the individual and the class make progress satisfactorily. The crucial role of good teaching practices is therefore central to both learning and good adjustment. Teaching is ineffective if it breeds pampering, for then the child is not being motivated to make maximal use of his native capacities. Moreover, the success achieved and recognized in satisfactory progress in school subjects augurs well for effective personal adjustment.

Of course, too much "pap" may be inserted into the school curriculum, but whether this is or is not the case is irrelevant to the question of whether the fundamental skills are being taught well, with good consequences for personality development—except if too much time and effort are devoted to irrelevant "subjects." The question concerning the amount of time necessary for adequate mastery of fundamental skills is a technical matter which should be largely, if not entirely, a matter for school officials to decide. The community, and particularly the parents, have a right to ask whether fundamental abilities are being learned adequately, and they have a right to participate in the general policy decisions concerning specific goals to be assigned to the schools, but the ways in which the basic skills and other skills and habits are to be taught is a pedagogical problem, best left to the "experts." It may turn out that some of the so-called "pap" is really significant in order to attain the very objectives insisted upon by the community. If it is not, or if it interferes with effective learning of both academic skills and personal adjustment, then it not only may but should be eliminated.

It is also important to point out that guidance and counseling programs are designed to implement the attainment of educational goals. Children need considerable guidance and counseling, particularly during such crucial periods as the eighth grade of elementary school when decisions about type of high school are being considered, and during the

upper grades of high school when many vocational and educational problems are being considered. Such types of guidance are important to the effective use of the capacities of pupils. They are offered to make the educational process more efficient. If they are employed improperly then their use should be improved. The problem here is the same as with the inefficient use of any educational process. But they are not more of a "frill" for the modern educational system than is the use of electricity or of central heating in the modern home or factory. If anything, they are an even more indispensable part of the truly effective educational program (5, 7).

SCHOOL GUIDANCE PROGRAMS AND SERVICES

The modern school or school system has, as an integral part of its services, a guidance program for all of its pupils. Some schools also provide the services of child-guidance clinics or have access to state or community clinics of this type. These facilities are designed to assist the teacher in the total process of education. When well organized they are manned by a properly trained professional staff and provide general consultation to all school personnel for decisions on matters of policy, diagnostic services for schools and individual pupils, and group and individual counseling for selected portions of the school population. Contrary to some opinion, they do not *relieve* the classroom teacher of any of her responsibilities and duties. Rather, they *supplement* her work with professional services when and as they are needed.

We shall begin our discussion by considering group programs of guidance, and then analyze some of the more common forms of individual guidance services. We shall leave for the last sections of this chapter our discussion of still more specialized guidance services, such as those provided by clinical psychologists, psychiatrists, and pediatricians. We can do no more than furnish a general survey of all these specialized programs since a detailed consideration of them would involve a whole book or even a number of books.

Social living classes

Many schools, particularly at the junior-high school and senior-high school levels, now offer classes in *social living,* or similar classes with other titles. The general philosophy of such programs is to utilize group methods of instruction to teach children how to cope with many of the common problems of daily living. If by *teaching* is meant imparting specific knowledge, testing for the effectiveness of the learning of this knowledge, and similar pedagogical goals, then one may seriously doubt the wisdom of such aims. If, however, by teaching is meant arousing interest in group discussion of common problems in learning and adjustment, providing opportunity for airing feelings and attitudes in an atmosphere designed to encourage objective and sober consideration, introducing children

to resources that contain information and wise counsel on relevant subjects, and presenting information in other ways when such sources are not readily available to students, such aims can be highly beneficial (7).

The chief function of such group experiences should be to provide opportunity for deliberate discussion of problems that are a source of conflict and worry. The chief function should *not* be to test for specific information that is learned about such matters. It is not the information, primarily, that is needed—although some kinds of information can be very helpful—but rather the *cathartic* value of sharing one's doubts and feelings with others who are experiencing similar problems in daily living. The teacher's role may be defined as that of a mature group leader, who is not there to judge or test what the pupils learn, but to help guide the discussion along fruitful lines, offer a sober and anxiety-reducing influence upon the group, and act as a resource person when the group needs one. Her value lies not in furnishing the correct answers, but in helping pupils to find more constructive and appropriate answers for themselves. Group discussion can be very salutary if it reduces anxiety about problems of living that interfere with learning and adjustment in the whole school area, if it provokes thoughtful evaluation of one's position and goals, and if the learning is not tinged with moralizing.

The content of such group meetings should be largely determined by the pupils themselves, with guidance and stimulation provided by the teacher. Such meetings can be most effective if problems of current urgency are the starting point. They can often lead to analysis of the relationship of present problems to future goals. At such times, specific information may be needed to lend substance to the discussion and to offer criteria for evaluation. Pupils may want to know how different types of school programs, and different subjects, relate to vocational and professional objectives, for example. In such instances, information may be extremely helpful and directly relevant. Sometimes the students may be referred to source materials in the library; sometimes the group may invite a representative of the profession or occupation to tell about his experience in training and working in his particular field; sometimes the teacher may give a talk on the local school offerings and their specific relationships to subsequent training possibilities. But most important of all, social living classes can devote themselves to problems manifested by the pupils themselves in their personal and interpersonal experiences, problems that are of current and direct concern to them.

As may be inferred from the preceding discussion, the teacher assumes a different role in such classes from those she assumes in classes focusing on subject matter. As a consequence, it can be seen that such specialized leadership requires both an appropriate personality and appropriate training. Not every teacher is suitable for the role of social living teacher. As minimal requirements the teacher should have: (a) a strong interest in such work; (b) a personality that will enable her to motivate and listen, provoke and tolerate the expression of con-

flicting emotional attitudes; (c) some training in group guidance or group discussion techniques. It would also be helpful if she had some training in counseling methods and in psychopathology or abnormal psychology. Experience has shown that discussions cannot be carried out effectively with large groups. Probably, the group should not be larger than 25 at the outside, and more profitable discussions would be likely if the group were closer in size to 15 students. Experience has also indicated that if the school is coeducational, the discussion groups should consist of members of both sexes. It is usually best to group pupils for discussion in terms of their chronological age levels (14).

Other forms of group guidance

Even though the functions of so-called social living classes come very close to and overlap considerably with those of professional group counseling procedures, when more intensive programs are desired professional counselors will be needed. We shall discuss the professional qualifications of the counselor in the next section, but we may anticipate this discussion by indicating that he has much more training than the minimal requirements suggested for the teacher of social living classes; he is specifically trained for counseling as a profession, whereas the social living teacher has obtained some relevant training but has not specialized in such a field.

Group counseling can provide both diagnostic and therapeutic services. At the diagnostic level, it can arrange for aptitude and interest testing so as to provide pupils with a more accurate basis for evaluating their potentialities along vocational and professional lines, it can offer group personality testing services, and it may include specialized evaluations in some fundamental school skills (reading skills of many high-school pupils are below their potential, and diagnosis is a first step in arranging for corrective experiences). The counselor is trained to know how to select, administer, and interpret the results of such tests. At the therapeutic level, the properly trained counselor is trained, in offering educational counseling, vocational counseling, or personal counseling. He deals with pupils who are in or near the normal range of adjustment, for the most part, leaving to the psychotherapist (see last section of this chapter for a discussion of his role) the more complicated problems of the severely disturbed individual. In group sessions, information relevant to vocational choice may be discussed, problems in improving study habits may be considered, and personal problems in adjustment that may interfere with maximal use of one's capacities may be analyzed.

Effective group counseling will consist of regularly scheduled sessions with a small number of pupils. Although some types of vocational information may be presented in large groups, the relevance of such data, and particularly the analysis of personal conflicts and anxieties, can best be dealt with in groups of about 8 or 10 pupils. The counselor may familiarize himself with the individual schoolwork and adjustment records of his pupils, he may have conferences with teachers and supervisors, and he may use such information toward gaining a better understanding of the individual needs and potentialities of each of the pupils. In some cases, group counseling may be supplemented with individual counseling sessions. The importance of the school counselor should not be underemphasized. The small school may be unable to afford him, but neither can the small or large school do its most effective job without his highly trained and specialized diagnostic and corrective services.

There are other kinds of group guidance available for the school. Most of these are utilized for very special kinds of school situations. Unique programs may be designed, for example, for schools with a large immigrant population, or special types of group guidance may be needed for schools with a large delinquency problem. The interested reader may find some discussion of these programs and further references about them in the excellent volume by Marzolff (7).

The school counselor and the visiting teacher

The school counselor, or as he may more properly be called, the clinical counselor, is, in the recent use of this term, a specialist in counseling as applied to educational situations. In many ways he is similar to the clinical psychologist or the school psychologist. In the past many types of individuals were assigned the functions of a school counselor, often with little consideration of their qualifications for this work, and as a consequence much confusion resulted and some harm was done. Today, the term *clinical counselor* has come to be widely accepted as representing a certain minimal level of training along specific professional lines. Although we have still not reached the stage when all counselors possess the Ph.D. degree in psychology (or in educational psychology), this is the desideratum that has been proposed for full certification by the American Psychology Association, by the American Board of Examiners in Professional Psychology, and by many State Civil Service Boards and State Departments of Education. During the present transitional period the majority of clinical counselors employed by school systems are individuals with a master's degree, and many of them, by virtue of professional training and extensive experience, are doing an

excellent job. It is recognized, however, that adequate training in the future will require a Ph.D. degree and certification based on supervised experience and further examination (15). Such training at the graduate level should include courses in: general psychology, personality development, evaluation and appraisal of the individual, sociology (or other courses about the social environment), counseling and psychotherapy, research methods, and cognate and elective subjects relevant to the professional objective. It should also include laboratory courses, work in clinics, hospitals or schools so that techniques may be mastered and applied in real-life situations under conditions of good supervision, and internship training. The whole train-

Sensory and motor skills are important in intelligence tests. (**U. of Mich.**)

ing program is projected on the basis of a full-time, four-year period. Persons with less than this minimal amount of training should not be expected to have the competency that is now required for such work although, as we have said, many people have previously acquired good training and wisely supplemented it by supervised field experience, without having gone through the formal academic requirements we have presented.

The school counselor can provide many useful, and in some instances essential, services. If he is properly trained in both educational and psychological theory and methods he can provide consultant service at the level of policy-making. His advice on technical problems of adjustment, vocational guidance, and vocational information may be sought when the principal or the school board is considering the formulation of policy decisions.

The visiting teacher is another type of specialist employed by some schools to assist with many kinds of problems. Since the training and functions of the visiting teacher vary throughout the several states, it is difficult to describe them in a precise manner. In general, however, the visiting teacher acts as a liaison person between the school and the community, trying in a number of ways to make the educational process more effective. The job may involve investigating home conditions to learn what bearing they may have upon a particular child's school difficulties, consulting with teachers about the problems pupils present, trying to integrate school and home efforts to make for more effective conditions of learning, assisting the family in cooperating with the school's aims, referring the child, when necessary, to various types of clinics and agencies that may provide diagnostic and treatment help along psychological or medical lines, and the like. The training usually is similar to that of a school teacher (although this is not necessarily the case in all instances), plus training in social case work. Assistance of the visiting teacher is sought for such varied types of problems as arranging for physical examination by specialists and for follow-up on their recommendations, investigating possibilities for special placement of children who cannot be taken care of at home, and helping parents to understand ways and methods by which they may contribute more effectively to the child's psychological growth and adjustment. This assistance can be a boon to the hard-pressed teacher, school administrator, and parent, as well as to the individual child.

In this connection we should point out that methods of obtaining reliable evaluations of home conditions, in general, and of interactions between parents and their children, in particular, require a basis in both adequate research analysis and in appropriate methods of interviewing and observation. As we have noted in earlier chapters, the findings of previous studies dealing with the influence of home climate or home training procedures are suspect because they are based upon dubious interviewing and observational methods. In recent years major strides have been taken to improve such methods (and thereby improve the

Interviews between teachers and parents are mutually helpful. (Merrill Palmer)

functioning of "home visitors" in obtaining relevant information) through research studies in this area. One of the significant efforts that is being made is an ongoing project at the Merrill Palmer School designed to evaluate methods of observing and interviewing parents with respect to the nature of child-parent interactions (16).

The school child-guidance clinic

Many large school systems now provide, as part of their services, the type of agency usually known as a *child-guidance clinic.* Other schools avail themselves of the services of somewhat similar agencies known variously as child-guidance centers, mental-hygiene clinics, and children's centers. It is probable that such an agency existing as an integral part of the school system can do a more effective job than one that is a part of the general community. When it is part of the school system, it has common objectives with the school, the problems of referral and communication between the two are vastly simplified, its personnel are familiar with the methods, possibilities, and limitations of the schools, and it can work directly with school officials and personnel in providing guidance for the formulation of policy to prevent the development of many types of problems.

The clinic usually consists of at least three types of specialized, professional personnel: a psychiatrist, a clinical psychologist, and a psychiatric social worker. Other types of personnel may be employed in larger school systems, such as pediatricians, neurologists, and the like—if not employed on a full-time basis, they may at least be available for consultation. The psychiatrist is a physician who has received special postgraduate training in the treatment of psychiatric disorders. Like any other physician he may prescribe and administer drugs, but his treatment methods may also involve psychotherapy. He is qualified to evaluate all medical and psychological findings in arriving at a final diagnosis of the disturbed individual. The fully qualified psychiatrist has been certified as a diplomate in psychiatry and neurology by the American Board of Neurology and Psychiatry. His major method of evalution, aside from assistance he may seek from other medical and behavior specialists, consists of interviews with (and observation of) the individual who is being examined. He may offer psychotherapy when indicated, thereby trying to assist the individual to a more effective adjustment in his whole way of life, or at least, when the goals of treatment are more limited, to the removal or alleviation of troublesome symptoms.

The clinical psychologist is a psychologist who has specialized in the problems of diagnosis and treatment of individuals with disturbances in their behavior adjustment. In this respect, the *goal* of his training is similar to that of the psychiatrist. But whereas most psychiatrists, especially in former years, were concerned with very grave problems of psychopathology (such as psychoses and severe psychoneuroses), and received a considerable portion of their field training in state mental hospitals for the psychiatrically ill, the clinical psychologist is concerned with the whole range of behavior patterns, from the normal through the psychopathological, and receives training with mildly disturbed people in clinics and school agencies, as well as in hospitals. The fully qualified clinical psychologist has earned the Ph.D. degree in psychology, and, on the basis of five additional years of suitable experience and a subsequent comprehensive examination, has obtained diplomate status from the American Board of Examiners in Professional Psychology. He is an expert in psychological methods of diagnosis (including the use of intelligence, ability, and personality tests), has had courses in personality theory and personality development, psychopathology, diagnostic methods, counseling and psychotherapy, sociology and social psychology, as well as experimental and research methods. His whole postgraduate training, usually for a period of four years, is devoted to study of human behavior, normal as well as abnormal. He is not qualified to employ somatic methods of treatment, although he may have gained understanding of their uses in his courses and field experience, and may evaluate their effectiveness in the treatment of behavioral disorders. Because of his intense familiarity with learning theory, research, and the psychological development of the human being, he is especially well qualified to assist in diagnosis and treatment of the problems presented by school children. Both the psychiatrist and clinical psychologist have been giving ever more attention and time to the problems of the normal or near-normal person. Many clinical psychologists have been trained in methods of group and individual psychotherapy. All have done research as part of their graduate work and are trained in the critical appraisal of research findings.

The psychiatric social worker is a specialist in the psychiatric aspects of social work. (Since most psychiatric social workers happen to be women we shall refer to them as "she.") She has received a master's degree in psychiatric social work from an accredited school of social work. Her training has included, besides the usual courses in social work, specialized courses in casework processes, interview methods, personality development, and psychopathology. She has been trained to work in the family setting, to investigate and evaluate home conditions, to know about referral procedures for referral of *clients* (as she prefers to call them) to various types of agencies, and the like. Her role is envisioned as that of assisting in the total casework treatment and is frequently but not necessarily restricted to the less deep aspects of psychotherapeutic treatment. Traditionally, she has

assisted the psychiatrist, often taking over casework treatment of the parent of a child who is in psychotherapy with the psychiatrist, although her assignment may be to the child if the parent is in need of deeper or more intensive treatment.

As can be inferred from the above, there is considerable overlap in the training of these three types of specialists, although each has his unique qualities and techniques. Because each can provide specialized types of professional help, the combined resources of the three, in consultation and treatment, acting as a so-called *neuropsychiatric team*, has been found to be most efficient (17).

The child-guidance clinic can evaluate a child's mental capacities, personality characteristics, special interests and aptitudes, educational achievement and disabilities, and physical and neurological deficiencies. It can offer individual and group treatment to the child or his parents as it is needed. As noted above, it can act as a resource agency for general consultation and advice for school personnel. Because it is "right on the spot," it can often help to prevent a relatively mild problem from becoming a more serious one.

ROLE OF THE PEDIATRICIAN

It is apparent that the best guidance for the physical well-being of the child can be offered by the person best qualified to diagnose and treat him: the physician or, more specifically, the pediatrician. Our reason for introducing the role of the pediatrician in this chapter on childhood disturbances is that the pediatrician can be a highly important resource person in the psychological care of the child. Since he is trained in the hygiene and diseases of childhood, his advice is eagerly sought by parents when the child's physical welfare is endangered, and in recent years

Getting acquainted. (U. of Mich.)

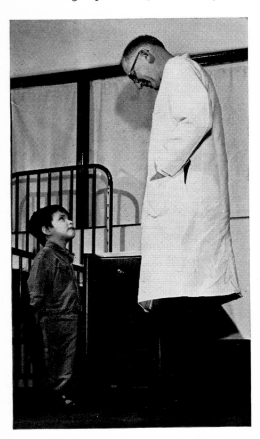

his role has become ever more important in preventing physical illness and in fostering maximum physical health and development. However, his advice is not sought so often, or if sought is not followed so often, in connection with psychological problems of the child. (See Chapter 3 and the discussion of Brody's study.) This is unfortunate because the pediatrician is in such a uniquely favorable position to exercise significant influence.

Because of the frequency of childhood illnesses, and because parents are so eager to promote the physical well-being of their children, the pediatrician becomes the professional person who is most regularly consulted by the parents. His advice is sought on such diverse matters as child nutrition and feeding, sleeping problems, behavior disturbances, sibling difficulties, hyperactivity, speech problems, enuresis, thumb-sucking, car sickness, nightmares, and many more. Since physical and psychological problems in the child are so closely interdependent, it is understandable that the physician's advice will be sought on both. If his advice is not always respected, the reason may be that he is sometimes not as well trained as he might be on matters of psychological development and adjustment. Unless he has made special effort, as so many pediatricians now do, to obtain special training along these lines, he will not be able to contribute very much, and this lack of his will soon be recognized by parents. Moreover, some pediatricians give only lip-service assent to the highly important interrelationships between emotional and physical phenomena; others will prescribe a drug or a diet, but will refrain from prescribing in the sphere of parent-child relationships even when this problem is central to the child's physical difficulties. Some pediatricians feel threatened when a child's emotional problems or the mother's related anxiety comes up during consultations; others feel highly inadequate when they cannot prescribe a specific type of medication, for they must have something quite tangible and quite obviously medical to bolster their feelings of competency.

It is undoubtedly true that pediatricians are constantly getting better training to cope with the whole range of problems of the development and adjustment of the child. Many leading pediatricians have been pointing the way for some time. The pediatrician can be helpful by simply giving time to the anxious mother in order to allay her understandable concern about problems (especially if she is discussing her first child) about which she knows very little. An opportunity for emotional support and some catharsis may do more to "treat the child," as well as the mother, than medication, in many instances. The pediatrician who has learned to listen with perceptive understanding will often find that it is not the obvious content of what the mother reports that is important, but her attitudes, her unconscious anxieties, her feelings of guilt, and the like that are basic to understanding the child's difficulties. The pediatrician who has become competent in the field of the psychopathology of childhood will be able to make better diagnoses of his patients, recognize his own assets and limitations more clearly, request the assistance of other child specialists in the

behavioral sciences more often, and become a tremendous asset to his patients and their mothers and fathers, with all the rewards therefrom (17).

PSYCHOTHERAPY FOR THE SCHOOL CHILD

We are now ready to consider psychotherapy in somewhat greater detail. Our aim will be to furnish the reader with an understanding of the *methods* and *goals* of psychotherapy, rather than to provide training in actual methods of psychotherapy. In previous years, psychotherapy (or psychiatric treatment, as it was more commonly called) was generally available only to persons suffering from very severe personality disturbances. Nowadays, with removal of much of the unnecessary stigma from both personality disturbance (we decry the use of the inexact and misleading term "mental illness") and psychotherapy, it is becoming ever more readily available for mild conditions of maladjustment and even for individuals who wish to learn to make more effective use of their capacities although they are not "disturbed" in the usual sense of the term. Whereas psychological disturbance formerly was regarded pretty much as "a skeleton in the closet," never to be revealed publicly, it is now no longer regarded as necessarily shameful. Moreover, if psychotherapy is provided *before* the problem in maladjustment becomes very severe, the possibility of complete or more effective recovery is greatly enhanced.

The presence of pets makes hospital experience more acceptable. (U. of Mich.)

Let us first consider the basic question of what psychotherapy is. Primarily, it is a process of relearning, so that poor habits of adjustment and unfavorable attitudes may be replaced by more effective patterns of behavior. In the normal processes of growth and development the individual is constantly changing his methods of adjustment. Psychotherapy is different from this mainly in that it is a *corrective* measure when, due to excessive stress or excessive anxiety, *ineffective methods of adjustment* have developed which then *tend to persist*. Since the difficulty is due to emotional problems arising from external or internal sources, the

process of psychotherapy is essentially a process of *emotional relearning*. The difficulties that the individual may present may take a great many forms, and they may involve disturbances in ideational, motor, educational, and vocational areas, as well as in emotional areas, but the basis of treatment rests on the rearrangement of emotional feelings and their consequent effects upon many other aspects of behavior (6). In the case of children, the difficulty may be perceived by the parent or the teacher, and not the child, or the child may develop certain symptoms such as excessive anxiety, headaches, gastrointestinal upset, sleeplessness, and learning disabilities that upset him, but in either type of case emotional difficulties are at the root of the problem, although other factors may contribute. Hence, psychotherapy is an emotional process of relearning in which improved behavior is sought in order to correct or eliminate symptoms or to produce more mature forms of adjustment, or both.

The preceding sentence suggests that there are many aims of psychotherapy, and it might be well to make this thought more explicit. The most direct and usually the simplest aim is to reduce or to eliminate some troublesome symptom. Sometimes this can be done quite readily, especially if the symptom is of recent origin, has not been "encapsulated" into the total personality, and the traumata are well focused. In such cases, direct attack on the symptom through *release therapy*, in which the traumata are re-experienced under favorable and supportive conditions of psychotherapy (18), or through suggestion or habit reeducation may be highly beneficial. Not only is the discomfiture of the symptom (or the undesirable trait) lessened or eliminated, but the *secondary* and unfavorable effects of the symptom are also eliminated. We can readily understand how a symptom can give rise to further difficulties, since its presence is unwanted and it may interfere with some other aspects of good adjustment, and so the individual may make considerable defensive maneuvers against it—and in the process acquire secondary symptoms. For example, consider a child who is markedly afraid of the dark. This symptom is directly uncomfortable, but, in turn, it limits his freedom of action in some

ways. Therefore, he may try to defend himself against his primary symptom by always insisting that someone be with him in the dark, or by avoiding being in dark places. In turn, his defense against his primary symptom may thus produce secondary symptoms, such as demanding that others stay with him when he anticipates being in the dark.

We may wonder why it is not always desirable to proceed in psychotherapy to the direct removal of symptoms. The reason for this is quite simple. Since the symptom has a *cause* (or a number of causes), it is often best to attempt to deal with the basic causation of the difficulty. Otherwise, the symptom may be removed only to have other, and perhaps more undesirable, symptoms take their place. The basic cause may remain, and thus the individual may become more maladjusted. Hence, removal of symptoms should only be considered in the light of their meaning or causation and only as their elimination contributes to the improved over-all adjustment of the individual.

Another aim of psychotherapy is to help the person resolve some of his current difficulties. The aim of usual counseling and the aim of this approach in psychotherapy are similar. The focus of the problem may be inability to get along with one's peers, fear in meeting new situations, phobic reactions to certain learning situations, and the like. In such instances, psychotherapy may be directed toward resolving the particular problem. In the process there may be some gain in maturation of the individual, but the basic personality may remain essentially unchanged. At most, reduction of conflict, more effective defense mechanisms, and somewhat greater capacity for general adjustment may be the consequences.

The most ambitious aim of psychotherapy is the *reconstruction* of the personality. When this is the aim, all pertinent areas of conflict are explored in psychotherapy, and basic ways of adaptation are learned or reconstructed so that the individual not only matures greatly, in the process, but develops a much more effective personality. He may not only overcome his specific symptoms, but he may also become much more capable of resolving new conflicts, when they arise, and of coping with life's problems, in general. He acquires new traits, new methods of defense, and new ways of adaptation. It is believed that this process involves increasing the strength of the ego and reducing, when relevant, the effect of undesirable aspects of the unconscious components of the personality —the id and the superego. A stronger ego is also a more mature ego. It is much more resilient and the individual is much more disciplined but spontaneous. He is able to gratify his needs in socially desirable ways without the expenditure of excessive efforts which the disturbed person must employ. He is able to balance effectively the needs of the situation with his own needs, delaying, inhibiting, compromising, or rebelling as circumstances warrant.

These, then, are the major types of aims of psychotherapy. But how are they to be achieved? A full discussion of the techniques of psychotherapy would involve, as we have said, a volume or several volumes on the subject. (The interested reader may refer to the appropriate chapters in our *Patterns of Abnormal Behavior* (6) for further discussion of this subject.) Some of the most effective psychotherapy with children is done in child-guidance clinics or agencies in which a team of specialists is available to offer psychotherapy simultaneously to (or advice for) each of the members of the family who may be directly involved in the problem. Often, it is necessary to evaluate both parent and child, and to provide help for each, since the child will continue to live in the home and the parent as well as the child needs to learn more effective ways of adjustment to internal problems and to the other person. Two books discuss in some detail various aspects of this total treatment process of several members of the family (19, 20). There are a number of "schools" of psychotherapy, each with its own unique characteristics, although there is considerable overlapping among the "schools," and the reader may wish to consult either of two works which discuss extensively the varieties of several approaches (9, 21).

We should like to make one additional point clear before discussing some of the elements common to all or most forms of psychotherapy: the meaning of psychoanalysis and its relationship to other forms of psychotherapy. Psychoanalysis may be considered a special form of psychotherapy, and it may be of Freudian, Jungian, Adlerian, Sullivanian, or other subforms. In general, psychoanalysis differs from other forms of psychotherapy in that it deals explicitly with the unconscious and therefore, presumably, goes to deeper levels and attempts a more complete reconstructive job than the others. The Freudian form of psychoanalysis, which is usually regarded as the classical form, makes extensive use of *free association* (or play analysis along with interviews, in the case of children), *dream analysis*, and the analysis of the *transference* (an evaluation and interpretation of the unconscious components of the relationships between patient and psychoanalyst). Because it is much more ambitious in scope than other forms of psychotherapy, and because the transference relationship is so important to its technique, the patient is seen many times per week (as many as six times per week in the psychoanalysis of adults) and for an extended period of time (as much as three or four years in the psychoanalysis of many adults). Anna Freud, the daughter of Sigmund Freud, has written an excellent study of child psychoanalysis (22). Because the classical psychoanalyst undergoes a personal psychoanalysis as part of his training, in order to understand more fully the nature of unconscious processes and to reduce the interference of unconscious processes in his subsequent psychoanalytic practice, he is presumably more competent than many other types of therapists to deal with such phenomena.

Returning now to psychotherapy, we may consider some of the elements of technique common to most "schools." In the first place, the psychotherapist attempts to establish a *good emotional*

relationship with his client. (We shall refer, henceforth, to the psychotherapy of children, only.) The *secure, accepting, nonmoral relationship* between psychotherapist and child may be regarded as an indispensable climate for psychotherapeutic work. The child must become able to express his thoughts and his feelings openly and without fear of criticism or other forms of moral judgment so that he can become aware of his own impulses. In this respect the therapist is different from all other members of society (and especially the parent, the teacher, and the religious leader). It is not for him to decide what is right or to predetermine what specific ways the child will learn to behave, but only to free him from his conflicts so that he may become more mature and finally more responsible. Quite often a child is brought for psychotherapy, not because he experiences any problem within himself, but only because others are dissatisfied with his ways of behaving. In such circumstances, the therapist must first ally himself with the child (and even, possibly, against the parent who brought him) and gradually motivate him to experience and to understand the nature of his internal difficulties. The therapist must start where the child is and first enable him to satisfy his neurotic or other disturbed expression of needs. Only in time can the child learn how to satisfy these needs in more appropriate social ways. At first the child may *act out* his needs or behave in aggressive or uncontrolled ways, however, as these needs are being experienced and dealt with in still immature ways.

The therapist offers *emotional support* and *observes* the child during these early sessions. The child may play and talk very little, or he may talk and play very much. In either case, the therapy room must be conducive to both play and talk. This means that the therapist will have available a variety of play materials and an adequate work surface as well as comfortable seating facilities for the child. Play may be highly important to the child in expressing his unconscious or preconscious needs when he is not yet able to talk about them.

During the process of therapy the child learns to *identify* with the therapist, and he takes over, both consciously and unconsciously, many of the therapist's attitudes, mannerisms, and traits. The process of identification is one of the means by which the child interiorizes some of the ego attributes that he may lack. In good therapy, he will learn to integrate these newly learned attributes and use them in his own unique ways.

As we have noted, the child learns to release repressed emotion-laden thoughts. In order that this may occur, he must be provided with a secure and accepting emotional climate, and an environment in which his feelings can be permissively expressed (23). The next part of the therapeutic procedure, although it will be understood that these "parts" overlap considerably, involves *reflection* and *interpretation* by the therapist of what the child is expressing. The trained and sensitive therapist, who understands the dynamics of child behavior, is able to detect expression of the child's defenses and to help the child to see and therefore deal with them. The therapist also interprets the child's unconscious or partially conscious needs and so makes them accessible for conscious inspection. During this process anxiety is reduced and the child learns to understand and accept himself more completely. He gains *insight* into the nature of his problems, and gradually finds ways of dealing with them more effectively. He *works through* many of the same problems (in different settings) and many other different problems in this way.

Thus, through the process of psychotherapy the child strengthens his ego as he gives up inappropriate methods of defense. As he solves his conflicts the arrest in his emotional growth is overcome and he returns to the normal path of further, healthy personality development from which he deviated. He can once more behave as a total, maturing, striving, and happily functioning individual.

GENERAL READINGS

1. Bettleheim, B., *Love is Not Enough*. Glencoe, Illinois: Free Press, 1950.
2. Biber, B., Murphy, L. B., Woodstock, L. P., and Black, I. S., *Child Life in School: A Study of a Seven-Year-Old Group*. New York: Dutton, 1942.
3. Fromm, E., *The Sane Society*. New York: Rinehart, 1955.
4. Hadley, J. M., *Clinical and Counseling Psychology*. New York: Knopf, 1958.
5. Havighurst, R. J., *Human Development and Education*. New York: Longmans, Green, 1953.
6. Hutt, M. L., and Gibby, R. G., *Patterns of Abnormal Behavior*. Boston: Allyn and Bacon, 1957.
7. Marzolff, S. S., *Psychological Diagnosis and Counseling in the Schools*. New York: Holt, 1956.
8. Murphy, L. B., *Personality in Young Children*, 2 vols. New York: Basic Books, 1956.
9. Symonds, P. M., *Dynamics of Psychotherapy*, 3 vols. New York: Grune & Stratton, 1956, 1957, 1958.

SELECTED BIBLIOGRAPHY

10. Rogers, C. R., *Client-Centered Therapy*. Boston: Houghton Mifflin, 1951.
11. World Health Organization, *Annual Epidemiological and Vital Statistics, 1930-1946*. Geneva, 1951.
12. Redl, F., and Wineman, D., *Children Who Hate*. Glencoe, Illinois: Free Press, 1951.
13. Hutt, M. L., and Miller, D. R., "Value interiorization and democratic education," *J. Soc. Issues*, 1949, 5, 31-43.
14. Redl, F., "Group emotion and leadership," *Psychiatry*, 1942, 5, 573-596.
15. Hutt, M. L., Menninger, W., and O'Keefe, D., "The neuropsychiatric team in the U.S. Army," *Mental Hygiene*, 1947, 31, 103-119.
16. Hoffman, M. L., "An interview method for obtaining descriptions of parent-child interactions," *Merrill Palmer Quarterly*, 1957, 3, 76-83.
17. Spock, B., *The Common Sense Book of Baby and Child Care*. New York: Duell, Sloan & Pearce, 1946.
18. Levy, D., "Release therapy," *Amer. J. Orthopsychiat.*, 1939, 9, 713-736.

19. Lippman, H. S., *Treatment of the Child in Emotional Conflict*. New York: McGraw-Hill, 1956.

20. Allen, F. H., *Psychotherapy with Children*. New York: Norton, 1942.

21. Wolberg, L. R., *The Technique of Psychotherapy*. New York: Grune and Stratton, 1954.

22. Freud, A., *Introduction to the Technique of Child Analysis*. New York: Nervous and Mental Disease Pub. Co., 1926.

23. Axline, V. M., *Play Therapy*. Boston: Houghton Mifflin, 1947.

Index of names

Index of subjects

Compulsion neurosis, 229
Concept, defined, 210
Conception, 24
Conceptual thinking, 209-212, 269
Conformity:
  in adolescence, 340, 344
  in group activities, 284, 327
  healthy personality and, 8-9
  in infancy, 99, 131
  in latency period, 229-230
  problem behavior and, 270
  in toddlerhood, 140
Conscience (see Superego)
Constipation, case study, 15
Constitution, 37-43
Constitutional problems, 272
Contagion in group behavior, research study, 253
Continuity, principle of:
  cultural experiences and, 58-59
  in infancy, 77-78
Continuous activity, principle of, 83
Cooperative play, 192
Coping behavior:
  in adolescence, 324
  anxiety and, 99
  defined, 96-97
  motor abilities and, 98
  sense modalities and, 98
Cortex, 109
Crawling, 111-112
Creative fantasy, 195
Crying, in infancy, 128, 129
Culture:
  adolescence and, 307
  child-rearing practices and, 73
  continuity and discontinuity, 58-59
  defense mechanisms and, 100, 294-299
  defined, 49-50
  emotional behavior and, 119
  hand preference and, 153
  home climate and, 180, 238
  individual reactions to, 50-51
  of infants, constancies in, 51-53
  language development and, 114-115, 187
  learning and, 254-255
  mental illness and, 63
  morality and, 246-248
  oedipal problem and, 165, 166, 169
  patterns, 50, 53-59
  play activities and, 149, 190, 232
  psychopathology and, 294
  puberty and, 316-322
  sex roles and, 230-234
  social class and, 59-63
  value conflicts, and childhood disturbances, 358-359

  values in competitive group behavior, 287-288
  values placed on intelligence, 202
Cumulative personality records, in school, 363

Dating, 321
Death, causes of, 244, 309
Defense mechanisms:
  child-rearing practices and, research studies, 295-299
  culture and, 294-299
  denial, 100, 101-102, 229
  incorporation, 97-98
  learning and, 294-299
  projection, 100, 101
  reaction formation, 229
  regression, 100
  repression, 100-101
  reversal, 100, 102
  psychopathology and, 345
  sex differences in use, 340
  social-class differences in, 294-299
Delight, as an emotion, 121
Delinquency:
  causes of, 300-304, 321, 343
  concept of, 300-301
  group membership and, 286
  periods of prevalence, 299-300
  school guidance programs and, 368
Dementia praecox, 347
Denial, 100, 101-102, 229
Deprivation:
  as factor in language development, 116
  as method of discipline, 68
Differentiated concepts, 211
Differentiation:
  conceptual thinking and, 210-211
  of emotional behavior in infancy, 120-124
  of infant's perceptions, 104
  language and, in toddlerhood, 155
  principle of, 78-81
Directional sequence of growth, 81
Discipline:
  in home, research studies, 235-238
  methods of, 68
Discontinuity, principle of, 58-59, 77-78
Disease:
  in early childhood, 186
  in early school years, 244
  marasmus, 85
  physical development and, 184
  reactions to, in early childhood, 218-221
  (see also Injury *and* Infections)

Neuropsychiatric team, in school child-guidance
    clinic, 373
Nightmares, 15, 277
Nonconformity (see Conformity)
Norms:
    cautions concerning, 76, 105, 117-118, 314
    concept of, 19
    height and weight, 314-315
    in infant development, 76, 105
    in language development, 117-118, 159
Nursery school:
    group experiences and, 360
    intellectual development and, 170
    language development and, 187-188
    objectives for, 213-218
    play activities in, 148, 151, 191-192
    toilet-training in, 216 -217

Obesity, 3
Obsessive-compulsive neurosis, 354
Oedipal complex, 166, 170
Oedipal problem:
    in adolescence, 326
    culture and, 165, 166, 169
    in early childhood, 164-169
    Freudian theory of, 165
    groundwork, in toddlerhood, 143
    intellectual development and, 205
    in latency period, 228-229
    resolution of, 169-172
Okinawans, breast-feeding, 51
Omnipotence, 96
Oral period:
    fixation in, 89
    frustration in, 89
    identification in, 88-89
    oral expulsive stage, 87, 88
    oral receptive stage, 87, 88
Oral zone, 45, 87-88
Ordinal position of child, 147, 180
Overlearning, 258
Ovulation, 24
Ovum, 23, 24, 38

Pacing, in growth, 353
Papilla, 316
Parallel play, 149
Parental overconcern, 16-17, 105, 141-142, 150,
    220, 235, 244
Passivity, 276-277, 344
Pediatrician, 373-375
Penis envy, 171
Percept, defined, 210
Perception:
    defined, 102
    infant's, 102-105

methods for studying, 103
    play and, 192
Permissiveness, 70-72, 237-238
Persistent non-adaptive problems, 271, 274, 338-
    347
Personality:
    culture and, 51-59, 316-322
    defined, 5
    disturbances in, 352-380
    in early childhood, 164-172
    family and, 181
    general observations, 5
    healthy, 8-9
    home discipline and, 238
    infant development, 46, 70-71, 84-86, 131
    as key to understanding child development, 2-4
    in latency period, 228-246
    maladaptive adolescent behavior and, 339
    minority-group membership and, 242
    neonatal, 44
    nursery-school attendance and, research studies,
        217-218
    physical factors and, in early school years,
        243-246
    psychopathology and, 345-346
    reconstruction, by psychotherapy, 378, 379
    school and, 259, 364-365
    social class and, 60-62, 240-242
    teacher's role in development, 266-267
    toilet-training and, 57-58, 91-92
    underachievement and, 292-293
    (see also specific periods and areas of interest)
Perverse sexual activities, 341-342
Phallic period (see Oedipal period)
Phonemes, 115
Physical development:
    in adolescence, 310-316
    basic trust and, 353
    compared with mental, 106
    disease and, 184
    in early childhood, 182-186
    in early school years, 243-246
    in infancy, 105-114
    maladjustment and, 274
    sex differences in, 107
    in toddlerhood, 150-155
Physical needs, of infants, 84
Placenta, 25
Play:
    concept of, 147-148
    culture and, 190, 232
    in early childhood, 190-194